Advance Praise for ***The Worst President in History***

"Barack Obama's legacy of failure isn't going anywhere. Margolis and Noonan's careful history and analysis will therefore prove an important touchstone for discussions on his Presidency in the decades to come. A must-read."

—Nick Adams, bestselling author of *Retaking America: Crushing Political Correctness*

"I've been following the writing of Matt Margolis and Mark Noonan for years and their takedown of Barack Obama is their best work yet. If you want to know why the history books will have a dim view of Barack Obama, this is the book to read."

—John Hawkins, *Right Wing News* and *Townhall.com*

"Matt Margolis and Mark Noonan's book *The Worst President in History: The Legacy of Barack Obama* should be required reading in America's schools."

—Robert Stacy McCain, veteran journalist and co-author of *Donkey Cons: Sex, Crime, and Corruption in the Democratic Party*

"The legacy of Barack Obama has become increasingly obvious since he left office. Terror attacks, Obamacare's failure, and eight years of economic pain are just now getting reversed. Margolis and Noonan effectively catalog the cost of feckless and corrupt governance."

—Dick Morris, author of *Power Grab: Obama's Dangerous Plan for a One-Party Nation* and *Armageddon: How Trump Can Beat Hillary*

"In clear and objective language and well-supported by facts, Margolis and Noonan have compiled a devastating series of indictments of Barack Obama's presidency."

—*Book Horde*

Tracy

937-405-5695

Also By Matt Margolis

The Scandalous Presidency of Barack Obama

THE WORST PRESIDENT IN HISTORY

THE LEGACY OF BARACK OBAMA

MATT MARGOLIS AND MARK NOONAN

BOMBARDIER
BOOKS

A BOMBARDIER BOOKS BOOK
An Imprint of Post Hill Press
ISBN: 978-1-68261-813-4

The Worst President in History:
The Legacy of Barack Obama

Cover Design by Cody Corcoran

BOMBARDIER
BOOKS

Post Hill
PRESS

Post Hill Press
New York • Nashville
posthillpress.com

Published in the United States of America

For my son, Isaac.
May your life not be burdened by the damage done during the Obama years. Hopefully, your generation will make wiser decisions, informed by history and reason, learning always from our mistakes.
—Matt Margolis

To my late father, George Childs Noonan, Jr. Marine, mathematician, philosopher, and patriot. Shortly before he died in 2009, he warned me that bad times were coming for America. He has been proved correct, and I pray that we recover his spirit so that we may restore our nation to greatness.
—Mark Noonan

TABLE OF CONTENTS

INTRODUCTION TO THE NEW EDITION

WHEN WE PUBLISHED THE FIRST edition of this book in July 2016, we knew that, with seven months left in Obama's presidency, there'd be more to say by the time he was done. *And boy, were we right!* Those seven months proved to be just as calamitous as the previous eighty-nine. We knew we'd have to publish an update; the only question was, how long should we wait? Even a full year after leaving office we're still getting new glimpses into just how bad things were during Obama's presidency. This updated and expanded edition aims to complete our original fact-based tome—as much as possible, since we'll be learning new details about the dumpster fire that was the Obama administration for years to come.

One thing we learned was that we underestimated just how important it was to build a complete and honest history of Obama's leadership. Obama's real record has been whitewashed by former members of his cabal, his supporters, the media, and academia. Obama still thinks his policies benefited the nation, and his supporters parrot those claims without skepticism.[1] If their fantasy version of Obama's presidency goes unchallenged, we will lose more than just the facts to history.

Despite all the failures and abuses documented in this book, Obama remains popular—people believe his two terms were scandal-free and think he meant well, even if they disagreed with his ideas. He won a second term despite an economy mired in stagnation and myriad scandals, and he's winning the war for history itself. Still, there is hope. On Obama's watch, the Democratic Party suffered widespread historic losses down ballot. Between state and congressional legislative seats, governorships, and the presidency, the Democratic Party suffered a net loss of 1,042 seats.[2] While he ruled, Americans were miserable and pushed Donald J. Trump—a political newcomer and harsh Obama critic—into the White House.

Though we think Obama set a dangerous precedent with his reliance on executive actions to enact his agenda, there's a silver lining—much of his legacy can be undone. Trump and his cabinet have made surprising progress cleaning up the mess Obama left in his wake, and there are measurable signs of improvement. In the first year after Obama left office, the economy finally turned a corner, small business confidence soared, deregulation swept through the executive branch, the individual mandate in Obamacare disappeared, median income climbed, North Korea felt real pressure to cooperate for the first time in years, and ISIS crumbled.

Our job, however, is to make sure no one forgets what happened. This book began as a cathartic response to Obama's reelection but became an important register of historical consequence. It's easy to relax when times are good and to let the political left paper over the past with gorgeous propaganda, but this is not the time to get complacent. Barack Obama was an undeniable phenomenon, and many invested everything in his success—including the journalists, filmmakers, and educators who dominate the narrative. But the fiction they're building doesn't stand up to scrutiny. The truth must be exposed.

In addition to updating and reorganizing the original book, we've added two new chapters—with this new edition, you have the most comprehensive compilation of facts detailing Obama's presidency available. My other book, *The Scandalous Presidency of Barack Obama*, documents how the press blinded America to dozens of the worst scandals in American history to protect their messiah. Both books will be indispensable references for those who still believe that facts matter.

—Matt Margolis

INTRODUCTION

WHEN AMERICANS ARE ASKED "WHO is the worst president in history?" and "Who is the best president in history?" one man ranks high on both lists: Barack Hussein Obama. How can he appear on both lists so frequently? The polls reflect dueling versions of history, one backed by objective research and the other by wishful thinking. In a December 2011 interview with *60 Minutes*, Obama said he would rank himself as *fourth* best president in terms of legislative accomplishments—an assessment so laughable the crew edited the comment out of the initial broadcast.[3] Obama knows that he needs to play a role in enshrining the version of his legacy he wants history to remember. His plan, after leaving the White House, was to raise $1 billion for his presidential library and a global foundation—double the amount raised by George W. Bush for his presidential library.[4] One billion dollars is *a lot* of money, but it's not enough to cover up the epic failures of his presidency, which we've compiled in the following pages. As opinionated as Americans are about how Obama measures up, history will be the ultimate judge...not recent polls, and certainly not Obama himself.

There's just one problem—history is a story, and our view of past events depends heavily on who is telling that story. Based on our research, however, we believe that honest historical accounts of Obama's presidency will *not* be kind. A truth-seeker will discover his lapses in judgment at home and abroad, failed policies, the radicalism of his appointees, his rejection of constitutional limitations, his demagoguery, the grotesque corruption of many of those in his inner circle, and, most important, his utter failure to lead on the world stage. The goal of this book is to make sure the truth about Obama's record is not forgotten so that future Americans are better informed about his presidency. Many will view Obama's legacy favorably because of the historic nature of his rise to the nation's highest office, but we are committed to truth, not enslaved by political correctness. Given everything we've learned throughout Obama's tenure, we decided it was time to compile a historical primer on his disastrous presidency. We've documented over two hundred reasons Barack Obama is the worst president in history. Some examples are more egregious than others, but each reveals inconvenient facts about Obama's real legacy. We took great care not to raise issues where we merely disagreed with Obama's political perspective and instead focus on failure and corruption backed by objective sources.

It's true that even our best leaders were flawed people with imperfect records. But, sometimes, history ignores the most valuable lessons of our most transformative political figures. Bill Clinton takes credit for a booming economy that would have never happened had it not been for Newt Gingrich and his Contract with America. Franklin Delano Roosevelt is credited with ending the Great Depression even though our best economists say he prolonged it. Today, we have a former president who claims credit for creating millions of jobs despite no increases in workforce participation and stagnant GDP growth throughout his two terms. So, while Obama works hard to tell the story his way, we will provide a fact-based narrative.

Unlike his predecessors, Obama must contend with a vigilant, informed opposition powered by alternative media outlets. No longer will any president be able to rely on a complicit, elite vanguard of media lackeys more interested in maintaining their status and access than in uncovering the truth. But this information age advantage is lost if we don't each contribute what we can to the proper recording of history. To that end, we have documented the truth about Obama's record for future generations so they will know what really happened under Obama's watch and won't repeat the mistakes of the past. History will be the ultimate judge; we just want to make sure that future historians have a fighting chance to get it right.

—Matt Margolis &
Mark Noonan

DOMESTIC ISSUES

GEORGE W. BUSH'S PRESIDENCY WAS defined by an event that forced Americans to look beyond their borders and consider a world overrun by anger, desperation, and want. Far beyond our safe and quiet homes, and our self-involved concerns, the world was increasingly hostile as strains of radical Islam came to dominate the peoples of the Middle East and northern Africa. Bush answered the devastating terror attack of 9/11 by crafting a foreign policy philosophy that would define him as a leader. Readers of this book can judge for themselves whether Bush handled the signature problems of his time in the White House well, but we begin here, in our analysis of President Obama, with a simple question: What were the defining problems of his time?

It turns out that this question has a more complex answer than it did for many former presidents, but we can say, with clarity, that the first problems he faced tilted toward the home front, at least in the minds of most Americans. Their leading concerns, when they voted in 2008, were far less likely to be the war on terror or the ambitions of China or Russia, and far more likely to be the recent economic collapse, the state of American politics, the ongoing debt crisis, or the perceived weaknesses of our education or healthcare systems. Obama campaigned as a man who would be the answer to those problems—a man who would unite Americans, answer populist calls for domestic reforms, revive our flagging economy and "nation-build at home, not in Iraq." Then, his focus seemed on point, even if you disagreed with his prescribed fixes. Then, he seemed to be an optimist—something Americans sorely needed.

Unfortunately, the position demands far more than shining rhetoric, calls for unity and optimism, and lofty ideals. The Obama we got bore little resemblance to the man who stood on that stage at the 2008 Democratic National Convention between soaring Roman columns and promised us he would look across the aisle, consider any reasonable proposal, comb every line item, and explain it all to every American. This man, instead, was divisive, insular, and self-absorbed. Despite his "hope and change" rhetoric, the man who took possession of the Oval Office was a pessimist, often accused of being antisocial and unyielding, who set an ugly tone for political debate and debased the honor of his position.

On matters of domestic policy, this man was far from a unifying populist who sought the council of Americans—he was beholden to special interests, and his policies were ideas that Americans loudly rejected when polled. His opportunistic flip-flops were a confusing array of partisan ploys and domineering lectures that left Americans more divided on social issues and domestic policy than they've been since the Civil War. His response to the rancor he brought to the political debate was to try to limit free speech and freedom of religion. Was Obama up to the task when confronted with those first defining problems? We think not.

1. THE NARCISSIST IN CHIEF

An important piece of a president's domestic policy is the tone he sets for the nation through his personal conduct and the manner in which he leads. Obama's presidency permanently coarsened American political discourse, weakened the respect many once held for the position, and left us feeling unimportant to a distant, detached Washington machine. Let's begin with a sampler of Obama's personal conduct around the White House—the sorts of antics Americans once thought were unbecoming of the presidency.

» In April 2009, Obama chose, as a gift to the Queen of England, an iPod loaded with his inauguration speech and his speech to the 2004 Democratic National Convention.[5] She already owned an iPod.[6]

» When Hawaii senator Daniel Inouye died in December 2012, Obama eulogized the senator and war hero by talking about himself, describing Inouye's life only as it related to his own, and devoting time to talk about his family vacation.[7]

» Neil Armstrong, the first man to step on the moon, died in 2012, and President Obama "honored" him by posting a picture of Obama looking at the moon.[8]

- When it came time to honor the great civil rights pioneer Rosa Parks, Obama posted a picture of himself sitting in the bus in which Parks bravely refused to give up her seat.[9]
- Likewise, he "honored" President John F. Kennedy on the fiftieth anniversary of his assassination with a photo of himself gazing at Kennedy's portrait.[10]
- A few weeks later, Nelson Mandela died. Obama tweeted a picture of himself hugging his daughter in Mandela's prison cell.[11]
- On the seventieth anniversary of the sinking of the USS *Arizona*, Obama commemorated the fallen heroes of Pearl Harbor with a picture of himself in the foreground, descending the stairs in front of the memorial site. The name of the ship was not fully shown in the image.[12]
- He even had the biographies of past presidents on the White House website updated to include references to himself and his policies. For instance, in the biography of Calvin Coolidge, the first president to address the nation via radio, Obama noted that he was the first to use Twitter at a town hall meeting.[13]
- He lectured Americans about the importance of going to public schools after benefiting from private schooling himself and sending his daughters to one of the priciest private schools in the country.[14]
- His respect for Americans depended on whether they could help his political messaging—he

> neglected to honor fallen soldiers killed in a Chattanooga, TN, terror attack but was quick to memorialize those killed in the Newtown, CT, school shooting.[15]

This has gone beyond just odd—it's Cult of Personality stuff, unworthy of a president of the United States. White House staffers reportedly gave Obama the nickname "Obam-me."[16] And this stuff is minor, if a bit creepy. The rest of this chapter will make you wonder just how much Obama cared for America compared to how much he evidently cared for himself.

2. BLAMING BUSH AND CONGRESS

Apart from his banal, vain personal conduct, the tone most Americans remember from Obama's term in office was one of divisive rhetoric and a polarized nation. Obama encouraged the worst in our political discourse, starting with his refusal to take ownership of the consequences of his actions. Every president casts at least some blame upon his predecessor, but, for President Obama, blaming George W. Bush became an exercise in the absurd, fitting a pattern of deflecting blame and criticism to a huge range of issues. During Obama's first term, he blamed Bush for the economy, for the botched Operation Fast and Furious, for the massive deficits, for our plummeting national wealth, for our problems in the Middle East—for just about everything that went wrong. At one point, he even blamed President Bush for things while standing right next to the man.[17] It became so reflexive he didn't know what else to say. Regardless of whether it was his first day or the end of his first term, Obama refused to take responsibility for the outcomes of his policies. Obama's administration even tried to blame the Solyndra scandal on Bush, even though Bush's Energy Department *denied* Solyndra's loan application two weeks before Obama took office.[18]

When Obama wasn't blaming Bush for his problems, he was blaming Congress—particularly Republicans. When Obama first took office, he inherited impressive advantages for Democrats in both the House and Senate and saw no need to court Republican support to achieve his agenda. Obama could have done whatever he wanted, and the Republican Party was nearly powerless to stop it. Yet four years later, while running for reelection, Obama endlessly blamed the GOP for his own lack of accomplishments on domestic issues. The economy was still limping along, despite his stimulus and Obamacare. He insisted the economy made real progress, but he needed more time to accomplish more because Republicans stalled his agenda.

He blamed the Republicans for his failure to pass immigration reform,[19] his unwillingness to compromise with Republicans,[20] his plans to ignore their concerns,[21] even for the impending lack of a deal on spending and taxes related to the so-called "fiscal cliff" when he was the one not willing to compromise.[22] When the government briefly shut down in October 2013, as Republicans in the

House of Representatives passed piecemeal funding bills that Harry Reid refused to even bring to the Senate floor for debate, Obama claimed it was Republicans unwilling to fund the government. Nothing that went wrong was ever on him, a far cry from Harry Truman's famous credo, "The buck stops here."

3. AN OVERTLY PARTISAN INAUGURAL SPEECH

Now we come to the tone of his rhetoric. He began his meteoric rise assuring us that he didn't believe in red states and blue states. A little over eight years after his soaring introduction to the national political scene at the 2004 Democratic National Convention, that Barack Obama was gone, replaced with a thin-skinned man who saw the nation as divided into two factions—his allies and his enemies. After being reelected with fewer votes than his first election, Obama started his second term with a country more divided than when he first took office. But, instead of signaling a shift towards the center, and a willingness to bring the two major parties together to address the country's problems, he gave what many described as the most partisan inauguration speech in our country's history.[23]

Republicans may have still been licking their wounds after the election just a couple months earlier, but the first step in breaching the partisan divide is for the country's chief executive to reach out to the opposition. Instead, as Senator John McCain noted, this was the first inauguration speech where such a call for both parties to work together was absent.[24]

Sarah Tanksalvala of *The Washington Examiner* called the speech "an ode to collectivism while quoting the founding fathers and documents. It was partisan while claiming to speak for the identity of the American."[25] *National Review*'s Yuval Levin described it as "the most partisan inaugural address in American history," noting that Obama accused Republicans "of desiring to throw the elderly and the poor onto the street, of wanting to leave the parents of disabled children with no options, of believing that freedom should be reserved for the lucky and happiness for the few, and of putting dogma and party above country."[26]

Ron Fournier of the *National Journal* wrote, "What happened to the idealistic young politician who argued against dividing the country into red and blue Americas? It seems we're not going to see him again."[27]

The Washington Post's David Ignatius called Obama's speech "flat, partisan and surprisingly pedestrian—more a laundry list of preferred political programs than a vision for a divided America and a disoriented world."[28] Ignatius explained that while Obama gave a speech that liberals would like, there were no "unifying or transcendent ideas that could help Obama do much more than continue the Washington version of trench warfare during his second term."[29]

It's telling that Obama spoke of unity in 2009 when his party controlled both Houses of Congress but did not in 2013 when he had divided government. It was a stark contrast to the attitude of his predecessor, George W. Bush, who had majorities in both the House and Senate at the start of his second term but still made extraordinary efforts to include Democrats on big issues, such as his goal to reform Social Security.

Obama signaled an unwillingness to compromise or even work with the Republican Party in his second term—he followed through far more than anyone imagined possible. As a result, Obama left office with an America even more divided than when he gave this cold, calculated speech—perhaps as divided as the years before the Civil War.

4. WORSENING THE PARTISAN DIVIDE IN CONGRESS

Obama had a similar effect on Congress. Despite his left-wing record, Obama promised to end partisanship in Washington by bringing "Democrats and Republicans together to pass an agenda that works for the American people."[30] But Obama forgot his promise when he took office without needing a single Republican vote to pass his agenda. *PolitiFact* reported, in August 2012, rather than bringing Congress together in a bipartisan fashion, he ignored the opposition and left Congress more divided than ever.

> *The House, led by a Republican majority that includes a slate of tea party members elected for the first time in 2010, set a record for the frequency of these party-line votes.*
>
> *The Senate, where Democrats were in charge, held far fewer partisan votes, but the average Democratic*

> *senator fell in line with his or her party's majority more than any time in the last five decades—another record.*
>
> *[...]*
>
> *"I don't think Obama ever brought the Republicans up to the White House in the way that (President Bill Clinton) would," said Sean Theriault, a political scientist from University of Texas at Austin. "It's unlikely it would have helped, but he didn't try as hard as he could have."*[31]

Obama put little effort into working with Congress to achieve a bipartisan agenda. By comparison, George W. Bush had many bipartisan successes on big issues like tax cuts, the Patriot Act, No Child Left Behind, Medicare reform, pension reform, and even the 2008 Stimulus and TARP. Obama, however, got zero support from Republicans for Obamacare and only three votes from Republicans in the Senate for his 2009 stimulus bill.

5. OFFICIALLY THE MOST POLARIZING PRESIDENT... EVER

Let's summarize Obama's impact on the nation's political discourse. Obama campaigned on a promise to unite the country and began his first term with approval ratings over 60 percent.[32] He quickly squandered the goodwill of those who took him at his word and carried the largest partisan gaps in approval of any president. His first four years in office "were the most polarized for any president's first, second, third, or fourth years." Gallup added, "Throughout his presidency, Barack Obama averaged 83% job approval among Democrats and 13% among Republicans. That 70-percentage-point party gap in job approval ratings easily eclipses the prior high—61 points for George W. Bush. All other presidents had party gaps of 55 points or less."[33]

Obama began his tenure with support even among Republicans but spent eight years demonizing conservative Americans and ignoring clear signs from the electorate that what they wanted was compromise and unity. After Republicans regained the Senate in 2014, he defied the voters, saying he heard the voices of the Americans that voted but also the even louder voices of the ones that stayed home—suggesting that the outcome of the 2014 midterms was not a repudiation of his policies, but a rejection of "business as usual" in Washington.[34] This tone deaf excuse-making recurred frequently, leaving even some of his initial supporters puzzled and angry.

6. DOMESTIC POLICY FLIP-FLOPS

Perhaps we could've come together as one nation if Obama governed with a coherent vision and explained that brighter future to the nation. But men lacking the ability to take responsibility for their choices and live up to their promises are fickle, and their most cherished beliefs easily fall away when they threaten to undermine their political prospects. Here are a few examples of Obama's domestic policy flip-flops:

- In 2006, then-Senator Obama called a proposal to raise the debt ceiling a "leadership failure" but, as president, Obama has requested multiple increases in the debt ceiling and unilateral power to raise it at his whim.[35]
- In 2008, Obama campaigned on cutting the deficit in half; through his first term, Obama raised the annual deficit to a trillion dollars or more per year.
- Obama said he would not hire lobbyists to serve in his White House but gave many waivers to allow lobbyists to work there.[36]
- Obama promised a robust, manned space program, even agreeing to the Bush administration policy of returning to the moon by 2020. But Obama killed funding for the Constellation space shuttle, which was to bring America back to the moon, meaning the United States no longer had a manned space program.[37]
- Obama promised that as president he would reduce earmarks "to less than $7.8 billion a year, a level they last achieved in 1993." Earmarks for FY2010, the last year before Republicans took control of the House, totaled $15.9 billion.[38]
- Obama promised that he would eliminate income taxes on American seniors making $50,000 or less. It never happened.[39]

- Obama promised to adhere to "pay-go" budgeting in which all new expenditures be paid for either by spending reductions elsewhere or tax increases.[40] At no time did Obama obey "pay-go" rules; he chastised GOP attempts to enforce it.
- Obama blamed President Bush for high gas prices, but when gas prices skyrocketed to record levels on his watch, Obama decided that the president had no power to affect gas prices, only to take credit when gas prices finally declined.[41]
- In 2008, Obama touted the use of gas pipelines across Canada to improve America's economy and reduce our dependence on foreign oil.[42] As president, he blocked the Keystone pipeline, which would bring oil from Canada into the United States and create thousands of jobs.[43]
- During the 2008 Democratic primary, Obama attacked Hillary Clinton's healthcare plan requiring an individual mandate.[44] Obamacare had an individual mandate.[45]
- After campaigning as opposed to the indefinite detention of American citizens,[46]when the piece of the NDAA authorizing indefinite detention of Americans was struck down as unconstitutional in court Obama got an emergency stay on the ruling and appealed it.[47]

7. EXPLOITING DISASTER AND TRAGEDY TO PUSH HIS AGENDA

If there's any time to put politics aside, it's in the wake of a national tragedy. But Barack Obama saw fit, more than once in his presidency, to take a national tragedy and use it to push his own agenda. Obama used the BP oil spill as cover for banning offshore drilling. He even compared the situation to the 9/11 terror attacks.[48] He turned the memorial service for the victims of the Tucson shooting of Rep. Gabrielle Giffords and other bystanders into a quasi-political rally and an opportunity to rail against Tea Party extremists and call for better gun control measures to boot.[49]

During a press conference several days after the shooting in Newtown, CT, at the Sandy Hook Elementary School, Obama invoked the massacre *and* Hurricane Sandy in a shameful plea for Republicans to agree to raise taxes. "After what we've gone through over the past several months," Obama said, regarding the hurricane and the shooting, "the country deserves the folks to be willing to compromise for the greater good."[50] Not that Obama ever showed any desire to compromise on taxes or entitlement reform during negotiations over entitlement reform or taxation. We'll get to some of these issues again before we're done, but here, we're highlighting the reality that Obama was preoccupied with messaging, even when cramming in that political talking point was in the poorest of taste or carried the whiff of exploitative opportunism at the emotional harm of the victims of tragedy.

After Hurricane Sandy ripped into the East Coast of the United States in the final week of the 2012 presidential election campaign, Obama sensed an opportunity to appear unifying and presidential. He and Republican Governor Chris Christie posed for a photo op and spoke to the press about the need to pull together as a nation to help the victims of this tragedy. With the photos taken and spread relentlessly around the mainstream media, Obama returned to campaigning and, judging by his subsequent actions, forgot all about the hurricane or its impact on New Jersey and New York.

While the Obama campaign basked in the warm glow of overwhelmingly positive post-Sandy coverage (which may have helped clinch the deal for Obama's reelection), the people of New Jersey and New York suffered through a level of government incompetence not seen since the Katrina disaster. On Staten Island, victims languished after FEMA packed up and left the area—a week after Obama promised, "No bureaucracy. No red tape."[51] Gas shortages throughout the region stranded tens of thousands in their homes up to three weeks after the storm hit.[52] It took nearly a month to restore power to the hardest hit areas, and many were short of food and clothing. Major streets remained impassable for up to three weeks. By April 2014, one federal recovery program had only rebuilt *six homes*, with 20,000 homeowners still on the waiting list.[53] These people lost everything but the clothes on their backs, but Obama only saw them as campaign props, leaving many feeling betrayed by Obama and his broken promises.[54]

Once he won reelection, did Obama grace the people of New Jersey with another visit or lend a presidential hand with relief efforts? Nope; he went golfing.[55]

In February 2014, Barack Obama visited California's Central valley to address an ongoing drought that had been devastating local farmers and families. While there, he promised millions in aid in the form of government handouts and pork for environmental activists, blaming the plight of the farmers on global warming.[56] There's just one problem: the water shortages, while exacerbated by an ongoing drought, primarily resulted from government mismanagement. Back in 2009, the Obama administration diverted water needed for irrigation away from central valley farmers and families to protect the delta smelt (a small, guppy-like fish) and salmon, citing the Endangered Species Act.[57] The government, not global warming, caused the problem.

A significant source of the nation's fruit, nuts, and vegetables, this region became fertile farmland because of irrigation.[58] While water usage in California was a constant issue for decades, Obama's environmental activism, not global warming, helped to destroy this important farmland. When Congress considered legislation to return water to the Central Valley, Obama threatened to veto it.[59]

8. THE GOVERNMENT RESPONSE TO THE BP OIL SPILL

On April 20, 2010, an explosion on the Deepwater Horizon drilling rig killed eleven workers and injured another sixteen. The rig burned and sank, resulting in what would become the worst oil spill in American history. The response of the Obama administration was shameful.

Louisiana Governor Bobby Jindal described the Obama administration's response as lackadaisical, with Obama far more concerned with his image and the criticism he was getting than addressing the actual problem.[60] Many within the administration were all too happy to appear in media interviews and blame Republicans and the oil industry for the problem, but the environmental rhetoric was full of sound and fury, signifying nothing.

In fact, the Obama administration's response to the BP oil spill was arguably much worse than the federal government's response to Hurricane Katrina. The 1988 Stafford Act says states are in charge during on-shore natural disasters, *not* the federal government.[61] The federal government's role in Katrina was to provide any resources requested by the governor. The BP oil spill happened in federal waters, placing the Obama administration in charge, but they weren't ready.

The National Commission on the BP Deepwater Horizon Oil Spill and Offshore Drilling (established by Obama via executive order) found that the Obama administration grossly underestimated the amount of oil flowing into the Gulf of Mexico, slowed response efforts, withheld its worst-case estimates from the public, and overstated the effectiveness of the cleanup efforts.[62] Obama railed against George W. Bush for his perceived failure to respond to Katrina, but when he faced disaster, his image was the only thing on his mind.

9. THE RACE-BAITING PRESIDENT

On matters of race, Obama went out of his way to divide Americans and inflame tensions most hoped would lessen with his historic electoral win. On policy matters, race was the first thing on Obama's mind at all times. He claimed an Arizona immigration enforcement passed in 2010 would cause harassment of Hispanic-Americans because of what they "look like."[63] In an interview with *The New York Times,* he even claimed that, if Congress didn't support his economic agenda, racial tensions "may get worse."[64] In an interview with *The New Yorker,* published in January 2014, he implied there was a racial component to his low approval ratings, saying, "There's no doubt that there's some folks who just really dislike me because they don't like the idea of a black president."[65] Obama made a race-based argument to justify his support of loosening enforcement of marijuana laws, stating, "African-American kids and Latino kids are more likely to be poor and less likely to have the resources and the support to avoid unduly harsh penalties..."[66]

Several times, Obama called press conferences to comment on criminal investigations involving African-American victims, breaking ranks with past presidents who mostly avoided such interference and speculation until the facts were in. In July 2009, Obama spoke out about the arrest of Harvard University Professor Henry Louis Gates Jr., who was mistakenly arrested while trying to enter his own home. A neighbor saw Gates struggle with his lock and thought it was a break-in attempt. Sgt. James Crowley of the Cambridge Police Department responded and, when the officer arrived, Gates refused to provide identification and was arrested for disorderly conduct as a result. A week later, Obama said that Crowley "acted stupidly" by arresting Gates, who is African-American, and cited "a long history in this country of African-Americans and Latinos being stopped by law enforcement disproportionately." Obama said all of this despite admitting that he didn't know all the facts or "what role race played."[67] He exacerbated an already tense situation, prompting him to invite Gates and Crowley to the White House for a "beer summit" to diffuse the controversy.

He also notoriously weighed in on the shooting death of Trayvon Martin before his body was even cold, claiming the nation needed to do some "soul searching." He concluded, "If I had a son, he'd look like Trayvon,"[68] giving credence to unfounded allegations that Trayvon's race was a factor in his death. The same story replayed following the death of Michael Brown in Ferguson, MO. Here again, Obama was quick to call for a "national discussion" on racial biases in law enforcement, long before the facts were in regarding whether Officer Wilson's actions were justified. Officer Wilson was acquitted by a grand jury when a federal investigation corroborated his claim that Brown attacked him and tried to grab his gun, but Obama issued no retractions or apologies.

His administration did virtually everything it could to racialize major issues of the day. Health and Human Services Secretary Kathleen Sebelius equated opponents of Obamacare with opponents of civil rights legislation in the 1960s during the 2013 NAACP convention. She even equated the fight for Obamacare to "the fight against lynching and the fight for desegregation."[69] Under the leadership of Attorney General Eric Holder, the Department of Justice selectively enforced laws on a racial basis. Whistleblower J. Christian Adams warned that Holder believed he was the arbiter of racial justice, leading him to perceive many cases through the ideological lens of racial politics and critical race theory and biasing the entire Obama administration.[70] He described Holder's dismissal of an open-and-shut case against the New Black Panther Party after they threatened white voters in Philadelphia, among other examples.

Obama claimed that racism was "deeply rooted in American society,"[71] and after years of inflammatory rhetoric, he had the gall to claim race relations improved on his watch.[72] But polling has shown that Americans are more racially divided now than they were when Obama took office.[73] According to a Bloomberg Politics poll at the end of 2014, a majority of Americans felt race relations have gotten worse since he took office.[74] Gallup surveyed Americans in April 2016 and found that more than a third of Americans are worried "a great deal" about race relations, more than doubling since 2014 to the highest level ever recorded.[75] If Obama wanted to drive a wedge between American ethnic groups—it worked.

10. RACIAL QUOTAS FOR SCHOOL DISCIPLINE

In the summer of 2012, Obama issued an executive order that effectively called for racial quotas in school discipline policies. The executive order, titled "White House Initiative on Educational Excellence for African Americans," linked the high dropout rate of African-American students with "methods that result in disparate use of disciplinary tools" and established a new bureaucracy to enforce proportionate outcomes in school discipline policies based on race.[76] Obama *assumed* that schools disciplined students differently because of their skin color, rather than their actions, and then proposed a solution that guaranteed the rules were based on race, not character.

According to Roger Clegg, the president of the Center for Equal Opportunity, Obama's executive order ignores the true source of the problem. Clegg told *The Daily Caller*, "A disproportionate share of crimes are committed by African Americans, and they are disproportionately likely to misbehave in school...[because] more than 7 out of 10 African-Americans (72.5 percent) are born out of wedlock... versus fewer than 3 out of 10 whites."[77]

Michael Meyers, the executive director of the New York Civil Rights Commission, said of Obama, "With the stroke of his presidential pen, Obama has ignored and denies the substantial and irreversible racial progress we as a nation have made; with great alacrity, and without any shame, he has embraced the separatists' mission, credo and agenda that dictate blacks should be regarded as different and educated differently, and treated differentially, from all other American students."[78] Martin Luther King Jr. would be very disappointed.

11. RELEASING CRIMINAL ILLEGAL ALIENS

Obama is not alone in his support of amnesty for illegal immigrants. But releasing convicted violent criminals who entered the United States illegally is not in the best interest of American citizens—this should not be a controversial position. Yet Obama, in his quest for amnesty, did just that.

The Center for Immigration Studies reported that U.S. Immigration and Customs Enforcement (ICE) released over 36,000 convicted criminal aliens awaiting deportation proceedings. Many were guilty of serious crimes, including 193 homicides, 426 sexual assaults, 303 kidnappings, 1,075 aggravated assaults, and an astounding 15,635 DUIs. Other convicts released committed robberies, arsons, assaults, sex offenses, larceny, and burglary.[79] Besides the 36,000 awaiting deportation proceedings, the Obama administration also caught and released 68,000 criminal aliens in 2013 who weren't put into deportation proceedings.[80]

According to Jessica M. Vaughn, the Director of Policy Studies at the Center for Immigration Studies, the policies of the Obama administration "frequently have allowed political considerations to trump public safety factors and, as a result, aliens with serious criminal convictions were allowed to return to the streets instead of being removed to their home countries."[81]

Obama argued that changing our immigration policy was "the right thing to do for our economy, our security, and our future."[82] Only in the Obama administration could releasing tens of thousands of convicted criminals back into the U.S. population just because they are illegal aliens be considered "the right thing to do" for our security.

12. RADICAL ATTORNEYS GENERAL

The Attorney General of the United States is charged with ensuring that the laws of the United States are strictly and fairly enforced for all Americans. Based on his choices to fill the position, Obama thought the primary job of the Attorney General was to provide cover for his administration's serial violations of law and precedent and to pursue a radical, racialized interpretation of the Civil Rights Act.

Attorney General Eric Holder's radical past ought to have disqualified him from being the nation's chief law enforcement officer. In 1970, Holder was a Columbia University freshman and a leader of a black separatist group on campus, the Student Afro-American Society (SAAS). With SAAS, Holder participated in a five-day armed takeover of an abandoned ROTC office on campus.[83]

Holder's radical past explains the actions of his Justice Department, described elsewhere in this book, from his failure to prosecute New Black Panther Party members over voter intimidation during the 2008 election, to his inappropriate involvement in the Trayvon Martin and Michael Brown shooting death cases, and his stonewalling of high-profile investigations (including Fast and Furious and the IRS Scandal), harassing reporters for doing their jobs, and allowing millions of illegal voters to remain on the voter rolls. Despite his tenure being marred by partisan actions, controversy, and scandal, Holder was one of the longest-serving members of Obama's original Cabinet.

After the disasters of Holder's tenure, Obama could have made a clean sweep, but instead, he turned to far-left radicals like Al Sharpton for advice on Holder's replacement.[84] Loretta Lynch replaced Holder as Attorney General for Obama's last two years in office. Lynch's racialist views on justice should have disqualified her too. She claimed that reasonable voter ID laws are racist and pledged to continue lawsuits against them. Lynch also said discipline in schools has a racist, disparate impact on minority children.[85] According to Lynch, being "tough on crime" is just code for being tough on blacks.[86] During her confirmation hearings, Lynch declared that she believes illegal aliens have the same rights to work as American citizens and that she didn't believe Obama's unilateral executive amnesty was, in fact, amnesty.[87]

Because Lynch was just like Holder in her radical views on racial issues, she was well-suited to continue Holder's policy of very selective law enforcement. As U.S. Attorney for the Eastern District of New York, Lynch signed off on mega-bank HSBC's avoiding prosecution for their massive money laundering for drug cartels and state sponsors of terrorism—a fact she omitted from her Senate questionnaire.[88] HSBC was, according to Lynch's then-boss Eric Holder, too big to prosecute. Lynch's tenure included many other bouts of radical partisanship, including a pledge to defend states that criminalize speech against climate change doctrine, a push to prosecute states that attempt to defend religious liberty on issues like gay marriage and gender identification, and an aggressive interventionist policy against states attempting to enact voter ID laws. None of this should surprise you, given her past views.

13. RADICAL SUPREME COURT NOMINEES

The Supreme Court of the United States experienced two vacancies during Obama's first term. Both of them occurred when Democrats controlled the Senate, meaning Obama had a clear path to confirmation. The two justices he chose are a monument to his radical leftist agenda, and their past made both of them questionable choices.

After the retirement of Justice David Souter in 2009, Barack Obama nominated Sonia Sotomayor to replace him. Controversy soon arose when Americans heard her past comments on gender and nationality in the judiciary. Sotomayor said, several times over the years, that she hoped that "a wise Latina woman with the richness of her experiences would more often than not reach a better conclusion than a white male who hasn't lived that life."[89] Her past writings and associations also raised questions about her attitude towards race and equal justice under the law. As a college student, Sotomayor described herself as a Puerto Rican nationalist and had clearly negative attitudes toward the United States.[90] Obama's own Department of Homeland Security classified Puerto Rican nationalists as potential domestic terrorists.[91]

Obama's second chance to nominate someone for the Supreme Court came when Justice John Paul Stevens retired. This time, he nominated his Solicitor General, Elena Kagan. Alas, she, too, had a radical past—this time as an activist opposed to the U.S. military. While the dean of Harvard Law School, Elena Kagan banned military recruiters from campus in protest over the military's now-defunct "don't-ask-don't-tell" policy regarding homosexuals. According to Elaine Donnelly of the Center for Military Readiness, Kagan's "only significant record indicates deliberate hostility and opposition to laws protecting the culture and best interests of the American military."[92] Veterans were not the only group outraged by the nomination. The group "9/11 Families" took issue with the fact that, as Obama's Solicitor General, she helped to shield the Saudi royal family from lawsuits for their alleged role in funding the terrorist attacks.[93]

Sotomayor's radical racialist views and Kagan's anti-military record cast them far outside the mainstream of American values and jurisprudence. That Obama selected them for lifetime appointments to the highest court in the country said a lot about just how out of the mainstream he was.

14. GIVING UP U.S. CONTROL OF THE INTERNET

We've shown how Obama placed himself at the center of every issue and treated half the country like his mortal enemies. The divisiveness and negativity of his governing style was bad enough, but his egocentrism also led to a myopic sequence of terrible domestic policy choices driven by ideology over pragmatism. What follows are some examples of his worst mistakes.

In March 2014, the Obama administration announced that the United States would gradually relinquish oversight of the Internet Corporation for Assigned Names and Numbers (ICANN), which oversees the assignment of domain names—paving the way for an international organization (most likely the U.N.'s International Telecommunication Union) to take over.[94] There are many good reasons this is a bad idea. *The Wall Street Journal*'s L. Gordon Crovitz explained: "Russia, China, and other authoritarian governments have already been working to redesign the Internet more to their liking, and now they will no doubt leap to fill the power vacuum caused by America's unilateral retreat."[95]

> *The U.S. role in protecting the open Internet is similar to its role enforcing freedom of the seas. The U.S. has used its power over the Internet exclusively to protect the interconnected networks from being closed off, just as the U.S. Navy protects sea lanes. Imagine the alarm if America suddenly announced that it would no longer patrol the world's oceans.*[96]

On October 1, 2016, the U.S. government officially relinquished control of ICANN. What can we expect if the International Telecommunication Union (ITU) takes over the role of overseeing the internet? Nothing good; nothing in favor of freedom, to be sure. During a 2012 conference, countries in the ITU voted in favor of a treaty giving governments the authority to block citizens' access to the global internet. But that's not all.

> *In the past few years, Russia and China have used [the ITU] to challenge the open Internet. They have lobbied for the ITU to replace Washington as the Icann [sic] overseer. They want the ITU to outlaw anonymity on*

the Web (to make identifying dissidents easier) and to add a fee charged to providers when people gain access to the Web "internationally"—in effect, a tax on U.S.-based sites such as Google and Facebook. The unspoken aim is to discourage global Internet companies from giving everyone equal access.[97]

If this was a gesture to the global community by Obama following the NSA scandal, internet freedom seems like a huge price to pay. Ceding oversight of the internet to an international agency will curtail freedoms, harm America, and make tyrannical regimes worldwide far more powerful in the arena of ideas.

15. NET NEUTRALITY

Obama's lack of understanding of the appeal of the internet, and its crucial role in promoting human freedom and flourishing, is even better highlighted by his administration's support of so-called "Net Neutrality." Ignoring the desires of the American people and Constitutional limits, in 2014 Obama began pressuring the Federal Communications Commission to regulate the internet as a public utility using authority granted under Title II of the Communications Act of 1934.

Net neutrality sounds innocuous and positive, but it would not only give the government more control over the internet, it would also tax internet usage itself.[98] According to Phil Kerpen, a leading free-market policy analyst and advocate, Obama's plan "includes a new 16.1

percent tax on your Internet bill that would automatically rise every three months—all without the approval of the people's elected representatives in Congress."[99] As the taxes increased, private investment would suffer, causing price increases to accelerate.

Michael Mandel, the chief economic strategist for the Progressive Policy Institute, said Obama's plan for Title II regulation of the internet is bad for the economy and "putting the Federal Communications Commission in charge of regulating broadband rates and micromanaging Web services, as the president proposes, would slow innovation and raise costs."[100] According to FCC Commissioner Ajit Pai, net neutrality advocates in the FCC deliberately misled the public about the scope of net neutrality. Pai explained that Obama's plans would give the FCC the "power to micromanage virtually every aspect of how the Internet works," including regulating prices.[101]

Obama claimed these new rules would "keep the Internet open and free," but, given that at the time a whopping 61 percent of Americans opposed his version of "net neutrality," it's clear that the public didn't buy it.[102] Of course, Obama has never been one to let public opinion or the Constitution get in his way. When Republicans in Congress attempted to build up support for legislation countering the excessive Obama-backed rules changes, the Obama administration declared the legislation unnecessary because the FCC already had authority to change the rules under Title II.[103]

In 2015, the Democrat-controlled FCC approved net neutrality in a 3-2 vote. Then-FCC commissioner Tom Wheeler originally opposed the plan but changed his mind after receiving pressure from Obama.[104] However, after President Donald Trump appointed a Republican to the FCC, they repealed net neutrality in December 2017. The debate over net neutrality certainly won't be over anytime soon, but Obama's dishonesty was on full display during the initial conflict.

16. POLITICIZING THE NATIONAL ENDOWMENT FOR THE ARTS

Brace yourselves—this is where it gets *really* creepy. In the summer of 2009, Patrick Courrielche, a contributor at *Breitbart*, participated in a conference call by the National Endowment for the Arts (NEA) that called on up-and-coming and well-known artists "to help lay a new foundation for growth, focusing on core areas of the recovery agenda - health care, energy and environment, safety and security, education, community renewal."[105] The call featured NEA Director of Communications, Yosi Sergant; Buffy Wicks, Deputy Director of the White House Office of Public Engagement; and Nell Abernathy, Director of Outreach for Obama's United We Serve campaign:

> *Backed by the full weight of President Barack Obama's call to service and the institutional weight of the NEA, the conference call was billed as an opportunity for those in the art community to inspire service in four key categories, and at the top of the list were "health care"*

and "energy and environment." The service was to be attached to the President's United We Serve campaign, a nationwide federal initiative to make service a way of life for all Americans.

[...]

We were encouraged to bring the same sense of enthusiasm to these "focus areas" as we had brought to Obama's presidential campaign, and we were encouraged to create art and art initiatives that brought awareness to these issues. Throughout the conversation, we were reminded of our ability as artists and art professionals to "shape the lives" of those around us. The now famous Obama "Hope" poster, created by artist Shepard Fairey and promoted by many of those on the phone call, and will.i.am's "Yes We Can" song and music video were presented as shining examples of our group's clear role in the election.[106]

There has been plenty of debate over the appropriateness of the government funding art, particularly when it's controversial or obscene. But there was something unAmerican about the Obama administration calling on the arts community to focus on creating propaganda for their agenda with government grant money. It was also illegal, as the conference call violated six federal laws, including the Anti-Lobbying Act and the Hatch Act.[107]

17. COMMON CORE THROUGH BRIBERY

Since the 2001 passage of the *No Child Left Behind Act* (NCLB), schools have had to meet certain requirements in mathematics, reading, and writing, as set by their state to maintain federal funding. Obama promised to reform the program to make it more effective by embracing "Common Core" standards—essentially establishing a federal monopoly on education standards. Obama's education department bribed states with *Race to The Top* grant money and with NCLB waivers if they adopted Common Core.[109] By 2015, all but four states had adopted Common Core standards, most of them in response to such bribes. Following negative reactions from parents, students, and teachers around the nation, ten states that initially adopted the standards withdrew from the program or made significant changes.

But, according to the Heritage Foundation, the Obama administration didn't actually have the power to bribe the states in this manner:

> *[...] the Secretary of Education has waiver authority under NCLB statute, but that authority does not extend to granting waivers in exchange for adopting Administration-approved policy. Rather than pursuing policy change through the reauthorization of NCLB, the Department circumvented Congress by granting waivers from the law.*[110]

From the start, there was plenty of criticism both from right- and left-leaning states about the Common Core curriculum and standards. Complaints are too numerous to list here, but they range from the absurd (*The Hunger Games* is considered more complex literature than *The Grapes of Wrath*)[111] to the frightening (getting the right answer to a math problem isn't as important as thinking about what they got wrong).[112] Even Common Core's earliest proponents have found themselves no longer supporting Obama's favored education standards and have called for changes and delays.[113] Sounds a lot like the botched Obamacare rollout...except, in this case, Obama couldn't share any blame with congressional Democrats.

18. SKYROCKETING COLLEGE COSTS

Under President Obama, the average cost of college tuition increased by 8 percent. This was true for public, private, two-year, and four-year schools.[114] These increases in college costs were more than double the rate of inflation,[115] and, combined with the decline of family incomes, significantly increased the burden of getting a higher education on Obama's watch. Yet, despite campaigning on increasing access to Pell Grants, Obama *cut* Pell Grants, which increased average college costs by nearly a thousand dollars per year per student.[116] Obama didn't mention this to all those youngsters who voted for his reelection.

Making matters even worse for college students, Obama's economic policies stymied the creation of jobs necessary to absorb each year's graduating class into the workforce. Youth employment rates fell dramatically in the Obama years. Full employment rates for recent college graduates dropped below 50 percent in 2011—the first time since tracking began.[117] Millennials were eager to vote for Obama, but he created an environment that led to a new moniker—the boomerang generation—as they returned to their parents' homes with mountains of debt and dim future prospects.

19. INACTION ON HOUSING FORECLOSURES

We've already covered a lot of ground, domestically, but what of the problem that caused the 2007/2008 financial collapse—what of home foreclosures? In 2006, there were 717,522 foreclosure filings on American homes. After the housing crash, this jumped to the 2.8 million range for 2009 and 2010 as the housing market appeared to hit a bottom.[118]

Throughout 2012, the media celebrated a coming housing recovery but, for 2012, the number of properties subjected to foreclosure was still a staggering 1.8 million.[119] The happy talk was, of course, at the service of Obama's reelection effort but around the country, foreclosures continue to affect Americans. Fifty-seven percent of the metro areas monitored by RealtyTrac showed an increase in foreclosure activity.[120]

In 2013, the overall picture of the housing market remained bleak despite modest gains. There were 1.36 million foreclosures, 19 percent of all homes were rated as "deeply underwater" on their mortgages, and overall foreclosures were still above the norm for a healthy economy.[121] RealtyTrac figures show that the pace of foreclosures rose again in early 2014 and struggled until late in 2016.[122] Too many people tried to save their homes but in Obama's stagnant economy, found few options. Unable to refinance, unable to sell, and unable to afford their homes due to job cuts, pay cuts, and tax hikes, many threw in the towel and gave their homes back to the banks.

Though Obama shoveled taxpayer dollars into General Motors and the big banks, for average American homeowners, he suddenly discovered that it was time to be cautious. He never backed legislation to force lenders to come to terms with borrowers whose homes were worth vastly less than the mortgage amount, nor did he pay attention to homeowners who found that lenders were being very uncooperative in working out deals to stave off foreclosure.[123] It seems strange that a populist figure like Obama would miss such easy chances to help struggling Americans deal with the loss of equity that came with the real estate market bust, but as we've already discussed, Obama isn't much of a populist once the campaign ends.

20. COLLAPSE OF HOME VALUES

In September 2012, the average value of an American home had climbed back to prices last seen in 2003[124] after falling to levels not seen since the 1990s. Most people who bought a home from about 2004 until the housing collapse in 2007 now owned a home worth less than they paid for it. A home is the largest source of wealth for most Americans, so this collapse in home values was devastating, especially to the middle class.

Bad news: the slight rise in home values since 2010 was built on financial sand. When the U.S. taxpayer was forced to bail out the failed Freddie Mac and Fannie Mae, the Federal Housing Authority used most of the government money to buy the bad loans, moving the disaster from federally insured lenders to the federal budget. If we'd had economic growth of 4 or 5 percent per year after the end of the recession, this would not have been a problem, but we didn't. Our anemic growth not only stunted American wages and reduced American employment; it also meant that the FHA needed repeated bailouts. In 2012, the FHA was over-leveraged as badly as Lehman Brothers was before its collapse triggered the 2008 financial crisis.[125] As a result, in 2013, the FHA needed a $1.7 billion bailout to cover their losses from troubled loans—it was the first time in its seventy-nine-year history that it needed a bailout.[126] And, following this bailout, the stagnation in real estate values continued, incurring even greater budget losses as home values stagnated.

21. CUTTING MEDICAID FOR STATES DEFUNDING PLANNED PARENTHOOD

Whatever your views on abortion, if you are fair-minded and ethical, when allegations of criminal wrongdoing surface, you take those allegations seriously. The states should take notice and investigate. In June 2015, a group of undercover investigative journalists calling themselves the "Center for Medical Progress" posted a series of "sting" videos[127] in a style similar to those once posted by activist

James O'Keefe. In these new videos, CMP investigators posed as agents for a biotechnology firm and attempted to form a business relationship with Planned Parenthood to facilitate the sale of tissue, organs, and intact cadavers extracted from second-trimester abortions. Should Planned Parenthood have profited from such sales, it would be a federal crime. As the evidence presented in the videos mounted, a number of states proposed measures that would strip state Medicaid funding from Planned Parenthood clinics. Obama warned officials in all states that such actions might violate federal law.[128]

We can debate the merits of CMP's research and the legality of responding with state-level cuts to Medicaid spending on Planned Parenthood, but there's a problem for Obama and his Justice Department. Following the election of far-right conservative governor Scott Brown in 2013, pro-life Kansas chose to eliminate state spending on Planned Parenthood clinics. The Obama administration took Kansas to court, claiming such cuts violated Title X funding laws by denying women equal access to reproductive healthcare. They lost because the claim that cutting funding to Planned Parenthood violated Title X depended on the assertion that those clinics provided services women couldn't get elsewhere, and Kansas disproved this by allocating those funds to valid alternatives.

Defeated in court, Obama issued an executive order cutting Kansas Medicaid payouts by roughly the same amount (around $400,000) that had been redirected from Planned Parenthood to other women's health clinics already.[129] Why would Obama punish women seeking reproductive care in Kansas for the state's decision to end its support of Planned Parenthood? Why was the administration picking one private sector entity to provide women with reproductive healthcare access? This abuse of executive orders was a constant theme of Obama's tenure. Later, we'll discuss one further petty effort by Obama to placate the abortion lobby via executive action.

22. ASSAULT ON RELIGIOUS FREEDOM

Under Obama, if your religion didn't align with his domestic agenda, even in small ways, you faced a vicious offensive against your right to live your faith. For example, the Catholic Church has long taught that healthcare is a basic human right—though it doesn't automatically follow that the government must provide access to care, many Catholics were initially supporters of Obamacare. When Obamacare became law, however, it had provisions that would require institutions such as Catholic schools and hospitals to provide birth control and abortion services to their employees—in direct violation of Church teaching. Obama held that these mandates were required because things like birth control and abortion were "basic" healthcare. His Justice Department further claimed that requiring a Catholic institution to carry health insurance that included abortion and birth control services was not the same thing as requiring the church to participate in those activities.[130]

Whatever your view on abortion, you should be willing to concede that a church knows more about the implications of its doctrine than government regulators. When Catholic institutions insist that carrying insurance that provides for abortion and birth control would be a grave sin; that is what they believe. In America, we don't curtail a person's right to believe as their faith commands and to live out that faith.

Despite the fact that freedom of religious expression is guaranteed by the First Amendment to the Constitution, American businesses found themselves being persecuted by the Obama administration for standing up for their religious beliefs.

By February 5, 2013, The Becket Fund for Religious Liberty had filed forty-seven lawsuits on behalf of hospitals, universities, and businesses with religious affiliations over the birth control mandate.[131] Groups ranging from orders of Catholic nuns to interstate companies with thousands of employees raced to lodge their grievances. One of those businesses was the Christian-owned Hobby Lobby, a chain of arts and crafts retail stores. After an attempt to get an injunction against the mandate failed, Hobby Lobby announced that the company would refuse to provide birth control coverage and would not pay the $1.3 million per day fine required by the Obamacare law.[132] In 2014, the Supreme Court heard their case and concluded that Hobby Lobby was a "closely held" corporation, rather than a partnership, and therefore had the right to limit access to birth control.

It's hard to believe that, in the United States of America, standing up for your religious beliefs would cause you to be fined by the government, but that was nearly the case here. In 2014, Hobby Lobby won their case before the Supreme Court with a narrow five-to-four margin. The administration also engaged in coordinated attacks on the freedom of religious believers to decline to offer expert services that would support same-sex marriages, attempted to listen in on sermons to ensure they weren't "too political," and carved out a narrow definition of religious liberty when Obama administration officials described it as a "right to worship." The Founding Fathers would not be pleased.

23. THE SO-CALLED "PEOPLE'S RIGHTS AMENDMENT"

The ultimate endpoint for Obama's policy toward the First Amendment, and especially toward freedom of the press and of speech, was a radical shift in precedent. He wanted the Constitution, through its amendments, to define protected speech as coming from an individual only. Many countries don't have free speech, freedom of the press, freedom of assembly, or freedom to petition, but these freedoms are fundamental American values. Barack Obama wanted to eradicate these freedoms and replace them with a carefully defined, limited freedom only to speak as an individual.

This is no conspiracy theory. David Axelrod, Obama's top political adviser, promised that, in a second term, the Obama administration would attempt, by any means possible, to overturn the landmark Supreme Court case, *Citizens United vs. Federal Election Commission.*[133] In that case, the Court held that the First Amendment prohibits the government from restricting the political spending of corporations and unions.[134] The "fix" the Obama administration saw to this problem was the so-called *People's Rights Amendment,* which explicitly declared that the First Amendment did not apply to "corporations, limited liability companies or other corporate entities established by the laws of any state, the United States, or any foreign state," and would enable Congress and the states to regulate the free speech of those entities. Such entities include newspapers, magazines, television networks, even churches, but, notably, did not include labor unions. According to UCLA law professor and law blogger Eugene Volokh, if the People's Rights Amendment were enacted, "Congress would have an entirely free hand to censor what is published in newspapers organized as corporations, what is published by book publishers organized as corporations, what is created by movie studios that are organized as corporations, what is distributed by music companies that are organized as corporations, and so on."[135]

That doesn't sound like something that would (or should) happen in "the land of the free," does it? Thankfully, it didn't.

24. MONITORING CREDIT CARD TRANSACTIONS

Judicial Watch acquired documents in 2013 via a Freedom of Information Act (FOIA) request that showed the Consumer Financial Protection Bureau "has spent millions of dollars for the warrantless collection and analysis of Americans' financial transactions."[136] Every time you used your credit card, the Obama administration knew about it.

The Consumer Financial Protection Bureau (CFPB) was formed in 2011, as authorized by the Dodd–Frank Wall Street Reform and Consumer Protection Act of 2010. It was supposed to protect consumers from predatory lending practices, but instead, it followed in the footsteps of Obama's National Security Agency and treated all Americans like criminals without due process. According to a (CFPB) strategy document, the agency's goal was to monitor 80 percent of all credit card transactions—about forty-two billion transactions a year, as well as 95 percent of mortgage transactions. But this never was the intention of the Dodd-Frank Act—which specifically prohibits the CFPB from collecting personally identifiable financial information on consumers.[137]

Making matters worse, Obama's CFPB Director, Richard Cordray, could *not* guarantee that the data being collected by the government was secure from fraud. The CFPB collected fifty-one terabytes of financial information on the American people, or enough to fill up fifty public libraries, by 2017. This data cache included FICO credit scores, credit balances, and borrowers' income and payment history.[138] Of course, this was for our "protection." How exactly does the government monitoring our credit card transactions "protect" us?

25. WAR ON COAL

We'll talk more about the economy later, but let's take a moment to consider the impact Obama had on our energy bills while he was in office, since it's a leading concern for many Americans who are struggling to get by. Coal is, by far, the largest source of electricity production in the United States. As of 2011, coal produced 42 percent of America's electricity, with the next highest source being natural gas at 25 percent. "Renewables," Obama's much-touted "green energy," provided only 13 percent. And while coal, as a source of electricity, has become less prevalent over the years (it was at a peak of 53 percent in the 1990s), it is still projected to provide 35 percent of our electricity in 2040 when "renewables" will still only account for 16 percent.[139] Given its ubiquity, the United States government must ensure a steady supply of coal in the short term. But that is not how Obama saw it: he believed that coal is a critical threat to the environment and did his best to cripple the coal industry before his two terms were up.

In fact, that was one of Obama's 2008 campaign promises: he stated that anyone could build a coal-fired electricity plant if they wanted but that his policies would bankrupt them.[140] In this, we have a definite promise kept by Obama: he went after the coal industry as if it were the source of all evil in the world. Using the heavy club of the Environmental Protection Agency (EPA), Obama forced more than two hundred coal-fired power plants to shut down over a five-year period.[141]

26. WAR ON OIL

While Obama lavished taxpayer money on "green energy," he was an enemy of the American oil industry. When Obama took office, the national average gas price was under $2.00 per gallon. Obama set about "correcting" this as soon as he could.

Using the 2010 BP oil spill in the Gulf of Mexico as a pretext, President Obama issued a moratorium on offshore oil drilling to ensure safety through a review of extraction procedures. But Obama's 2010 budget proposal, submitted to Congress two months before the BP oil spill, indicated that government revenues from offshore oil drilling would drop from $1.5 billion in 2009 to $413 million in 2015. Obama envisioned big restrictions on offshore drilling; he just needed an environmental disaster to use as political cover.[142]

After the moratorium, already rising gas prices spiked to nearly $4.00 a gallon.[143] The national average gas price would stay above $3.00 per gallon for a record 1,410 days, which stymied the struggling economic recovery.[144]

Obama also opposed the Keystone XL pipeline, which would deliver 700,000 barrels a day of crude oil from Canada to coastal Texas oil refineries and create an estimated 20,000 jobs. Obama delayed making a final decision until after the 2014 midterm elections. After Republicans won control of the Senate, Obama threatened to veto any bill approving construction of the pipeline.[145] Later, he made good on that threat, stating:

> *Because this act of Congress conflicts with established executive branch procedures and cuts short thorough consideration of issues that could bear on our national interest – including our security, safety, and environment – it has earned my veto.*[146]

Never mind a State Department environmental impact study on the proposed pipeline that concluded the pipeline would have a minimal impact on greenhouse gas emissions and posed little threat to the surrounding ecosystem.[147]

Obama's war on oil didn't stop there. He did as much as possible to slow down, if not stop, oil production in the United States. His administration cut back the amount of federal land available for shale oil production[148] and blocked oil exploration in Alaska, a potential source of about twenty-seven billion barrels of oil and thousands of jobs.[149] Federal drilling permits were delayed. It's no surprise that, on Obama's watch, oil and natural gas production on federal land dropped 6 percent and 28 percent.

Oil and natural gas production on *private* and state land, however, increased by 61 percent and 33 percent respectively thanks to innovations that made previously inaccessible oil and natural gas available to extract at low cost.[150] But Obama tried his best to interfere in private sector efforts too. In 2011, he proposed more than $60 billion in tax and fee increases on American energy production.[151] A year later, Obama proposed exempting oil and gas companies from eligibility to receive a tax credit that encourages domestic manufacturing.[152]

Thanks to the boom in private oil and natural gas production, Americans got much-needed relief at the gas pump in 2014. According to AAA, the plunge in gas prices saved American drivers more than $500 million per day.[153] It's a good thing Obama's war on oil failed; otherwise, the slim economic recovery we managed may never have happened at all.

27. CLIMATE CHANGE RADICALISM

This book is not an indictment of left-wing ideas and policies, per se, but a condemnation for the particularly unlawful, ineffective, or otherwise bafflingly illogical approaches that Obama and his administration took to achieve their goals. This tendency toward extremism and unlawfulness was most apparent when he formed his policies regarding climate change. Obama's "Colosseum" speech at the Democratic National Convention in Denver in 2008 included a now-infamous promise, "We'll be able to look back and say [...] this was the moment when the rise of the oceans began to slow and our planet began to heal [...]."[154]

He fancied himself the savior of the Earth's climate system in those days and went to extraordinary lengths to leave a legacy of climate change activism despite opposition from Congress, the courts, other nations, and the American people. In service to Obama's belief that climate change is our biggest threat, even as ISIS marched through the Middle East slaughtering by the thousands, he spent his entire presidency pushing policies that defied decency and common sense. We've already mentioned his foolish war on fossil fuel energy, but here are some more examples of his environmental extremism:

» He and his representatives and appointees, including Secretary of State John Kerry, repeatedly made the claim that climate change is a bigger threat than terrorism.[155]
» His administration often linked Islamic terrorism to climate change, making the ludicrous claim that jihadis would be less prone to violence if there weren't a Syrian drought.[156]
» He and his cronies throughout the green energy sphere wasted billions on renewable energy boondoggles from ABC batteries to Solyndra to solar and wind projects now in the process of shutting down.[157]
» Obama ordered the Defense Department to implement directives that made climate change preparedness a priority for U.S. troops.[158]
» While claiming the right was anti-science, he filled the budget of NASA with climate change pork, denying the agency its core mission: space exploration.[159]
» The Department of Energy and the EPA targeted the coal country for extermination—the former head of the EPA even said people resisting the anti-coal push should be "crucified."[160]
» Attorney General Loretta Lynch indicated that her DOJ would act to support state initiatives to target climate "deniers" with prosecution and civil lawsuits and intended to defend states pursuing such laws in court.[161]

» The Obama administration shifted funds intended for military improvements to climate change causes.[162]

» He made carbon dioxide a pollutant by executive fiat despite its healthful benefits to biomass productivity, subjecting the entire energy sector to massive regulatory burdens and limits on their productivity.[163] The EPA pursued that policy, branding carbon dioxide a pollutant in 2009. Subsequent efforts heavily focused on using this designation to control the energy sector.[164]

» When he failed to get "Cap and Trade" legislation passed through Congress, he tried to start the process in the energy-guzzling Northeast Corridor by creating an interstate energy cooperative.[165] The Supreme Court issued a stay on this so-called "clean power plan"—which boils down to a regional cap-and-trade system—in February 2016.[166]

» Without the approval of Congress, he entered the U.S. into an international Paris Climate Treaty in 2015. Such an action is illegal by the United States Constitution.[167] After taking office, Donald Trump rescinded our participation pledge.

» In 2016, he diverted funds that were initially earmarked for infectious disease control to climate change research, just as the Zika virus

> was threatening to break across the U.S. border into Texas and Florida and Congress was forced to appropriate further discretionary spending to combat Zika.[168]

Doing even a few of these things would mark Obama a zealot on this issue, and this list is hardly exhaustive. The entire Obama presidency was marked by a dogmatic obsession with climate change as the go-to explanation for every wrong, the first argument in favor of every new regulation, and the first deflection for every personal failing. The lengths to which Obama and his surrogates went—the logical gymnastic they employed—to bring the conversation back to climate change often defied belief. But, more importantly, the law seemed to be no object to a man that obsessed.

28. DECLINE OF AMERICAN OPTIMISM

The worst consequence of Obama's naked partisanship, self-aggrandizing personal conduct, and lack of personal responsibility was the swift decline in Americans' belief in themselves and their country. A Gallup poll, taken two weeks before Obama's second inauguration, showed only 39 percent of Americans had a positive view of the country, the smallest number since 1979.[169]

> *The challenges President Obama faces as he begins his second term in office are evident from the fact that less than four in 10 Americans rate the nation's current situation on the positive end of a zero to 10 scale and*

> *that slightly less than half project that the state of the nation will be positive in five years. Both of these assessments are among the more negative Gallup has measured since the Eisenhower administration.*[170]

To compare, at the start of George W. Bush's first term, 73 percent of Americans had a positive view of America, and that number remained above 50 percent until Obama's presidency.[171] By the end of Obama's presidency, less than a third of Americans thought the nation was headed in the right direction, according to *RealClearPolitics* aggregates of polling data on the question—and never during his presidency did a majority of Americans think we were making progress.[172]

PERSONAL CORRUPTION

MANY OF THE MOST-DISCUSSED POLITICAL scandals to shake the Obama administration during his tenure were bureaucratic failures, failures of leadership, the incompetence of government agencies, or corruption not linked to Obama alone. We'll talk much more about those examples of government corruption and bloat in later chapters. But first, we'd like to focus on Obama's personal corruption and moral bankruptcy—much of which has flown under the radar.

Obama, more than any past president, has lived a life of privilege, opulence, and self-involved petulance that Americans viewed with increasing disgust the longer he reigned. His self-absorbed, narcissistic approach to every problem led to a general disrespect for his position, for civic duty, and for the rule of law and of the Constitution. We've tracked down some of the finest examples of his corruption, greed, moral cowardice, and opportunism. This list is far from exhaustive but should give you a feel for the quality of Obama's character once he got a seat at the golden banquet table. We trust you'll agree with us—it wasn't pretty.

29. AN OPAQUE ADMINISTRATION

We'll start by discussing the tone Obama set for his administration. It was from his personality that his senior advisers and handlers took their cues, and a keen observer can tell a lot about a leader's character by how he runs his affairs. In 2007, then-U.S. Senator Barack Obama said, as president, he would have the most transparent and accountable administration in history—a promise that liberty-minded Americans dearly hoped he'd keep. He even promised that he would post all bills online for five days prior to signing them. This would allow the American people to see each proposal and comment on it, letting Obama know whether Americans wanted him to sign it. It would have been a great precedent to set for the presidency, but Obama managed to break his promise a mere nine days after assuming office.

On January 29, 2009, President Obama signed the *Lilly Ledbetter Fair Pay Act*, passed by Congress only two days earlier. When Obama broke his promise the second time, by signing an expanded S-CHIP law on February 4, 2009, a few honest reporters asked why. The White House claimed it was "too difficult" to post the legislation online for five days prior to signing and that they were working on the problem. Apparently, they never solved it, because no bill was ever posted on the White House website five days before he signed it.

Obama's broke his vow to run a transparent executive branch in more ways than one though. On his first day in office, Obama issued a presidential memorandum instructing federal agencies "to usher in a new era of open Government."[173] He also issued an executive order reversing changes to the *Presidential Records Act* made by the previous administration, claiming to hold himself and his records "to a new standard of openness."[174] In retrospect, this seemed to have more to do with implying that his predecessor ran a secretive government than with making his own government transparent. A 2012 analysis by *Bloomberg News* found that the Obama administration failed to meet his own alleged standard of transparency.[175] Despite that seemingly sincere call on his first day for a more open government, the Obama White House also spent years fighting the release of the White House visitor logs from the period between his inauguration and the end of September 2009.[176]

Obama also didn't let the media photograph certain events, preferring instead to have the White House release official photos. According to the White House Correspondents Association, this practice sets "a troubling precedent with a direct and adverse impact on the public's ability to independently monitor and see what its government is doing."[177] When the president of the United States is requiring the press to use propaganda in its reporting on White House business, we're in a heap of trouble already. And we're just getting started.

30. THE KNOW-NOTHING PRESIDENT

One way that Obama tried to spin events to fit a picture of him as a heroic crusader besieged by unreasonable adversaries was to deflect blame when things that should be under his purview went haywire. His skill in this area was epic, as you'll see. We know that the president of the United States has information resources available to no one else in the world. Despite this, Obama often claimed to be unaware of what was going on in the world, or even within his own administration.

Whenever a scandal arose within his administration, Obama *claimed* to have found out about them the same time everyone else did, the exact same way: through the media. That's how it was for Fast and Furious, the NSA spying on world leaders, the IRS targeting conservative groups, the Department of Justice stealing phone records from the Associated Press, the VA waiting list scandal, and many other events that would have toppled any Republican presidency. We were asked to believe Obama was just as shocked and angered as the rest of us.[178]

He even said media reports on Hillary Clinton's private email server were news to him.[179] That was another lie. *Politico* reported the White House was aware of the possible scandal involving her emails six months before *The New York Times* broke the story.[180] In this case, as in every other, the official White House explanation for what Obama knew and when was dubious.

When he wasn't denying knowledge of the corruption in his government, he was ignoring his most important job as commander in chief—protecting American interests abroad. The self-proclaimed smartest man in the room got blindsided by consequential events in foreign affairs countless times, including the Arab Spring,[181] the North Korea rocket launch,[182] the rise of ISIS in Iraq, Russia's invasion of the Ukraine,[183] and the collapse of the U.S. backed government in Yemen.[184] Between his apparent disinterest in world affairs, which was the stuff of legend, and his professed obliviousness to what was going on in his own administration, there was little reason to be confident in his competence as chief executive of the United States. But apparently Obama couldn't be bothered to pay attention even as the world around him burned to the ground and as his administration was being plagued by endless scandals. One thing is for sure, corrupt men often spend more time denying their own misdeeds than doing their jobs.

31. EQUAL PAY DECEPTION

All presidents lie or spin statistics at least a little to make their points and push their agendas, but Obama's particular brand of lying was uniquely corrosive and narcissistic. As president, Barack Obama championed the cause of equal pay. In fact, the first bill Obama signed as president was the *Lilly Ledbetter Fair Pay Act*. In his 2014 State of the Union address, he said, "Women make up about half our workforce. But they still make seventy-seven cents for every dollar a man earns. That is wrong, and in 2014, it's an embarrassment."

But his passionate rhetoric on pay equity didn't match his record. According to a *Washington Post* analysis in 2014, "The average male White House employee currently earns about $88,600, while the average female White House employee earns about $78,400 [...] That is a gap of thirteen percent."[185] This gender-based gap remained unchanged throughout his presidency.

The White House fought back against the accusation, claiming that "men and women in equivalent roles earn equivalent salaries."[186] This explanation makes sense, so much sense that it also debunks the alleged gender pay gap nationally: men and women working similar jobs make similar pay. The "gap" only exists when you compare all men with all women without considering all the facts. Obama's claim that women only make seventy-seven cents for every dollar a man makes for doing the same work is false. His defense of White House staffing policy proved he knew his rhetoric was bogus. That didn't stop him from continuing to champion a battle against a nonexistent problem. If Obama were honest, he'd concede that, just as in his White House, the national statistic he cited doesn't account for differences in education, occupation, position, or even hours worked. But the rules of fair debate do not apply to Obama, and the truth matters far less than the cause. Obama's deliberate deception and "war on women" rhetoric was the real embarrassment.

32. EXCESSIVE AND LAVISH TAXPAYER-FUNDED VACATIONS

The presidency is probably the most stressful job in the world, and each president has found the need to vacation while in office. No one complains about that, and everyone understands that if a president doesn't sometimes decompress and renew his energy, he will not be an effective leader. But with Obama, vacations became so frequent and lavish that we must question whether Obama viewed the presidency as the most important job in the world or as a way to live a swanky lifestyle.

How many times per year does even the most avid of golfers take to the links? Ten? Twenty if they're lucky and have the money? Obama's predecessor, George W. Bush, considered himself an avid golfer and got a reputation for spending a lot of time teeing off to relax during his two terms. He went golfing about one hundred times, most of which were in his first year in office. Obama more than quadrupled his greens fees, sporting the visor and a fine set of clubs more than four hundred times in eight years—just about once a week. He should turn pro!

But that's petty time-wasting compared to the Obama family travel schedule. By March 2015, Obama and his family had taken thirty-eight vacations, according to one estimate. Obama's defenders are quick to point to Obama's predecessor, George W. Bush, for his frequent trips to his ranch in Crawford, Texas. They neglect to mention that Bush conducted White House business there on almost every trip, including hosting foreign dignitaries and members of his cabinet, a stark contrast to the lavish vacations of the Obamas.

Those vacations were not only numerous but also costly to the taxpayers. Some of the most notable vacations included Michelle Obama's luxury trip to Spain in the summer of 2010, which cost taxpayers $467,585,[187] and the African safari in June 2011 that cost $424,000.[188] The Obama family went on a twenty-day vacation in Hawaii in December of 2012 that cost American taxpayers a whopping $4 million dollars.[189] Showing his complete contempt for the American taxpayer, during the height of the "fiscal cliff" negotiations, Obama spent taxpayer dollars flying back from his Hawaii vacation to DC and then spent more flying back to Hawaii after Congress enacted the "fix" to the fiscal cliff. The estimated cost of all this jet-setting: $3 million.[190]

In 2013, Obama averaged more over a vacation per month,[191] including trips to Hawaii and Martha's Vineyard, and an appearance on *The Tonight Show with Jay Leno*—those extravagances cost taxpayers $7.4 million.[192] Between November 2014 and February 2015, the Obamas took another *three* vacations.[193] They booked another $12 million mansion on Martha's Vineyard for the summer of 2015.[194] Travel records examined by Judicial Watch put the final tally for Obama and his family's known travel expenses at a whopping $105.7 million over eight years.[195]

The worst aspect of the Obama family's frequent and expensive vacations is the insensitivity shown towards Americans who were struggling to get by because of Obama's inability to fix the economy. In 2009, the term "staycation" was added to Merriam-Webster's Collegiate Dictionary due to the popularity of local day trips or home vacations in lieu of longer trips away from home because of the sluggish economy under Obama.[196] But staycations are for little people.

33. CAMPAIGNING ON TAXPAYER MONEY

Presidents of the United States are provided taxpayer-funded security and the use of Air Force One—both are job necessities. But when a president runs for reelection, their campaigns are expected to pay the costs of campaign trips, including those costs borne by local governments to provide security. However, there is a gray area. An unscrupulous politician can merge campaign trips with presidential business and get the taxpayers to share the cost or pay the bill outright. Barack Obama wasn't the first sitting president to do this, but he made this practice an art form during his reelection campaign.

When Obama attended a lavish celebrity-studded fundraiser in Manhattan, which raised $4.5 million for his campaign, the trip was partially funded by taxpayers because he briefly visited Ground Zero for an official event.[197] It was one of many such instances for which Obama had the taxpayers share the burden of paying for him to campaign around the country.

When George W. Bush ran for reelection in 2004, he held a mere fifty-seven fundraisers. In the year following the launch of his reelection campaign, Barack Obama held 124, or about one every three days.[198] A formal complaint by the Republican National Committee noted that alleged government-business events were occurring in battleground states and often resembled campaign rallies.[199]

Often, neither Obama's campaign nor the Democratic National Committee would pay struggling cities for the costs they incurred for extra security provided for Obama. Some examples include:

» In the city of Westport, CT, Obama held a $35,800-per-person fundraiser in August 2012. This resulted in additional costs to the city of $14,812 in overtime payments for police officers and firefighters. The Obama campaign refused to pay these costs.[200]

» In December 2012, the Obama campaign refused the request by the city of Portsmouth, NH, to reimburse $30,000 in costs for a campaign stop in September.[201]

- When both Barack Obama and Mitt Romney held separate fundraisers at Newport Beach, CA, in 2012, both campaigns got a bill for the security costs for those political events. Romney's campaign paid their bill. Obama's campaign did not.[202]

So, when Obama wasn't having all taxpayers share the cost of his campaigning, he was sticking it to small cities and towns that had been struggling on his watch. These sorts of "perks" are unnecessary for the government to function and unbecoming of a man who rails against the largesse of corporate CEOs.

34. CAMPAIGNING WITH YOUR PRIVATE DATA

Even if you weren't an Obama supporter in 2012, depending on your online activity, you may have been flagged by his campaign as a potential voter and unwittingly provided them with personal data. According to a March 2012 *Politico* report, Obama's campaign "invested millions of dollars in sophisticated Internet messaging, marketing and fundraising efforts" that relied on personal data that wasn't always provided voluntarily. This information was compiled in a centralized digital database containing personal information on millions of potential Obama voters.[203]

There was enough concern about this data-mining operation that Obama's campaign data director penned an op-ed denying any Orwellian intentions.[204] Ironically, Obama did this while talking up the need to protect the privacy of the American people on the internet.[205] We trusted him with our privacy about as much as we trust wolves with our sheep.

35. REMOVING GOD AND JERUSALEM FROM HIS PARTY PLATFORM

It is a staple of American politics to call upon the blessings of God for our efforts. Even today, the overwhelming majority of Americans express belief in God, and a majority of them adhere to the Judeo-Christian concept of God. So honoring God is, in practical terms, considered uncontroversial in American politics. But at the 2012 Democratic National Convention, all mention of God or Jerusalem was removed from the party platform. When a few among them proposed to reinsert them, they were showered with boos. Former L.A. Mayor Antonio Villaraigosa then crammed them into the platform using an up-or-down vote and some very generous estimates of the yes votes. The "bad optics" of the Democratic Party delegates booing God and Jerusalem, however, is not the point of this entry.

Once the media reported the story, the Democratic National Committee went into full damage control. The media aided and abetted, and the bad situation was spun into a positive for Obama, suggesting he personally intervened to get the mention of God and Jerusalem as Israel's capital back in the party platform. But Obama was aware of the change before the convention. *Politico* reported that Obama "had seen the language prior to the convention

[...] but did not seek to change it until after Republicans jumped on the omissions..."[206] Obama couldn't admit that he approved of this change and then got caught by a disapproving public. When the citizens deemed his positions out of line, Obama refused to own them and make a case in their defense.

36. GIVING CLASSIFIED INFORMATION TO FILMMAKERS

With the media and Hollywood in his corner, Obama didn't have to worry much about how his actions were portrayed to the masses. But that didn't stop him from taking some ill-advised actions to boost his image. Prior to the 2012 election, the Obama administration gave classified information to filmmakers behind *Zero Dark Thirty*, a film about the Osama bin Laden raid conducted by SEAL Team Six. They denied providing director Kathryn Bigelow and screenwriter Mark Boal classified information until after the election, at which point they admitted their misdeed and agreed it could have caused an "unnecessary security and counterintelligence risk."[207]

Ironically, when some senators and Obama administration officials were given an advance screening of the film, there were objections to the portrayals of enhanced interrogations (which Obama opposes) playing a key role in finding bin Laden. The film was a critical flop but a fantastic way of reminding the few who saw it about Obama's role in the death of Osama bin Laden, and that's all that mattered.

37. NO WALL STREET OR BANKER PROSECUTIONS

In 2008, during the financial crisis, candidate Barack Obama promised to bring a "new era of responsibility and accountability to Wall Street and to Washington."[208] When he took office in 2009, he had a mandate to prosecute the Wall Street bankers responsible for the systemic fraud that contributed to the crisis. But there were no arrests or prosecutions of any banker involved in the fiscal collapse.[209] The criminal fraud was undeniable; yet in 2012, Barack Obama defended the lack of prosecutions because "a lot of that stuff wasn't necessarily illegal, it was just immoral or inappropriate or reckless."[210]

Even though Obama publicly promised to hold Wall Street accountable, the so-called "architects of the financial crisis" gained historic protections.[211] He handed the largest banks bulletproof vests when he signed the *Dodd-Frank Wall Street Reform and Consumer Protection Act*, which gave the lenders with the most assets federal protections that make them nearly immune to competition.[212]

Wall Street donated a lot of money to Obama's campaign in 2008 and has since gained significant influence in his administration. "President Obama has repeatedly turned to nominees with close Wall Street ties for high-level economic positions," wrote Senator Elizabeth Warren (D-MA) in *The Huffington Post* in November 2014, including Jack Lew, Obama's Treasury Secretary during his second term. No wonder a report by the Government Accountability Institute cited cronyism inside the Department of Justice and political donations made to the Obama campaign as likely reasons Attorney General Eric Holder failed to charge anyone from Wall Street with a crime.[213]

One of Holder's deputy Attorney Generals actually got paid $20 million for work done for AIG Insurance—the firm at the heart of the 2008 financial crash.[214] Obama even collected more donations from Wall Street than any of the Republican candidates for president. From the GAI report:

> *In the weeks before and after the Senate report on Goldman Sachs, several Goldman executives and their families made contributions to Obama's Victory Fund and related entities, and some contributors maxed out at the largest individual donation allowed, $35,800. Five senior Goldman Sachs executives wrote more than $130,000 in checks to the Obama Victory Fund. Two of these executives had never donated to Obama before and had previously only given small donations to individual candidates.*[215]

For Obama, a check made out to his campaign with a lot of zeros on it became the difference between right and wrong, legal and illegal.

38. THE PAY TO PLAY ADMINISTRATION

During his 2012 State of the Union address, Barack Obama criticized the "corrosive influence of money in politics."[216] We're confident he was being disingenuous since, both during his initial presidential campaign and after he took office, his attitude was "Show me the money!" He made sure to award his most generous donors with influence and perks. For example:

- Donors to Obama's campaigns got back $21,000 in taxpayer money for each dollar they gave to Obama.[217]
- Obama's donors disproportionately gained major government contracts for their firms and positions to advise his administration on government spending.[218]
- Obama donors literally got a seat at Obama's table during the "fiscal cliff" meetings at the end of 2012.[219]
- Major corporations lobbying the American government were permitted to donate at least $283 million to Obama's second inauguration.[220]
- Obama established a permanent campaign group, Organizing for Action, to give corporations and individuals access and influence in exchange for donations.[221]
- Top donors and fundraisers were getting plum government jobs, often with none of the credentials needed to hold the position on offer. Ambassadorships, czarships, leading advisory roles, and other appointments became like feudal titles for loyal vassals of the king.[222]
- 80 percent of Obama's "green energy" loans went to his own donors.[223]

According to a *New York Times* analysis, about 75 percent of Obama donors who gave $100,000 or more got to visit the White House.[224] Some of them were first-time donors to Obama or the Democratic Party, and their donations sometimes coincided with their visits.[225]

One such donor was Sanjiv Ahuja, the CEO of LightSquared, a Virginia-based satellite broadband company. Ahuja donated more than $30,000 to the Democratic Party. His White House meetings often coincided with his attendance at Obama fundraisers.[226] *The Daily Caller* reported donations also coincided with Obama's Federal Communications Commission giving "favorable regulatory decisions and other special treatment while driving its competition out of business," after getting documents and communications on the matter.[228]

Rewarding donors and pay to play and schemes were the standard operating procedure in the Obama administration. Here's another prime example of just how corrupt it was: Even though the U.S. government had stockpiled $1 billion in smallpox vaccines at $3 a dose, the Obama administration aggressively pushed through a no-bid contract for Siga Technologies to provide 1.7 million unnecessary experimental smallpox vaccine doses costing taxpayers $255 per dose. Did the experimental vaccine even work? No one knew. But the controlling shareholder of Siga, Ronald O. Perelman, is a long-time Democrat party donor. Andy Stern, the onetime boss of the Service Employees International Union (SEIU), which donated about $27 million to Obama's political campaigns, also sits on the Siga board.[229]

The Pritzker family of Chicago have long been generous donors to Obama. In 2011, they got a sweet deal from the FDIC forgiving $144 million they owed after one of their banks failed in 2001. One thousand, four hundred depositors of that bank never recouped over $10 million they lost after the bank's closure.[230]

Obama's rather blatant pay-to-play activities were too much even for some Democrats to stomach, with such liberal Democrat stalwarts as Senators Al Franken and Elizabeth Warren complaining when Obama's pick to head up the Treasury Department ended up being Antonio Weiss, one of Obama's major campaign donation bundlers.[231]

We haven't even discussed the mother of all pay-to-play scams Obama had running; he branded the most offensive example as a Super PAC, but that's not how it functioned while Obama was in office. Just before his second inauguration, Obama announced that his presidential campaign was not going to disband, a stunning break from tradition for second-term presidents. Instead, it would relaunch as a nonprofit group called Organizing for Action (OFA), which would mobilize supporters of his agenda during his second term.

Organizing for Action was run by former Obama White House and campaign staffers, with Obama's 2012 campaign manager, Jim Messina, serving as national chairman. Despite claims the organization would be the next step in a grassroots movement, something more sinister was afoot. With OFA not subject to campaign finance laws, the organization can accept unlimited personal and corporate donations.[232] And big donations bought big influence. Giving or raising at least half a million dollars earned donors a spot on a national advisory board, which met quarterly with Obama at the White House.[233]

While technically legal, this group enabled Obama to skirt campaign finance and ethics regulations designed to prevent outside influence from corrupting government officials. Obama claimed to be an advocate for the little guy, but it was the folks who wrote the big checks who got a ticket to Obama's inner circle and the ability to influence the White House agenda. Given all of this shady activity in Obama's administration, we think Obama's 2011 executive order requiring government contractors to disclose their political donations was just a means of making it easy for Obama officials to identify those who have paid the price to gain influence or receive favors.

39. OBAMA'S UNQUALIFIED AMBASSADORS

Presidents sometimes give ambassadorships to big donors and bundlers, and Barack Obama was no exception. Some donors outright expect such assignments as a reward for their loyalty. Prior to his second term, Obama found so many fundraisers expecting appointments that he established rules for applicants: volunteer for more than one country and be ready to serve for only two years so he could award the post to someone else who donated big money.[234]

According to an analysis by the American Foreign Service Association, 30.7 percent of Obama's ambassadorships went to political appointees.[235] Many of these were campaign bundlers who collectively raised millions of dollars for Obama.[236] However, the problem with these nominations wasn't that they were political. Many of his political picks were grossly unqualified for the posts they filled. Here are some gems from Obama's second-term ambassadorial nominees:

- **Caroline Kennedy** was nominated as ambassador to Japan, despite having no foreign policy experience, knowing next to nothing about the country, and not speaking Japanese.[237]
- **George Tsunis** was an Obama bundler nominated as ambassador to Norway; he proved during his nomination hearing that he didn't know what system of government the country had.[238]
- **Noah Bryson Mamet** was nominated as ambassador to Argentina; he'd never even visited there.[239]
- **Max Baucus,** the retired Democratic Senator, was nominated by Obama to be ambassador to China. He painfully admitted to the Senate Foreign Relations Committee that he was "no real expert on China."[240]
- **Colleen Bell**, yet another Obama bundler and a soap opera producer, was nominated as ambassador to Hungary; she had no knowledge about the country.[241]

According to Christian Whiton, a former State Department adviser in the Bush administration, while sending donors to be ambassadors is nothing new, sending people "that have no idea what they're doing or about the regions they're going to" is.[242] Henri J. Barkey, a former State

Department official in the Clinton administration, was also critical of Obama's ambassadorial picks. "The Obama administration's appointments suggest that the president isn't being honest when he says that diplomacy is important to him."[243] It certainly was not as important to him as his campaign coffers.

40. AN ADMINISTRATION OF RADICALS

During his first presidential campaign, Obama buried his decades-long friendship with the racist Reverend Jeremiah Wright and domestic terrorist Bill Ayers. Obama may have distanced himself from Ayers and Wright during the campaign but as president, he openly embraced individuals just as radical and out of the American mainstream as his former pastor and political mentor and appointed or nominated them for high positions in his administration. That happens when those who support your candidacy with contributions get the plum assignments, and those who are close to you are far outside the mainstream. Here are some zealots not mentioned elsewhere in this book:

» **Charles Freeman** was nominated as director of the National Intelligence Council (NIC). Even Nancy Pelosi objected to the pick.[244] His ties to Saudi and Chinese interests, his anti-Israel positions, and his prior criticism of "America's lack of introspection about September 11" regarding "what might have caused the attack"[245] aroused so much opposition that Freeman had to withdraw his name from consideration.

- **Donald Berwick** was appointed by Obama in 2010 as Administrator of the Centers for Medicare and Medicaid Services (CMS). He sparked controversy, not only because he got the position via a recess appointment after it was clear his nomination wouldn't get the consent of the Senate, but also for his forthright advocacy of healthcare rationing and for his admiration of the way the British national health system denies care to people whose quality of life (as determined by bureaucrats) isn't worth spending money on.[246]
- **Nawar Shora** was a member of the fanatically anti-Semitic Arab-American Anti-Defamation Committee when Obama appointed him, in 2010, as senior advisor to the Transportation Safety Administration (TSA) on civil rights and civil liberties matters.[247] What justification is there for putting such a person in a position to advise the TSA—our only line of defense against jihadist terrorism targeting public transit—on protecting civil rights? There isn't any.
- **Debo P. Adegbile,** a former NAACP Legal Defense Official, was nominated by Obama to head the Civil Rights Division at the Department of Justice. He's an unapologetic supporter of convicted cop-killer Mumia Abu-Jamal and helped spare him the death penalty on appeal.[248]

His controversial nomination was blocked by the U.S. Senate in March 2014.[249]

» **Jeh Johnson** was nominated by Obama to be his new Secretary of Homeland Security after the departure of Janet Napolitano. His main qualification was the $100,000 he gave to Obama and Democrat candidates and groups.[250] Johnson's lack of experience on immigration was concerning.[251] But his experience in other areas was downright scary. As general counsel of the Department of Defense, he proposed changes for military tribunals that gave captured terrorists *more* protections.[252] In November 2012, he claimed that "the core of al-Qaeda is today degraded, disorganized and on the run."[253] Whether he foolishly believed this or intended to mislead Americans, such a claim spoke ill of his ability to defend the homeland. In January 2014, Johnson said illegal immigrants residing in America had "earned the right to be citizens."[254]

41. CZARS EVERYWHERE, AND ALL OF THEM RADICALS

Beyond executive appointments to head up established federal departments, the modern president will also surround himself, in theory, with subject-matter experts who can help him respond to issues with sound policy. Despite his original campaign promise of unprecedented transparency, Obama's czars took on a much greater significance than in any previous administration as a group, and most of them completely bypassed the nomination process, which would have provided the transparency that Obama had promised. Without the advice and consent of the Senate, Obama was free to place some of the most radical individuals in high positions of the government, and many of them knew virtually nothing about the subject on which they advised the President. Here are a few of Obama's most radical czars, most of whom got their positions without the Senate's consent:

» **Van Jones** was an admitted radical communist with connections to black nationalism and anarchism. In 2009, he became Obama's **Green Jobs Czar** without nomination or Senate approval but was forced to resign six months later when he could no longer deflect questions about his radical past. His use of crude language to describe Republicans in a speech prior to taking his post and his signature on a petition alleging the U.S. government had a role in the 9/11 terrorist attacks didn't help matters.[255] Jones is also a supporter of convicted cop-killer Mumia Abu-Jamal.[256]

» **Cass Sunstein** advocated for the government to outlaw hunting and eating meat. In a book published in 2004, he wrote that animals should have the right to sue in a court of law.[257] This is the man Obama nominated as his **Regulatory**

Czar. After gaining Senate approval, he served in that capacity from 2009 to 2012.

» **Kevin Jennings**, Obama's appointed **Safe Schools Czar** from 2009 to 2011, is a radical LGBTQ activist who founded the Gay, Lesbian, and Straight Education Network (GLSEN) in 1990. His group has promoted radical homosexual lesson plans and curricula in K-12 schools.[258] Jennings was the keynote speaker at a GLSEN conference in Boston, MA, in 2000, where his fellow activists gave young children (as young as twelve years old) graphic instructions for performing various homosexual sex acts.[259]

» **John Holdren** was a 1960s radical whose writings have shown support for forced abortions and sterilizations to combat overpopulation and for a massive campaign to regress the economies of the United States and other Western nations for the sake of the environment.[260] He served as Obama's **Science Czar** throughout his tenure after gaining Senate approval in 2009.

» **Adolfo Carrion** served as Bronx Borough president and pocketed thousands of dollars in kickbacks from developers in exchange for getting projects approved or funded with taxpayer dollars.[261] This urban machine politician has much in common with Obama and was, therefore, a natural fit to be his **Urban Czar**. He served in that capacity from 2009 to 2011, all without Senate approval.

- **Vivek Kundra**, appointed as **Information Czar** from 2009 to 2011, had a criminal history. At twenty-one, Kundra was convicted of misdemeanor theft for stealing shirts from JC Penney after he attempted to evade arrest by running from police. Soon after starting his position at the White House, his former place of employment, the D.C. technology office, was raided by the FBI. Two of his former aides were arrested on a slew of charges, including bribery and taking kickbacks.[262]
- **Carol Browner,** head of the EPA under Bill Clinton, helped destroy the agency's computer files and email backups on her last day in office, in violation of federal law.[263] In January 2009, we learned that Browner was a member of the Commission for a Sustainable World Society, the climate change action arm of Socialist International.[264] She served as Obama's **Global Warming Czar** throughout his first term. The Senate was not consulted.
- **Mark Lloyd** was Obama's appointed **FCC Diversity Czar** from 2009 to 2012. While working for a left-wing thinktank prior to joining the Obama administration, Lloyd encouraged activists to harass conservative and Christian radio stations by filing complaints with the FCC in hopes of shutting them down.[265] Lloyd has also advocated for white media executives be *forced* to step down from their positions so

that blacks, gays, and other minorities can have power.[266]

- **Ron Klain** was appointed as **Ebola Czar** in 2014 after a massive outbreak of the Ebola virus killed thousands of people in West Africa. Because it struck hardest in Nigeria, an important trading partner with the West, cases of the virus made their way to the United States, and Obama tapped Klain to plan a strategy to contain an outbreak at home. But Klain was not a medical professional nor someone with any expertise in infectious diseases and epidemiology. He was a money-moving Democrat operative.[267] The outbreak subsided in 2015, and Klain quietly moved on, having never produced any sort of strategy.
- **Rob Malley** was Obama's **ISIS Czar**, appointed in December 2015, but that wasn't his first stint working for the president. The Obama administration already fired him once for meeting with the Palestinian terrorist group Hamas and sympathizing with Islamist extremists.[268]

So much for Obama's campaign promise to create a team of rivals. These are all people who think and act the same way. Do they represent American values? Not even close. Are these the people you hire if you want to unite the country? Hardly. Do we want our president *choosing* to welcome corrupt zealots into his administration? Most certainly not. But Obama's goal was to fundamentally transform America, and these were most definitely the kinds of people who could help him do that.

42. THE WORST RECORD WITH THE SUPREME COURT

While running for president in 2007, then-Senator Barack Obama said: "I was a constitutional law professor, which means, unlike the current president, I actually respect the Constitution." He had a funny way of showing it. There are many examples of Obama flouting the Constitution, and the vast majority involve his tendency to bypass Congress to legislate via executive action. We'll talk more about that in a later chapter, but few things show Obama's lack of respect for the Constitution better than the slew of unanimous rebukes he suffered in the Supreme Court.

In *NLRB v. Noel Canning*, the Supreme Court ruled that Obama had made three unconstitutional appointments when the U.S. Senate was not in recess. In *McCullen v. Coakley*, the Obama administration filed an amicus brief in favor of a Massachusetts law banning free speech within thirty-five feet of an abortion clinic. The law was unanimously found to be unconstitutional. They also filed an amicus brief supporting warrantless searches of cellphones of American citizens in *Riley v. California*—and lost. In *U.S. v. Jones*, Obama's Justice Department tried to convince the Supreme Court that the federal government doesn't need a warrant to track your car with a hidden GPS device for any reason and was laughed out of court.[269]

Obama's record with the United States Supreme Court is the "worst record of any modern presidency," according to Ilya Shapiro of the CATO Institute. "In the first 6.5 years of Obama's presidency (January 2009 to June 2015), the government lost unanimously at the Supreme Court 23 times, an average of 3.62 cases per year." Obama's unanimous defeats are double that of George W. Bush and one-and-a-half times as many as Bill Clinton. The government had an average win rate of 70 percent before the Supreme Court before Obama arrived, while Obama won less than 50 percent of his cases.[270]

It says a lot when the highest court in the land, so often split along ideological lines in their rulings, reached unanimous decisions so frequently *against* Barack Obama's extremist positions. Obama may fancy himself a president that "actually respects the Constitution," but the Supreme Court (and even two of his own Supreme Court nominees) clearly thought otherwise.

43. UNCONSTITUTIONAL RECESS APPOINTMENTS

Presidents have the power to nominate and appoint individuals to various federal positions, with the advice and consent of the U.S. Senate. However, when the Senate is not in session, the chief executive is also given the authority to fill federal positions temporarily without consent. The Senate checks this power by being the sole body capable of declaring itself in recess. We mentioned that Obama lost a court battle over recess appointments before the Supreme Court. Here's why.

When Obama's controversial nominees to the National Labor Relations Board (NLRB) and Consumer Financial Protection Bureau stalled in the Senate, he bypassed their constitutional role and declared his nominees appointed via recess appointment when the Senate was not in recess. Majority leader Harry Reid declared the Senate to be in "pro forma" session, a tactic he already used to prevent George W. Bush from making recess appointments at the end of his second term. Experts from across the political spectrum warned of the dangerous precedent Obama was setting.[271]

The Senate later approved Obama's appointment of Richard Cordray as director of the Consumer Financial Protection Bureau in a confirmation deal, but the legitimacy of his three "recess" appointments to the NLRB was debated in court. Days after his second inauguration, a federal appeals court overturned those appointments, saying, "Allowing the president to define the scope of his own appointments power would eviscerate the Constitution's separation of powers."[272] A second federal appeals court agreed in May 2013.[273] A third federal appeals court also agreed a couple months later that Obama violated the Constitution with his three NLRB "recess" appointments, effectively invalidating all the decisions made by the NLRB with the illegally appointed nominees.[274]

The U.S. Supreme Court took up the case in 2014, and one of Obama's own nominees, Justice Elena Kagan, found herself questioning Obama's abuse of power, saying, "It really is the Senate's job to determine whether they're in recess or whether they're not," during oral arguments.[275] They ruled unanimously against Obama and rejected those appointments as invalid.

44. SELECTIVE ENFORCEMENT OF THE LAW

Sometimes it wasn't Obama's crafting of a new law by executive order that smacked of the worst corruption. Sometimes it was his refusal to enforce laws already on the books. The president of the United States doesn't just sign new bills into law; he also has to enforce existing laws. Unfortunately for the rule of law, this president had a hard time enforcing laws he didn't like.

In February 2011, Barack Obama decided that the Defense of Marriage Act (DOMA), signed by President Bill Clinton in 1996, was unconstitutional and instructed his Department of Justice to stop defending the law in court.[276] In August 2011, the Obama administration announced a decision to suspend deportation proceedings against illegal immigrants "who pose no threat to national security or public safety." According to *The New York Times*, "The new policy is expected to help thousands of illegal immigrants who came to the United States as young children, graduated from high school and want to go on to college or serve in the armed forces."[277] Obama's actions, *The New York Times* conceded, would improve his image with Latino voters before Election Day. A week prior to this announcement, Obama was criticized by Hispanic organizations for not doing enough on issues important to Latino voters, particularly immigration.[278] Obama's refusal to enforce all immigration laws helped him win reelection. According to exit polls, Obama won 71 percent of the Hispanic vote,[279] up from 67 percent in 2008.[280]

It may be easy for some to excuse Obama's selective enforcement of the law because they feel the ends justify the means. Selective enforcement of the law can only lead to trouble. Dr. Milton R. Wolf, a *Washington Times* columnist and cousin to Barack Obama, called selective enforcement of the law "the first sign of tyranny."[281] We agree. If Obama could pick and choose what laws to enforce, all future presidents will see no reason not to do the same, to the great detriment of all Americans.

45. VIOLATING HIS OWN LAWS

It wasn't just existing laws that gave Obama trouble. He often chose not to enforce laws he himself signed. For example, Section 1513 of Obama's economic stimulus required the executive branch to submit quarterly reports on the impact of the stimulus. These reports, which were meant to prove just how transparent the Obama administration was, would continue until the third quarter of 2013, but the last report ever submitted came in 2011, when it became impossible to sugarcoat how little the stimulus helped.[282]

Obama often violated even his most important legislative achievement, the Patient Protection and Affordable Care Act, hereafter referred to as Obamacare. The Galen Institute published an analysis of Obama's execution of Obamacare in January 2016. They documented forty-three unapproved changes to the bill, including multiple delays of the employer mandate, delaying the individual mandate, delaying the online insurance marketplace, expanding subsidies, covering abortions, delaying and eventually canceling Medicare cuts, and many others.[283]

In 2012, Barack Obama signed the Magnitsky Act, a bipartisan bill sanctioning human rights abusers in Russia. Eighteen Russian officials were sanctioned under the law in 2013, and the Obama administration promised to expand the list later that year. But Obama refused to enforce the law—a law he signed—by not adding twenty new human rights abusers (as vetted by the Treasury and State Departments) to the list of those banned from traveling into or doing business in the United States.[284] One Obama official thought this might be a payoff to Russian President Putin for his "help" brokering a deal for Syria to give up its chemical weapons.[285] Human rights abusers worldwide breathed a sigh of relief knowing that, under Obama, the United States' foreign policy for promoting human rights could be so easily manipulated.

When Obama agreed to a deal purporting to curb Iran's nuclear ambitions, he violated the Constitution by not seeking the approval of Congress. But he also violated another existing law he signed.[286] A provision in the deal allowed for foreign subsidiaries of U.S. parent companies to do business with Iran. This violated the Iran Threat Reduction and Syria Human Rights Act of 2012, which closed a loophole enabling foreign subsidiaries of U.S. parent companies to do business with Iran.[287] We'll have much more about the deal with Iran later in this book; it suffices to say that Obama bent many rules and made many unwarranted compromises on behalf of the United States to make the deal, including laws he personally signed into law.

THE ECONOMY

ON ELECTION DAY 2008, THE biggest issue was the economy. With the economic meltdown that September fresh in everyone's memory, many Americans voted for Obama because he promised to get our economy back on track after the perceived failure of Republican fiscal policy. He would later claim actions he took prevented a second Great Depression, but the record proves otherwise. The changes Obama delivered included: higher gas prices, spending increases, tax increases, record-breaking deficits, historic debt, stubbornly high unemployment and low workforce participation, and a slew of other failures at home.

By the end of 2013, Obama had already "pivoted" his focus back to the economy over twenty times, without success.[288] His constant need to announce that he was returning his attention to the economy came from the undeniable fact that, for most Americans, his policies didn't make things better. Let's tackle a few of his biggest-ticket items and discuss their efficacy. As you'll see throughout this chapter, Barack Obama answered most economic problems with calls for an immediate federal response to the crisis. His recommendations revolved around regulation, market manipulation, and central planning, and when he was able to implement his policies, they usually made matters worse.

46. MISSED BUDGET DEADLINES

Obama's priorities never aligned with the needs of a struggling American economy. From the start, he proved his lack of concern in large ways and small. As a presidential candidate and as president-elect, Obama promised to "go through our federal budget—page by page, line by line—eliminating those programs we don't need, and insisting that those we do operate in a sensible, cost-effective way."[289] This promise suggested Obama was very serious about the nation's budget and getting the country's fiscal house in order.

But as president, the budget became such a low priority for him that, not only did he break his promise to go line-by-line to eliminate waste, he rarely submitted an annual budget proposal on time as required by law. The Budget and Accounting Act of 1921 says the President of the United States must submit his annual budget by the first Monday in February. Since its passage, no president ever missed the legally mandated deadline more than once. That is, until Barack Obama became president.

Obama's budgets for FY2011 and FY2016 were both on time, but the others were all late:[290]

FY2010: 98 days late
FY2012: 7 days late
FY2013: 7 days late
FY2014: 66 days late
FY2015: 30 days late
FY2017: 8 days late

This was a minor offense, but his repeated violation of budgetary law was a symptom of his general lack of concern for keeping America's financial house in order. The boondoggles and ill-conceived policy blunders that littered his administration came from the same lack of orientation to detail and fiscal responsibility. Let's now discuss some of those failures.

47. FEDERAL TAKEOVER OF STUDENT LOANS

We begin our exploration of Obama's economic legacy with one of the leading issues for millennial voters who helped to propel him to prominence in 2007 and 2008: the cost of a college education. The young supported his presidential bid by a larger than two-to-one margin, but they paid a steep price for their naiveté. Under Obama, the cost of going to college increased faster than ever before. On Obama's watch, the average student loan debt for an undergraduate roughly doubled. How did this happen?

On March 30, 2010, President Obama signed a law taking over the student loan program from private lenders to prevent predatory high-interest loans. In the short term, this move lowered student loan interest by 1 or 2 percent; however, by federalizing student loans, the government profited immensely from student loan interest. And, as so often happens when government gains a monopoly on any service, those writing the rules stopped defending the people they claimed to serve. To maximize profits for the federal government, the Obama administration fought vigorously against bankruptcy safeguards for student loans. The law shackled America's young people in the bonds of government dependency and blocked any hope for more innovative methods of financing a college degree.

Total outstanding student loan debt in the United States is over $1.2 trillion, making it second only to mortgage debt. The average student loan debt for college graduates in 2009 was $24,000.[291] In 2016, it exploded to $35,000. Burdened with record debts, students entered the workforce only to face an economy hostile to the young. Due to an increasing number of college graduates that couldn't find a job after leaving school in the Obama economy, student loan delinquency rates skyrocketed; by 2016, 11 percent of all student loans were ninety days or more delinquent, nearly double the rate it was in 2003.[292] Gone were the days when young people could expect to gain their independence and make their own way in the world after they finished college. We alluded to this previously when we described millennials as the "boomerang generation." Millennials now boomerang as often as 30 percent of the time, and that number is on the rise.[293]

Alan Collinge, founder of StudentLoanJustice.org, said, "To say that the federal government now sits atop the most predatory lending system in our nation's history is not an understatement."[294] He added, "This all happened on Obama's watch. He cannot avoid accountability for what is shaping up to be among the largest financial catastrophes this country has ever seen."[295] For all of his big talk about the injustice being done to young people at American colleges, Obama made things far, far worse.

48. PROPOSED FEDERAL TAKEOVER OF COMMUNITY COLLEGES

Obama wasn't satisfied with handing the college lending industry over to federal managers. With his support among millennials dropping as they struggled to enter the workforce and pay off their debts, Obama proposed that community colleges should be free to attend (at taxpayer expense) nationwide in 2015.[296] He argued funding the entire community college infrastructure would cost less than driving many youths into four-year colleges for the entire term and forcing them to take on large student loans and accumulate debt.

There are several problems with this line of reasoning however. First, the average student who completes a two-year degree, and then finishes completing a four-year degree thereafter, takes about three semesters longer to finish both degrees than the students who just complete a four-year degree, saving only one semester of tuition at a more expensive four-year institution.[297] Credits don't always transfer well, the students who begin at a community college tend not to be the high-achievers who will advance quickly through a full bachelor's degree, and the students who start at a community college often join the workforce during or after their experiences. Second, the vast majority of people who complete a two-year degree never finish a four-year degree and already avoid having debts since community colleges aren't very expensive. Third, community colleges vary wildly in quality and tend not to prepare students all that well for four-year degrees or the workforce unless they offer programs directed at a specific trade.

This proposal amounted to a multibillion-dollar speculative investment in a system that is much, much weaker and less equipped to educate our youth and prepare them for the workforce than the four-year college system. In fact, the nonpartisan American Action Forum released a report late in 2015 that suggested the community college subsidy plan will be a perverse incentive and will have the opposite impact that Obama intended. Rather than improving access to post-secondary education, it would have the effect of reducing graduation rates and squandering over half the money invested in students who don't obtain degrees.[298]

And the debt the federal government would accumulate to promote this program would be the tip of the iceberg. How long would it be before Obama and the left leaned on the electorate to support the full takeover of the university system? When the government was struggling to keep paying their own employees and their interest charges on outstanding debt, attempting to fully manage the college and university system was folly.

49. CASH FOR CLUNKERS

Speaking of speculative investments with little in the way of upside potential, this one was a doozy. Many of Obama's attempts to stimulate the economy were *probably* well-intentioned, but they weren't well thought out. Government programs often have unintended consequences and, ultimately, do more harm than good. The *Car Allowance Rebate System* (more commonly known as Cash for Clunkers) was a program meant to stimulate the auto industry by enticing car owners to purchase newer, more fuel-efficient vehicles by offering a rebate on their older, less fuel-efficient vehicle. The program was such a "success" that the original $1 billion allocated for the program wasn't enough, and the system required another $2 billion to run.[299]

Based on the results, Cash for Clunkers was not worth the hefty price tag. According to an analysis by Edmunds.com, owners bought 690,000 vehicles while the program ran, but "only 125,000 of the sales were incremental. The rest of the sales would have happened anyway, regardless of the existence of the program."[300] Despite the environmental justification for the program, it hurt the environment, as vehicles traded in were destroyed, not resold, creating vast material waste.[301]

Obama called Cash for Clunkers "successful beyond anybody's imagination."[302] If spending $3 billion to fail at stimulating the auto industry and hurting the environment was a success, we would prefer not to see what failure looked like.

50. THE BIGGEST GOVERNMENT SPENDER IN HISTORY

Speculative spending like the above was just a minor symptom of a much bigger problem with Obama's economic policy. There is a firm fascination in the far-left with spending our way out of problems. While running for reelection in 2012, Obama claimed: "Federal spending since I took office has risen at the slowest pace of any President in almost 60 years." That was a deliberate deception based the belief that a new president has no control over spending during his first year in office because that year's budget was approved by the previous president and Congress. It's a very convenient axiom that enables Obama and his defenders to distort his spending record. It also couldn't be more wrong.

Obama's first year in office was not constrained by the budget approved by President Bush. In fact, only three of Fiscal Year 2009's twelve appropriations bills passed under Bush because the Democrats in Congress, confident that Obama would win in 2008, waited until Obama took office before going on a spending binge. So most of the spending that took place in 2009 was, in fact, approved by President Obama.

This spending, which included Obama's failed stimulus and bailouts, resulted in a 17.9 percent increase in spending over Fiscal Year 2008 compared to the 3 percent increase proposed by Bush.[303] This increase in spending was the highest annual spending increase since the Korean War. By the end of his first year in office, Obama's spending as a percentage of GDP was 25.2 percent, the highest in history, except for during World War II.

Obama's reckless spending could have been a short-term aberration following the financial crisis of 2008, but instead, Obama maintained that higher level of spending. Obama's spending far outpaced his predecessors and the historical post-WWII average.[304] By ignoring his first year in office, Obama and his defenders can claim he maintained the status quo, shirking responsibility for his record deficits and for skyrocketing the nation's debt. No matter how much he tried to pass the buck, Obama was the biggest government spender in history.

51. LARGEST DEFICITS IN HISTORY

If you spend as much as Obama did, annual deficits will skyrocket. Not only did it skyrocket, but Obama gave us the highest U.S. deficits in history. Here are the top ten deficits in history adjusted for inflation in 2009 dollars:

FY 2010	$1.54 trillion (Obama)
FY 2009	$1.4 trillion (Obama)
FY 2011	$1.23 trillion (Obama)
FY 2012	$787.39 billion (Obama)
FY 2015	$683.51 billion (Obama)
FY 2013	$680.29 billion (Obama)
FY 2014	$648.53 billion (Obama)
FY 1943	$602.19 billion (FDR)
FY 1945	$599.82 billion (FDR)
FY 2017	$588.29 billion (Obama)[305]

When adjusted for inflation, Obama owns the seven highest deficits in history, which surpass the debts incurred during World War II. Obama's smallest deficit was for FY 2016 ($524.61 billion, in 2009 dollars), which was still higher than the deficit for FY 2008 ($462 billion), George

W. Bush's last full year in office.[306] Yet, since Obama takes no responsibility for the cost of doing business in 2009, he claims that he reduced the annual deficit by two-thirds. *Politifact* gave this claim a stamp of "mostly true," but they yield some important caveats, notably that he compared his performance to his dreadful performance in 2009 when he added a huge stimulus package to the budget whose impacts we'll discuss at greater length shortly.

52. MORE DEBT THAN ALL PAST PRESIDENTS... COMBINED

As a presidential candidate in 2008, Obama called President George W. Bush "unpatriotic" and "irresponsible" for adding $4 trillion to the national debt during his two terms. But here are the facts about our nation's debt from the day Obama took office, to the start of his second term, to his last day in office:

Publicly Held Debt
January 20, 2009: $6.31 trillion
January 22, 2013: $11.57 trillion (+83%)
January 20, 2017: $14.4 trillion (+128%)

Gross Federal Debt
January 20, 2009: $10.6 trillion
January 22, 2013: $16.43 trillion (+55%)
January 20, 2017: $19.95 trillion (+88%)[307]

Obama accumulated almost as much gross federal debt as all previous U.S. presidents in history *combined*. In fact, under his administration, the debt to GDP ratio surpassed 100 percent for the first time since World War II. Unlike the temporary expense of running a massive war campaign, Obama's exploding debt was permanent, as the current deficits mostly came from entitlement spending, which went up on Obama's watch.[308] This unsustainable growth of America's debt continued unabated and, by the end of FY2016, the Debt-To-GDP ratio was 106.1 percent.[309] Most economists agree that, if U.S. dollars didn't back the entire global lending industry, such levels of debt, relative to GDP, would lead to hyperinflation and economic ruin.

He often blamed Republican obstruction for slowing his plans for deficit reduction by blocking tax increases on the wealthy. There's just one problem: if every penny were taken from people making $250,000 per year, the deficit reduction, even assuming no one fled the country to protect their assets, would be smaller than the rate of mandatory spending increases forced on the budget by Medicare, Social Security, and Medicaid. To get enough tax revenue to make a real dent in the debt without cutting spending—something Obama never suggested doing in any of his budgets, many of which were unanimously *rejected* in the Senate—he would have to tax the middle class and the wealthy to such levels as to make everyone poor.

53. CREDIT RATING DOWNGRADE

In modern history, many nations have had their credit ratings downgraded; nations like Argentina and Zimbabwe, which have a long history of economic troubles and lack the influence of the United States on global monetary policy. But on August 5, 2011, Standard & Poor's downgraded the U.S. credit rating from AAA to AA+. This was the first time the United States ever had its credit downgraded.[310] Democrats have been quick to blame conservatives, claiming that our downgrade was a result of uncertainty over whether the U.S. would increase its debt ceiling or shutter the government, rather than accepting "compromises" dictated by Democrats. Compromise isn't compromise if you don't give up something in return for getting something. And S&P's report lists multiple causes for the downgrade, including the above Democrat talking point and the lack of seriousness by Washington's leftists in tackling entitlement deficit spending.

This meant that the financial world was starting to doubt whether the United States, under Obama, could generate enough money, long-term, to pay down the massive and rapidly rising U.S. debt. With Obama's record high annual deficits, the questions remain: will we be able to repay Obama's debts? Will there be future downgrades to America's credit rating?

54. REFUSAL TO COMPROMISE ON THE "FISCAL CLIFF"

After his reelection, Obama decided compromise was no longer necessary. Even when Republicans gave him something he wanted, he wouldn't give them something back in return. Obama wanted to see "the rich pay their fair share" and promised to end exemptions and deductions for high-income earners. He couldn't fulfill this promise before the election but, with the "fiscal cliff" looming at the end of 2012, Republicans offered to close loopholes for the wealthy, hoping Obama would accept their concession and offer one of his own to complete the deal.

The GOP offered a balanced compromise: reduce or eliminate various exemptions and deductions for high-income earners in exchange for making all of the Bush tax cuts permanent.[311] With this deal, Obama could keep his promise and could do so with bipartisan support and the overwhelming support of Americans. But this wasn't good enough for Obama, who rejected the deal because he still wanted an increase in tax rates.[312] There would be no halfway with him, just *his* way or the highway. After a contentious election, Obama had a chance to prove he could unite the country and score an easy, popular victory. Instead, he established, once and for all, he was no uniter.

55. EXPLOSION OF MILITARY FOOD STAMP USAGE

Let's talk about entitlements. We can raise concerns over the price of Obama's many boondoggles, his economic stimulus plan (more to come on that one), and his experimental attempts to give the government more control over business. But the biggest source of debt, by far, is entitlement spending. So why would Obama cut military benefits enough to force able-bodied, patriotic Americans onto food stamps when a sensible politician would look for ways to "bend the cost curve down" on these social safety net programs?

At the end of 2013, Defense Secretary Chuck Hagel warned of looming cuts to military pay and benefits.

Our brave men and women in the military already make much less than civilian federal employees, yet Hagel called the cuts necessary for "military readiness."[313] Once the ill-advised deed was done, the cost of providing active and retired military families with food stamps increased dramatically, nearly doubling from $52.9 million in 2009 to $103.6 million in 2013.[314] Civilian federal employees typically got wage hikes every year under Obama.[315] It makes no sense to us that the military should fare any differently. The least any nation can do for their warriors (who have volunteered to be put in harm's way in service of their country) is to make sure their families don't have to endure financial hardships that make them dependent on government support.

56. THE FOOD STAMP PRESIDENT

If you want to understand why Obama would throw our military into the Supplemental Nutrition Assistance Program (SNAP), have a look at the bigger picture. On the day Obama took office, there were 31.94 million Americans participating in the food stamp program.[316] By Election Day 2012, the number of Americans on food stamps rose to a record-high 46.7 million people[317] and, for each person who found a job in the Obama Economy, seventy-five went on food stamps.[318] At the end of FY2015, there were 45.77 million. The program cost $37.6 billion in FY2008 and peaked at $79.87 billion in FY2013. By the end of his time in office, the SNAP program was cost $70.93 billion, still almost double what it was before he took office.[319]

How did this happen? We need look no further than Obama's 2009 "Stimulus," which increased the benefits of the program and relaxed eligibility. The "Stimulus" was intended to encourage economic growth but encouraged government dependency instead. Robert Rector, senior research fellow at the Heritage Foundation, found that able-bodied adults without dependents (ABAWDs) were the fastest-growing category of new food stamp users under Obama.[320]

There's another problem contributing to the massive cost increases of the SNAP program. When almost five times as many ABAWDs started getting food stamps, food stamp fraud also increased. Compared to other federal programs, SNAP has one of the lowest rates of fraud, but when the program is running around $75 billion annually, even a small amount of fraud translates to millions of dollars.[321] The cost of food stamp fraud more than doubled during Obama's first term, costing taxpayers $750 million in 2012 despite Obama administration plans to crack down on food stamp fraud in 2011.[322]

Fraud aside, most Americans support the food stamp program, but people who become dependent upon government for a long time lose the incentive to work and improve their own lives, especially since, the moment they get a job, their benefits are cut, and it rarely pays as well to work an entry-level job as it does to collect from Uncle Sam. Obama showed no urgency to improve the lives of the less fortunate. Instead, he placated them with a meager subsistence diet and called it social justice.

57. THE DISABILITY PRESIDENT

Unemployment benefits only last for a finite period, but many Americans that were unable to find work instead discovered an alternative to unemployment checks: Social Security Disability. Under Obama, Social Security Disability claims rose at a 4.5 percent annual rate—until it peaked in May 2014—even though the incidences of workplace injuries had been declining for many years.[323] When Obama took office, 9.3 million Americans were receiving Social Security Disability payments; he left office with 10.6 million Americans receiving Social Security Disability benefits.[324]

Because dependent people are easier to control, the Obama administration made it easier for people to become dependent. The Social Security Administration stopped verifying disability claims with anywhere near the rigor of prior years. The Senate Permanent Subcommittee on Investigations found in 2012 that a large percentage of disability claims were not properly reviewed, making it hard to track fraudulent claims.[325]

58. POVERTY AND INCOME INEQUALITY

In looking for an issue to resonate with his base for the 2014 midterm elections and take some attention away from the botched Obamacare rollout, Obama talked about income inequality—which he described as the "defining challenge of our time." In a speech at an event hosted by a liberal thinktank, Obama declared that the "combined trends of increased inequality and decreasing mobility pose a fundamental threat to the American Dream, our way of life, and what we stand for around the globe."[326] While honoring the fiftieth anniversary of the war on poverty, Obama said there was more work to do, lamenting that "far too many children are still born into poverty, far too few have a fair shot to escape it."[327] Such rhetoric sounds nice, but Obama was the real threat to the American dream.

Child poverty was catastrophic under Obama, with UNICEF reporting 1.7 million more American children were living in poverty in 2012 than in 2008 (a 2 percent increase), bringing the total to 24.2 million—nearly a third of America's children.[328] Nearly 40 percent of African-American children lived in poverty during Obama's presidency.[329] As of December 2014, 65 percent of American children were living in households receiving federal aid.[330] Poverty reached record levels on his watch. In 2009, Obama's first year in office, the overall poverty rate was 14.3 percent thanks to the Great Recession. The poverty rate then held at or above 15 percent for three years for the first time since the mid-1960s.[331]

While the income gap was stable under President Bush, under Obama, the richest 20 percent of Americans got richer while the bottom 80 percent got poorer every year. When Ronald Reagan was president, everyone, rich and poor, got richer every year.[332] Even the liberal *Huffington Post* admitted that, under Obama, the wealthy have taken home a greater share of the nation's income than they did under President Bush.[333]

Obama often decried the so-called Bush tax cuts "for the wealthy," but the fact is that Obama's policies were more "pro-rich" than the ideas put forth by Republicans. Since Obama became president, the richest 1 percent have seen their share of America's wealth skyrocket to 25 percent of all income, while the bottom 90 percent have seen theirs drop below 50 percent of the nation's income for the first time.[334] In Obama's America, the middle class dwindled while the millionaires and the poor drifted further apart.

To understand why, we look to the median household income. If an economy is in recovery, median income adjusted for inflation should rise over time until the recession ends. But "The Obama Recovery" saw a net *reduction* in worker pay. The American median annual household income declined for six years straight under Obama, despite the end of the recession in 2009. Even those Americans fortunate enough to hold jobs weren't seeing the benefits of the recovery.

The only people who've reaped the benefits work on Wall Street. Stock prices are doing just fine, fueled by speculation and the success of the wealthiest Americans under Obama. While the average pay of the American worker fell for six straight years, the incomes of the top 5 percent went up.[335] If Obama cared about income inequality, he didn't show in how he governed, choosing to support policies that proved harmful to the middle class for ideological reasons.

59. RECORD LONG-TERM UNEMPLOYMENT

We now know that Obama was terrible for deficit spending, income inequality, and the cost of entitlements, but how did he do at creating jobs? We can begin to learn the answer by finding out how many people lost work and then failed to find new jobs. The "long-term unemployed" are those persons who stay unemployed for twenty-seven weeks or longer. When Obama first took office, the number of long-term unemployed was 2.6 million. That number more than doubled during the recession, peaking at 6.8 million people in April 2010.[336]

When Obama took office in January 2009, the average (mean) duration of unemployment was 19.8 weeks. It continued to climb even after the recession ended, peaking at 40.6 weeks in July 2011.[337] Under Obama, the long-term unemployment rate reached its highest levels since World War II[338] and didn't recover to pre-recession levels until well into his second term—far too long.[339]

60. DECLINE IN LABOR FORCE PARTICIPATION RATE

Context is vital when assessing economic figures. The official unemployment rate, the U3 rate, measures only people who are both out of work and actively looking for work. This unemployment number does not include those underemployed or those who have given up looking for work. Although Obama trumpeted a slowly falling U3 unemployment rate as progress, the workforce participation rate argues otherwise. The workforce participation rate is calculated by the Bureau of Labor Statistics and indicates the percentage of Americans sixteen years of age and older who are working or looking for work.

In December 2007, when the Great Recession began, the labor force participation rate was 66 percent and declined to 65.7 by the end of it. However, the labor force participation rate did *not* improve even after the recession ended. By May 2015, the participation rate was 62.9 percent, the lowest since Jimmy Carter's presidency, and still went lower.[340] The decline in the labor force participation rate has been the most significant factor in the decline of the official unemployment rate during Obama's presidency.[341] Even though the official unemployment rate for May 2015 was 5.5 percent, the seasonally adjusted U6 unemployment rate (which includes discouraged workers who stopped looking for work and part-time workers who want full-time work) was 10.4 percent, which is significantly *higher* than it was before the recession.[342] By the time Obama left office, the labor force participation rate was still only 62.7 percent.[343]

61. STIMULUS FAILURE

Now, let's look at Obama's signature employment bill—the omnibus spending appropriation he hoped would create jobs and halt the recession. To hear Obama tell it, in 2009, passing the American Recovery and Reinvestment Act would usher in a new era of American prosperity. Obama promised the American people that by spending hundreds of billions of dollars we would keep unemployment low, reduce poverty, create a new green economy, and provide shovel-ready projects that would rebuild our crumbling infrastructure.

None of that happened. All we got for our huge investment was a mountain of new debt,[344] a long list of failed "green energy" companies,[345] more poverty,[346] and a still crumbling infrastructure.[347] There was a recovery, but it was a "recovery" marked by fewer new jobs than we needed to keep up with population growth and record low levels of workforce participation. As for those shovel-ready projects, even Obama had to admit they didn't exist.[348]

Despite Obama administration forecasts of robust GDP growth of 4.3 percent in 2011 and 2012, GDP only grew 1.3 percent in 2011 and 2.4 percent in 2012.[349] Anemic GDP growth would continue for five years before showing real, however brief, signs of improvement.[350] By the summer of 2016, GDP growth was still in a slump at around 1.5%.

The stimulus failed at getting Americans back to work also. The Obama administration had predicted that the official unemployment rate would be 5 percent by January 2014—*without* the stimulus. Yet, after the stimulus passed, 6.6 percent of Americans were officially unemployed, and the only reason the unemployment rate got that low was because millions of Americans left the workforce entirely. Despite Obama's stimulus, it wasn't until May 2014—a whopping seventy-seven months after the start of the recession—before non-farm employment returned to pre-recession levels, making Obama's economic recovery the slowest since the failures of the last massive community investment projects known as the alphabet soup pushed forward by FDR.[351]

Maybe the spending would have done more to help the middle class had the funds been sent where they were needed. Instead, richer blue states with lower poverty, unemployment, bankruptcy, and foreclosure rates received the bulk of Obama's stimulus money while poorer red states got shafted.[352] It is difficult to provide shovel-ready jobs when you're rebuilding the infrastructure in places where most of the people are already employed or possess significant personal wealth. Perhaps that is why unemployment stayed above 8 percent for an unprecedented forty-three months.

62. DECLINE OF ENTREPRENEURSHIP

Not even Barack Obama would argue that entrepreneurship is not critical for the American economy. "Entrepreneurs embody the promise of America," Obama said in January 2011. "In fulfilling this promise, entrepreneurs also play a critical role in expanding our economy and creating jobs."[353] And you would think, with Obama investing billions of federal dollars in startups and scientific research, there would be a surge in entrepreneurship. After all, Obama often called his stimulus bill an investment in the future.

Not so much. In January 2015, Jim Clifton, the CEO of Gallup, revealed that America now ranked "12th among developed nations in terms of business startup activity. Countries such as Hungary, Denmark, Finland, New Zealand, Sweden, Israel and Italy all have higher startup rates than America does."[354] Clifton also noted that "for the first time in 35 years, American business deaths now outnumber business births."[355] The last time that was true was under Jimmy Carter. Small businesses were forced to freeze hiring, cut jobs, even scale back growth because of Obamacare, and Obama's financial regulations have dried up startup capital.[356] Despite Obama's lip service to entrepreneurs, his policies nearly killed America's entrepreneurial spirit. In the wake of the election of Donald Trump, small business confidence exploded and, riding a wave of tax cuts and deregulation, the nation came back fighting. What a difference pro-growth leadership makes.

63. TAX HIKES AFTER PROMISED TAX CUTS

As a candidate for president in 2008, Barack Obama promised to cut taxes for the middle class. He promised that "no family making less than $250,000 a year will see any form of tax increase. Not your income tax, not your payroll tax, not your capital-gains taxes, not any of your taxes." It was a lie, of course. No politician, no matter their intentions, can keep tax rates low, increase government spending by 20 percent, and keep deficits under control. Americans for Tax Reform found that Obama's budget proposals from FY2010 through FY2015 included a total of *442 tax increases!*[357] Even the left-wing fact-checking site *PolitiFact had* to concede that Obama didn't keep his promise to cut taxes on the middle class.[358]

Despite his love for tax increases, Obama often claimed he was a tax *cutter*. He claimed his stimulus bill cut taxes for 95 percent of Americans. It was a lie oft-repeated and rarely challenged by the media. Obama's "stimulus" package didn't cut taxes, as veteran journalist and blogger Robert Stacy McCain explained, it merely included: "a temporary two-year tax credit that reduced payroll withholding by—brace yourself—a whopping $8 a week."[359] That didn't stop

Obama from claiming it was "the biggest middle-class tax cut in history," a claim debunked by *The Washington Post*'s fact checker as "ridiculous."[360]

Obama may want history to remember him as a friend to the middle class, but every single budget Obama proposed included significant tax hikes. From his expensive climate policies, to tobacco taxes, to limits on tax deductions, Obama proposed tax increases amounting to trillions of dollars, many of which hurt the middle class.[361] And we haven't even discussed the biggest tax hike of them all: the *Affordable Care Act.*

64. ANEMIC GDP GROWTH

Obama pitched his tax increases and spending sprees as investments in economic growth and sustainability, but the economy didn't grow much as a result. The Gross Domestic Product (GDP)—a measure of the economic output of a country—is perhaps best gauge of the strength of America's economy, and when you look at Obama's economy in terms of GDP, there is no way to sugarcoat how awful it has been. Despite seven years of Obamanomics, economic growth in the first quarter of 2016 was a dismal .5 percent, the slowest in two years.[362] That continued a trend of anemic production year after year. Annual GDP growth rates averaged 1.55 percent during his two terms, with the following yearly figures:

2009	-2.8%
2010	2.5%
2011	1.6%
2012	2.2%
2013	1.7%
2014	2.6%
2015	2.9%
2016	1.5%[363]

This means Obama is the *only* president in U.S. history to have never had a single year of 3.0% or greater GDP growth.[364] *Entrepreneur* and *Forbes* contributor Louis Woodhill said his abysmal average growth rate only outperformed Herbert Hoover (-5.65 percent), Andrew Johnson (-0.70 percent), and Theodore Roosevelt (1.41 percent).[365] So...congratulations?

65. THE DECLINE OF ECONOMIC FREEDOM

In order for there to be economic growth, there has to be economic freedom. Just look at the nations that have none—in the communist dictatorship of North Korea, the people eat tree bark to survive.[366] Zimbabwe, which used to be self-sufficient in food, has suffered a 70 percent reduction in food production since dictator Robert Mugabe gained power.[367] Venezuela sits on an ocean of oil and overflows with other valuable natural resources. Yet the country suffers from food and power shortages.[368] The common denominator in these examples is a government that has taken control over the economy. Every time this is tried, economic disaster results.

Economic freedom allows people to start and expand businesses as they see fit. It allows people to take risks and earn rewards. People decide for themselves what is in their best interests. Freedom and ingenuity create more success than top-down attempts to increase national wealth. It's basic human nature—we do not strive to improve ourselves without incentives.

Under Barack Obama, the United States experienced a significant decline in economic freedom. According to the Heritage Foundation's Index of Economic Freedom, the United States had the 5th freest economy in 2008, the year before Obama took office, but fell to 11th place in 2016, his last year in office. "The U.S. score declined repeatedly during the Obama years thanks to dramatically increased government spending and regulations, a failed stimulus program that enriched the well-connected but left average Americans behind, and laws such as the Affordable Care Act, which denied the right of individuals to keep the health plans they already had, and as the president had promised."[369] The Fraser Institute's economic freedom rankings showed a similar decline over the Obama years too.[370]

66. THE WORST ECONOMIC RECOVERY

So let's total this all up for you, readers. What was the net result of increased taxes, increased spending, decreased labor force participation, a hobbling GDP growth rate, increased dependence, and serial attempts to hand the government more control over business?

If you listen to Obama, you'd think he was the first president ever to inherit an economy in recession. But both George W. Bush and Ronald Reagan inherited recessions.

There have been eleven recessions since World War II, each of which was followed by a recovery. Even Obama has experienced economic recovery...it just happens to be the worst one.

All jobs lost in post-World War II recessions were recovered after about twenty-five months on average. It took seventy-seven months for non-farm employment to return to pre-recession levels, making Obama's recovery the slowest recovery of them all (by a wide margin).[371]

The labor force participation rate trended downward for the entirety of Obama's presidency—never recovering to pre-recession levels.[372] The employment-population ratio remained virtually flat since the end of the recession. In December 2007, the employment-population ratio was 62.7 percent. By the time the recession ended in June 2009, it had dropped to 59.4 percent. In December 2014, it was even lower, coming in at 59.2 percent, which is also below the average Employment-Population Ratio for the entire eighteen-month recession, and the 60.6 ratio when Obama took office.[373] Jim Clifton, the CEO of Gallup, said in early 2015, "The number of full-time jobs, and that's what everybody wants, as a percent of the total population, is the lowest it's ever been. [...] In the recession we lost 13 million jobs. Only 3 million have come back."[374]

As we noted, wage growth wasn't good either. Prior to the recession, annual wage growth was above 3 percent but averaged about 2 percent for Obama.[375] GDP growth has hovered in the tepid 2 percent range after the so-called recovery.[376] In early 2016, Steven Ricchiuto, the chief economist at Mizuho Securities USA, said, "There is no acceleration in underlying economic activity."[377]

The middle class suffered the most in the Obama economy. After six years of Obama's economy, the middle of the road wage earners still made less than they did before Obama took office and have a lower net worth.[378] Median income in 2013, down 8 percent from 2007, still hadn't recovered from the 2008 recession.[379] While most of the jobs lost in the recession were medium or high wage jobs, nearly half of the jobs created in the Obama recovery were low-wage jobs.[380] Home ownership has declined and, in 2014, reached a nineteen-year low.[381] Nearly two-thirds of Americans live paycheck-to-paycheck with no emergency fund to cover unexpected expenses.[382]

The Obama recovery was particularly hard on women and minorities. Even though women make up 46.8 percent of the workforce, only 38.6 percent of all new jobs added under Obama went to women.[383] According the Bureau of Labor Statistics: "women have experienced weaker job growth after the end of the 2007-2009 downturn than they had experienced in the previous three recessions."[384] The wealth gap between whites and minorities also got worse since the end of the recession.[385]

America's young people are also "experiencing hardships like never before under the Obama administration," according to an analysis by Young America's Foundation. The Youth Misery Index (YMI), which is calculated "by adding youth unemployment, student loan debt, and national debt (per capita) numbers," reached a record high in 2014. The Youth Misery Index increased 53.7 percent under Obama, which is "the highest increase under any President, making Obama the worst President for youth economic opportunity."[386]

Obama often claimed that he inherited "the worst recession since the Great Depression," but even that's not true. The economy Ronald Reagan inherited was in rougher shape after the disastrous Carter years.[387] The slow recovery was not because the recession he inherited was "the worst recession since the Great Depression," but because his approach to getting the economy back on track failed miserably. Some jobs did arrive for Americans during Obama's presidency, but he can't claim responsibility for them. The oil industry created more jobs in the United States than all other industries combined between 2008 and 2013 despite Obama's war on oil (more on this later)—Obama was openly hostile to the energy sector.[388] Making Obama's job record even worse, job growth in just one state accounted for the nationwide net gain in jobs since the recession. From December 2007 to December 2014, Texas added 1,444,290 jobs, while the forty-nine other states and the District of Columbia were still 275,290 jobs below pre-recession levels.[389]

Obama thinks—or at least claims—that he *saved* the economy. And while he may cherry-pick numbers to claim the economy bounced back well, the Obama Recovery is not worth bragging about. Millions of people lost jobs and never got rehired. Those who were able to find work mostly got lower wage jobs. Household wealth remained below its 2007 peak. In fact, Obama's economic growth gap topped two trillion dollars in GDP in the summer of 2015. According to *Investor's Business Daily,* Obama's so-called economic recovery "is far worse than all the previous 10 stretching back 70 years."[390]

BULLY TACTICS

THE LAST THING AMERICANS EXPECTED when they elected Obama was a mafia-style government. His campaign touched on the general concern people felt for the overreach of George W. Bush's Department of Homeland Security, that sense they were at the mercy of their government, rather than in command of it. He seemed to have a sunny, charitable disposition. He even restrained his criticism of Bush to respectful disagreement devoid of malice.

But once he took office and settled in, Obama's actions said, "That's a fine-looking business you've got there. It'd be a shame if something happened to it." Substitute government agency, monument, newsroom, lifestyle, healthcare plan, or some other cherished American value or privilege for business and the line still worked. When Obama didn't get his way in Washington, the American people paid the price. His temper erupted into bursts of irrational saber rattling, petty bullying, and bitter rhetorical spasms that left even his supporters mystified.

After three years of contending with a Republican-controlled House of Representatives, Obama aired his dirty laundry on national television during the 2014 State of the Union address, when he declared if Congress didn't play ball, "I have a pen, and I have a phone." Perhaps we should add the Constitution to the list of items it would be a shame to lose for not acquiescing to his demands. We've tallied a few of his nastiest tactics to bully the nation to his way of thinking for your perusal.

67. DESPOTIC VETO THREATS

The Founding Fathers had an amazing insight into human nature. They foresaw the coming of men like Obama who would threaten the liberties guaranteed by their Constitution. So they built a system of checks and balances and carefully enumerated the powers of every piece of the government, giving the executive branch few ways to influence lawmaking. Throughout Obama's two terms in office, his unconstitutional actions and power grabs outraged millions of American citizens, including members of Congress. But we'll discuss some of his attempts to legislate with executive orders later in this book.

Lawmakers tried everything they could, short of impeachment, to reign in Obama and stop his excesses. After a long train of usurpations and abuses by Obama, they drafted two separate pieces of legislation to reign him in. The *Faithful Execution of the Law Act* of 2014 would require executive agencies to submit a legal justification from the Attorney General whenever they chose not to enforce a law. The *Enforce the Law Act* would give Congress the power to sue the president when he changed a law or failed to faithfully execute it.[391] Obama threatened to veto both bills rather than risk any limits on his ever-expanding legislative authority.

In December 2014, Obama advisor Dan Pfeiffer told *The Huffington Post* that Obama "would veto a bill to fund the Department of Homeland Security if it included a rider that nullified his executive action on deferred deportation."[392] In other words, Obama threatened to imperil national security for the sake of an illegal action he felt was justified.

The Founders gave the president veto power to use as a last resort when Congress enacted laws that defied the Constitution to prevent legislative overreach. Obama, instead, threatened to use his veto power to defend his own unlawful acts against a legislature rightfully asserting its authority to make laws. In both cases, Obama never vetoed a bill—the threat of a veto was enough to kill both bills—but Obama's inversion of the Framers' intent amounts to a declaration that he alone, and not Congress, would dictate policy.

68. CARD CHECK

Democrats rely on financial backing from big labor—eleven of the top twenty donors to political causes during the 2012 elections were unions.[393] Obama has always counted on the support of unions, and unions relied on Obama to support their efforts to increase their power and influence. When it suited him to bludgeon union workers to maintain funding for Democrats, he did it by supporting "Card Check" and opposed laws guaranteeing the right of all workers to get a job in their trade.

In order for a company to unionize, there is a secret ballot election among the workers. When their ballots are secret, workers are more likely to vote their conscience, which may or may not be in favor of joining a union.

So Democrats, in support of their big labor donors, put forward the deceptively titled *Employee Free Choice Act*, commonly referred to as "Card Check," to deny workers a secret ballot. Supporters of Card Check say, in a secret ballot, voters may be fed misinformation by coordinated anti-union forces from company management, robbing them of their freedom to form groups and associate as a union. Card Check gives union organizers an excuse to twist arms and force a de facto public vote by distributing cards requesting the authorization of a union; if a majority of the employees request the union, the employer can skip the secret ballot and recognize the union.[394] Barack Obama, responding to a rapid decline in union participation with typical brute force, supported Card Check at the federal level.

Right-to-work laws make it illegal for a company to force union membership and dues as a condition of employment. Any worker can belong to any union he likes, but no firm may *require* them to belong to a union. Obama opposed this basic protection of workers, dubbing them "right to work for less" laws.[395] By 2012, states with right-to-work laws created four times as many jobs as forced-unionization states.[396] From 2009 to 2012, right-to-work states accounted for 72 percent of the new jobs created, even though they didn't quite make up 40 percent of the population.[397]

If putting people to work transcended politics for Obama, he'd have supported right-to-work laws because they *encourage* job growth. If he supported liberty, he'd have favored workers doing as they wish, rather than being forced to fund the Democratic Party with their hard-earned wages. Instead, he supported the right of unions to harass and intimidate some workers and exclude others from good jobs because they disagree with his agenda.

69. WHITE HOUSE SNITCH LINE

In August 2009, a disturbing blog post on the official White House blog called on Obama's supporters to submit "scary chain emails and videos," "rumors," "emails," and even "casual conversation" to a specific White House email address so the Obama administration could "keep track of all of them."[398] This was Obama's third weapon of mass intimidation—the three Ds of silencing debate, as chronicled by Kirsten Powers in her recent bestseller *The Silencing: How the Left Is Killing Free Speech.* Those three Ds are: delegitimize, divide, and dehumanize. Obama used them all to perfection. The snitch line divided Americans into tribes and calls on his supporters to rat out their illegitimate opposition, for example.

Later Obama's reelection campaign would follow suit with an "Attack Watch" page, on which registered Obama supporters could denounce their fellow Americans for expressing anti-Obama opinions.[399] This was not a clearinghouse where Obama supporters could get talking points to refute attacks against Obama—it was a page for Obama supporters to report on fellow citizens who were speaking ill of the president. It was filled with grotesque depictions of inhuman caricatures that represented conservatives and Republicans and moderated by White House staffers.

This kind of thing might be typical in countries ruled by dictators, but not America. In made Obama look tiny, thin-skinned, and imperial. After conservative media got wind of the story, Obama's campaign aides apologized and removed the site. Treating American citizens like children who need a chaperone or criminals guilty of wrongthink is straight out of *1984* or Soviet Russia.

70. THE GIBSON GUITAR RAID

On August 24, 2011, armed federal agents raided the Gibson Guitar headquarters in Tennessee. They shut down production, sent employees home, and confiscated wood. Gibson was accused of illegally importing woods from India, but Gibson had not violated any American law. The Department of Justice was enforcing the laws of India, even though the Indian government approved the exports. According to Gibson, the government of India did not support or consent to the actions of the Justice Department.[400]

Gibson had fully complied with foreign laws, and the wood seized by the government conformed with industry-recognized, independent standards for "responsible management of the world's forests."[401] But that didn't stop the Obama administration from going after Gibson, and the reason might be political. Both C.F. Martin Guitars and Fender use wood from the same source as Gibson, but neither were raided by the government or forced to pay any fines. Martin and Fender both contribute money to Democrats. Gibson's CEO is a Republican donor.[402]

Motive aside, the raid on Gibson fits a pattern of the Obama administration being openly hostile to non-union companies or union companies that have moved their operations to right-to-work states.[403] In fact, Seattle's largest employer, Boeing, nearly lost an opportunity to expand into South Carolina–a right to work state–when the National Labor Relations Board voted to disallow the company's deal to construct a $2 billion manufacturing plant in the state. Obama's appointees to the NLRB were the difference in the vote.

In 2012, Gibson settled its case with the federal government for $300,000. This amounted to a forfeiture of $262,000 in seized wood and $50,000 in the form of a donation to promote the conservation of protected tree species.[404] The wood was eventually returned to Gibson. The company used it to craft Government Series II Les Paul special edition guitars in a glorious act of defiance of the Obama administration.[405]

71. ARRESTING AN INNOCENT MAN AS A FALL GUY

What did Obama do when he needed someone to blame? Perhaps you should ask Nakoula Basseley Nakoula, the man behind the anti-Islamic video that the Obama administration tried to blame for inciting the attack on the U.S. consulate in Benghazi. The Obama administration knew al-Qaeda was connected to the attacks early on, but they made a strong effort to blame Nakoula's little-seen YouTube video, "Innocence of Muslims," for the violence. On September 12, 2012, Egyptian President Mohamed Morsi called on the U.S. government to arrest Nakoula. Three days later, authorities brought him in for questioning. He was arrested on September 28, 2012, for allegedly violating the conditions of his probation.[406]

Nakoula's arrest caused alarm for some who believe Nakoula was targeted so that the Obama administration could make an example of him and avoid taking responsibility for the Benghazi disaster. According to George Washington University law professor John Turley, this move was very suspicious. "As someone who has had clients accused of violating conditions of probation, this is not standard operating procedure for these violations. It is relatively rare to see people incarcerated on relatively minor violations." He added, "It seemed obvious to many of us that the administration wanted a picture of this man being handcuffed and put in the back of a cruiser so it would play around the world and in the Arab street."[407]

The day after Obama was reelected, after spending months in jail without due process, in violation of the Fifth Amendment to the Constitution, Nakoula was sentenced to spend a year in jail.[408] Those actually responsible for the attack on the consulate that killed four Americans have yet to be brought to justice.

72. TELLING JOURNALISTS HOW TO REPORT HIS POSITIONS

On April 27, 1961, President John F. Kennedy said, "Without debate, without criticism, no Administration and no country can succeed—and no republic can survive."[409] Times have changed. Instead of extolling the virtues of freedom of the press, Barack Obama instead sought to minimize debate and criticism.

While speaking at the Associated Press luncheon, on April 3, 2012, Obama told an audience of journalists how to report his positions. He said, "So, as all of you are doing your reporting, I think it's important to remember that the positions I'm taking now on the budget and a host of other issues, if we had been having this discussion 20 years ago, or even 15 years ago, would have been considered squarely centrist positions."[410]

Obama influences his media coverage in other ways. While running for reelection, Obama granted many interviews to local media. By August 2012, Obama had done fifty-eight local media interviews, but only eight national media interviews.[411] We learned later that Obama was doing this so he could set ground rules for his local media interviews. He couldn't do this with the national press, but smaller media outlets were desperate for access, and Obama could often dictate the topics allowed for discussion.[412] Kennedy's words, over fifty years ago, seem like an ominous warning now. And Obama was just getting started with the press.

73. PROPOSING GOVERNMENT MONITORS IN NEWSROOMS

For Obama, the free press was only free to think like he did. Not content with the fact that nearly all of the mainstream media was on Obama's side, the Obama administration made many efforts to ensure that their actions and policies were only viewed in the most favorable light. For instance, the Obama administration tried "very hard" to discourage Fox News from reporting extensively on the Benghazi attack in 2012.[413] The threat wasn't enough to stop the network from investigating and reporting on it, but the Obama administration didn't stop trying.

Less than a year later, the FCC proposed a new program called "Multi-Market Study of Critical Information Needs (CIN)." CIN would involve placing FCC agents in America's newsrooms to determine how stories were selected, whether there was bias in reporting, and whether "critical information needs" were being met.[414] And the FCC was not planning on just monitoring broadcast news, but also placing agents in print media outlets—over which the FCC has no regulatory authority.

The clear intent of CIN was to intimidate the news media. The FCC controls the licensing of broadcast media and placing FCC agents to monitor the America's newsrooms would put immense pressure on media outlets to report news as the government wishes or risk losing their FCC licenses. After FCC commissioner Ajit Pai exposed the existence of the proposed program in February 2014, outrage caused the FCC to back down.[415] But Obama would find other ways to intimidate the media.

74. ASSAULT ON FREE PRESS

When Barack Obama took office, he promised that his administration would create "an unprecedented level of openness in government."[416] What we got instead was what *The New York Times* public editor Margaret Sullivan described as "unprecedented secrecy and unprecedented attacks on a free press."[417] According to Sullivan, the ability of the press to report freely on its government was "under siege" by the Obama administration.

They began their offensive against freedom of the press with threats and intimidation. In 2012, when the so-called sequestration budget "cuts" were looming, Barack Obama tried to blame the cuts on Republicans during his third debate with candidate Mitt Romney. It wasn't true, according to legendary journalist Bob Woodward, who pointed out, both in his book *The Price of Politics* and in an opinion piece in *The Washington Post* in early 2013, that automatic spending cuts were proposed by the White House and personally approved and signed into law by Obama.[418] Less than a week after that piece was published, Woodward revealed, during an appearance on CNN, that a senior White House official warned him that he would "regret" criticizing Obama for his true role in the genesis of the sequester.[419]

Soon after Woodward's story came to light, other journalists started coming forward with similar stories about threats and abusive treatment they'd received for merely asking tough questions of members of the administration, or for unflattering coverage.

The *New York Post*'s Maureen Callahan spoke with several reporters. David Brody, the chief correspondent for CBN News told her, "I can tell you categorically that there's always been, right from the get-go of this administration, an overzealous sensitivity to any push-back from any media outlet." Liberal journalist Jonathan Alter also said he'd been subject to similar abusive treatment from the

Obama administration for writing something they didn't like. A young female reporter was called crude names in an email for merely asking important questions of an Obama Cabinet Secretary.[420]

Ron Fournier, editor-in-chief of *National Journal*, also came forward, stating, "I received several emails and telephone calls from this White House official filled with vulgarity, abusive language, and virtually the same phrase that Woodward called a veiled threat."[421]

The Washington Times columnist Lanny Davis, a centrist Democrat and Obama supporter, was threatened with having his access to White House officials limited for being critical of the administration's policies.[422]

This kind of thuggery from the White House, which flies in the face of our First Amendment rights to freedom of the press, was standard operating procedure in the Obama administration. But they weren't satisfied with mere threats. After Obama was reelected, he and his cabal got *really* nasty.

In May 2013, the Associated Press revealed that Obama's Justice Department secretly obtained two months of phone records of AP reporters and editors. AP President and CEO Gary Pruitt said, "There can be no possible justification for such an overbroad collection of the telephone communications of The Associated Press and its reporters. These records potentially reveal communications with confidential sources across all of the newsgathering activities undertaken by the AP during a two-month period, provide a road map to AP's newsgathering operations and disclose information about AP's activities and operations that the government has no conceivable right to know."[423] The Obama administration wouldn't say why it gathered the records, but it may have been connected to a government investigation into the source for an AP story of a foiled terror plot.[424] As a result, longtime sources stopped talking to the Associated Press and other news organizations.[425]

Soon after the AP phone records story broke, *The Washington Post* reported that, in 2010, the Justice Department secretly obtained Fox News reporter James Rosen's phone records, tracked his movements, and read his emails while investigating possible leaks of classified information to Rosen for an article on North Korea's nuclear program published in 2009. The Justice Department justified their actions by labeling Rosen a "co-conspirator" with Stephen Jin-Woo Kim, a State Department contractor who was charged with violating the Espionage Act of 1917 for leaking the information to Rosen.[426] The secret warrant was approved by Attorney General Eric Holder.[427]

Michael Barone, senior political analyst for *The Washington Examiner*, said, "Presidents and attorneys general of both parties have been reluctant to use the Espionage Act when secret information has been leaked to the press because they have recognized that it is overbroad." But not Barack Obama and Eric Holder. "They have used the Espionage Act of 1917 six times to bring cases against government officials for leaks to the media—twice as many as all of their predecessors combined."[428]

A report by the Committee to Protect Journalists, a nonprofit organization that promotes press freedom worldwide, was highly critical of Obama's aggressive and unprecedented attacks on the free press. "In the Obama administration's Washington, government officials are increasingly afraid to talk to the press. Those suspected of discussing, with reporters, anything that the government has classified as secret are subject to investigation, including lie-detector tests and scrutiny of their telephone and e-mail records," the report says.[429] Longtime *New York Times* reporter David Sanger called the Obama administration, "the most closed, control freak administration I've ever covered."[430]

75. OBAMA'S ENEMIES LIST

Believe it or not, Obama's 2012 campaign team stooped to even uglier tactics than "Attack Watch." Democrats remember Richard Nixon's "enemies list" with justified terror, but Obama created something similar when he used a campaign fact-checking microsite to identify and vilify several private citizens who were donors to Mitt Romney's campaign in 2012.

Campaign staffers identified the donors on Obama's list on Twitter and disseminated via email to his supporters. One such Romney donor was Sheldon Adelson. In the summer of 2012, the Obama campaign emailed supporters vilifying Adelson and his wealth—the same day Obama's Justice Department began investigating alleged money laundering by several executives of the Las Vegas Sands Corporation, owned by Adelson.[431]

Obama also tweeted a call for his supporters to demand that the Koch brothers make the names of donors who had joined them in setting up political action committees for the 2012 campaign public.[432] Obama attempted to intimidate anyone working with the Koch brothers by urging his most rabid supporters to denounce the donors and cast them as pariahs worthy of exile from polite society. Even Democratic pollster, strategist, and commentator Douglas E. Schoen called this a "misuse of government power to vilify private donors," which "diminishes the prestige of the Oval Office and damages our social consensus."[433]

76. MILITARY LABELING OF CHRISTIANS AND CONSERVATIVES AS EXTREMISTS

During the 2008 campaign, Obama referred to his opponents as people who bitterly cling to guns and religion.[434] With an attitude like that, it came as no surprise that Obama's Defense Department classified Catholics and Evangelical Christians as religious extremists in their training manuals, lumping them in with groups like al-Qaeda, Hamas, and the Ku Klux Klan.[435] A Defense Department teaching guide, obtained by Judicial Watch via a FOIA request, labeled the Founding Fathers and conservatives as extremists and equated conservative values with the Ku Klux Klan: "Nowadays, instead of dressing in sheets or publicly espousing hate messages, many extremists will talk of individual liberties, states' rights, and how to make the world a better place."[436]

Tom Fitton, the president of Judicial Watch, criticized the Obama administration for having "a nasty habit of equating basic conservative values with terrorism."[437] But the Obama administration went beyond conservative values and demonized bedrock *American* values. Obama administration officials turned the military against the opponents of his policies with anti-conservative agitprop. We found that horrifying; you should too.

77. THREATENING GALLUP FOR UNFAVORABLE POLLS

Every politician seeks to control the debate, to set up coverage in the most favorable light to himself and the worst for his opponent. But when the Obama administration faced a series of negative polls from Gallup during the 2012 campaign, they taught Gallup a lesson.

First, David Axelrod, one of Obama's senior advisors, contacted Gallup to complain about Gallup's polling methods. When Gallup defended their methods, the Department of Justice joined a lawsuit which had initially been filed against Gallup in 2009 by a disgruntled former Gallup employee.[438] That sent a powerful message to the entire polling industry: if they didn't turn in polls favoring Democrats, they would pay the price. Not long after the DOJ got involved, Gallup changed their polling methods and, miraculously, Obama moved up in favorability and in head-to-head matchups at the national and state levels against Mitt Romney. And, wouldn't you know it, the Justice Department dropped their lawsuit not long after.

78. THREATENING S&P FOR CREDIT RATING DOWNGRADE

Barack Obama didn't just weaponize the Justice Department to target political enemies. Sometimes he used it for payback. In February 2013, the Justice Department accused credit rating agency Standard & Poor's of using a subjective, fraudulent credit rating system. In January 2014, court filings showed the Obama administration had warned Harold McGraw, the chairman of Standard & Poor's parent company McGraw-Hill Financial, that they'd be held accountable for their 2011 decision to downgrade the United States credit rating from AAA to AA+.

In response to the downgrade, the Justice Department sought $5 billion in damages. No other credit rating agencies were included in the lawsuit.[439] The government was investigating all three major credit rating companies but focused solely on S&P after the 2011 downgrade of the United States credit rating.[440] According to McGraw's deposition, then-Secretary of Treasury Timothy Geithner told him the government would look at S&P's conduct very carefully. "Such behavior could not occur, [Geithner] said, without a response from the government," McGraw said in his deposition.[441]

79. OPERATION CHOKE POINT

On March 20, 2013, Michael J. Bresnickat, head of the Financial Fraud Enforcement Task Force at the Department of Justice, announced they had launched a new initiative to investigate banks that did business with companies the Obama administration believed were at a higher risk for fraud and money laundering.[442] Dubbed "Operation Choke Point," the investigation soon took on a partisan slant as Obama's Justice Department "forced banks to terminate relationships with a wide variety of entirely lawful and legitimate merchants," according to the House Committee on Government Oversight and Reform.[443] Some of these businesses were in the adult entertainment industry, or pawn shops and payday lenders. The largest group of businesses impacted, however, were firearms distributors.

Gun retailers of all sizes felt the Obama administration breathing down their necks as they saw their assets frozen, their lines of credit cancelled, and their online presence forbidden—even though they were properly licensed and had good credit. Thousands of small gun-shop owners reported having their accounts frozen by their banks or being dropped altogether. "This is an attempt by the federal government to keep people from buying guns and a way for them to combat the Second Amendment rights we have," said Kelly McMillan, owner of McMillan Group International, which had its account dropped by Bank of America in 2012. "It's a covert way for them to control our right to manufacture guns and individuals to buy guns."[444]

Don't think we included this just because the firearms industry was victimized. The operation gave businesses no due process before stripping them of their livelihoods. They had no evidence that any of the affected businesses did anything illegal. In response to pressure, the FDIC admitted, in January 2015, they were attacking legal businesses because the Obama administration considered them politically incorrect, and promised more transparency, by requiring bank examiners to put their recommendations to end banking relationships in writing, with legal justification.[445] Operation Choke Point ended in the summer of 2017.[446]

80. UNPRECEDENTED ATTEMPTS TO INFLUENCE THE SUPREME COURT

Obama, more than most presidents, thought it was his job to comment on judicial matters; many times, he attempted to influence the Supreme Court prior to major rulings using the bully pulpit. Josh Blackman, a constitutional law professor at the South Texas College of Law, noted, "Very few Presidents have spoken about pending Supreme Court cases after arguments were submitted. Even fewer discussed the merits of cases. Only a handful could be seen as preemptively faulting the Justices for ruling against the government. President Obama, however, stands alone in his pointed and directed arguments to the Supreme Court."

His public comments about two cases involving the constitutionality of key aspects of Obamacare serve as fine examples of this tendency. Those cases were: *NFIB v. Sebelius*, which addressed the individual mandate, and *King v. Burwell*, which addressed federal subsidies.

Of *NFIB v. Sebelius*, Obama said, "Justices should understand that, in the absence of an individual mandate, you cannot have a mechanism to ensure that people with preexisting conditions can actually get healthcare." He also said it would be "unprecedented" for the Court to overturn the law. In *King v. Burwell*, Obama said the case "shouldn't even have been taken up."[447] In both cases, the Supreme Court ruled in Obama's favor.

Whether or not Obama's preemptive public attacks on the Court influenced any Justices, it is not the job of any president to comment on the Supreme Court. Obama's own college law professor, Laurence Tribe, pointed out that "[p] residents should generally refrain from commenting on pending cases during the process of judicial deliberation. Even if such comments won't affect the justices...they can contribute to an atmosphere of public cynicism."[448] For Obama, though, such risks were worth it—the good of his legacy mattered more than the good of the nation.

81. MAKING THE SEQUESTER AS PAINFUL AS POSSIBLE

The last desperate refuge for anyone who cannot get their way is to throw a fit. Tantrums don't get most of us anywhere, but Obama has allies who call a fit a principled stand, hide the evidence of his immaturity, and provide cover. Locked in battles with Congressional Republicans placed there by the American people to slow him down, he collapsed into two separate fits of rage where the victims were ordinary people, and the outcome would have been different if the bad actor was conservative.

In the early months of Obama's second term, the man-child in chief continued his campaign, ignoring the unpleasant business of governing a divided nation by working with the opposition party. Hoping that the American people would blame Republicans for the sequester cuts, Obama instructed various agencies to ensure that the cuts would be as painful as he promised they would be. *The Washington Times* reported:

> *The Obama administration denied an appeal for flexibility in lessening the sequester's effects, with an email*

> *this week appearing to show officials in Washington that because they already had promised the cuts would be devastating, they now have to follow through on that.*
>
> *In the email sent Monday by Charles Brown, an official with the Animal and Plant Health Inspection Service office in Raleigh, N.C., Mr. Brown asked "if there was any latitude" in how to spread the sequester cuts across the region to lessen the impacts on fish inspections.*
>
> *He said he was discouraged by officials in Washington, who gave him this reply: "We have gone on record with a notification to Congress and whoever else that 'APHIS would eliminate assistance to producers in 24 states in managing wildlife damage to the aquaculture industry, unless they provide funding to cover the costs.' So it is our opinion that however you manage that reduction, you need to make sure you are not contradicting what we said the impact would be."*[449]

A whistleblower in the National Parks Service said supervisors denied plans to deal with budget cuts while minimizing the impact on the public and were instead instructed to cancel special events, tours, and educational services provided by park rangers.[450]

Immigration and Customs Enforcement (ICE) released several hundred illegals in their custody "to ensure detention levels stay within ICE's current budget," according to an ICE spokeswoman.[451] Many saw the move as politically motivated to increase public opposition to sequestration and the Republican Party. Is this what an administration does when it's looking out for the best interests of the American people?

82. MAKING THE GOVERNMENT SHUTDOWN AS PAINFUL AS POSSIBLE

From 1976 to 2009, there were seventeen government shutdowns: one time during Ford's presidency, five times during Carter's, seven times during Reagan's, once under George H.W. Bush, and twice under Clinton.[452] All prior shutdown disputes ended when the President and Congress met and hashed out a compromise. But when a government shutdown occurred on Obama's watch, he *refused* to negotiate with Congress to end it. The issue at the center of this shutdown was Obamacare. Republicans wanted to defund it, but the Democrat majority in the U.S. Senate, following Obama's dictate, refused to even debate the notion.

As the budget deadline approached, in September 2013, Congressional Republicans retreated to one demand on the president: in return for a one-year delay implementing the requirement that all Americans must buy health insurance, Congress would provide a continuing resolution to keep the government open. This would give average Americans a similar delay to the one Obama illegally granted to big business. Obama refused to agree to this very reasonable demand, and when the government shut down, he blamed *Republicans* for it.

The American people watched as Obama and congressional Democrats (with the help of the mainstream media) went on a tirade the likes of which they'd never seen. They called Republicans "terrorists" and "hostage takers" with "a gun pointed at the head" of the country. Most of us would hesitate before using such vile language against avowed foreign enemies of the United States. When not fomenting anger towards his fellow Americans who disagreed with him, President Obama was doing whatever he could to make the shutdown "as painful as possible," as he'd also done with the sequester.

National parks and war memorials closed, barricaded and guarded by U.S. Park Service Rangers to prevent access. A supposedly shuttered government had money to print signs and rent fences to close off parks normally open twenty-four hours a day, seven days a week. The Obama administration even barred aged veterans from visiting the open-air World War II and Vietnam War Memorials. Veterans resorted to breaking through the barriers to pay their respects. According to leaked emails obtained by *National Review Online*, the National Park Service knew the veterans were coming but put up the barricades anyway.[454] A tour group of senior citizens was not only kicked out of Yellowstone National Park but treated to frightening, brutal police intimidation until they left the park.[455]

Never missing a chance to be vindictive, Obama forced national parks not even funded by the federal government to close, including the Claude Moore Colonial Farm in Virginia, privately funded campgrounds in Arizona, the Ford's Theatre, and Mount Vernon.[456] Private property owners within the Lake Mead National Recreation Area in Nevada couldn't get to their own homes because Lake Mead was closed.[457] It got so bad and so absurd that even ultra-liberal House delegate Eleanor Holmes Norton (D-DC) confronted Obama about the absurdity of his actions.[458]

Obama made the shutdown out to be an existential crisis and took his ire out on the American people to direct their anger at the Republican Party. After just over two weeks of watching Obama throw a childish tantrum, Congressional Republicans gave Obama everything he wanted for the good of the country. Obamacare rolled forward, and Obama gave no ground.

As bare-knuckle political brawling, Obama's actions might impress the ill-informed, but there is a delicious irony in all this for those who believe in justice: The Obamacare roll-out (which also started on October 1, 2013) was such a disaster that Obama would have been better served had he agreed to the one-year delay of Obamacare as Congressional Republicans demanded.

FOREIGN POLICY AND MILITARY AFFAIRS

AT THE G20 SUMMIT IN London, England, in 2009, the first international summit of his presidency, Obama was asked about previous comments he made regarding America's "diminished power and authority" over the last decade. He said, "I would like to think that with my election and the early decisions that we've made, that you're starting to see some restoration of America's standing in the world."[459] Despite coming into office with no foreign policy experience, Obama believed he would arrive on the scene, restore the world's faith in the U.S. as a reliable partner, convince die-hard enemies of the West to negotiate in good faith, and end the many regional wars and intractable ideological differences that divide the world, or at least, begin the healing process.

The reality, however, looked much different. His lack of foreign policy experience opened him up to many embarrassing, insulting, or otherwise inexcusable gaffes. For example, in September 2012, Obama said of Egypt, "I don't think that we would consider them an ally, but we do not consider them an enemy." White House aides and the State Department had to scramble to correct the record that Egypt is, in fact, a major non-NATO ally and has been since 1989.[460]

But the mistakes ran much deeper than confusion over America's complex relationships around the world. His vanity and naiveté came back to hurt him most when he applied a warped, backward strategy of befriending our adversaries and holding our friends at arm's length. This frightful combination emboldened our enemies, damaged our friendships, and destabilized the entire world, from the Middle East to South America. We'll deal with radical Islam, the Middle East, and the global fight against terrorism in a later chapter. First, however, let's review Obama's general approach to matters of foreign policy and discuss his confusion about the difference between friend and foe and his often disrespectful and dictatorial management of the U.S. Armed Forces. If there were a pattern to the choices he made, we struggled to find it, unless you counted taking the common sense solution to every problem and doing the *exact opposite*.

83. FOREIGN POLICY FLIP-FLOPS

We're leading off this chapter by shining a light on his tail-chasing and lack of conviction because it explains everything else on this list. The man built no coherent vision for how to make the world safer for democracy and economic freedom. He responded to each problem with half-baked reactionary choices depending entirely on the political necessity of the moment. Now, not every policy change was bad for America—he campaigned against Bush's tactics in the war on terror but found, once he arrived in the Oval Office, that some of Bush's policies were unavoidable without serious consequences.[461] But most often, when he changed his mind, he made things worse for America and its allies. Here are a few examples:

» Obama promised to recognize the 1915 Turkish genocide against the Armenian people but later squashed congressional efforts to pass a resolution recognizing the genocide.[462]

» In 2007, Obama stated that the president does not have the power to unilaterally authorize military action but did not seek congressional approval for sending our troops to Libya or Syria.[463]

» Early in his administration, Obama called Egyptian President Mubarak an ally and a "force for good."[464] When Mubarak came under fire during the Arab Spring, Obama called for Mubarak to surrender power.[465]

» Obama said he would not turn a blind eye to the ongoing genocide in the Darfur region of Sudan but did nothing about it as President.[466]

» He claimed, in a speech in front of the American Israel Public Affairs Committee, the United States "will always have Israel's back" but effectively retracted the statement days later during a press conference.[467] His presidency was marked with constant rejections of Israel.

» After Venezuela descended into economic ruin in 2015, Obama claimed he was looking into sanctions against the Maduro regime. The head of the Organization of American States, Luis Almagro, pleaded with Obama to take immediate action, but Obama ignored him and took no action.[468]

- The Obama administration talked tough about Panama's role in drug trafficking and its policy of holding the Panama Canal hostage in exchange for international favors but in 2011, they signed a free trade agreement with them that offered little benefit to the U.S. Later, we learned that the change of heart probably had something to do with creating a tax shelter for the political class with the release of the Panama Papers.[469]
- Obama campaigned on renegotiating the North American Free-Trade Agreement (NAFTA) and even opting out if he couldn't get a better deal for America. He later became one of NAFTA's strongest advocates.[470]

We're just scratching the surface here—this is but a taste of the total chaos that was Obama's foreign policy. Every administration changes positions now and then but, when they cluster like this, they tell the world we don't know what we're doing and make us easy targets for opportunists. They give credence to the Islamist propaganda that the United States is a blind, petulant empire indiscriminately killing innocent people and destabilizing nations for no reason and leaving nothing but misery behind.

84. THE GLOBAL APOLOGY TOUR

Obama began his foreign policy with an international junket conservatives dubbed the "Global Apology Tour."[471] He hoped to rebrand the United States as less arrogant, less entitled, and more willing to compromise with the rest of the world. In his view, the U.S. acquired a bad reputation under George W. Bush and other prior administrations, and the way to fix it was to announce that he would govern differently. The various appearances met with favorable reactions from world leaders and the international press. That would be great if those plaudits earned the U.S. any benefits, but the tour accomplished nothing. Obama's rhetoric showed weakness to our enemies and branded the country as unreliable—if you didn't like America's position on some issue, wait for the next president and it would change.

While in France, in April 2009, Obama said, in America, there was "a failure to appreciate Europe's leading role in the world." He followed that up with: "America has shown arrogance and been dismissive, even derisive."[472] A week later, while speaking to the Turkish Parliament, Obama claimed America was still "working through some of our own darker periods in our history," citing slavery and segregation.[473] At the Summit of the Americas later that same month, he conceded that America has played a key role in promoting peace and prosperity but added, "...we have at times been disengaged, and at times we sought to dictate our terms."[474]

Obama's apologies for the United States continued through his final year in office. In 2016, just before Memorial Day weekend, Obama became the first U.S. president to visit the Hiroshima Peace Memorial and, while not making a direct apology, called the United States' use of atomic weapons on Japan, the same ones that resulted in Japan's surrender and the end of World War II, "mistakes of the past."[475] Likewise, when he toured Havana on his diplomatic mission to Cuba, he praised Castro's regime for getting it right on healthcare and education and said America could learn from the Cuban example on human rights, all while sidestepping Castro's boldface lie that Cuba held no political prisoners[476] and forgetting that people still boarded driftwood rafts to get away from Castro's humanitarian haven.

Obama took a dim view of American history, but the commander in chief of the armed forces shouldn't use his influence to denigrate the nation without expecting negative consequences throughout the world. America paid the price for his historical illiteracy.

85. CUTTING FUNDING TO FIGHT AIDS

Obama entered the White House with plenty of political capital around the world. Despite his conviction that George W. Bush had left us without a friend in sight, America had many allies and ran many successful programs to fight the world's most pernicious problems. Somehow, Obama turned those advantages into old memories and many of our longstanding friends into neutral observers. Let's look at a few examples.

George W. Bush's initiative to fight AIDS around the world, the President's Emergency Plan for AIDS Relief (PEPFAR), saved millions of lives in Africa and elsewhere. From the program's launch in 2003 to the time Bush left office, the number of HIV-infected people in Africa getting proper treatment went from fewer than fifty thousand to two million.[477] His efforts didn't go unnoticed by the people of the African continent. When President Bush took a farewell tour of Africa near the end of his second term, massive crowds of grateful Africans cheered for him.[478]

Despite massive spending increases spearheaded by Obama, he cut funding for PEPFAR[479] and deprived hundreds of thousands of people around of treatment. This inexplicable decision had a devastating effect on Africa, where most AIDS deaths occur.[480] The AIDS Healthcare Foundation was highly critical of Obama's cuts, which came after he had promised to expand the fight against AIDS months earlier:

> *"This latest action merely confirms what people with HIV/AIDS and their advocates have long suspected—the President simply is not committed to fighting global AIDS. Coming on the heels of the President's flowery rhetoric last December, the cynicism is simply breathtaking," said Michael Weinstein, President of AIDS Healthcare Foundation, which provides free HIV/AIDS medical care to over 125,000 people in 26 countries abroad."*[481]

The lesson for Africans: American friendship was fickle and patronizing and they couldn't trust our promises. And we wonder why ISIS propaganda was so attractive to North Africans.

86. HURTING OUR SPECIAL RELATIONSHIP WITH BRITAIN

Since the American declaration of war against Imperial Germany in 1917, Britain has been America's most consistent and staunchest ally around the world. While there have been differences, when the United States found itself in difficulties, we could always rely upon the support of Britain. This friendship was forged by common priorities, shared values, and bloodshed in joint military missions for a century.

Almost as soon as Obama took office, he set about cutting ties by offering insults to our British friends. After the 9/11 terrorist attacks upon the United States, the British government loaned a bronze bust of Winston Churchill to the U.S. as both a pledge of British friendship and an invocation of resolve in the face of adversity. This bust of the greatest Briton of the past century—and the first foreigner ever accorded honorary American citizenship—stayed in the Oval Office during President Bush's term. Weeks after taking office, Obama had packed up the bust and sent it back to Britain.[482]

And the insults didn't stop there. Obama made a series of gaffes and insults at the expense of our ally. In March 2009, Obama gave Prime Minister Gordon Brown a most lackluster presidential gift: a boxed set of classic American films. This uninspired gift was even more insulting since the discs were incompatible with British DVD players.[483] Obama snubbed Prime Minister Brown throughout the year, at one point forcing Brown to settle for an impromptu chat in a kitchen at the United Nations building.[484] In May 2011, while a guest at Buckingham Palace, Obama continued toasting the Queen as the orchestra played "God Save the Queen,"[485] a major faux pas that left a thick air of awkwardness in the room.

Later that year, Obama abandoned all pretense when he declared, "We don't have a stronger friend and stronger ally than Nicolas Sarkozy, and the French people."[486] As America's relations with Britain deteriorated, in March 2012, a panel of British lawmakers wanted to end the "special relationship" with the United States because the phrase was no longer an accurate description of reality.[487] Obama White House officials dismissed the notion that our alliance was anything remarkable. According to the London newspaper *The Daily Telegraph*, "The reality, right now, is that, in the White House's eyes, Britain is not so much 'special' as rather annoying."[488]

In March 2016, Obama, rather than accept responsibility for the destabilization of Libya, blamed British Prime Minister David Cameron for allowing the country to become a "s*** show."[489] Even *TIME* described the relationship between the U.S. and the UK as "less special than ever."[490] With his bridges burnt to a crisp, Obama went to work poisoning the river below. When the British government decided they would hold a vote on whether or not to stay in the European Union, Obama threatened to put them at the "back of the queue" in future trade talks if they voted against staying in the Union.[491] This threat resulted in a significant backlash[492] and, when the United Kingdom voted in favor of Brexit, Obama ended all attempts to broker a free-trade agreement with both the EU and the UK.

87. BETRAYING POLAND

On September 17, 2009, Obama, a longtime opponent of missile defense, killed plans for joint missile defense with Poland and the Czech Republic. These countries, once under Soviet rule, still fear Russia today. Obama had pledged support for the program just six months earlier.[493] According to Dr. Paul Kengor, author and political science professor at Grove City College, "Obama's action was a shocking betrayal of these two allies, and it was done to mollify Vladimir Putin and the Russians."[494] According to Kengor, "Poles and Czechs were stunned. Poles especially were aghast at the timing of Obama's decision," announced on the 70th anniversary of the day Stalin's Red Army invaded Poland. "Back then, too, in September 1939, Poland was virtually defenseless, and Uncle Sam didn't help."[495]

Obama's infamous hot mike moment, during which he told Russian President Dimitri Medvedev he'd have more flexibility to accommodate Russia's demands regarding U.S. involvement in Eastern Europe, came twenty-nine years after Ronald Reagan announced his Strategic Defense Initiative in 1983. Obama's misguided attempts to "reset" relations with Russia have come at the expense of a close ally and our own national security.

When Obama awarded the Presidential Medal of Freedom to a Polish resistance fighter, he outraged the country by calling a Nazi death camp a "Polish death camp."[496] But Obama's treatment of Poland took an extraordinarily insulting turn when Obama played golf on the day of the funeral of the Polish president, first lady, and nearly one hundred senior officials who died in a plane crash and didn't visit the Polish embassy afterwards.[497]

88. THE FIRST ANTI-ISRAEL PRESIDENT

Since the State of Israel formed in 1948, each president has reinforced the United States' commitment to the safety and liberty of the Israeli people. But under Obama, the United States has taken a different direction in its policy towards Israel. With Obama in the White House, America aligned itself more with Israel's enemies. In 2009, during a meeting with Jewish leaders, Obama acknowledged that his administration's policies would put "daylight" between America and Israel.[498] Indeed, Obama's anti-Israel record speaks for itself. Here are a few examples:

» He called on Israel to return to the "1967 borders," which Israel considers indefensible.[499]

» He called on Israel to stop all Jews from moving into the West Bank without a reciprocal request that Muslim populations stay out of the region.[500]

» He legitimized the U.N. Human Rights Council; they called Israel the world's worst human rights violator while ignoring nations that behead people for having the wrong faith, being homosexual, or choosing the wrong Muslim sect.[501]

- He refused to accept Jerusalem as the capital of Israel.[502]
- He told Iran if Israel defends herself and strikes at Iran's nuclear facilities, then Israel is on her own and we had nothing to do with it.[503]
- He snubbed and insulted the Prime Minister of Israel when he was visiting the United States.[504]
- He met with representatives of Hamas, a terrorist group responsible for launching missiles into Israel, but frequently dodged Prime Minister Netanyahu.[505]
- He nominated anti-Israel Chuck Hagel as his Secretary of Defense for his second term.
- He never visited Israel during his first term, despite visiting several of its Middle East neighbors.[506]
- He excluded Israel from his Global Counter-Terrorism Forum while inviting eleven Muslim countries.[507]
- Although Palestinian Authority President Mahmoud Abbas stated, in no uncertain terms, he wouldn't accept any peace deal recognizing Israel as a Jewish State, Obama and Secretary of State John Kerry pressured Israel into accepting a new framework that would have Israel to recognize the Palestinian State with an implied threat of America abandoning Israel if they didn't comply.[508]

- His second Secretary of State, John Kerry, claimed Israel risked becoming "an apartheid state" without a two-state peace deal with Palestine.[509] Despite the uproar that followed this offensive comment, Obama did not repudiate Kerry's remarks.
- Obama's State Department used insulting language to describe Prime Minister Netanyahu's speech before a joint session of Congress.[510]
- He sent campaign operatives to Israel in January 2015 attempting to defeat Netanyahu in Israel's elections.[511] His State Department also sent hundreds of thousands of taxpayer dollars to aid that effort.[512]
- He exposed top secret information about Israel's nuclear program to the world.[513]
- He ended a forty-year-old program that guaranteed Israel oil supplies in case of a cutoff.[514]
- Obama's Federal Aviation Administration (FAA) attempted to ban American flights to Israel following a rocket strike by Hamas. Israeli and American leaders criticized the ban as unjustified, and they cancelled it after widespread outrage.[515]
- He even spied on Israeli Prime Minister Benjamin Netanyahu during the ongoing nuclear negotiations with Iran and used information he took from private conversations to influence public debate about the treaty.[516]

American Jews have long supported Democrats, and despite Obama's anti-Israel record, they still do. The late Ed Koch, former mayor of New York City and lifelong Democrat, supported Obama's reelection despite acknowledging that he knew Obama "would renege on what he conveyed on [sic] his support of Israel."[517] Did he ever. He saved his final insult for his final days in office—we'll discuss that later in the book.

89. NOMINATING CHUCK HAGEL AS SECRETARY OF DEFENSE

Now let's turn our attention to Obama's management of the U.S. Armed Forces. Over the next several entries, you'll see that our servicemen had many reasons to be skeptical of Obama's commitment to national security or to the well-being of veterans and active duty personnel. We begin with his choices to lead the Departments of Defense and State and implement his vision for foreign affairs.

To replace Leon Panetta as Secretary of Defense in 2013, Obama chose Chuck Hagel—a man with none of the qualifications needed for the job. When Hagel testified before the Senate for his confirmation, he revealed himself ignorant of the workings of the Department of Defense and woefully unprepared to take on one of the hardest jobs in government. Hagel was confirmed but drew forty-one "no" votes—a modern record.[518]

Hagel's positions were inconsistent to say the least. He co-sponsored a resolution to give then-President Clinton retroactive approval for the Kosovo War but later called President George W. Bush—who got Congressional approval before going to war—"reckless."[519] He flip-flopped on both the War in Iraq and the PATRIOT Act. During the 2008 presidential campaign, he said he'd be happy to serve in either a McCain or an Obama administration, yet he denounced Republican lawmakers backing McCain's aggressive foreign policy positions on a regular basis.

Hagel was often on the wrong side of foreign policy issues. He called the ultimately successful "surge" of troops in Iraq our worst mistake since Vietnam. He was one of only two senators to oppose sanctions against Iran in 2001.[520] In August 2006, he refused to sign a bipartisan Senate letter calling on the EU to declare Hezbollah a terrorist organization.[521] Hagel also was always wrong about American policy for relations with Israel. In October 2000, he refused to sign a Senate letter in support of Israel. In November 2001, he refused to sign a letter to President Bush urging him not to meet with Yasser Arafat until his forces stopped attacking Israel. In March 2007, he claimed that there was a "Jewish lobby" intimidating American government officials into doing Israel's bidding.[522] In March 2009, he signed a letter urging Obama to open direct talks with Hamas leaders. When Israel tried to stop Hamas from firing rockets at them from Lebanon, Hagel condemned President Bush for not stopping them from defending themselves. In April 2010, he accused Israel of becoming an apartheid state.[523]

Hagel was forced out of the Pentagon in November 2014. David Sedney, the deputy assistant secretary of defense for Afghanistan, Pakistan, and Central Asia from 2009 to 2013, confirmed Hagel was forced out "because of criticism the administration has faced over its national security policies and because of the overall weakness of those policies."[524]

90. THE WORST SECRETARIES OF STATE

Obama's first Secretary of State was Senator Hillary Clinton, who had zero experience in foreign affairs and who achieved next to nothing in the U.S. Senate. She flew around the world a lot, much to her satisfaction, but diplomatic relations with Syria, Venezuela, and all of our allies, even Canada, suffered on her watch.[525] The Russian "reset" was a complete failure.[526] Relations with Israel deteriorated, Japan and South Korea feared we wouldn't defend them against Chinese aggression, and America's enemies saw no reason to fear us. Perhaps the biggest stains on her record as Secretary were the disastrous intervention in Libya, and the Benghazi attack of September 11, 2012,[527] both of which we'll discuss in further detail later.

Clinton left the State Department after Obama's first term and was replaced by Senator John Kerry. On paper, Kerry had substantial foreign policy experience, but his record is atrocious, filled with moments where he was on the wrong side of history. From his adherence to the anti-American "Winter Soldier" program of the far left during the Vietnam War, to his well-documented string of terrible misjudgments of proper strategy against USSR during the Cold War, to his 2003 vote against a campaign in Iraq that he once voted for.[528]

Under John Kerry, crises abounded. From failed ceasefire negotiations between Israel and Hamas, to the rise of the Islamic State in Iraq, it's been one bad headline after another.[529] His policy in Syria was also a continuing disaster, with some indications that U.S. policy in Syria evolved toward helping Iran to restore their alliance with Bashar al-Assad.[530] In early 2014, Kerry failed miserably to bring Russia and the Ukraine to the negotiating table and made no major initiatives to resolve that growing crisis.[531] While the world was burning around us, Kerry's top priority was the negotiation of a climate change treaty.[532] Whatever your position on global warming, it is difficult to understand the connection between international relations and global warming unless your objective is to create global economic controls in the name of mitigating it.

Without a doubt, the Obama-Clinton-Kerry foreign policy record was disastrous. In a September 2014 poll, Americans said they felt less safe six years into Obama's presidency than they did a year after the 9/11 terrorist attacks.[533] They understood better than Obama that weakness invites enemy action. If the average American knew this, how do you suppose experienced combat officers viewed the actions of their superiors?

91. CUTTING MILITARY HEALTHCARE BENEFITS

Aside from cutting our country's defense budget, Barack Obama proposed cuts that raised TRICARE premiums—veterans and active duty servicemen relied on TRICARE as their health insurance guarantee. The White House estimated that the higher fees would generate $6.7 billion in revenues over a decade.[534] Premiums increased by up to 345 percent after five years. Pentagon officials warned this change would hurt military recruitment as health benefits were a key incentive to joining America's military.[535]

Interestingly enough, Obama's cuts didn't affect unionized civilian defense contractor benefits.[536]

One of the more popular provisions of Obamacare is a rule change that allows young adults to stay on their parents' coverage until the age of twenty-six. However, this provision did *not* apply to military families under the military healthcare plan. Children between twenty-two and twenty-six years old cost an extra $200 a month in premiums to insure. By August 2012, only 9 percent of eligible young-adult dependents of service members eligible for the TRICARE extension signed up.[537]

92. POLITICAL CORRECTNESS IN THE MILITARY

America's armed forces must be the best fighting force in the world, equipped to outfight, outwit, and outlast any who would oppose them. With Barack Obama as commander in chief, the military instead became the latest place where the most bizarre and absurd ideas of liberal political correctness took root with no thought to how such actions might affect our ability to fight and win a war.

In 2013, Obama lifted the ban on women serving in combat, despite undeniable biological differences that make women less likely to meet the existing physical demands.[538] Case in point: in January 2014, the majority of female Marine recruits couldn't meet the minimum fitness standards for combat duty. Rather than admit that not all women were capable, the Obama administration delayed implementing the requirement to allow time to reevaluate the standard to give women a better chance to pass.[539]

Concurrently, the Obama administration announced plans to make the Marine Corps uniforms gender-neutral.[540]

Barack Obama's military also became far more hostile toward God and Christianity to make sure a select few were not offended. In 2013, the Pentagon recruited Mikey Weinstein, an anti-Christian extremist, to develop a religious tolerance policy for the military.[541] Soon afterward, the Department of Defense announced that service members who proselytize their faith could face court-martial.[542] In 2015, Lance Cpl. Monifa Sterling was court-martialed for posting a Bible verse on her desktop computer.[543] With Obama as commander in chief, our armed forces abandoned time-honored traditions in favor of a politically correct agenda, sacrificing morale and military readiness.

93. KEEPING MILITARY BASES AND FACILITIES "GUN-FREE ZONES"

Military bases have been "gun-free zones" since 1993. Regardless of the intentions of the ban, the disarming of soldiers on military bases had terrible consequences. After the 2009 shooting at Fort Hood—when Nidal Hasan killed thirteen people and injured thirty-one others—this absurd policy should have been instantly reevaluated by Obama. It wasn't.

In 2011, Congressman Peter King (R-NY), House Homeland Security Committee, warned that military bases, recruitment stations, and other armed services facilities "have become the most desirable and vulnerable targets for the violent homegrown Islamist extremists seeking to kill Americans in their homeland."[544] According to a counterterrorism and security report released during the hearings, "at least 33 threats, plots and strikes against U.S. military communities since 9/11 have been part of a surge of homegrown terrorism." The report also noted "serious gaps" in the "military's preparedness for attacks against its personnel, dependents, and facilities—such as a lack of adequate and clear training in spotting indicators of violent Islamist extremism in individuals who wear the same uniform as those they may target." Yet military facilities remained "gun-free zones."

After the Washington Navy Yard shooting on September 16, 2013, when lone gunman Aaron Alexis killed twelve and injured three, the rule didn't change. Alexis was, according to the FBI, under "the delusional belief that he was being controlled or influenced by extremely low-frequency electromagnetic waves."[545] Military facilities were still "gun-free zones" on April 2, 2014, when there was another deadly shooting at Fort Hood, and soldiers were again defenseless and facing a deadly threat. Over a dozen soldiers were shot, and three were killed before the gunman shot himself. The shooter, Ivan Lopez, an Iraq war veteran, reportedly "snapped" after being denied his request for leave, and the shooting may have been connected to post-traumatic stress disorder.[546] And, when a Chattanooga, TN, military base was shot up by an Islamic jihadi, it was also "gun-free."

Barack Obama should have made sure that soldiers in the most powerful military in the world were no longer reliable "soft targets" for crazed gunmen or terrorists by changing this ill-advised and dangerous rule. He wasn't responsible for military facilities becoming "gun-free zones," but he kept them that way when there were many reasons not to. For that, there was no excuse.

94. PURGING DISSENT IN THE MILITARY

The Obama administration wasn't content to reduce morale in the ranks of the military by slashing their benefits, making them bow to a doctrine of political correctness that often defied common sense, and disrespecting them by failing to honor their service and sacrifices. He also wished to change military culture, by force if necessary. Under Obama, many senior military officers were dismissed without explanation or warning. J.D. Gordon, a retired Navy commander and former Pentagon spokesman, reported by mid-November 2013, the defense department dismissed over two hundred military leaders, or one every 8.8 days, despite decades of loyal service and experience.[547] This suspicious rise in military brass firings led many to speculate that Obama was purging commanders he didn't agree with or threatening those who still served into submission.[548]

According to retired U.S. Army Maj. Gen. Paul Vallely, Obama was "intentionally weakening and gutting our military, Pentagon and [sic] reducing us as a superpower, and anyone in the ranks who disagrees or speaks out is being purged."[549] An anonymous source in the Pentagon said even "young officers, down through the ranks, have been told not to talk about Obama or the politics of the White House. They are purging everyone and if you want to keep your job —just keep your mouth shut."[550]

Further confirmation came in March 2014, when *BuzzFeed* posted a video in which Coast Guard Commandant Admiral Robert Papp claimed Obama had called all five service chiefs into the Oval Office and presented them with an ultimatum: support the repeal of "don't ask, don't tell" (DADT) or resign. "If any of us didn't agree with it—we all had the opportunity to resign our commissions and go do other things," Papp said in the video.[551]

As a presidential candidate, Obama claimed he wanted members of the Joint Chiefs of Staff to decide military matters "based on what strengthens our military and what is going to make us safer, not ideology."[552] Back then, Obama claimed he didn't want to surround himself with yes-men telling him what he wants to hear all the time. "That's part of what happened with George Bush," he claimed. "He surrounded himself with people who were of the same mind."[553] But, as president, his ideology and agenda were far more important than military strength and readiness.

95. CUTTING WEAPONS PROGRAMS

To ensure that our service members go into battle with the very best weapons and equipment possible, the U.S. budgets a significant amount of discretionary spending toward the development and procurement of equipment and weapons. Because we didn't do this during the years prior to World War II, when we went into the war, we had torpedoes that wouldn't explode, aircraft that were sitting ducks, and ammunition that was corroded and useless. We paid in blood for that lack of foresight. Because of this, each post-World War II president has ensured that the budget for new weapons and equipment meets the needs of the moment.

But Obama took a different approach. He cut defense budgets to spend the money elsewhere. The bulk of his defense cuts fell on development and procurement. All told, 40 percent of Obama's defense cuts came from this area.[554] Obama wasn't only tormenting our troops with his personal agenda or putting them at risk with bad foreign policy; he defanged them and stole their capability to defend themselves in combat.

96. KILLING SUCCESSFUL MISSILE PROGRAMS

If you aren't yet convinced that Obama was determined to turn the U.S. military into a small-time operation, we have more evidence for you. In 2014, he announced his intention to eliminate two successful Navy missile programs. Obama's 2015 budget proposed cuts to the Tomahawk missile program budget and an end to production in 2016. The Hellfire missile program was canceled in 2015. So what would have replaced them? The Obama administration invested in a different missile system that won't be combat-ready for at least ten years.[555]

Obama's decision came as a shock to Congress and military experts. Former Pentagon staffer Mackenzie Eaglen, who analyzes military readiness, called the move "short-sighted, given the value of the Tomahawk as a workhorse." Seth Cropsey, the director of the Hudson Institute's Center for American Seapower, said Obama's proposal didn't make sense. "This really moves the U.S. away from a position of influence and military dominance." According to Cropsey, depriving the Navy of Tomahawks is the best way to "reduce the U.S. [sic] ability to shape events" in the world.[556] Obama was quick to remind the public that he was the Commander-in-Chief, but he never embraced the role and advocated for the needs of his military. Thankfully, cooler heads prevailed, and the Tomahawk program continued serving U.S. interests in warfare, including critical operations in Syria in 2017.[557]

97. MASSIVE MILITARY CUTS

If all of the above comments on the state of the military under Obama weren't enough, we offer his 2014 military budget. In his February 2014 announcement of proposed military budget cuts, Secretary of Defense Hagel said, "This is the first time in 13 years we will be presenting a budget to the Congress of the United States that's not a war-footing budget."[558] In this, Hagel declared that, to the Obama administration, not only were there no wars for us to fight, but we had no enemies out there threatening us and our allies. To Obama, the world was at peace. Others looked at the chaotic and violent state of the world and wondered just where Obama got that idea.

This was not a time to be cutting our military budget. Syria descended into civil war, Libya fell apart completely, conditions deteriorated in Afghanistan and Iraq, al-Qaeda advanced in the Middle East and Africa, ISIS claimed a large piece of land in Iraq and Syria and declared themselves a caliphate in the heart of the region, and Iran continued to try to develop nuclear weapons. Ben Shapiro of *The Daily Wire* said the 30 percent cut in the military budget was immense compared to most other periods in American history—comparable to the post-Soviet defense cuts, except that those cuts took place over an eleven-year period, rather than Obama's three-year window. The post-Soviet defense cuts also "paved the way for the rise of al-Qaeda," which ultimately led to the 9/11 terror attacks.[559]

Despite the many potential national security threats that we faced, Obama did significant damage to our military, in terms of size, readiness, effectiveness, and power. After damaging America's alliances, encouraging America's enemies, and helping turn the world into a roiling cauldron of hatred, fear and resentment, Obama's *coup de grâce* was hollowing out our military. Heritage Foundation military expert Dakota Wood said the military was in a "death spiral" following Obama-era spending cuts.[560] He went on to describe the many shortfalls in equipment and personnel the military faced by the end of 2017:

> *The U.S. Air Force is 24 percent short of the fighters it needs. It is also short 1,000 pilots and over 3,000 maintainers. Only four of its 32 combat-coded squadrons are ready to execute all wartime missions. The Marine Corps "is insufficiently manned, trained and equipped across the depth of the force to operate in an ever-evolving operational environment," according to Gen. Glenn Walters, assistant commandant of the Marine Corps. Only 41 percent of the Corps' aviation platforms are considered flyable. At only 276 combatants, the Navy has two-thirds the ships it did near the end of the Cold War. It now has the smallest battle fleet since*

> *before World War I. Of its 18 classes of ships, only seven are currently in production. The recent spate of ship collisions and a grounding imply problems in basic ship-handling skills. Currently, of the Army's 31 brigade combat teams only three would be available to immediately deploy to a conflict. As recently as 2012, the Army had 45 brigade combat teams and nearly the entire Army was involved in the rotational base supporting combat operations in Afghanistan and Iraq.*[561]

Donald Trump took a different approach upon his arrival and, as of this writing, increased military spending by about 3 percent and placed the emphasis back on battlefield readiness, but it may be too little, too late. He has his work cut for him—it should never have come to this.

98. TRIPS TO TYRANNICAL REGIMES

When Obama wasn't busy distancing himself from allies or savagely curtailing our military battle readiness, he was cozying up to long-time enemies of the U.S., of human rights, and of liberty. The next few entries show examples of this disturbing trend.

After winning his second term, Obama made trips to Burma and Cambodia—two nations long run by brutal, tyrannical regimes. People who cared about human rights were appalled by the action. Though Democrats were hard-pressed to criticize Obama, several House and Senate Democrats, including Senator Dick Durbin from Obama's home state of Illinois, criticized Obama's actions in a letter to the White House.

> *By taking a strong and public stand in support of human rights and democracy during this first-time visit by a U.S. President to Cambodia, your words would encourage and embolden the Cambodian people and send a clear message to the entire region about American values and expectations, particularly in the wake of the Arab Spring. However, failure to speak out will serve to undermine America's narrative of support for Asian democrats.*[562]

When the United States mutes its support for human rights and gives legitimacy to tyrants by treating them as rational, civilized members of the world community, freedom fighters get discouraged—and tyrants are more apt to be brutal, as they become convinced that the United States won't interfere.

99. CONDONING THE USE OF CHILD SOLDIERS

In 2008, President George W. Bush signed the *Child Soldiers Prevention Act*, which imposed sanctions on countries whose governments used child soldiers. Despite the law, several countries using child soldiers continued receiving military assistance under Obama. The law, which went into effect in 2010, gives the president of the United States the power to waive the penalties as he sees fit. Obama considered his waivers in "the national interest."[563] The Obama administration claimed the law penalized countries that were crucial to the fight against al-Qaeda. So several countries in northern and central Africa have continued using child soldiers, with the blessing of Barack Obama.

And what did Obama get out of condoning the use of child soldiers in those countries? If the fight against al-Qaeda was the justification, then these waivers were all for naught. Al-Qaeda's influence in the region increased on his watch.

100. ILLEGAL SCIENTIFIC EXCHANGES WITH CHINA

It took twenty-two years for the United States to develop and deploy the new F-22 Raptor. The F-22 is a superb aircraft, which looked likely to maintain U.S. aerial superiority for years to come. But in September 2012, China unveiled two new fighter jets that bore an uncanny resemblance to the American F-22.[564]

How did China do it? They got the technology from us. China gets technology like this by any means necessary. They'll buy it when it's for sale and steal it when it's not.[565] Congress has said our military technology is not for sale. Obama, by his actions, said it was.

It turns out that Obama facilitated *illegal* scientific exchanges between the United States and China.[566] In 2011, Congress, as part of a spending bill, prohibited using government funds to pay for scientific exchanges between the United States and Chinese governments. Obama's administration ignored Congress, claiming that a prohibition on the use of federal funds for something does not prohibit federal employees from doing it, so long as no funds are allocated expressly for that purpose. Obama learned how to splice words to his advantage from Bill Clinton, we think, but that doesn't mean the Obama administration didn't break the law. But it's even worse knowing they broke the law to help China—and there is no good explanation for wanting to do that.

101. RUSSIA'S INVASION OF UKRAINE

Sarah Palin predicted Obama's weakness on the world stage in 2008, saying then-Senator Obama's reaction to Russia's invasion of the Republic of Georgia was so weak and indecisive that it might encourage Putin to invade Ukraine.[567] She was mocked for her statement, but the world came face to face with her prescience in 2014, when Russia invaded Ukraine.

What had the Russians to fear from the United States, after all? Obama warned Putin to keep out of Ukraine, but what of it? What did Obama ever do that would convince Putin, or any other world leader, to pay heed to his empty bluster? As Putin was unwilling to lose control of the Ukraine, Russian troops poured into the Crimean Peninsula and other parts of eastern Ukraine to secure Russia's interests.[568]

According to Charles Krauthammer, Obama showed "weakness" in his statement on the developing situation in Ukraine and implied that "we're not really going to do anything" about it. Krauthammer observed that Putin "knows he has nothing to fear from the west, because it's not led by anybody. It used to be led by the United States."[569]

The world knew Obama wouldn't do anything that required a long-term military commitment and the buy-in of the American people. Putin had Russian troops in Ukraine within days of his allies being forced out of power there. Obama then skipped a national security team meeting on the situation with Russia and Ukraine on March 1, 2014.[570]

As "punishment" for the invasion, Obama imposed small, targeted sanctions against certain Russian and Ukrainian officials. Russia's deputy prime minister mocked the measure—a rather unfortunate reminder of just how weak Obama is perceived to be by the rest of the world.[571]

102. THE LIBYAN QUAGMIRE

The Arab Spring was a series of protests across North Africa, from Somalia to South Sudan to Egypt to Libya to Morocco, varying in severity and violence in proportion to the level of control the leaders of each nation could exert. Mubarak in Egypt was unpopular and, with no involvement from the U.S. beyond rhetoric, that regime collapsed into a violent struggle between the Muslim Brotherhood and the moderates. In Libya, however, there was little sign that anything more than localized violence had erupted in the spring of 2011 when Barack Obama inexplicably decided that the regime of eccentric dictator Muammar Gaddafi must end. Gaddafi previously had the favor of the United States because he'd proven a strong ally in the fight against terrorist groups like al-Qaeda.

Despite no vital security threats to the United States and, counter to after-action claims by the left, no indication that Gaddafi's regime was in any danger of collapse, Obama meddled in Libyan affairs.[572] Rather than taking a leading role, he stepped back and let NATO handle strategic planning in the region, and the results were disastrous.[573] After Gaddafi toppled, the country collapsed into civil war between radicals and what was left of Gaddafi's military. Obama refused to help the military train soldiers and police to fight terrorists or provide material aid to them, leading to the rise of the Islamic State and al-Qaeda in the country.[574]

In short, Obama and then-Secretary of State Hillary Clinton took a stable, albeit repressive country that had been an ally in the fight against terrorism and turned it into a breeding ground for the most radical of jihadis in a feeble attempt at nation-building. The Obama/Clinton misadventure was everything many disliked about the war in Iraq only much, much worse. Unlike Iraq, Obama committed U.S. forces for the intervention in Libya without a congressional declaration of war, violating the War Powers Act of 1973.[575] Libya, like Iraq, suffered greatly at the hands of Obama's foreign policy decisions, turning the once stable and prosperous country into a terrorist haven.[576]

Obama had defended the mission to the American people, saying he acted to "prevent a massacre" and inaction would have been "a betrayal of who we are."[577] It sure seems that, far from preventing a massacre, he created one; and that blood is on his hands.

103. THE SYRIA DEBACLE

During a press conference on August 20, 2012, President Obama asserted that, while he had no plan for a U.S. military intervention in Syria, the "moving around" or use of chemical weapons would be a "red line" that would "change my calculus; that would change my equation."[578]

Once Obama drew his "red line," he was caught in a bind. If Bashar al Assad used chemical weapons, he'd have to do something or look like the biggest fool and weakling in the world. You'll be stunned to know the Assad regime laughed off Obama's empty threats. Over the next year, reports trickled in hinting at Assad's use of chemical weapons. In April 2013, Defense Secretary Chuck Hagel and Secretary of State John Kerry admitted the Assad regime used chemical weapons, crossing Obama's "red line."[579] Senate Intelligence Committee Chair Dianne Feinstein said, "It is clear that 'red lines' have been crossed and action must be taken to prevent larger scale use."[580] But he took no action. Obama's "red line" became rather pink and blurred.

The White House acknowledged the use of chemical weapons by the Assad regime in various sites outside Damascus on August 21, 2013, a year and one day after Obama's "red line" speech. That attack killed more than 1,400 people.[581] Obama, by his own words, had to do something. What followed was nothing less than an embarrassing display of incompetence, with the entire world watching.

Obama failed to garner enough global support for an attack on the Assad regime. Soon after attack plans were finalized, the British government backed out, putting Obama in the awkward position of having to go it alone, if at all.[582] Obama found the American people equally unwilling to support military strikes against Syria. A vote in Congress looked like it might fail.[583] Obama then claimed he had a right, as commander in chief, to order a military strike against Syria without congressional approval and backpedaled on his "red line" remarks, falsely claiming, "I didn't set a red line; the world set a red line." He also asserted, "My credibility is not on the line. The international community's credibility is on the line. And America's and Congress's credibility is on the line."[584]

Opposition to military action against Syria grew. Polls showed that the American people strongly opposed a strike.[585] In order gin up support, Obama had Secretary of State Kerry "reassure" the public that a strike against Syria would be "unbelievably small."[586] This did little to move public opinion but certainly proved to Assad that any action by Obama would be negligible. With the promised military strike in doubt, Obama waived a federal ban on arming terrorists in order to provide aid to Syrian rebels linked to al-Qaeda.[587]

In the end, and to the detriment of American prestige and military might, Russia came to Obama's rescue and brokered a deal which got Obama off the hook for military action in return for a promise by Syria to surrender their chemical weapons.[588] The deal was a humiliation for the United States. Obama's red line vanished; Russia got a massive increase in influence as they got their ally, Assad, out of a tight spot; Iran kept funneling money, fighters, and weapons to the Assad regime. Then the Assad regime failed to honor the agreement, as he ignored the first deadline for the surrender of his stockpile of chemical weapons. Obama downplayed Assad's non-compliance.[589] In February 2014,

Obama's own Secretary of State, John Kerry, admitted that Obama's Syria policy was a failure.[590]

Obama was partially right, though. America's credibility worldwide was on the line, but, as president and commander in chief, the damage done to America's credibility was *his* fault and responsibility. His misguided provision of weapons to Syrian rebels handed material to ISIS. Not until Trump took the reins did the bleeding stop.

104. LOSING AFGHANISTAN

Even though Barack Obama considered the war in Afghanistan "the right war," he failed to execute it with any skill.[591] He never considered the war in Afghanistan his responsibility and, according to Secretary of Defense Robert Gates, he was more concerned with getting out of Afghanistan than achieving a long-term victory. "The president doesn't trust his commander, can't stand Karzai, doesn't believe in his own strategy and doesn't consider the war to be his," Gates wrote in his memoir. "For him, it's all about getting out."[592]

Despite shifting resources to Afghanistan, conditions in the country declined significantly after he became commander in chief. Three-quarters of U.S. fatalities in Afghanistan occurred on his watch.[593] A burgeoning opium trade (despite U.S. efforts to curtail it) and government corruption threaten the country's long-term stability even now.[594] Relations with Afghanistan also deteriorated under Obama, culminating with threats of full U.S. troop withdrawal by the end of 2014 due to an impasse over a security agreement.[595] He made good on his threat and began withdrawal, only to reverse his decision in October 2015 after "extensive, lengthy review." Or when it became clear the Taliban had risen in prominence.[596]

Obama may not have wanted to be a wartime commander in chief, but he asked the American people to make him one in 2008 and again in 2012. It was his job to ensure American victory, but victory was never his objective, and Afghanistan is worse off because of it. According to Elise Jordan of *The Daily Beast*, "Afghanistan today is much more violent than when Obama came into office. Fewer Americans may be dying. But many more Afghan civilians are being killed, according to U.N. statistics. More guns, more warlords, more militias—that's Obama's probable legacy. It's what happens when you can't deal with reality and commit one way or the other in wartime—you lose."[597]

105. LOSING IRAQ

When Obama took over as commander in chief, things were looking up for Iraq. The country was relatively stable, thanks to the hard fighting of both American and Iraqi forces and the troop surge then-Senator Obama opposed in 2007.[598] Radical Islamist groups inside were in retreat, and the level of violence was down to a place where Iraqi forces, backed up at need by American troops, could secure the peace. The war was over and America won. All Obama had to do was to maintain U.S. support for Iraq and things would be fine.

Obama's main anti-Bush promises in the 2008 presidential campaign had been to close the Guantanamo Bay prison and the get U.S. out of Iraq. Disinterested in the whole affair and viewing it as Bush's mistake, not his, he bungled the negotiations with Iraq over a "status of forces agreement." An agreement would have allowed twenty thousand U.S. troops to remain in Iraq for training, support, and (in an emergency) to fight.[599]

When the Obama administration announced a full withdrawal of U.S. troops by the end of 2011, there was a promised commitment to Iraq's future stability.[600] But experts worried that, without American backup, the still-maturing Iraqi military and government would not repel a renewed attack by Islamist militants, especially if such militants got help from Iran.

It took less than a year for levels of violence in Iraq to rise after the American withdrawal.[601] Massive sectarian erupted between Iraq's religious and ethnic groups. In January 2014, the Islamic State of Iraq and Syria (ISIS) violently captured of the city of Fallujah, where U.S. forces exterminated most of al-Qaeda in 2005.[602] The leader of ISIS, Abu Bakr al-Baghdadi, was in U.S. custody in Iraq, but Obama freed him in 2009.[603] After Fallujah, ISIS made more progress. In June 2014, they acquired a stockpile of chemical weapons when they took over a military base in northern Iraq, raising fears that those weapons could be used as dirty bombs.[604] By the summer of 2016, ISIS was stepping up terror attacks on Baghdad itself and had captured about 40 percent of Iraqi territory, including four of Iraq's six largest cities.

The United States lost four thousand lives and spent around $800 billion in Iraq over an eight-year period to bring peace, stability, and freedom to the beleaguered nation. Because President Obama did not take Iraq seriously, viewing it as no more than a Bush mistake, all the blood, treasure, and effort we expended in Iraq nearly went to waste. When Donald Trump arrived, he turned over control of the Iraqi theater to Secretary of Defense "Madman" Maddux and told him to do whatever he thought would win the war against ISIS. Less than a year later, coalition forces drove the terrorists out of their last stronghold in Iraq and surrounded them in small pockets within Syria. As of this writing, the group is, for all intents and purposes, destroyed, forever underscoring what a pathetic, feckless strategy Obama employed.

106. DECLINING RESPECT FOR AMERICA'S POWER

Foreign media often described Obama as an "embarrassing amateur on the world stage," with a "weak-kneed, confused, and strategically incoherent" foreign policy.[605] Between his foreign policy fumbles and leadership failures, it is no surprise that respect for American power declined significantly on his watch.

Obama may think he restored America's standing in the world, but the American people disagree. In 2013, the Pew Research Center found that, for the first time in forty years, a majority of Americans, 53 percent, believed the United States had less power and prestige in the world—more than double the amount measured in 2004. A majority also believe the United States is less respected internationally than it was ten years ago.[606]

This decline of respect for America's power manifested itself in alarming ways throughout Obama's reign. According to British defense advisor Sir Hew Strachan, Obama "devalued the deterrent effect of American military capability."[607] Unfortunately, he was right.

Obama's repeated snubbing of Israel and his lack of success containing Iran's nuclear program led Israel and Saudi Arabia, nations that don't see eye-to-eye, to devise a contingency plan for a joint strike on Iran.[608]

In December 2013, a U.S. Navy guided missile cruiser in the South China Sea took evasive action after a Chinese warship on a collision course refused to stop despite a radio warning. Sources told CNN this was "a highly unusual and deliberate act by China."[609]

In February 2014, Iran, emboldened by their dominant position over Obama in negotiations surrounding its nuclear program, sent warships close to American maritime borders in response to U.S. naval deployments in the Persian Gulf—a first.[610] John Bolton, former U.S. ambassador to the United Nations, argued that Iran was building up its capabilities for the future and could one day be a real threat. "It shows they could put a weapon on a boat or freighter, and if (Iran) has ballistic missiles it could put it anywhere on the U.S. coast."[611]

As Obama began his second term, North Korea, full of renewed confidence, developed a flourishing arms trade.[612] China also flexed its military muscle against the Philippines, another U.S. ally in the Asia-Pacific region.[613]

Because of Obama, there were serious fears of war in that area, with some drawing a parallel between Southeast Asia in 2014 and Europe in 1914, on the eve of World War I.[614] U.S. relations with Afghanistan also deteriorated, which threatened the gains we made there in stopping the spread of international terrorism and ousting the Taliban.

Obama surrendered our position as the world's greatest peacekeeper, a position won through with unthinkable blood and treasure during World War II. Most of those gains were gone in eight short years. That's what happens when your foreign policy consists of befriending tyrants and mullahs, abandoning your promises to allies, and disrupting or destroying your own military at every level.

EXECUTIVE OVERREACH

WHILE RUNNING FOR PRESIDENT, OBAMA claimed he was a constitutional hardliner who would reign in the excesses in the Bush executive branch. "I was a constitutional law professor," he said, "which means, unlike the current president, I actually respect the Constitution."[615] He gave up the ruse when he became president, especially when he found himself frustrated by a Congress that wasn't a rubber stamp for his agenda. During his first Cabinet meeting in 2014, Obama declared, "We're not just going to be waiting for legislation in order to make sure that we're providing Americans the kind of help they need. I've got a pen and I've got a phone, and I can use that pen to sign executive orders and take executive actions and administrative actions that move the ball forward..."[616] Obama could not have been clearer: under the guise of "helping" Americans, Obama planned to impose his agenda, constitutional checks and balances be damned.

But Obama's overreach didn't stop with abusive executive orders. Even that wasn't enough for him. He also sought scary expansions of presidential power that were well outside the enumerated powers set forth in the Constitution—assuming powers he didn't have out of convenience or because the ends justified the means. We have to wonder about the quality of his legal education, because, if this was his way of showing respect to the Constitution, he never understood it.

107. DACA VIA EXECUTIVE ORDER

In 2012, when Congress blocked the DREAM Act, he signed an executive order creating the Deferred Action for Childhood Arrivals (DACA) program instead. DACA allowed illegal immigrants who came to the United States as minors to stay in the United States via renewable two-year periods of amnesty, protecting them from deportation.

Obama had no authority to do this via executive action. The program required funding to operate—those funds must be appropriated by Congress through legislation. The order contradicted multiple laws—laws that must be repealed or replaced by Congress. And Congress had just finished rejecting the exact same measure, demonstrating that it did have the support of lawmakers and couldn't possibly follow naturally from existing laws. Despite this usurpation of the Constitution, he called it "the right thing to do." With the federal government no longer deporting young illegal immigrants, what's the worst that could happen?

How about a massive wave of over 100,000 "unaccompanied minors"[617] crossing the border into the United States in 2014 and 2015?[618] These unaccompanied young illegal aliens included innocent young children and toddlers, but also criminal gangs.[619] They were often ill, sometimes with diseases like tuberculosis and measles.[620] Some had family or friends in the United States already, but others went north hoping their families could follow once Obama granted them amnesty. Border Patrol forces were overwhelmed, local communities felt the bite of increased spending on law enforcement, public schooling, and healthcare for the kids, and, in the chaos, criminals flooded into the United States.[621]

In response to the crisis, Obama refused to visit the border; he went on vacation instead.[622] Democrats pointed their fingers at George W. Bush and the Republicans for the ongoing crisis.[623] When not blaming Bush and the GOP, the White House claimed, "Today, border security is stronger than it ever has been."[624] So those who followed at home learned that Republicans were to blame for an order given by the president, expressly rejected by Republicans in Congress, and challenged by Republicans in the courts—an order that created great border security! They were so far out on a limb they couldn't decide which lie to tell.

A joint report from the Department of Homeland Security (DHS) and Immigration and Customs Enforcement (ICE) contradicted the administration's claims about the cause of the crisis. The authors cited the lack of deportations is a significant factor for the influx of Central American minors coming into the United States illegally.[625] The Obama administration even anticipated the crisis well before it exploded. In January 2014, the Department of Homeland Security posted a Request for Information (RFI) for "Escort Services for Unaccompanied Alien Children."[626]

A bad policy enacted illegally by Obama via executive action made Americans less safe, but Obama refused to accept any responsibility for the crisis and, by all appearances, never took it seriously. Without a remedy, unaccompanied minor aliens continued to trickle across the border right through the 2016 election. When Donald Trump took office, he ended Obama's unconstitutional DACA program in September 2017, allowing a six-month period for Congress to address the issue.

108. EXECUTIVE AMNESTY

Obama went even further with immigration. He argued DACA was within the limits of his authority, though many people doubted his claim.[627] Regarding full-scale immigration reform, Obama made the case he couldn't unilaterally change immigration laws for two more years, insisting it was a problem for Congress to solve.[628] However, after Congress failed to pass immigration reform, Obama threatened to use executive action to grant amnesty to illegals.[629] Worried that such a move would make an already treacherous electoral environment even worse for Democrats, Obama waited until after the 2014 midterms to announce *another* executive action on immigration. This time, he granted amnesty to about five million illegal immigrants.[630]

President Obama stretched his executive authority beyond the breaking point with this order. But you need not take our word for it; take it from Barack Obama. As a candidate for president, he said, "I take the Constitution very seriously. The biggest problems that we're facing right now have to do with [the president] trying to bring more and more power into the executive branch and not go through Congress at all. And that's what I intend to reverse when I'm President of the United States of America."[631] For years as president, he acknowledged the limitations on his executive powers, including acting alone on amnesty. "I am president, I am not king. [...] I can't just make the laws up by myself."[632]

When he no longer faced any electoral accountability, he changed his tune. Mark Krikorian, the executive director of the Center for Immigration Studies, said, unlike Obama's unilateral executive amnesty, previous executive actions on immigration by Ronald Reagan and George H.W. Bush "were modest attempts at faithfully executing legislation duly enacted by Congress."[633] Leaked documents also showed border patrol agents were told the vast majority of illegal immigrants were off-limits to deportation.[634]

The consequences of Obama's amnesty were serious. States lost significant revenue when illegal immigrants granted amnesty protections used state services and benefits, including unemployment benefits, at the expense of taxpaying citizens and legal immigrants.[635] The IRS also ruled that illegal immigrants granted amnesty would be eligible for tax refunds even if they didn't pay taxes.[636] Illegal immigrants could also get driver's licenses and social security numbers, making it easier for them to vote in elections.[637] That is no coincidence.

In February 2015, federal judge Andrew S. Hanen blocked implementation of Obama's amnesty.[638] That didn't stop Obama from threatening Immigration and Customs Enforcement (ICE) officials with unspecified "consequences" if they didn't follow his amnesty rules.[639]

In April 2015, Hanen refused the Obama administration's appeal of his earlier ruling.[640] According to Hanen, Obama's threat of punishment for those who enforce our immigration laws amounts to "total non-enforcement" of the law. He also accused the Obama administration of misleading him when they claimed they hadn't yet implemented any part of Obama's amnesty. The Supreme Court blocked the order in 2016, ending the fight, one of many legal skirmishes Obama lost there.[641]

109. TITLE IX ABUSES

In George Orwell's famous dystopian tale *1984*, the Ministry of Truth has, as its primary aim, the job of manipulating the language to suit the needs of the bureaucracy (not to mention rewriting history to create a narrative that suits those same needs). Obama sometimes embodied this vision with alarming accuracy by altering an existing law through creative interpretation, then using the full force of the federal government to impose his new definition of the text on the country. Perhaps his most blatant foray into the rewriting of decades-old legislation was his treatment of Title IX and the Civil Rights Act regarding gender issues.

The Obama administration expanded Title IX's definition of sexual harassment as "any unwelcome conduct of a sexual nature," making colleges and university responsible for sexual harassment and assaults that occur both on- and off-campus, and lowering the standards of evidence to prove the guilt of the accused. Former DOJ senior policy advisor Jessica Gavora said Obama's new standards killed protections for academic freedom and free expression on college campuses.[642]

When North Carolina's House Bill 2 (H.B. 2) brought gender expression and bathroom usage into the national spotlight in 2016, the Obama administration again overstepped its authority by redefining existing laws. On May 4, 2016, Obama's Justice Department, headed by Loretta Lynch, wrote a letter to Governor McCrory informing him that "as a result of compliance with and implementation of North Carolina House Bill 2 ("H.B. 2"), both you and the State of North Carolina are in violation of Title VII of the Civil Rights Act of 1964." While Title VII makes it unlawful to discriminate based on (biological) sex, it does not say or imply that individuals can use whatever bathroom or locker rooms they want based on "gender identity" or "gender expression."[643] This newspeak conflated sex with gender, bore no resemblance to the meaning of sex written into the CRA, and is rejected by modern gender theorists.

The Obama administration doubled down just over a week later when it declared that the Departments of Justice and Education would both "treat a student's gender identity as the student's sex for purposes of enforcing Title IX," and issued a directive to all public school districts in the country to allow students to use the bathrooms matching their "gender identity." Let's leave aside the implications a decision like this has for states exercising their 10th amendment right to define their public education systems as they see fit. Title IX only makes reference to *biological* sex, not "gender identity" or "gender expression;" ergo, this decree amounts to rewriting Title IX without the assent of

Congress.[644] Even though Obama believed sex and gender were entirely different, that didn't stop him from treating them as the same to redefine a decades-old law when it suited his needs.

Obama defended his directive by stating, "I think that it is part of our obligation as a society to make sure that everybody is treated fairly, and our kids are all loved, and that they're protected and that their dignity is affirmed."[645] The dignity and privacy of women and young girls who didn't want to share bathrooms and changing facilities with men, however, wasn't relevant. *The New York Times* noted that the Obama administration directive "does not have the force of law, but it contains an implicit threat: Schools that do not abide by the Obama administration's interpretation of the law could face lawsuits or a loss of federal aid."[646] Despite that threat, state and local officials across America pushed back against Obama's transgender bathroom decree. By the summer of 2016, governors from twelve states, including North Carolina, spoke against Obama's instruction and promised to challenge it.[647]

According to Mario Loyola, a senior fellow at the Wisconsin Institute for Law, Obama's reinterpretation of Title IX, was an egregious abuse of power. "In order to 'change the law,' the Obama administration simply pretends that a 1972 act of Congress means whatever the latest progressive fashion trend requires it to mean—even though not a single member of Congress in 1972 would have supported the new 'interpretation,' much less voted for a law expressly stating what the Obama administration now claims the law says."[648]

110. THE EXECUTIVE ORDER ON OVERTIME PAY

In a move that stunned the business community, in March 2014, President Obama changed the regulations in the Fair Labor Standards Act of 1938 through executive order to move about ten million "executive and professional" employees into a category that requires their employers to pay them overtime for working more than a certain number of hours per week.[649] There was no congressional debate, no legislative vote, no recognized limit on his authority. It was another blatant abuse of executive power that raised the ire of business groups who warned that these changes would vastly increase the cost of doing business.

As Marc Freedman of the Chamber of Commerce put it, "Changing the rules for overtime eligibility will, just like increasing the minimum wage, make employees more expensive and will force employers to look for ways to cover these increased costs."[650] Companies offset such costs by having fewer employees and/or increasing prices for consumers. A federal judge blocked the order in November 2016, a week before it was to take effect, though, sparing Americans those costs.[651]

111. CLAIMING EXECUTIVE AUTHORITY TO UNILATERALLY RAISE TAXES

In March 2015, White House Press Secretary Josh Earnest stated that Obama was "very interested" in raising taxes via unilateral executive action. "The president certainly has not indicated any reticence in using his executive authority to try and advance an agenda that benefits middle-class Americans," Earnest explained. What should make Obama reticent is Article I, Section 7, Clause 1 of the Constitution, which states, "All Bills for raising Revenue shall originate in the House of Representatives, but the Senate may propose or concur with Amendments as on other Bills." In other words, the president does *not* have the power to raise taxes on his own.

Hans von Spakovsky, the manager of the Election Law Reform Initiative and senior legal fellow at The Heritage Foundation, said Obama's consideration of executive tax hikes is another sign of how arrogant and dangerous Obama is. "He believes he can rule by executive fiat and that the restrictions and limitations in the Constitution on the executive can just be ignored or shrugged off. The president has no authority to raise taxes whatsoever. Only the House of Representatives can originate bills for raising taxes, and this would be just the latest unilateral, abusive, and unconstitutional action of the president."[652] Although he never attempted to raise taxes with an executive order, it is alarming that he even considered it a possibility.

112. WANTING UNILATERAL POWER TO RAISE THE DEBT CEILING

On March 16, 2006, then-Senator Obama said the debate over raising America's debt ceiling was a sign of leadership failure. "It is a sign that the U.S. Government can't pay its own bills. It is a sign that we now depend on ongoing financial assistance from foreign countries to finance our Government's reckless fiscal policies." We wonder what became of this Obama, so concerned with reckless spending he questioned whether they had the authority to raise the debt ceiling. As president, he tried to grant himself that power.[653] Obama made the outlandish demand that he should have the power to raise the debt ceiling on his own as part of a "deal" he offered to House Republicans during negotiations over the sunset date of the tax cuts passed under George W. Bush—the so-called fiscal cliff. The proposal was so absurd that it was met with laughter by Republican leaders when presented on Capitol Hill.[654] But there's nothing funny about a president who continually seeks to increase his own power beyond the limits set by the Constitution.

113. KILLING THE WELFARE WORK REQUIREMENT

Our history with entitlement reforms has involved many choices that led to increased costs, increased dependency, and increased complexity of the safety net, but few choices that improved the viability and effectiveness of such programs. There is, however, one shining example: the Republican-led *Welfare Reform Act* of 1996. Few people would claim this landmark legislation was anything but a huge win in the fight against poverty and the battle against government deficits. Welfare caseloads declined, child poverty declined, and the poverty rate for black children fell to its lowest level ever.[655]

Despite the success of welfare reform, Obama filled the Department of Health and Human Services with opponents of the system. In July 2012, Obama put forward a plan that would effectively end the work requirement from welfare, a key element of its success.[656] Obama and his supporters vehemently denied that his plan would gut Welfare Reform or end the work requirement. But even Ron Haskins—the de facto author of the bill as a congressional staffer in 1996—conceded that, if there was any way to undermine the work requirement, Obama's plan was the "way to do it."[657]

But did Obama even have the legal authority to make these changes? The Government Accountability Office said no. Rep. Dave Camp (R-MI), chairman of the House Ways and Means Committee, and John Kline (R-MN), chairman of the House Committee on Education and the Workforce, explain that the Temporary Assistance for Needy Families (TANF) program created by the 1996 welfare reforms, which include the work requirements, can't simply be rewritten:

> *A Ways and Means Committee summary of the 1996 reforms issued shortly after the law was signed is explicit on this point: "Waivers granted after the date of enactment [of the 1996 law] may not override provisions of the TANF law that concern mandatory work requirements."*
>
> *The president's plan to waive the work requirements is not only illegal, it also is being implemented through an unlawful end run around Congress. The GAO determined the Obama administration's proposal to waive work requirements should have been submitted to Congress for review and possible disapproval. The administration didn't do that and said it does not need to.*[658]

114. ASSASSINATING U.S. CITIZENS WITHOUT DUE PROCESS

Drones have proven to be an effective weapon in fighting terrorist groups around the world. The advantages of speed and stealth in attacking the enemy without risking American are undeniable, even if controversial. Drone strikes often come with collateral deaths of non-combatants. Further adding to the controversy are the deaths of American citizens by drone attacks overseas.[659]

But what of their use inside the United States, against American citizens? Obama's Attorney General Eric Holder asserted, in congressional testimony on March 6, 2013, that, under "extraordinary" circumstances, the president has the legal authority to use drones to kill Americans *inside* the territory of the United States.[660]

Drones are risky enough as a tactic overseas, but to use them on Americans on American soil denies many constitutional rights, including the vital right to due process.

How can the president of the United States pretend he has the right to kill Americans without giving them due process? John Brennan, Obama's CIA Director and the architect of Obama's drone policy, argued that due process is *unnecessary* if the person targeted for elimination is suspected of planning potential future acts of terrorism against the United States.[661]

Potential future acts?

Holder eventually stepped back from his claim after Senator Rand Paul filibustered Brennan's confirmation.[662] Obama never attempted to exercise this imaginary authority... but he believed he could, and that should chill you to the core. Imagine a scenario where a future president claims a political opponent is a domestic terrorist holding the government at gunpoint (already happened!) and has them blown away by drone strike.

The Guardian reported in February 2014 that Obama had weekly meetings with his national security team to approve a "kill list" from among suspected terrorists.[663] Obama refused to provide any details of this, other than his assertion that he has the legal authority to do it. One cannot help but shudder at the thought that Obama believed he had the right to kill American citizens, maybe citizens on a secret kill list for crimes they might someday commit!

115. UNILATERALLY NORMALIZING RELATIONS WITH CUBA

Communist Cuba is an oppressive regime that the United States has kept at arm's length for more than half a century. Given that the Cuban government talks a lot about social justice—while imprisoning and killing anyone who steps out of line—plenty of American liberals have a soft spot for that antique Communist regime. In line with starry-eyed leftist fantasies of a Cuban Utopia, Obama decided, with no notice or debate, to restore American relations with Cuba. It began in a secret deal when Obama leveraged the swap of some Cuban spies in return for an imprisoned American aid worker as an initial means of starting negotiations with Cuba over normalization of relations. The deal was so secret that the Obama administration gave members of Congress no notice about the decision, nor of justification for the release of the Cuban spies, claiming executive privilege.[664]

Even Senator Robert Menendez (D-NJ) slammed Obama over the deal. "President Obama's actions have vindicated the brutal behavior of the Cuban government," he said in a statement. "There is no equivalence between an international aid worker and convicted spies who were found guilty of conspiracy to commit espionage against our nation." Menendez also said the swap set "an extremely dangerous precedent."[665]

After testing the waters with Cuba, in a surprise announcement in mid-December 2014, Barack Obama announced that the United States would restore full diplomatic relations with Cuba, including opening an embassy in the communist country. True to form, Obama's strategy for reversing over a half-century of U.S. foreign policy did not include going through Congress. The move followed the aforementioned spy swap and formalized the Obama administration's stance that America should accept and embrace Cuba. Senator Menendez again protested, saying that Obama's actions "vindicated the brutal behavior of the Cuban government."[666]

While Obama could not change all aspects of U.S. policies towards Cuba overnight, he did whatever he could, including going out of his way to shake hands with Cuba's dictator Raul Castro and nixing Cuba from the U.S. list of state sponsors of terrorism. Obama justified his decision by saying that Cuba had not provided any support to terrorists in the prior six months, and he also guaranteed that Cuba would not support terrorism in the future.[667] A day after the announcement, Cuban-backed FARC terrorists in Colombia murdered ten Colombian soldiers.[668]

Normalizing relations with Cuba, including weakening the trade embargo and allowing for tourism, had one other significant, negative impact in the Western Hemisphere. Cuba and Venezuela have been small-time trading partners for decades,[669] but the infusion of cash Cuba gained from American trade and tourism allowed them to step up purchasing oil from Venezuela at prices set by a brutal Maduro regime that has overseen the near-total collapse of one of the wealthiest nations of South America.[670] Obama's actions in Cuba propped up Maduro in Venezuela and, in so doing, prolonged the suffering of the Venezuelan people, many of whom live with little access to food, water, electricity or basic sanitation. The average Venezuelan lost seventeen pounds in 2016—the starving people refer to it as the Maduro diet.[671] Cuba and North Korea even sent elite forces to aid Maduro in Venezuela, with no comment from the Obama administration on Cuba's role.[672]

Obama claimed we had to change our policy towards Cuba because isolation wasn't working. This was an odd way to look at it. The policy may not have brought down the Cuban regime, but it certainly affected the Cuban economy and prevented them from exerting much influence on global political matters. The Cuban government is an evil, brutal regime, but a small one, thanks to the embargo. In the past, both Presidents Carter and Clinton, buying the theory that Cubans only struggle to survive because the

United States crippled their economy, tried to improve relations with Cuba, and each time, the Cuban government accepted the U.S. favors and then committed acts against U.S. interests.[673] They sponsored terrorism, worked with international drug traffickers, and undermined the United States and our allies for nearly six decades. Opening up to Cuba is a foolhardy act fostered by progressive propaganda and wishful thinking. It is, in a way, the perfect capstone to Obama's foreign policy of turning us away from friends and towards our enemies, and he didn't have the authority to do any of it.

116. MASSIVE INCREASES IN FEDERAL REGULATIONS

When it came to governing, Barack Obama hated working with Congress and instead chose to enact his agenda with regulations. Lots of them. In fact, according to analysis from *The Washington Examiner*, Obama "implemented more costly rules and swamped America with more federal red tape than any other administration."[674] According to analysis from the American Action Forum, the economic cost of Obama's regulations is staggering: "$2,496 per person, per year, an amazing four times higher than the average annual household heating bill."[675]

> *"The Obama administration has set several notable records in the regulatory world: 600 major regulations and counting, more than 10 billion hours of federal paperwork, and the costliest single year in regulation in recent history. It's time for another record: 101 unfunded regulatory mandates imposed on states, local governments, and businesses," said the new AAF report.*

> *"Broadly, an unfunded mandate is defined as a regulation, without explicit Congressional consent or adequate federal funding, which may displace state or local priorities. President Obama managed to easily top 13 years of unfunded mandates in less than eight," said the report.*
>
> *The explosion of regulations and unfunded mandates was predicted by Obama when he threatened congressional Republicans that if they ignored his requests he would act alone.*[676]

Obama's unfunded mandates cost nearly $600 billion and saddled the nation with over one hundred million hours of bureaucratic paperwork every year by the time his work was done. "For perspective, it would take 50,506 individuals employed by states and businesses (working 2,000 hours annually) to complete a single year of these new paperwork requirements."[677]

117. USING THE EPA TO BYPASS CONGRESS

To say Obama's environmental agenda was a disaster is an understatement. From 2009 to 2012, a fifth of the nation's coal plants shut down.[678] Obama's coal regulations cost the U.S. economy an estimated 1.65 million jobs between 2012 and 2020.[679]

The negative impacts of these regulations aren't the whole story. Obama's Environmental Protection Agency (EPA) imposed these regulations without Congressional oversight or review. They crushed the coal industry, killed jobs, inflated energy prices, and ignored the Constitution to do it.

In his 2012 State of the Union address, Obama promised even more "executive action" on the environment, declaring that if Congress didn't enact his environment agenda, he would do so by executive action.[680] And he made good on that promise. One of the more well-known regulations he pushed through the EPA after Congress rejected the idea was cap-and-trade. The 2014 rule set limits on emissions but also allowed companies to "trade allowances or credits for emissions as a way of staying under different benchmarks the EPA sets for each state."[681]

No debate. No congressional approval. No checks and balances. Obama wanted to impose cap-and-trade no matter what the cost and regardless of whether the Congress approved. According to a 2015 study by the Chamber of Commerce, "The EPA's climate rule could cost $50 billion annually and about 40 percent of the U.S. coal fleet could be retired by 2030."[682] But Congress was denied the opportunity to do their job and debate the merits and faults of the proposal.

The EPA issued about four thousand new regulations under Barack Obama, and they came at a high price. According to Americans for Tax Reform, "The compliance costs associated with EPA regulations under Obama number in the hundreds of billions and have grown by more than $50 billion in annual costs since Obama took office."[683] These costs kill jobs and make consumer goods more expensive. Obama abandoned a legislative approach to his climate agenda in favor of executive fiat to avoid compromise once Congress began opposing him. If every president acted this way, the Constitution would be irrelevant.

118. BYPASSING CONGRESS TO MANDATE "BLACK BOXES" IN ALL VEHICLES

When Obama wanted something, he got it—by any means necessary. After the 2012 election, he engaged in a campaign to expand the accepted limits of executive discretion and crafted all sorts of creative new laws without congressional oversight. For example, a new regulation imposed by Obama's Department of Transportation required that all automakers install event data recorders (EDRs) to collect data on passenger vehicles starting on September 1, 2014.[684]

The alleged intent of EDRs (commonly referred to as "black boxes") was to understand how drivers respond in a crash and give the federal government the "critical insight and information" they need to save more lives, according to Obama's Transportation Secretary Ray LaHood.[685] But Horace Cooper of the National Center for Public Policy Analysis called the requirement "an unprecedented breach of privacy for Americans."

> *"Contrary to what is now being claimed, EDRs can and will track the comings and goings of car owners and even their passengers," Cooper said. "EDRs not only provide details necessary for accident investigation,*

> *they also track travel records, passenger usage, cell phone use and other private data. Who you visit, what you weigh, how often you call your mother and more is captured by these devices. Mandating that they be installed and accessible by the DOT is a terrible idea."* [686]

Cooper explained that, since the system would run whenever the engine was on, there was no guarantee that the information collected by EDRs would only be relevant to an auto accident. The AAA auto club and the Alliance of Automobile Manufacturers also expressed privacy concerns. Congress *rejected* this mandate in 2011, but Obama never let Congress get in the way of imposing his agenda. So he bypassed Congress and subverted the Constitution, imposing the mandate through Department of Transportation.

119. ABUSIVE INTERPRETATIONS OF FOIA

The *Freedom of Information Act (FOIA)*, signed into law on July 4, 1966, by President Lyndon Johnson, empowers private citizens to request the disclosure of government documents, as long as they aren't too sensitive for release. There have been changes to the law since it was first enacted, but Obama's Justice Department proposed a disturbing change to the law. When FOIA requests are denied, the law requires that the agency provide a reason. But the new rule, proposed by the Obama administration, would "direct government agencies who are denying a request under an established FOIA exemption to 'respond to the request as if the excluded records did not exist,' rather than citing the relevant exemption." Both left and right-leaning government transparency advocates called the proposed rule change "Orwellian."[687] The outcry over the mere suggestion of such changes caused the Obama administration to backtrack, but they later proposed new rules that allowed agencies to deny FOIA requests with any trivial reason they could come up with.

Obama's track record regarding FOIA requests was bad from the start. Documents released in 2014 showed that, back in 2009, the Obama White House secretly rewrote a portion of the *Freedom of Information Act* (FOIA) to suppress politically sensitive documents. Any documents involving "White House equities" now had to pass a review by White House officials before being released, allowing the White House to indefinitely delay the release of documents it preferred remain hidden.[688] This explains why a 2014 analysis by the Associated Press found that the Obama administration denied, censored, or stonewalled FOIA requests at record rates.[689] In March 2015, the White House exempted itself from FOIA requests entirely.[690] One can only wonder what Obama wanted to hide during his last two years in office. We think ugly little tidbits will continue trickling into the public consciousness for years to come.

And the politicization of FOIA went far beyond stonewalling to hide scandals. Obama also directed executive agencies to keep allies in the know and enemies in the dark about the workings of their government. *PJ Media* found documents in 2011 showing FOIA requests from liberal groups and Democrats were "often given same day turnaround by the DOJ," while requests from conservatives or Republicans were stonewalled or denied.[691] One agency was particularly unscrupulous with FOIA requests—the EPA, which we will cover in more detail later.

Obama claimed he was committed to creating "an unprecedented level of openness" in government. Instead, we got an unprecedented level of partisanship in government, with selective "transparency" given only to those whom Obama considers political allies and administrative bullying tactics covered up by euphemistic non-answers and outright lies.

120. EXECUTIVE GUN CONTROL

Obama *claimed* he believed in the Second Amendment to the Constitution, but he certainly didn't act that way. Instead, he chipped away at the rights of gun owners while quashing the constitutional system of checks and balances. When Obama's gun control agenda failed to pass Congress, he took executive actions to achieve his goals. In January 2013, using the Sandy Hook shooting a month earlier for political cover, Obama signed a whopping twenty-three executive actions related to gun control, grossly overstepping his executive authority.[692] Many state leaders immediately announced plans to resist compliance with any executive action that violated the Second Amendment.[693] He added two more executive actions on gun control in August of that year[694] and two more the following January.[695]

Not satisfied, Obama announced plans to ban a widely used bullet for the AR-15 semi-automatic rifle in 2015. The Bureau of Alcohol, Tobacco, Firearms, and Explosives (BATFE) justified the ban with the claim that the "armor-piercing" ammunition *could be* used in semi-automatic handguns that posed a significant threat to police, though they provided no evidence of police getting shot with a semi-automatic handgun using this ammo. The Obama administration tried to ban the popular ammunition because his attempts to ban the sporting rifle through legislation failed.[696] After ferocious public outrage, the BATFE backed away from the ammunition ban.[697]

When another tragedy struck, Obama went back to his old playbook. Following the ISIS-inspired terrorist attack in San Bernardino, CA, in December 2015, Obama took to the airwaves to decry the attacks as a sign that America needed tougher gun control—because terrorists are *eager* to obey gun laws. Obama used the event to pressure Congress to pass legislation making it illegal for people on a terrorism watch-list to purchase firearms of any kind. When the GOP-led Congress refused to do so, he signed an executive order on February 8, 2016, that lacked teeth but recommended the same measures he'd advertised the previous December, including a moratorium on terror watch list suspects buying guns, an end to the non-existent "gun show loophole," and other measures opposed by gun rights lobbyists.[698]

121. ILLEGAL EXECUTIVE "FIXES" TO OBAMACARE

The Obamacare rollout was an abysmal failure—not just for Obama, but the entire Democratic Party. When millions of Americans discovered they would lose the plans they had and would have higher premiums and higher deductibles, something had to be done to reduce the political fallout. On November 14, 2013, Obama announced that insurance companies could continue to offer plans that violated the requirements of his signature healthcare law for an additional year. Democrats called the same adjustment "terrorism" and shut down the government to stop it.[699]

Obama trampled on the Constitution in a futile attempt to save his party from electoral slaughter, and Democrats like former DNC Chairman Howard Dean questioned whether Obama had the legal authority.[700] Eugene Kontorovich, a constitutional law professor at Northwestern University School of Law, said Obama's fix "exceeds the president's discretion in implementing the law and amounts to legislation from the White House. The president has no constitutional authority to rewrite or unbundle statutes, especially in ways that impose new obligations on people, as the fix does."[701] UC Berkeley law professor John Yoo wrote that Obama's fix "amounts to a suspension power that the Framers consciously rejected by including the Take Care Clause in Article II of the Constitution."[702] The "Take Care" clause instructs the President to ensure that all laws are faithfully enforced, whether or not the president agrees with it or finds it politically expedient.

In response to Obama's illegal action, House Republicans announced the Keep Your Health Plan Act, which would have accomplished the same thing Obama called for, just in a constitutional manner. But Obama, not wanting Republicans to benefit from stench of his administration's failure, said he would veto the bill.[703]

Obama's illegal fix was neither his first nor last. He already delayed the employer mandate. By the end of 2013, Obama had made fourteen changes to Obamacare without consultation or approval from Congress, with the last change of the year making it possible for people to sign up for bare-bones "catastrophic" health coverage via a so-called "hardship exemption."[704]

As 2014 began and polling suggested an impending electoral disaster thanks to his signature law, Obama went even further to delay the effects of the law. He delayed the employer mandate for medium-sized businesses—again, without congressional approval.[705] But that didn't go far enough to ease electoral concerns. Someone in the Obama administration must have figured out that the original one-year delay to allow consumers to keep existing health-care plans that didn't comply with Obamacare wasn't long enough to prevent cancellation notices from being mailed out prior to the 2014 midterm elections. So in March 2014, Obama officials announced, without congressional approval, he would delay this provision of the law for *two* more years.[706]

The means by which Obama insisted on "correcting" its many flaws (purely for political cover) were gross abuses of a president's power. At a House Judiciary Committee hearing, Jonathan Turley, a professor of public interest law at George Washington University stated, "The problem with what the president is doing is that he's not simply posing a danger to the constitutional system. He's becoming the very danger the Constitution was designed to avoid. That is the concentration of power in every single branch."[707]

ADMINISTRATION CORRUPTION

THE OBAMA ADMINISTRATION DWARFED ALL others in its mastery of systemic corruption and obfuscation. He made Nixon look like a rank amateur. The men and women he chose to form the backbone of his executive branch abused their authority, forsaking all prior notions of civic responsibility, honor, and temperance in a power-mad quest to achieve every imaginable leftist goal without regard for the wants of the people they claimed to serve. Their ideological blinders, naked greed, and cronyism led to some of the most blatant attacks on the credibility of government ever seen and to spectacular ineptitude along the way.

Whether Obama ordered the scandalous practices that blighted his administration like the plague or merely appointed political contemporaries raised in the same cesspool of machine politics and radicalism, the onus was on him to run an executive branch free of corruption or hold the guilty accountable. He did the opposite, stonewalling investigations, weaponizing entire executive agencies against his political enemies, and, when caught, retaining the culprits or allowing them to retire with their generous pensions rather than rotting in prison. Obama's corruption far eclipsed that of Nixon, Harding, or Johnson. This chapter gives the sordid details in full.

122. ABUSING EXECUTIVE POWER TO MANIPULATE THE NEWS

One of Obama's most powerful weapons in the war on inconvenient truths about his presidency was his mastery of the news cycle and the broader ongoing conversation about current events. He and his administrative appointees found every little advantage they could as they worked to keep Americans from noticing the signs that his ideas didn't work. Most presidents do a bit of this, but Obama and his cronies took much greater liberties with their authority. Here are a few examples.

You probably never thought your tax dollars would pay for bloggers to troll websites and harass political opponents, but the Obama administration squandered real treasure to do just that. Obama's Justice Department hired bloggers to carry out a secret propaganda campaign by posting anonymous comments on newspaper websites with stories critical of Obama, Holder, and the Justice Department.[708] This was a gross misuse of taxpayer dollars for an agency tasked with upholding the nation's laws without political bias.

As the 2012 election neared, Obama needed to claim the economy was recovering, but must to his chagrin, the stubborn facts showing a sluggish, miserable economy kept popping up in mandatory government reports. For example, food stamp data is usually released around the end of the month, but the October 2012 numbers were grim—food stamp usage rose to a record high 47.1 million people.[709] We should have received the last pre-election food stamp report about a week before the election, but we didn't get it until November 10, four days *after* the election.

In his bid for reelection, Obama tried to walk a tightrope between his aggressive regulatory agenda and Americans' growing frustration with regulatory burdens that harmed the economy. He "systematically delayed enacting a series of rules on the environment, worker safety, and health-care to prevent them from becoming points of contention before the 2012 election."[710] Administration officials denied any political motive behind the move, but seven current and former officials disagreed in a report released by the Administrative Conference of the United States (ACUS), which found that internal reviews of proposed regulatory changes "took longer in 2011 and 2012 because of concerns about the agencies issuing costly or controversial rules prior to the November 2012 election."[711]

About a month before the presidential election, Virginia-based defense contractor Lockheed Martin announced that, in response to a White House request, they would delay layoff notices until *after* the election. Company representatives told ABC News that, at first, they intended to issue notices about possible layoffs in the fall of 2012 based on speculation that the defense budget would get a $500 billion haircut if Congress couldn't agree on a budget compromise, but Obama administration officials requested they wait.[712] The law requiring layoffs to be announced in advance was passed with a veto-proof majority in a Democrat-controlled Congress in 1988.[713] That was before it benefited Democrats to violate the law to eke out a 116,000 vote win in a vital swing state.

123. POLITICIZING THE 2010 CENSUS

The decennial census of the United States is mandated by our Constitution. Every ten years, there is to be an enumeration of the people of the United States so that representation in our House of Representatives can be apportioned among the states. Modern legislation, however, also ties federal funding for certain lucrative social programs to population. To gain advantages for certain liberal interest groups, Obama moved the census from the Commerce Department to the White House, under Obama's then-chief of staff, Rahm Emanuel. White House officials didn't describe Emanuel's role, but the conflict of interest was indisputable.[714]

The Huffington Post reported the census sought to reach out to gays and lesbians, in order to tally the number of same-sex marriages. Same-sex couples in states where same-sex marriage was not then legal were advised to consider themselves married on the census form.[715] They also tried to get as many illegal immigrants as possible to participate in the census.[716] The White House even told census workers to slow down and extend their work to improve jobs reports in the run-up to the 2010 midterm elections.[717]

124. SESTAK JOB OFFER SCANDAL

If that wasn't bad enough for you, Obama also attempted to manipulate the election process itself. When Senator Arlen Specter sought reelection to the United States Senate in 2010 as a Democrat, Congressman Joe Sestak felt compelled to challenge Specter for the Democratic nomination, thinking the Democratic Party's best interests weren't served by having a recent convert to their party in the U.S. Senate.

But the Obama administration felt that Specter's chances of being reelected were better. Sestak said a White House official approached him offering a high-ranking job if he would drop out of the race. The White House later admitted they had former president Bill Clinton approach Sestak with the job offer[718] but claimed they didn't violate any laws. Except 18 U.S.C. § 600 makes it illegal to promise "any employment, position, compensation, contract, appointment, or other benefit" to any person as a "consideration, favor, or reward for any political activity or for the support of or opposition to any candidate or any political party...in connection with any primary election."[719]

Further, 18 U.S.C. § 211 states that "whoever solicits or receives" such an offer "shall be fined and/or imprisoned for no more than a year."[720] Sestak—who ultimately won the Democratic primary but lost the general election to Republican Pat Toomey—didn't accept Bill Clinton's offer, but the Obama administration broke the law. If Obama ordered Clinton to make the offer, it would be an impeachable offense. Obama's Justice Department rejected a request by Congressman Darrell Issa (R-CA) for a special counsel to investigate, and the scandal got swept under the rug.[721] No one in the Obama administration was ever held accountable for breaking the law.

125. OBAMA'S TAX CHEATS

For a man who often lectured Americans on the importance of the rich paying their fair share, Obama created quite a safe haven for tax code violators. After Obama nominated Timothy Geithner to be his Treasury Secretary, we learned that Geithner failed to pay payroll taxes for several years on income he made working for the International Monetary Fund. He called the omissions careless even though he was aware, at the time, that he was responsible for paying those taxes. During his confirmation hearings, Geithner blamed TurboTax software for his failure to pay, forcing him to pay $42,702 in back taxes before taking his new post.[722]

Obama originally nominated Tom Daschle to be his Health & Human Services Secretary, but he was forced to drop out after reports showed he failed to pay over $100,000 in income taxes. Kathleen Sebelius replaced him as Obama's pick for the position. Shortly after she testified before the Senate Health, Education, Labor, and Pensions Committee, we discovered she owed over $7,000 in back taxes—she got confirmed anyway.[723]

The confirmation vote for Hilda Solis to be Obama's Labor Secretary was postponed when media sources found her husband paid $6,400 in tax liens from sixteen years prior.[724] Nancy Killefer withdrew her nomination to be Obama's Performance Czar after reports revealed she had a nearly $1,000 lien on her property for failing to pay property taxes in 2005.[725] In early 2012, we discovered thirty-six Obama aides owed $833,000 in back taxes.[726]

But he didn't just employ his tax-evading allies, he paid private citizens records of tax evasion using stimulus grants. By law, tax cheats were not eligible to receive any money from the government's mortgage insurance program. But the Federal Housing Administration (FHA) had no means to determine which applicants owed back taxes and should have their applications denied. In the end, $1.4 billion in stimulus loans and $27 million in tax credits were given to tax delinquents.[727]

126. PROTECTING HIS ALLIES FROM JUSTICE

Under Obama and his radical Attorneys General, the Justice Department became a hotbed of political favoritism. The trouble began within mere weeks of Eric Holder's appointment. In 2009, when the new Attorney General dropped a voter intimidation case against the New Black Panther Party (NBPP) that started under George W. Bush. On Election Day in 2008, NBPP members wore paramilitary clothing and carried clubs in front of polling places, intimidating potential voters entering polling places. The Obama administration refused to explain why Attorney General Holder dropped an open-and-shut case and this blatant violation of civil rights went unpunished.[728]

By the summer of 2010, the U.S. Commission on Civil Rights declared there was evidence of "possible unequal administration of justice" by the Justice Department.[729] Holder denied there was a racial motivation during a House Appropriations subcommittee hearing in March

2011, justifying the decision not to prosecute the NBPP by citing the roadblocks African-Americans endured when trying to vote in the South during the era of Jim Crow laws.[730] He made the case that there was no racial bias by invoking a racial motive.

Along with selective enforcement of the law, Obama used the Justice Department to protect his political allies from criminal and ethical probes that would likely have resulted in convictions or ended careers. When Harry Reid was still Senate Majority Leader, Obama prevented a federal investigation of a corruption probe that implicated Harry Reid as one of two U.S. Senators who may have taken money and benefits from political donors in return for political favors.[731]

When Inspector General Gerald Walpin began investigating the misuse of AmeriCorps grant money by St. HOPE, a nonprofit organization of Sacramento Mayor Kevin Johnson, the former NBA star and a friend and supporter of Obama's, Obama stepped in to protect Johnson by firing Walpin. The *2008 Inspector General Reform Act*—a bill then-Senator Barack Obama co-sponsored—gave Walpin certain protections, including a right to thirty-days' notice and a written explanation to Congress before he could be dismissed. Neither was provided.[732] He got a phone call from the White House counsel's office; they told him he had an hour to resign or be fired.[733]

Why did they fire Walpin so abruptly? Well, Walpin's investigation exposed an apparent cover-up of sexual abuse accusations against Johnson, and he pressed for Johnson's criminal prosecution.[734] Obama fired him before he could report his findings, and the White House offered Johnson a deal to avoid prosecution. The White House then began a smear campaign against Walpin.[735]

Eric Holder took part in a scandalous, incompetent gun-running project known as "Fast and Furious" from 2009 to 2011. We'll discuss the scandal more shortly, but for now, we want to highlight how Holder avoided prosecution. During the Congressional investigation into Fast and Furious, Obama protected Attorney General Eric Holder by asserting executive privilege over thousands of requested documents just before the House Oversight and Government Affairs Committee voted on a motion to declare Holder in contempt of Congress for withholding those documents from the committee.[736]

Later that year, Obama's Department of Homeland Security requested that Immigration and Customs Enforcement (ICE) delay the arrest of a campaign intern for Senator Robert Menendez (D-NJ) until after the 2012 elections. Menendez was up for reelection, and this move saved him from a potentially damaging pre-election scandal.[737]

Obama's Justice Department did not see fit to investigate New York City's Sanitation Department after whistleblowers revealed that union bosses ordered drivers to botch snow cleanup after a major blizzard in 2010 in order protest budget cuts.[738] Nor did the Department of Justice investigate after the city's new mayor Bill de Blasio was accused, by residents of the affluent Upper East Side of Manhattan, of deliberately leaving the neighborhood unplowed as retribution for not supporting him.[739] We wouldn't expect the feds to investigate urban political scandals, but, as you'll see shortly, Holder's Department of Justice pursued political adversaries involved in local or personal imbroglios several times.

Obama also protected a member of his own Cabinet instead of demanding her resignation after she broke the law. On February 25, 2012, Health & Human Services Secretary Kathleen Sebelius endorsed Barack Obama for reelection during a taxpayer-funded event. Her political position wasn't surprising, but by making a partisan political remark at such an event in her official capacity as a member of the Cabinet, she was in violation of the *Hatch Act* of 1939. The *Hatch Act* prohibits federal employees from engaging in partisan political activity. Less than two months before the 2012 presidential election, the Office of Special Counsel (OSC) issued a report that found that Sebelius was indeed in violation of the *Hatch Act*.[740]

According to the OSC report, Sebelius was very much aware of the *Hatch Act* when she made her violation and should have been punished. "An employee who violates the *Hatch Act* shall be removed from their position, and funds appropriated for the position from which removed thereafter may not be used to pay the employee or individual."[741] Obama never fired her for breaking the law. She didn't resign until 2014—soon after Obamacare's open enrollment period ended.

None of the above compares to the lengths to which Obama and his surrogates went to protect his heir apparent, Hillary Rodham Clinton—but we'll go into that later.

127. PARTISAN PROSECUTIONS

When not selectively enforcing the laws or giving his friends a pass from lawbreaking, Obama weaponized the Justice Department to target his political enemies. Senator Menendez (whom Obama previously protected) learned this the hard way when, in 2015, the Department of Justice moved forward with criminal charges against him on a five-year-old case. Washington, D.C., insiders believed the decision was politically motivated, since they charged him after Menendez spoke out against Obama regarding his plan to normalize relations with communist Cuba and his nuclear deal with Iran.[742]

If Obama was willing to go after Democrats who got out of line, naturally his Republican critics were also targets. In 2014, when the Democratic mayor of Fort Lee, NJ, accused staffers and political appointees of New Jersey Governor Chris Christie causing a major traffic jam on the George Washington Bridge, the Obama administration took up the case.[743] Christie was cleared of wrongdoing, but "Bridgegate" dogged him even unto his 2016 presidential campaign.

In January 2014, Dinesh D'Souza, the conservative author and speaker who wrote several books critical of Obama and produced the widely popular anti-Obama documentary *2016: Obama's America*, was indicted for campaign finance violations for having orchestrated $20,000 in straw donations to the campaign of a friend who ran for U.S. Senate.[744] Conservatives and liberals alike questioned the motivation behind the indictment. Legal experts saw it as a partisan selective prosecution. Harvard Law School professor and Obama supporter Alan Dershowitz said, in an interview with *Newsmax*, "This is an outrageous prosecution and is certainly a misuse of resources. It raises the question of why he is being selected for prosecution among the many, many people who commit similar crimes." Dershowitz believed the indictment came from high up in the Obama administration. "This sounds to me like it is coming from higher places. It is hard for me to believe this did not come out of Washington or at least get the approval of those in Washington," he said.[745]

National Review's Andrew McCarthy also noted, by charging him with making illegal donations and making false statements to the government, the Justice Department prosecuted D'Souza twice for the same crime to maximize his punishment. According to McCarthy, "By gratuitously piling on another felony, Obama and Holder portray D'Souza as a serious crook and subject him to the onerous potential of seven years in prison—all for an episode that ordinarily would not be prosecuted at all."[746]

D'Souza was the not the only conservative activist that Obama targeted for selective harassment. James O'Keefe, founder of the undercover journalism outfit known as Project Veritas, videotaped himself dressed as a terrorist and crossing back and forth from the United States to Mexico and back again without getting stopped as part of a video series on the lack of security along the southern border. The video went viral and fueled Tea Party-backed demands to scuttle all talk of further discussion of any immigration reform bill in 2014. U.S. Customs officers were quick to detain O'Keefe and, incredibly, place him on a terrorism watch-list that exposed him to intense scrutiny each time he traveled internationally.

The way Obama pulled the blindfold off Lady Justice should be troubling to all Americans. When a president weaponizes the Department of Justice to go after his political enemies, everyone, regardless of party, should be afraid.

128. THE PIGFORD SCANDAL

The Justice Department also became a feeding trough for supporters of Obama. *Pigford v. Glickman* was a 1997 lawsuit alleging the United States Department of Agriculture (USDA) discriminated against ninety-one African-American farmers by denying them loans. The farmers won the case, and each were paid $50,000 from a judgement fund originally set at $120 million. Over time, the number of claimants grew into the thousands. Fraudulent *Pigford* claims didn't start under Obama, but he did everything in his power, starting from his days as a U.S. Senator, to use it to his advantage in what would become a huge taxpayer-funded vote-buying scheme costing billions.[747]

In 2010, the Obama administration increased the judgement fund by $1.15 billion, then expanded *Pigford* settlements to include Hispanic, Native American, and women farmers who claimed discrimination—groups crucial to his electoral prospects. With Obama and Attorney General Eric Holder managing the *Pigford* judgement fund, the number of discrimination claimants exploded. The Justice Department required no hard evidence of discrimination to approve a payment, thus setting up a system *during an election year* that allowed anyone (of the right ethnic group or gender, of course) to make a *Pigford* claim even if they never farmed or experienced discrimination.[748]

The New York Times exposed evidence of countless fraudulent claims, including multiple claims by one individual, claims on behalf of children, and claims made by people on behalf of the deceased. The Obama administration even reminded thousands of prospective voters to submit their claims before time ran out.[750] Thanks to the efforts of the Obama administration, the cost of *Pigford* payouts exploded to $4.4 billion by 2013—nearly a thousand times more than the original settlement paid out.[751]

129. FEDERAL ENERGY LOAN SCANDAL

The next few entries will cover examples of ineptitude of government service on Obama's watch. We assure you, this is not a complete list. If we were to attempt that, we would need to write an entirely new book on the subject. Let's begin with Obama's green economy.

To propel us toward a "green energy" future, Obama used federal loans as carrots for development but granted those loans in a highly politicized process that produced abysmal results as a direct result of Obama's meddling. The 2009 Stimulus earmarked $80 billion for clean energy loans, grants, and tax credits. On October 31, 2012, previously undisclosed emails revealed the White House pressured Department of Energy officials into approving many of these government loans.

The emails, made public by the House Oversight and Government Reform Committee, showed personal involvement by President Barack Obama and Vice President Joe Biden. Obama previously claimed, in a television interview less than a week earlier, the Department of Energy made all decisions on loan grants, and politics played no role. Well, both claims were lies, as the emails also revealed loan money was used to help Senator Harry Reid's 2010 reelection campaign answer criticisms that he didn't get enough federal money for Nevada.[752]

Officials at the Department of Energy grew concerned that Obama's personal involvement was putting taxpayer dollars at risk. Still, that didn't stop Obama from repeatedly claiming the process was not politicized. One lawsuit against the DOE, filed in January 2013, alleged not only were these loans granted to donors of Obama and other Democrats, but the DOE transferred proprietary technology from these companies to the Obama's cronies who were awarded the loans.[753]

These politicized loans proved to be terrible investments. At least fifty Obama-backed clean energy companies went bankrupt or found themselves in major financial trouble. One such company was Solyndra. Solyndra, a solar energy company, went bankrupt on September 6, 2011, and 1,100 workers were laid off. Solyndra received a $535 million DOE loan in 2009 championed by the White House, despite concerns by the DOE that the company was on track to go belly up.[754] Why would the White House push for a loan of more than half a billion dollars to a start-up

DOE officials knew was heading toward bankruptcy? Solyndra employees were Democratic donors, and one of Solyndra's largest investors, billionaire George Kaiser, was a campaign fundraiser for Obama in 2008.[755]

130. STIMULUS JOBS SAVED OR CREATED IN PHANTOM DISTRICTS

Despite a weak economy still suffering from high unemployment, Obama argued that his 2009 Stimulus worked. Regularly referring to jobs "saved or created" by the stimulus, Obama portrayed himself as the man who single-handedly saved our economy. To help document the success of the stimulus, the administration built a government website, recovery.gov, to track how and where the stimulus money was spent and how many jobs were "saved or created."

There was, however, a major problem. The website showed money spent and jobs "saved or created" in congressional districts that did not exist.[756] According to *Watchdog.org*, there were 440 non-existent congressional districts that received $6.4 billion in stimulus funds to "create or save" nearly thirty thousand jobs.[757] And, according to recovery.gov, a single lawn mower purchased with stimulus funds to cut grass at an Arkansas cemetery "saved or created" fifty jobs. *Really*?

Despite the absurdity of the data, the Obama administration used the recovery.gov stats to prove that the stimulus bill was a success. They blamed stimulus recipients for faulty input.[758] Instead of being a beacon of government transparency, recovery.gov became a propaganda site, relying on faulty data overstating the success of the stimulus bill in order to mislead the public.

131. THE OPM HACK

The Office of Personnel Management (OPM) is charged with managing information related to all federal employees. The agency maintains a database filled with sensitive, personal details about the employees and, sometimes, their families—precisely the sort of information two different sorts of people would love to have: identity thieves and foreign spies. Chinese intelligence hacked that database—you won't believe how they did it.

If you think a specialized group of super-hackers working for years to crack our security did the job, think again. OPM hired contractors to manage their security, and some of the people working for the contractors were, incredibly, physically located within the borders of the People's Republic of China.[759] These contractors had access to every line of data in OPM's system. All the Chinese government had to do—if they weren't the actual contractors hired in the first place—was order the hackers to hand over the data.

When the story broke in June 2015, the administration claimed that only about four million people were affected.[760] A month later, the figure was revised upward to thirty-two million Americans whose personal information was stolen by China.[761] To save some face, Obama's administration tried to claim OPM discovered the hack during an aggressive effort to beef up cybersecurity. But that claim was false; the hack was discovered by chance.[762]

How does something like this happen? According to Paul Conway, who served as Chief of Staff of OPM during the Bush administration, it was "a devastating example of the poor personnel judgment exercised by President Obama" in appointing Katherine Archuleta as OPM director.[763] Archuleta, a political appointee, was grossly unqualified for the position. She "ignored repeated written warnings from OPM Inspector General Patrick McFarland regarding the vulnerability of key personnel IT systems to hacking." Archuleta resigned, but according to Obama's spokesman, she still had the president's confidence.[764]

While Obama's failures are manifold over his term of office, there is something particularly outrageous about this one. Obama put the wrong person in charge of the agency, and the direct result of that mistake was largest breach of government data in America's history.

132. EPA RUN AMUCK

Soon after Obama was reelected, we learned that Obama's EPA Administrator, Lisa Jackson, was using several secret alias email accounts to conduct official business in violation of federal law in order to avoid potential exposure and scrutiny of the EPA's activities to FOIA requests.[765] One such alias was Richard Windsor. Jackson's deception was so detailed that EPA records showed he earned certificates for completing various training courses required by the agency and even got commended as a "scholar of ethical behavior" three years in a row from 2010 to 2012.[766] How ironic. Jackson announced her resignation soon after these allegations surfaced.[767]

The scandals involving Obama's EPA didn't end there. In May 2013, on the heels of the scandal involving the IRS targeting conservative groups during the 2012 election cycle, reports suggested the Environmental Protection Agency gave preferential treatment to environmental groups over conservative groups attempting to obtain government records under the Freedom of Information Act (FOIA). They got caught waiving FOIA fees for environmental groups but not conservative groups.[768] The Competitive Enterprise Institute also found, of the eighty-two FOIA requests made by environmental groups, 92 percent were granted fee waivers, while of the twenty-six requests made by conservative groups, 81 percent were *rejected*—effectively stopping the requests.[769] AP Washington Bureau Chief Sally Buzbee said the Obama administration routinely forwarded FOIA requests to political appointees and used those requests "as a tip service" to learn what news organizations were investigating.[770]

As if that wasn't enough, the EPA took a page out of the IRS playbook and illegally leaked the personal information of over eighty thousand private farms and ranches to various left-wing environmental groups, which prompted a bipartisan group of senators to demand answers, not only about why this private information was released, but also why it was collected in the first place.[771] It's clear, given the stained record of the EPA on Obama's watch, that he turned the Environmental Protection Agency into a device for enforcing his radical environmental agenda without congressional approval or oversight.

While the EPA went to extraordinary lengths to protect itself, protecting actual Americans was clearly not a priority. When a careless EPA crew breached the Gold King Mine, which was holding back three million gallons of toxic waste, the mine failed, unleashing the toxic waste into the Animas River, poisoning drinking water in three states. The supposedly environmentally friendly Obama administration lied about what happened, delayed notifying the public about the spill, refused to prosecute the EPA worker responsible, and stonewalled investigations... all to protect the image of the EPA.[772]

And, in a shocking case bearing too many similarities to the Tuskegee syphilis experiment of 1972, a report obtained by *The Daily Caller* on the Environmental Protection Agency's particulate matter experiments revealed that the EPA exposed people with health problems to particulate matter fifty times more concentrated that the upper limit of safety. They did this without informing all the participants of the risk involved or the material to which they were being exposed.[773] As the EPA director put it in 2011, "Particulate matter causes premature death. It doesn't make you sick. It's directly causal to dying sooner than you should." Despite this, Obama's EPA sought out Americans with underlying health problems and lured them into the experiments with promises of payment.[774] In addition to particulate matter, subjects were exposed to diesel exhaust and ozone.

So why would the Obama administration deliberately expose American citizens to substances they knew could kill them? They believed particulate matter was lethal but needed proof to justify more stringent clean air regulations.[775] To complete the horror of the Obama administration's actions, Obama's EPA defended the study by claiming "the exposure risk for healthy individuals is minimal."[776] Even if this didn't contradict previous statements made by the EPA, the people being used as test subjects were not healthy individuals. The ends justified the means—whatever was necessary to move forward with his radical environmental agenda, Obama and his cabinet would do.

133. THE VETERANS AFFAIRS SCANDAL

None in America deserve more respect and care than our veterans, especially those who have been injured in connection with their service. Obama promised to end the horrendous backlog in VA benefit claims (some claims languished for years without resolution) and said he would be a President who would fight for veterans "every hour of every day."[777]

But the backlog of VA claims increased massively on Obama's watch, with unprocessed claims often exceeding 900,000, and around two-thirds of all claims idling for 125 days or longer.[778] Claims took an average of 272 days to process in 2013, up 40 percent from 2011.[779] The number of veterans who died waiting for care and benefits also skyrocketed on Obama's watch.[780] The surge in claims resulting from aged Vietnam veterans and the wars in Afghanistan and Iraq went unaddressed by the Obama administration.

It wasn't until April 2014, when stories surfaced claiming roughly forty veterans in a VA hospital in Arizona died while spending an eternity on a hidden waiting list, that this issue started to gain the attention it deserved. Senior officials at the hospital deliberately hid the long wait times for care and the 1,600 veterans who waited months for an appointment. Outraged, several senators called for a full investigation into the fraud and mismanagement (and the resulting deaths) plaguing Veterans Affairs Hospitals.[781] Whistleblowers came forward alleging similar problems and deceptions at seven other VA hospitals around the country.[782] Yet Obama's Justice Department showed no interest in launching their own investigation.[783] Instead, whistleblowers found themselves targets of retaliation by the agency.[784]

The White House claimed Obama was unaware of the problems in the Department of Veterans Affairs, allegedly learning about them "on the news" when the scandal exploded in May 2014.[785] But after Obama won his first election, VA officials informed his transition team of the sorry state of the department.[786] Obama had ample opportunity to work out a plan to improve the care of our veterans. But instead of making things better, as he pledged to do during his campaign, he moved on to his real priorities, yielding no action on behalf of veterans in need. According to an internal Veterans Affairs report released in July 2015, nearly three years after the scandal broke, 238,647 veterans waiting for VA healthcare died before receiving treatment.[787] This is far worse than a broken promise; this was a national disgrace and a complete betrayal of the men and women who volunteered to serve our country. It took a new administration with a real commitment to solving the problem to end this nightmare.

134. OPERATION FAST AND FURIOUS

The Bureau of Alcohol, Tobacco, Firearms, and Explosives (ATF) created Project Gunrunner to track and interrupt the flow of American firearms to Mexican drug cartels. Operations began under the Bush administration and were continued under the Obama administration. Operation Fast and Furious (2009-2011) was the largest gunwalking operation under the project, delivering roughly two thousand firearms across the border. But the operation was seriously compromised; the ATF lost track of hundreds of firearms, and an unknown number of these firearms would later be linked to various crimes, including the murder of U.S. Border Patrol Agent Brian Terry.[788] The Mexican government claims that at least 150 Mexicans were killed or wounded with "Fast and Furious" weapons and that not a single cartel leader has been caught using one.[789]

Of course, the Obama administration tried to cover it up. They even tried blaming President Bush for the operation, even though Operation Fast and Furious started nine months after Obama took office.[790] Attorney General Eric Holder claimed to have no knowledge of the operation. When a congressional investigation took place, Obama asserted executive privilege and refused to provide any documents about it, resulting in an historic vote by

Congress to hold the Attorney General in contempt, which passed with bipartisan support.[791]

Over a hundred people, including Border Patrol Agent Brian Terry, were murdered with firearms provided by the U.S. government. Obama and Holder not only lied about the operation but did whatever they could to stonewall the investigation. So much for transparency.

135. OBAMA'S SLUSH FUND FOR LIBERAL GROUPS

For years, big lenders issued mortgages to people who couldn't afford them—these mortgages featured higher than normal interest rates, low monthly payments that caused debt to *increase* rather than fall as payments were made, and payments that ballooned suddenly after a few years. When struggling homeowners defaulted on these loans in ever-increasing numbers, the resulting pressure on the entire lending market culminated with the subprime mortgage crisis during The Great Recession.[792] The crisis had been brewing for thirty years thanks to initiatives aimed at helping the poor achieve home ownership, but these predatory lending practices were jaw-dropping in their brazenness.

At first, Obama made good on campaign promises to punish predatory lenders. His Justice Department sued the major lenders for these unscrupulous practices, claiming they were scoring victories for minorities and the poor. Bank of America's settlement alone was $16.6 billion, and just about every major lender had hefty settlements to pay.[793] But Obama's concern for the little guy evaporated when he and his allies in Washington realized that these settlement deals could fund left-wing activism without congressional approval.

In 2010, we learned that the Obama administration was funneling leftover money to various groups, some of which were partisan political groups allied with the Obama administration.[794] By 2013, Obama's Justice Department was *instructing* defendants to pay to liberal political groups directly, by including language in the settlement agreements that forgave two or more dollars owed for every one dollar given to groups approved by Obama administration officials. Bank of America got $194 million reduced from their penalty by donating $84 million to groups on Obama's approved nonprofit list.[795] Other lenders such as Citigroup, Morgan Stanley, and Goldman Sachs had settlements with similar language. And Obama's allied groups profited significantly as a result. For example, $1.5 million that should have gone to predatory lending victims went instead to the National Council of La Raza. Another $1.1 million went to the National Urban League. Dozens of other leftist groups also received hefty payouts at the expense of the victims.[796]

The reason we have a civil justice system is to resolve disputes and make victims of fraud, defamation, and other financial violations whole again. When a court found big lenders guilty of damaging and predatory lending practices and awarded billions of dollars in compensatory damages, it did so intending to give the victims justice, not to shake down businesses for political protection money and fund left-wing activism of the most extreme sort. It would be equally wrong for a conservative president to offer companies a sweetheart deal if they would only pay protection money to conservative groups like the Family Research Council, LiveAction, the Heritage Foundation, the Foundation for Individual Rights in Education, and Americans for Prosperity, and the left would never stand for it. Look all you want through the pages of this book; you will not find a more blatant example of racketeering for political purposes in it.

Rather than use the practice to enrich allied groups of their own, the Trump administration officially put an end to the Obama-era slush fund for political groups in June 2017.[797]

136. THE IRS SCANDAL AND COVER-UP

On May 10, 2013, the former Director of the IRS Exempt Organizations division, Lois Lerner, admitted during an American Bar Association meeting that the Tea Party and other conservative groups had been improperly scrutinized by the IRS between 2010 to 2012.[798] Ms. Lerner did this hoping to control the narrative about the brewing scandal, since the Inspector General investigating complaints by conservative groups would soon release a report detailing the improper activity, but outrage immediately followed.

Despite the Obama administration's attempts to blame rogue "low-level" employees in one office for the scandal, as many as twelve different IRS offices across the country targeted conservative groups in the two-year period leading up to the 2012 election,[799] and documents obtained by Judicial Watch via a FOIA request showed the DC headquarters of the IRS orchestrated the crackdown on Tea Party groups.[800] There was also evidence of White House involvement,[801] with some IRS employees claiming that Obama wanted the crackdown.[802] IRS Commissioner Douglas Shulman was at the White House at least 157 times while the IRS targeting occurred. That's more visits than any of Obama's Cabinet members.[803] Emails obtained by the House Oversight and Government Reform Committee also revealed the IRS exchanged confidential taxpayer information with the White House in 2012.[804]

According to the Treasury Department's Inspector General, 292 Tea Party groups were targeted by the IRS, compared with only six liberal groups that were similarly scrutinized.[805] But none of those liberal groups were given the same scrutiny as any Tea Party group.[806] According to the House Committee on Oversight and Government Reform, 10 percent of Tea Party donors were audited by the IRS—ten times higher than the average annual rate of Americans who are audited.[807] Two pro-life nonprofit groups were also denied tax-exempt status by the IRS. One of these groups, the Coalition for Life of Iowa, was told by an IRS agent that their application would only be approved if they signed a letter promising not to protest outside of Planned Parenthood, the nation's largest abortion provider.[808]

The IRS also targeted private individuals critical of Obama, GOP candidates, and Romney donors. As a result of congressional hearings, we learned the IRS covered up the scandal until after the 2012 election. When Barack Obama was asked when he first knew about it, he dodged the question.[809] An analysis by the American Enterprise

Institute suggested that the IRS's actions may have influenced the results of the election.[810]

The Department of Justice promised their own investigation into the scandal. However, a year and a half later, Congress had not yet been briefed on their progress, and groups victimized by the IRS had not yet been interviewed—hardly surprising, considering that Barbara Bosserman, an Obama donor, had been secretly chosen by the Obama administration to lead the investigation.[811] In an additional attempt to delay the investigation, Congressional Democrats demanded an investigation of the IRS Inspector General who had discovered the illegal activity.[812] Bosserman's sham investigation allegedly found no criminal activity by the IRS. The widespread targeting of conservative groups was instead absurdly blamed on "a mismanaged bureaucracy enforcing rules about tax-exemption applications it didn't understand," and it was announced, on January 13, 2014, that no criminal charges were expected to be filed.[813]

The Obama administration didn't have any interest in shedding any light on the IRS's illegal activities, but a report by the House Committee on Oversight and Government Reform implicated Lois Lerner specifically for her role in targeting Tea Party groups and for giving false statements to the committee during their investigation.[814] She also gave confidential tax information on the anti-voter fraud group True The Vote to Democratic Congressman Elijah Cummings (the ranking Democrat on the House Ethics Committee), and she colluded with Obama's Justice Department regarding possible prosecution of conservative tax-exempt groups.[815] Lerner's refusal to testify resulted in the House of Representatives voting to hold her in contempt.[816] Later, the IRS claimed two years' worth of Lerner's and other IRS officials' emails had been lost.[817] While the IRS blamed a crash of Lerner's hard drive for the lost emails, IRS regulations required Lerner to keep printed copies of her emails.[818] The IRS also conveniently cancelled a contract with an email-storage contractor a few weeks after the potentially damaging emails were "lost."[819]

Despite all the evidence of illegal activity, and the blatant attempts to cover up the scandal with a phony internal investigation, Obama and his allies in the media tried to label this a phony scandal.[820] But the fact that the IRS was weaponized against Obama's critics is downright frightening.

OBAMACARE

WE'VE GONE THROUGH QUITE A remarkable list of transgressions, failures, and general malfeasance thus far, but now it's time to tackle Obama's most important, and most reviled, domestic law—the *Patient Protection and Affordable Care Act* (hereafter, Obamacare).

While we'd like to believe that Obama at least meant well by this bill, the tactics he used and the people he employed in the service of the cause suggest otherwise. But, good intentions or not, this bill was a perfect storm of government incompetence, overbearing nanny-state thinking, radical ideology, violations of civil liberties, unconstitutional acts, and crippling economic policies combined in one sickening, blatantly dishonest, life-threatening behemoth of a package. The coils of this leviathan may never be loosed—the new administration made one attempt to wholesale destroy the beast but is reduced to hacking off one tiny piece at a time.

Not only does Obamacare perfectly describe Obama's presidency, but Americans' reactions to it, from supporters and dissenters alike, perfectly describe the state of civil discourse in this polarized nation. What was laughingly called "debate" on this bill, though it dragged on for over a year, was an exercise in team sports, with one side demanding that the other side shut up (guess which side was which!). As we walk you through the horrendous details of Obamacare, be on the lookout for the misbegotten themes you've seen throughout the rest of this book—they're all represented. It is a testament to what a man like Obama can accomplish when he sets his mind to the task of "fundamentally transforming" the country.

137. A PARTISAN HEALTHCARE BILL

When Barack Obama won the presidency in 2008, he promised to make healthcare reform a bipartisan effort. But there was nothing bipartisan about how Obamacare became law. In fact, Democrats were so desperate just to get it passed and signed that when Scott Brown won a special election to fill Ted Kennedy's former seat—and end the Democrats' filibuster-proof majority—Democrats used a legislative process called reconciliation to limit debate in order to fast track the bill's passage in both chambers. But according to The Heritage Foundation, reconciliation "was not intended to be the procedure of last resort when other means fail, and to do so would be a complete abuse of reconciliation rules."[821] It appears their desperate attempt to pass Obamacare created an unfortunate precedent that will only increase dysfunction and partisanship in Congress.

Despite his campaign promise to bring Democrats and Republicans *together* to reform healthcare, Obama signed a trillion-dollar government takeover of one-sixth of the United States economy that passed with zero Republican votes in the Senate and only one Republican vote in the House.[822]

But it's actually worse than it sounds—not only did Obama get the bill passed with essentially no GOP support, but he refused to include GOP legislators and conservative analysts when designing, drafting, and proofreading the bill. The end result of this sort of exclusivity and bullish partisan ramrodding was a Republican Party that felt betrayed and powerless, thus guaranteeing that conservatives would make repealing the bill a central plank in election platforms and galvanizing the grassroots against Obamacare.

Even if you think Obamacare was a good idea—and if you do, we advise you to keep reading—this was a shortsighted failure of leadership, and it cost his party dearly. Democrats suffered two of the worst shellackings in modern political history at the ballot box in 2010 and 2014, costing them the entire southern U.S., many of the gains they'd previously made in the Midwest, and even some ground in the Northeast. They owned Obamacare and everything that happened because of it.

138. LACK OF HEALTHCARE TRANSPARENCY

Healthcare affects all Americans, and at current rates of inflation, the cost of healthcare to the federal government, and to the taxpayers, will soon become so large that conservative and liberal economists all agree it will amount to a national crisis. Despite years of research, there is no clear consensus on how to fix this burdensome issue, though there is no shortage of ideas. America is a large and diverse nation with varied healthcare needs. It is also the central hub for the world's most promising medical research, and Americans shoulder much of the cost of developing new drugs and therapies by paying higher prices than the developing world. That being the case, there are many competing interests in the healthcare market, and they all need a seat at the table when we discuss major reforms. The only chance to find a rational solution for our healthcare system is to include all perspectives in debate and planning. This is what Obama promised—in fact, he promised to broadcast the final negotiations live on C-SPAN.

Sadly, that was just another broken Obama promise. Because of an alleged need to "fast-track" the final Obamacare bill, Obama agreed with then-House Speaker Nancy Pelosi that the final negotiations would be held behind closed doors.[823] While the administration claimed that failures of the healthcare system demanded immediate action, Obama likely feared he would lose his filibuster-proof majority in the Senate before the final bill could be passed.

It was this lack of transparency that was crucial to Obamacare getting passed, according to Obamacare architect Jonathan Gruber, because the details would have been politically unpopular. "Lack of transparency is a huge political advantage. And basically, call it the stupidity of the American voter or whatever, but basically that was really, really [sic] critical for the thing to pass..."[824] Nancy Pelosi put it best when she infamously said, "We have to pass the bill to find out what is in it."

139. THE OBAMACARE CO-OP DEBACLE

An obscure provision in Obamacare allocated $2.4 billion in taxpayer-funded, tax-free loans to establish twenty-three Obamacare co-ops nationwide to compete with private health insurance providers. The Obama administration approved each loan, so you might think they created some basic standards before doling out the money if you didn't read the rest of this book and, therefore, know better.

The Washington Examiner's Richard Pollack reported on some of the loans the Obama administration approved:

- $62 million to Maine Community Health Options; the company's president molested teenage boys for more than three decades.[825]
- $65 million to Louisiana Health Cooperative; CEO Terry Shilling was sanctioned by the Securities and Exchange Commission for insider trading.[826]
- $112 million to CoOportunity Health; CFO Stephen Ringlee had at least three businesses fail since 2009.[827]
- $129 million to Florida-based Community Health Solutions of America for an Obamacare co-op in Ohio. The principal investors for this co-op had histories of failed companies, bankruptcy, and tax problems.[828]

But the largest loan, $340 million, went to Freelancers Insurance Company, which is based out of New York and run by Sara Horowitz, an old Obama chum from his days as a state senator. This might not seem so terrible if her company had a reputation for quality service, but it didn't. Freelancers Insurance Company had an extremely high rate of consumer complaints and, for two consecutive years, was rated the "worst" insurer by state regulators.[829] Why did these companies get so many of our tax dollars? There's no good answer.

Due to gross mismanagement, by January 2016, more than half of Obamacare co-ops had failed, costing a quarter of a million Americans their insurance and leaving the taxpayers $1.2 billion in unpaid loans.[830] By January 2018, only four Obamacare Co-ops remained.[831] The Obamacare co-ops were the health insurance version of the Solyndra boondoggle, but bigger.

140. FUDGING THE ENROLLMENT NUMBERS

Despite the fact that millions had their existing plans canceled and millions more would eventually share the same fate, Obama called his healthcare law a proven success when he announced that by end of its first open enrollment, the Obamacare exchanges had allegedly signed up 7.1 million people.[832] But who, exactly, counted as a successful Obamacare enrollee? Like Bill Clinton's famous request to define the meaning of "is," it depends who you ask.

For starters, there were duplicate enrollments, counted as unique, from consumers advised to create new accounts and re-enroll because of problems with the health exchange website.[833] Various studies raised serious doubts about the number of enrollees touted by Obama. The RAND Corporation found there were only 3.9 million legitimate exchange enrollees in a 2014 analysis. You might think Obama would be interested in the number of *newly insured* Americans who purchased an exchange plan. If you do, you should go back and read this book again. The same study by RAND found only 1.4 million enrollees were previously uninsured.[834] Another study by McKinsey & Company in 2014 found that of those signing up for Obamacare, only 26 percent were previously uninsured.[835]

Many people signing up for Obamacare either previously had insurance plans cancelled by Obamacare rules or were merely signing up for Medicaid. And future plan cancellations still loomed for millions more Americans even though Obama repeatedly promised it would never happen.

141. DO-NOTHING OBAMACARE CONTRACTORS

In the summer of 2013, the British firm Serco was awarded a five-year contract worth over a billion dollars to process Obamacare paper applications.[836] The Obama administration must have figured they'd be pretty busy. But in the spring of 2014, whistleblowers came forward from Serco offices in four states admitting that they were paid taxpayer dollars to do nothing.

One employee reported, over a six-month period, he processed only forty applications. Another, who quit her job in frustration, said she processed only six applications in the entire month of December. She reported the company kept her on the clock from 9 pm to midnight but forbade her to make any calls or do any work. In a Serco office in Arkansas, workers were required to be on the clock and get paid but stay off the phones. That office was *still* hiring too.[837]

Where was the oversight and accountability? Why were taxpayer dollars being wasted so frivolously? The nonpartisan, nonprofit Sunlight Foundation found the likely answer. Of the forty-seven companies awarded contracts by the Obama administration, seventeen spent a cumulative $128 million on lobbying in 2011 and 2012. Twenty-nine of these contract winners had employees or PACs that contributed a total of $32 million to federal candidates and parties during the same period. Barack Obama's reelection campaign received nearly $4 million from employees and PACs from Obamacare contract winners. Serco spent more than $1 million on lobbying and donations prior to being awarded its Obamacare contract.[838] Money certainly does talk.

Making matters worse, Serco came under investigation by Britain's Serious Fraud Office a few days after being awarded the Obamacare contract. An audit revealed Serco and another company had overbilled the United States government by more than $80 billion.[839] Despite this, the Obama administration defended their decision to award the contract to Serco.[840]

142. THE MANDATE EFFECT

As Obamacare took effect, the law put businesses across the country in a tight squeeze, forcing employers to lay off workers in order to reduce costs and stay afloat. To minimize the political fallout of the implementation of his signature healthcare law, Obama twice delayed the employer mandate for businesses with fifty to ninety-nine employees, once in 2013 and again in 2014.[841] But delaying the onset of the mandate did nothing to convince businesses that they should employ more than those benchmark levels, and they became a perverse incentive to lay off employees. As James Taranto of *The Wall Street Journal* explained, "For a company on the cusp, the marginal cost of hiring the next employee could run into the tens of thousands of dollars—or, for one just above the threshold, the marginal savings from firing a worker can be considerable."[842]

Realizing this but unwilling to risk political fallout from these layoffs in the crucial midterm election year, the Obama administration did what any totalitarian regime would do: it wrote new regulations making it clear that employers could not lay off workers to get below the 100-employee threshold and qualify for exemption from the mandate. Employers who did lay off workers were required to certify to the IRS—under penalty of perjury—that avoiding the costs of Obamacare was not a motivating factor in those layoffs.[843] The president tried to silence critics of his signature bill with threats of jail time unless they remained silent about how Obamacare hurt their business.

143. WAIVERS FOR OBAMACARE'S PROPONENTS

If Obamacare is great, why would anyone want a waiver, and why would the government grant them one? It's a fair question, seeing as 1,231 companies, employing just under four million people, received waivers, according to the Department of Health and Human Services.[844] Most federal employees got waivers too.

The majority of the waivers granted were given to Obama's allies in Big Labor—who overwhelmingly supported the law.[845] It wasn't just Obama's Big Labor allies getting Obamacare waivers either. Sally Jewell, the CEO of REI, was always a supporter of Obamacare. In 2009, she participated in an Obama administration roundtable on healthcare reform. That didn't stop her from seeking and receiving an Obamacare waiver for REI's health coverage back in 2011.[846] An Obama cabinet nominee also received an Obamacare waiver.

144. AMERICANS DELAYED MEDICAL CARE OVER OBAMACARE COSTS

Obamacare triggered a series of massive hikes in insurance premiums and deductibles, and this had negative consequences. Gallup surveyed Americans on their healthcare decisions in November 2015. 31 percent of Americans reported "that they or a family member have put off any sort of medical treatment in the past year because of the cost." A full third of Americans said the same in 2014—the *highest* number ever reported since Gallup began polling on it in 2001. Despite the passage and implementation of Obamacare, the number of people reporting they or a family member had put off medical treatment because they couldn't afford it was higher than it was before Obama took office (29%) and much higher than it was when Gallup first asked the question in 2001 (19%).[847]

How is this possible? Obamacare was supposed to *increase* access to healthcare. The middle class took the biggest blow since the poor could get Medicaid for free and the wealthy could afford to buy private insurance. For the middle class, though, health insurance premiums and deductibles increased because of Obamacare, straining already-limited budgets. Gallup found people who put off treatment were more likely to do so for a serious condition (19 percent) than a non-serious one (12 percent).[848] For most Americans, things were better *before* Obamacare.

Only low-income families with less than $30,000 annual household income saw a decline in delaying healthcare over costs, according to Gallup.[849] Obama didn't spread the wealth; he redistributed it. It's quite obvious that Obamacare made the problem it was trying to solve worse. A Gallup poll from the summer of 2017 found that 17 percent of Americans cited the cost of healthcare as the top financial problem facing their family—making it the most cited financial concern of Americans, up a whopping seven points since 2013.[850] Is that what Obama calls success?

145. FUNDING ABORTIONS UNDER OBAMACARE

Even with large majorities in both Houses of Congress, getting enough *Democrats* on board to pass Obamacare came with a few challenges. Corrupt deals and promises had to be made just to secure an essentially party-line vote on the controversial legislation.

After party leaders purchased enough votes with amendments to the bill that rolled out the pork barrels to every corner of the nation, there remained one final roadblock for Obamacare's passage in the House of Representatives. Congressman Bart Stupak's coalition of pro-life Democrats could not support Obamacare while it contained language allowing for taxpayer-funded abortion medications under the law. Stupak, under pressure from both sides of the abortion issue, negotiated an executive order that effectively banned public funding of abortions in Obama's healthcare law.[851] Without this compromise, Obamacare would have never passed the House of Representatives.

Stupak paid a huge political price for his support for Obamacare and, ultimately, the compromise he made in good faith with President Obama was a sham. Less than a month after Obamacare was signed into law, Bart Stupak, seeing the writing on the wall, announced his retirement.[852] Obama broke his promise to Stupak, and language in the final regulations for Obamacare *required* coverage of medications that cause abortions.[853] At the 2012 Democratic National Convention, Stupak, speaking to a Democrats for Life panel, said, "I am perplexed and disappointed that, having negotiated the Executive Order with the President, not only does the HHS mandate violate the Executive Order but it also violates statutory law."[854]

146. THREATENING DRUG MAKERS TO SUPPORT OBAMACARE

Thanks to a year-long investigation by House Republicans, we learned the truth behind the pharmaceutical industry's support for Obamacare. Despite Obama's promises of transparency, the nation's top drug companies faced secret threats of higher taxes if they didn't endorse the law. The House released internal documents from the investigation on May 31, 2012. *The Washington Times* reported that these documents showed, in June 2009, White House officials told drug company representatives if they didn't show their support, Obama would "demand a costly 15 percent rebate on Medicare drugs and push for the removal of the tax deduction for direct consumer advertising, which would cost the industry $100 billion over the next decade." The threats worked, and "drug companies agreed to pay higher Medicaid rebates and a new healthcare reform fee to raise $80 billion for the legislation, and promised to run positive television ads about it."[855] We find it strange that a man who promised to be transparent and accountable mastered the art of secret extortion.

147. OBAMACARE HOSPITAL LAYOFFS AND CLOSURES

If the true goal of Obamacare was to make healthcare more accessible, something went terribly wrong. In addition to higher premiums and deductibles, cancelled plans, and a website that didn't work, Obamacare found other ways to be an obstacle to getting access to healthcare.

The world-renowned Cleveland Clinic announced in September 2013 they would be cutting their annual budget by 5 to 6 percent and cutting jobs to prepare for Obamacare reforms.[856] Hospitals across the country cut thousands of jobs in 2013 because of Obamacare, and the number grew in 2014. The healthcare sector has typically been a reliable source of job growth, even when the economy is in recession. But now, thanks to Obamacare, it is entering into a recession of its own.[857]

In some cases, hospitals closed for good. In Georgia alone, four hospitals closed over a two-year period because of Obamacare-related payment cuts.[858] In addition to closed hospitals and reduced staff, many doctors refused to take patients enrolled in Obamacare programs for fear of increased costs and reduced payments for medical services.[859] In January 2017, we learned, because of Obamacare, rural hospitals closed at a rate of one per month since 2010.[860] Health insurance is not automatically healthcare access; it's tough to access quality care when you can't find a doctor, the nearest hospital closed, and you have to pay through the nose until your massive deductible is gone.

148. A BILL THAT HURTS BUSINESSES

In 2012, for the first time ever, employer-provided health insurance costs for a family of four exceeded $20,000.[861] Obama promised that his bill would lower costs for businesses, but employer healthcare costs increased by 6 percent between 2016 and 2017, continuing a trend of exploding costs for businesses and their employees.

Brian Marcotte, CEO of the National Business Group on Health, called these cost increases "unsustainable and unacceptable." Employers pushed the added costs onto their employees by charging them more for premiums and deductibles, lowering their salaries, or offering lower-cost plans. In fact, over a third of companies offered less expensive high-deductible plans to keep their costs down, meaning their employees were left with no choice but to pay thousands of dollars for their medical costs before their insurance kicked in.[862]

Obamacare didn't just force businesses to make their employees or customers pay more to offset the extra costs. Smaller businesses that couldn't afford to provide coverage as mandated by Obamacare laid off employees or cut their hours to avoid heavy penalties. Florida restaurant owner John Metz, who ran roughly forty Denny's Restaurants and owned the Hurricane Grill & Wings franchise, decided after Obama was reelected to add a 5 percent surcharge to customers' bills and cut hours of employees to under thirty hours a week to avoid the $2,000 per employee penalty for not offering a government-approved insurance plan as required under Obamacare. According to Metz, the cost of covering employees under the law would be more than most of his restaurants make in a year.[863]

149. CUTTING MEDICARE TO PAY FOR OBAMACARE

Obama assured us Medicare would be unaffected by his health plan, but Obamacare *cut* $716 billion from Medicare. Medicare actuary Richard Foster said these cuts would not be viable in the long term.[864] Foster also projected that about half of Medicare recipients enrolled in highly popular private Medicare Advantage plans—that's seven million customers—would have to find other coverage because of the cuts.[865] These cuts would ultimately force seniors to pay higher premiums and see a reduction in benefits.[866]

Seniors weren't happy about this, and the issue became a huge liability for Obama and the Democratic Party. In April 2014, Obama, via executive fiat, scaled back the cuts in a futile effort to save his party in the upcoming midterm elections.[867] Considering that seniors are a large, reliable voting block, why was a huge cut in Medicare ever part of Obamacare? It appears the cuts were a budgetary gimmick designed to make the costs of Obamacare appear low enough that the Congressional Budget Office (CBO) would score Obamacare as having minimal impact on the nation's debt and pave the way for its passage by reconciliation.[868]

150. RATIONING HEALTHCARE

About the only common ground between Republicans and Democrats in the debate over Obamacare was their mutual opposition to the Independent Payment Advisory Board (IPAB), the fifteen-member government agency created by Obamacare with the stated purpose of finding savings in Medicare without compromising coverage or the quality of care. By design, this board of unelected bureaucrats was protected from Congressional review.[869] It wasn't just members of Congress raising objections to the IPAB. Even the American Medical Association, whose support was crucial to getting the bill passed, called for the IPAB's repeal.[870] We think calling the IPAB a "death panel" is a bit extreme, but many Democrats agreed with the concern that the IPAB would reduce access to care. Julie Reiskin, who was nominated to serve on the Legal Services Corporation Board of Directors by Barack Obama, said that the IPAB would "ration care or increase consumer cost sharing."[871]

151. OBAMACARE-CAUSED LAYOFFS

Many American business owners, struggling under the Obama economy, held out for the results of the 2012 presidential election before making major decisions about the future of their companies. They were hoping a change in administration might give them some relief, but they were denied. When Obama won reelection, the chance of Obamacare being repealed vanished. With new regulations and higher taxes looming, businesses across the country announced sweeping layoffs. Here are just a few:

Boeing: 30 percent of executives.[872]
Energizer: about 1,500 employees.[873]
Murray Energy: 156 employees.[874]
Groupon: 80 employees.[875]
Stanford Brake: 75 employees.[876]
Rocketdyne: 100 employees.[877]

According to the Bureau of Labor Statistics, in November 2012 there were 1,759 "mass layoff actions" from firms with more than fifty employees, affecting nearly 165,000 workers.[878] Mass layoffs *declined* the prior three years, meaning this new wave of layoffs related to the results of the election.

Some companies didn't even wait until the election to make their moves. Medical companies like Boston Scientific, Medtronic, Abbot Labs, Covidien, Kinetic Concepts, St. Jude Medical, Welch Allyn, Hill-Rom, and Stryker, Smith & Nephew had previously anticipated massive layoffs in 2013 due to the new medical device tax in Obamacare.[879]

152. THE OBAMACARE ROLLOUT DISASTER

On October 1, 2013, millions of Americans tried to shop for their new "affordable" government-approved healthcare plans by visiting *HealthCare.gov* or their state's insurance exchange sites. Massive system failures not only prevented access to the sites or stalled the application process, especially at *HealthCare.gov*. Sources in the insurance industry said, because of software problems, only about 1 percent of applications contained enough data to successfully enroll the applicants in a plan.[880]

A mere six people succeeded in signing up for Obamacare on its launch day.[881] According to the nonpartisan research firm Millward Brown Digital, less than half of 1 percent of the visitors to the federal healthcare website were able to complete enrollment in the first week.[882] The early sign-up numbers were awful. At times, it looked like it would be nearly impossible for the Obama administration to meet its goal of seven million enrollees during the six-month enrollment period.

To call the Obamacare rollout a disaster is an understatement. And the Obama administration was aware that the site couldn't handle the anticipated load long before launch day. According to a confidential report obtained by CNN, the Obama administration "was given stark warnings just one month before launch that the federal healthcare site was not ready to go live."[883] Why, then, did the Obama administration let the rollout (which was destined to be a total failure) occur at all, especially after refusing the House Republicans' compromise to delay Obamacare for a year?

The site also had major security flaws, putting the private information of millions of Americans at risk of being stolen. The Obama administration knew of these flaws and vulnerabilities but did nothing, according to documents provided to the House Committee on Government Oversight and Reform.[884] One top Obamacare official recommended the site be shut down over the security risks but was overruled—directly contradicting the claims that they were not aware of any security concerns prior to the site's launch.[885]

Obamacare enrollees also discovered that it was nearly impossible to add a newborn baby to an already purchased plan. Nor could they address other common life changes affecting premiums, such as marriage, divorce, and death of a family member.[886]

The architect of the site, CGI Federal, was given a $678 million no-bid contract, even though there were several companies qualified to perform those services. Why? Perhaps it was because Princeton classmate of First Lady Michelle Obama's was a top executive at CGI. Or maybe the fact president of the company's North American operations became a donor for Obama's reelection campaign after receiving the contract to build *HealthCare.gov* played a role.[887] Either way, the $678 million no-bid contract was a total loss; the government paid another developer to rebuild *HealthCare.gov*.

153. MASS POLICY CANCELLATIONS

"If you like your health-care plan, you will be able to keep your health-care plan, period."

Obama repeatedly made this claim as he campaigned for public support of Obamacare. Unfortunately, Americans would learn the hard way that this promise was a lie, as millions discovered their current health plans didn't meet Obamacare standards and couldn't be offered again.

To call this a broken promise would be inaccurate. It was, in fact, a deliberate deception meant to ensure the law's passage and, eventually, his own reelection. Obama administration officials estimated in 2010 that ninety-three million Americans would *lose* their healthcare plans under the new law.[888] By the end of February 2014, just five months after the Obamacare rollout, 6.3 million people lost their existing plans.[889] Obama also quietly pursued new regulations to make "fixed benefit" plans—which are less expensive than more comprehensive plans—illegal, resulting in another wave of policy cancellations.[890]

Knowing that millions would lose their plans didn't stop Obama from regularly promising the opposite while running for reelection. It turns out, if it wasn't for that one big lie, the 2012 election would have turned out differently. According to a Wilson Perkins Allen Opinion Research survey, when voters were asked if they would still have voted for Barack Obama knowing they'd actually lose their healthcare plans, nearly one out of four said they would not. An *ABC/Washington Post* poll conducted a month and a half after the botched Obamacare rollout found that if voters had an election do-over, Romney would have won with 49 percent to Obama's 45 percent.[891]

As millions of Americans received cancellation notices, Obama denied he ever made that promise. "What we said was you could keep it if it hasn't changed since the law was passed," was Obama's absurd claim. Caught in one of the most brazen lies in American history, Obama's recourse was to present another lie to cover up the first. Unfortunately for Obama, video recordings prove he made the unequivocal promise that Americans could keep their plans, no matter what, at least twenty-nine times.[892] An investigation by CNN revealed that the Obama administration threatened insurance company executives to keep quiet about the cancellations.[893] They also scolded liberal pundit Bob Beckel for advocating a year-long delay of Obamacare in order to address its many problems.[894]

Americans might have accepted the problems with the rollout of Obamacare had they found their coverage better or, at least, more affordable as Barack Obama promised. That turned out to not to be true either. Millions of Americans found the new plans were *more* expensive and had higher deductibles before. College students who could previously buy cheap health insurance through their college or university no longer could—another lovely gift from Obama to his biggest fans.[895] Cancer patients lost their existing plans and found themselves paying more than double for their new Obamacare-compliant plans.[896] Even a single mother whose story was cited by Obama as an Obamacare success after buying insurance off her state's exchange website found the plan she picked wasn't actually affordable.[897] There were many stories of real Americans losing their coverage and finding out they had to pay higher premiums for plans with higher deductibles. So egregious was Obama's lie about keeping your plan that the left-wing fact-checking site *PolitiFact* crowned it the Lie of the Year for 2013.[898]

154. HIGHER HEALTHCARE PREMIUMS AND DEDUCTIBLES

Obama promised his healthcare reform would lower insurance premiums by $2,500 per family per year. The Congressional Budget Office (CBO) found Obamacare actually raised annual premiums per family by $2,400 by 2014.[899] And it only got worse. In October 2016, the Obama administration admitted there would be double-digit premium hikes in 2017, with an average increase "of 25 percent across the 39 states served by the federally run online market."[900]

The CBO had predicted Americans would feel sticker shock when they browsed the exchange website, and boy were they right. Not only were new premiums much higher than promised, but their new deductibles were unaffordable.[901] Jonathan Gruber—Obama's healthcare advisor and the architect of Obamacare—said, in 2009, Obamacare would *not* be affordable and added, in 2012, that Obama was fully aware of that fact.[902] The hardest hit are the middle class, since they don't qualify for subsidies.

155. THE LARGEST TAX INCREASE ON THE MIDDLE CLASS IN HISTORY

Aside from being a government takeover of healthcare, Obamacare is also the largest tax increase on the middle class in history. When the Supreme Court upheld the law by declaring that the individual mandate was constitutional only as a tax, *The Wall Street Journal* explained the implications of the decision:

> *It is now undeniable that Mr. Obama has imposed the largest tax increase in history on the middle class. Individuals who don't buy insurance will have to pay several hundred dollars, depending on income. The Congressional Budget Office says that 76% of those who pay the mandate tax will make less than 500% of the federal poverty level, estimated to be $24,000 for a family of four in 2016. That means 76% of the payers will earn less than $120,000 a year.*
>
> *So much for Mr. Obama's promise not to raise taxes on anyone earning less than $200,000. And this initial mandate tax will only be a teaser rate when it becomes clear it isn't nearly enough either to finance the bill or drive individuals to buy insurance. Millions will wait to buy insurance until they need expensive treatment, knowing they can always buy it when they show up at the hospital.*[903]

Whether you want to call it a tax or a mandate, the middle class paid *more* because of Obama's policies. Yet, during a *60 Minutes* interview, Obama not only insisted he hadn't raised taxes, but he had the nerve to claim he had *cut* taxes.[904] For the record, Obamacare had eighteen new tax hikes, with $36.3 billion in taxes hitting the American people in 2013, alone, not counting the penalties some paid for not complying with the individual mandate.[905] In their landmark tax reform bill in 2017, Congress eliminated the individual mandate and spared the middle class from billions of dollars in punitive taxes.

TERRORISM

IN 2008, OBAMA CAMPAIGNED AS a peacemaker. He knew Americans were tired of war, and so he promised them he'd end the wars in Iraq and Afghanistan and nation-build at home while still being tough on terrorism. Unfortunately, a combination of poor decisions and misguided policies left us less safe by the time he left office. We've talked about his terrible record in the foreign policy sphere, but now we're going to focus on his record fighting terrorism. Under his leadership, terrorism around the globe surged, old enemies returned to the battle, America suffered over a dozen major terrorist attacks at home, and when he tried to end the wars, it only led to more terrorism.

And yet, with a dismal economy, Obama needed to pump up his foreign policy record while running for reelection. He claimed credit for killing Osama bin Laden, saying, "Al-Qaeda is on its heels." We wish it were so but knew better and, after al-Qaeda was linked to the attack on the U.S. Consulate in Benghazi, and reports of a comeback of al-Qaeda in Iraq[906] and North Africa emerged,[907] he had to drop it from his speech. Gen. Jack Keane, a retired four-star general and former vice chief of staff of the U.S. Army, gave the real story. In testimony before the Senate Armed Services Committee in January 2015, he said radical Islam had "grown fourfold in the last five years,"[908] and later added that the Obama administration "became paralyzed by the fear of adverse consequences in the Middle East after fighting two wars."[909]

Obama was unable able to admit we were (and still are) at war with radical Islam. This refusal to acknowledge reality certainly had a hand the explosion of radical Islam on his watch, which engulfed most of North Africa, the whole of the Middle East, and parts of Southeast Asia, Europe, and the Pacific Islands. Former allies of the United States in the affected areas tumbled and fell or allied with the most powerful Islamic theocracies, Iran and Saudi Arabia. Muslim factions took sides in what may soon become a regional war powered by weapons of mass destruction, including nuclear bombs. This was one of Obama's greatest failings—he pursued a badly incoherent, morally timid, and illogical strategy in the fight against radicalism and terrorism, and we may soon pay for it with our freedoms or even our lives.

156. NOMINATING JOHN BRENNAN AS CIA DIRECTOR

John Brennan served as Obama's Homeland Security Advisor during his first term. He was Obama's original pick for CIA Director in 2009 but was forced to withdraw because of Democratic opposition. Liberated by his reelection, Obama nominated him for the position again in 2013. But Brennan's road to heading the CIA would still not be easy. Brennan, the architect of Obama's controversial drone program, also "helped construct and justify the administration's claim that it could kill people, including American citizens, abroad, on its own authority, even when those people are not in countries with which we are at war."[910] During his Senate Committee Hearing, Brennan claimed that due process was not necessary to kill Americans for their potential future acts.[911]

There were other reasons Brennan was a bad choice for the job. According to Steven Emerson, the executive director of The Investigative Project on Terrorism, Brennan has "shown a tendency to fall for the bait from radical Islamists."

> *Globally, [Brennan] repeatedly expressed a hope that "moderates" within Iran and its terror proxy Hezbollah would steer their respective constituencies away from terrorism.*
>
> *Domestically, he claims that radical Islam does not pose its own, unique threat to American security. He has helped strip language about "radical Islam," "jihad" and similar terms from government vernacular, choosing instead to refer to "violent extremism" in an attempt to deny terrorists religious credibility.*
>
> *When it comes to jihad, he stubbornly maintains the word does not belong in conversations about terror, no matter what terrorists themselves say.*
>
> *Likewise, he also yielded to demands from American Islamists to purge law enforcement and intelligence training material of the terms "jihad" and "radical Islam."*[912]

Brennan also claimed that terrorists were motivated by economic and political factors, not religious ones, despite evidence to the contrary.[913]

Brennan's political correctness blinded him to potential threats. In 2010, Brennan allowed a sheik linked to Hamas to participate in an FBI-hosted "Citizens Academy," which gave him a tutorial on the National Counterterrorism Center and other secure government facilities.[914] Brennan was confirmed by the Senate but received a record-breaking thirty-four votes *against* his confirmation for the position.[915]

157. SKIPPING THE PARIS ANTI-TERRORISM RALLY

George W. Bush famously said in his 2002 State of the Union Address, in which he laid out a vision for his response to the 9/11 Terror Attack: "To all nations who have sponsored terrorists or given them safe harbor, I have a simple message. You are either with us, or you're against us." He was roundly mocked by leftists for his "simplistic" worldview, but there are certain times when a question arises for which there must be a simple answer or no answer at all. This is one of those questions: does the United States stand opposed to terrorism in the name of religion or not?

In the aftermath of the Islamic Jihadist massacre conducted in the offices of the French satirical paper *Charlie Hebdo* for running cartoons of the Islamic prophet Muhammad, the world united in outrage against the attack and in solidarity with the French people. On January 11, 2015, an historic rally against terrorism and in support of free speech took place in Paris, bringing together 1.3

million people, including forty-four heads of state from around the world. One very glaring absence from the event was Barack Obama.

Obama's muted response to the shooting at the *Charlie Hebdo* offices, where twelve people were killed, stands in sharp contrast to his remarks following the death of Michael Brown, killed resisting arrest in Ferguson, MO, in 2014. Obama sent three representatives to Brown's funeral.[916] But this rally against terrorism, a worldwide expression of solidarity, was not important enough to attend. What was Obama doing that kept him away from joining hands with other world leaders, including German Chancellor Angela Merkel, Israeli Prime Minister Benjamin Netanyahu, and British Prime Minister David Cameron? According to an administration official, Obama had an open schedule and spent part of the afternoon watching football on television.[917]

With all the world leaders present, security could not have been a legitimate concern. Obama should have been there, or at least a high-ranking official in his administration. But none were there. Vice President Biden, whose public schedule was also open, did not attend. Secretary of State John Kerry was in India. Attorney General Eric Holder, who was *in Paris* at the time for a terrorism summit, didn't participate either.[918]

Outrage over the snub forced the Obama administration to apologize and admit that it should have sent a high-ranking official to the event. Security concerns were blamed for Obama's absence—though, according to a former Secret Service agent, if Obama *wanted* to go, the Secret Service could have made it work.[919]

In 2012, the Obama administration condemned *Charlie Hebdo* for featuring cartoons of Muhammad as offensive and potentially inflammatory.[920] Obama also declared, in a speech to the U.N., that "the future must not belong to those who slander the prophet of Islam."[921] The Obama administration was even reluctant to call the attack "terrorism" and avoided any language associating violence with Islam.[922] Every time Obama had the chance to stand up for free speech and Western egalitarian values in the face of radical extremism, he was on the wrong side; and if you think complaining about a symbolic gesture not made is splitting hairs, we recommend you keep reading. This was just a symbol, but a symbol of an intellectual rot at the core of Obama's worldview that threatened everything we hold dear.

158. DOUBLE-TALK ON LOCKERBIE BOMBER RELEASE

On July 25, 2009, Abdelbaset al-Megrahi, the Lockerbie bomber, was released from prison on compassionate grounds. Al-Megrahi was dying of prostate cancer. He was also responsible for the deaths of 270 people and, naturally, outrage ensued. Of those 270 victims, 189 were Americans. Barack Obama publicly denounced the decision. A year later, in a joint press conference at the White House with the British Prime Minister, Obama reiterated that sentiment, with the claim, "My administration expressed, very clearly, our objections prior to the decision being made and subsequent to the decision being made. So we welcome any additional information that will give us insights and a better understanding of why the decision was made.[923]

Obama knew exactly how and why the decision was made. Less than a week later, it was revealed that the Obama administration had secretly advised Scottish ministers to free the Lockerbie bomber rather than jail him in Libya.[924] Not only did Al-Megrahi receive a hero's welcome upon returning to Libya, he lived for another two years, much longer than the short few months expected when he was released.

159. IRAN DRONE ATTACK COVER-UP

On November 1, 2012, the Iranian air force attacked an unmanned U.S. drone aircraft in international airspace. News of Iran's deliberate act of war was not released to the American people until November 8, two days *after* the presidential election.[925] The Pentagon dubiously argued that they couldn't tell us about the attack until after the election because of "security concerns."

The Pentagon denied any political motivation for keeping the incident secret; however, key Republican leaders, who would normally be briefed about such an incident, were not informed. Nor was Mitt Romney, who had been receiving intelligence briefings at the time.[926] Political expediency cannot be tolerated as an excuse for failing to respond immediately—and with conviction—to such acts by enemy combatants.

160. ISLAMIC RADICALS AT THE WHITE HOUSE

The nature of Islam according to the founder of the Muslim Brotherhood, Hassan al-Bama, is "to dominate, not to be dominated, to impose its law on all nations and to extend its power to the entire planet."[927] That is pretty clear and straightforward. The Muslim Brotherhood believes if you are non-Muslim, then you are their enemy. If any group should be watched and opposed by the United States—the champion of pluralist government and freedom of conscience in the world—then the Muslim Brotherhood is it. We treated them as an enemy in practice until Obama became president. He seemed incapable of telling friend from foe, especially in the battle against radical Islam.

In April 2012, we learned White House officials had met with members of Egypt's Muslim Brotherhood. The White House justified the meeting, saying that the Muslim Brotherhood would play a "prominent role" in Egyptian affairs going forward.[928] Indeed, they would. After all, the White House had played a key role in ousting the Mubarak regime, paving the way for the Muslim Brotherhood to grab power.

But that's not all. The Investigative Project on Terrorism reported, "Scores of known radical Islamists made hundreds of visits to the Obama White House, meeting with top administration officials."

> *The IPT made the discovery combing through millions of White House visitor log entries. IPT compared the visitors' names with lists of known radical Islamists.*

> *Among the visitors were officials representing groups which have:*
>
> - *Been designated by the Department of Justice as unindicted co-conspirators in terrorist trials; Extolled Islamic terrorist groups including Hamas and Hezbollah;*
> - *Obstructed terrorist investigations by instructing their followers not to cooperate with law enforcement;*
> - *Promoted the incendiary conspiratorial allegation that the United States is engaged in a "war against Islam"—a leading tool in recruiting Muslims to carry out acts of terror;*
> - *Repeatedly claimed that many of the Islamic terrorists convicted since 9-11 were framed by the U.S government as part of an anti-Muslim profiling campaign.*
>
> *Individuals from the Council on American-Islamic Relations (CAIR) visited the White House at least 20 times starting in 2009. In 2008, CAIR was listed as an unindicted co-conspirator in the largest terrorist money laundering case in U.S. history—the trial of the Holy Land Foundation in which five HLF officials were convicted of funneling money to Hamas.*[929]

These are hardly the types of people that should be given access to the White House, meeting with top administration officials and influencing the administration's foreign policy.

161. ALLOWING TERROR-LINKED REFUGEES INTO THE U.S.

Continuing in his foolhardy belief that, if he is nice to the people who despise America, they will change their minds, Obama changed our immigration laws—without Congressional authorization—to relax restrictions on refugees and asylum seekers who provided "limited" material support to terrorists and terrorist organizations. Obama's team called this law change "common sense."[930]

One of the excuses offered for waiving the restrictions was some people might have helped terrorists under duress.[931] Obama felt that the safety of Americans was less important than giving possible terrorists the benefit of the doubt. This is what Obama called "common sense"? This level of incoherence was but a taste of what was to come, however.

In 2015, as millions of Syrian and Iraqi refugees—and by refugees, we mean able-bodied, fighting-aged young men, predominantly—poured into Europe and overwhelmed the EU's resources, world leaders began pressuring the United States to take some of them. Obama was all too happy to oblige, and he began making plans to order Immigration and Naturalization Services to drastically expand its program for refugees in order to accept ten thousand Syrians in 2016,[932] justifying the move on humanitarian grounds and claiming that they would be heavily vetted.[933]

The problems with this were threefold. First, the refugees pouring into Europe were rampaging through the continent leading to huge spikes in rape rates,[934] armed robberies, and assaults and inspiring a nationalist political pushback throughout eastern Europe.[935] Second, his own security experts told him and the American people that the vetting process could not be thorough enough to screen out terrorists.[936] And third, Americans overwhelmingly opposed the idea, and thirty-one state governors signed executive orders or bills passed by state legislatures declaring their refusal to accept them.[937] But since when did Obama care about the will of the people?

162. ATTEMPTS TO PROSECUTE KHALID SHEIK MOHAMMED IN THE UNITED STATES

Barack Obama made it clear that he wanted 9/11 mastermind Khalid Sheikh Mohammed and four co-conspirators to be tried in the U.S. federal court system. This was a terrible idea on many levels: Security costs would have been enormous, it would have given terrorists a public platform to denounce America, and it could have jeopardized intelligence sources. Yet Obama, an outspoken critic of military tribunals, was determined to have a public trial in New York City.

The plan was so bad that there was bipartisan opposition from Congress. New York City officials were also opposed to it.[938] The administration did eventually reverse its policy—not because it realized the error of its ways, but because Congress refused to provide the funds for a trial on American soil.[939] International terrorism is not a federal crime; it is an act of war. Federal authorities have no jurisdiction to prosecute Khalid Sheik Muhammed, and it revealed a stunning lack of common sense for Obama to make a public spectacle out of the handling of a war criminal.

163. IGNORING WORLDWIDE CHRISTIAN OPPRESSION

In 2007, Obama promised, "As a president of the United States, I don't intend to abandon people or turn a blind eye to slaughter." They were fine, noble words but totally devoid of substance in the years that followed. According to a report by the bipartisan United States Commission on International Religious Freedom released in May 2014, the Obama administration indeed ignored the persecution of Christians worldwide.[940] This is particularly outrageous as, throughout his presidency, Obama was quick to condemn what he perceived as persecution, as long as the alleged victim fit certain criteria. Whenever it appeared that an American minority person was being ill-treated—even if the accusation of ill-treatment turned out to be false—there was Barack Obama condemning the crime. But when it came to the world's most oppressed religious group, Obama was curiously silent.[941] In 2012, Christian villages in Sudan were bombed at Christmastime by the country's own military.[943] In Pakistan, Christians were routinely accused of anti-Muslim blasphemy on trumped-up charges—often resulting in death for the accused. ISIS forced the Christian population of Mosul, Iraq, to flee for their lives.[944] Coptic Christians in Egypt found their places of worship burned and their lives endangered constantly.[945]

Christian oppression around the world is very real, particularly in Muslim nations, and it's gotten worse every year after the Arab Spring. With the situation darkening, Obama did nothing to stand against *this* slaughter. He even allowed his administration to press forward with the deportation of a Christian German family that sought asylum in the United States so they could homeschool their children,[946] while also denying refugee status for some of Egypt's Coptic Christian minority fleeing persecution.[947]

164. TAX DOLLARS FOR TERRORIST GROUPS

On a Friday night in April 2012, sources reported that Barack Obama bypassed Congress in order to send $192 million in aid to the Palestinian Authority (PA). Funding for the PA was frozen by Congress after PA president Mahmoud Abbas requested the U.N. recognize a Palestinian state. Obama claimed his waiver was important to the national security of the United States. A bizarre claim indeed, since his actions came just months after the terrorist group Hamas became a partner with the PA. In other words, Obama bypassed Congress to give nearly $200 million of our tax dollars to a terrorist organization.[948]

Five months later, Obama informed Congress that he would provide $450 million in emergency aid for Egypt's new government, now controlled by the Muslim Brotherhood, a group with a history of supporting terrorism.[949] No one bothered to explain to Congress or the American people what emergency forced the delivery of nearly half a billion dollars to terrorists. To put it into perspective, Osama bin Laden, his top deputy Ayman al-Zawahiri, and 9/11 mastermind Khalid Sheikh Mohammed all once belonged to the Muslim Brotherhood before bin Laden formed al-Qaeda. Hamas considers itself the Muslim Brotherhood's Palestinian branch.[950] Indeed, Egypt designated the Muslim

Brotherhood as a terrorist group prior to the fall of the old Mubarak regime. The left claimed that the Muslim Brotherhood was more moderate than its affiliates, but their own charter made clear that their goal was to spread Sharia Law throughout the world.[951] In 2012, Obama sent the Muslim Brotherhood $1.5 billion in military aid over the objections of Congress.[952] Obama's actions were hard to explain and impossible to justify. Going around Congress in order to provide aid to an enemy of America just doesn't sound like the actions of a president who had our nation's values and interests at heart. But what happened when a revolution (backed by overwhelming numbers of the Egyptian people[953]) overthrew the Muslim Brotherhood government? Obama moved to cut aid to Egypt![954]

165. PURGING GITMO

As a candidate in 2007, Obama promised he would close the terrorist detention facility at Guantánamo Bay, Cuba, (Gitmo) as soon as he was elected. He promised it so many times that it was a given: both Obama's supporters and opponents assumed that Gitmo was gone at the earliest moment possible once Obama was elected. Opponents of this plan had many legitimate concerns and questions. Where would the prisoners go? How would they be tried? Where would we hold any terrorists captured after Gitmo was closed?

But Obama was less concerned about the logistics and more concerned with fulfilling his promise. He signed an executive order on January 22, 2009, requiring Gitmo to close within one year[955] But he failed to carry out his own executive order because of opposition from Congress. This Congressional opposition eventually led Obama, on January 3, 2013, to sign the National Defense Authorization Act (NDAA), which barred the use of federal funds to transfer Gitmo prisoners to the United States, despite a promised veto.[956]

Though Obama couldn't close Gitmo, he systematically purged the prison of its terrorist inmates, as a sort of end-run around Congressional opposition to closure. In 2003, there were 680 prisoners. By early January 2015, there were fewer than 130. According to *The New York Times*, Obama's goal for his last two years in office was "...to deplete the Guantánamo prison to the point where it houses 60 to 80 people and keeping it open no longer makes economic sense."[957]

While the Obama administration claimed only 6 percent of terrorists released from Gitmo returned to fight for the enemy, retired CIA officer Gary Berntsen said it was at least 50 percent. "Many of these people that we captured would tell us right to our faces: We're going to be released and kill you and your families when we get out. That's their attitude. Because they don't believe the United States is going to act harshly against them. They see the light at the end of the tunnel, they want to continue the fight against us."[958]

So strong was Obama's desire to close Gitmo that his former Secretary of Defense, Chuck Hagel, admitted that he felt pressure within the administration to accelerate the release of prisoners against his better judgment.[959]

The Obama administration claimed that all those released were low risk, but five Yemeni detainees were released in January 2015 even though they were all medium- or high-risk detainees.[960] The reality was that Gitmo housed some of the most evil and dangerous men in the world. They were given regular meals and exercise time. They were also allowed to freely practice their religion.

Obama's efforts to purge Gitmo continued through the end of his presidency. Though he was unable to close it altogether, most of its inmates were released and in the final weeks of his presidency, Obama raced to release as many more as he could. According to *The Wall Street Journal*, nearly a third of Gitmo detainees who were released returned to terrorist activities.[961]

None of us know how many lives were lost because Obama had more sympathy for avowed radical terrorists than his own military, but we do know—thanks to testimony from Paul Lewis, Obama's Special Envoy for Guantanamo Closure—that "there have been Americans that have died because of Gitmo detainees" who were released.[962]

166. NEGOTIATING WITH TERRORISTS

In January 2012, *The New York Times* reported that "Several Taliban negotiators [had] begun meeting with American officials in Qatar, where they [were] discussing preliminary trust-building measures, including a possible prisoner transfer[.]"[963] According to Judicial Watch, "As part of 'Taliban reconciliation efforts,' the terrorists would be transferred to Qatar, a Middle Eastern Arab state where [the Taliban] will soon open an office. The Obama administration sold the preposterous deal to Congress by saying that the prisoners wouldn't actually be released but rather transferred to the custody of the Qatari government and they will remain in jail."[964]

With bipartisan opposition in Congress to the plan, the Obama administration's negotiations failed. It seems rather strange that the Obama administration would be willing to negotiate directly with a terrorist organization. Except the State Department revealed the U.S. strangely did not consider the Taliban a terrorist group.[965]

The Obama White House's habit of making deals with terrorists reached a new low in 2014 as five high-ranking jihadis were released into the custody of Qatar in exchange for the return of Army deserter Bowe Bergdahl. The U.S. military has long followed the admirable code: leave no one behind. Without their code of honor, military forces would find it far more difficult to keep up morale and build trust between soldiers, but honor is a two-way street, and those who desert, especially in the face of the enemy, betray that trust as surely as a commander who abandons his men in battle. Given this, the circumstances surrounding Bowe Bergdahl's release from Taliban captivity came under immediate scrutiny.

Soldiers who had served with Bergdahl claimed that he deserted his post of his own accord.[966] Next, soldiers reported being threatened by the Obama administration to remain silent about what they knew about Bergdahl's disappearance.[967] A private intelligence agency contracted by the Defense Department discovered Bergdahl also converted to Islam and declared jihad while in captivity.[968] The Army launched multiple search and rescue attempts to recover Bergdahl, and six men lost their lives in suspicious ambush attacks along the way, with many others badly wounded.[969]

Between the increased jeopardy of Americans worldwide each time Obama negotiated with terrorists, the threat that those five high-risk jihadi prisoners we traded could have returned to the battlefield, the doubts over whether Bergdahl was captured or deserted, the lopsidedness of the swap, and not informing Congress of the details of the planned exchange, Obama suffered a major black eye. Administration officials tried to deflect responsibility for the swap away from Obama, claiming that Secretary of Defense Chuck Hagel made the final call on the swap.[970]

The Obama administration justified the swap by quoting the aforementioned code of honor, but it was empty pablum. This is the same administration that left four soldiers in Benghazi with no air support and abandoned Marine Sgt. Andrew Tahmooressi in Mexican captivity for seven months. To add insult to injury, by January 2015, military and intelligence officials suspected that one of those released rejoined the fight.[971]

Obama clearly thought he'd be considered a hero for securing Bergdahl's freedom and enjoy more political capital to spend on his agenda at home. Instead it became yet another foreign policy blunder—a blunder that encouraged our enemies and endangered all Americans. On March 25, 2015, ten months after his release, Sgt. Bergdahl was charged with desertion and pleaded guilty in October 2017. Even though he faced up to life in prison, he was merely sentenced to dishonorable discharge and avoided prison time.[972]

167. THE BOSTON MARATHON BOMBING

What if we told you the Obama administration could have prevented the Boston Marathon Bombing on April 15, 2013?

Just a few days after the bombing, the FBI identified two suspects: Chechen brothers Tamerlan Tsarnaev, 26, and Dzhokhar Tsarnaev, 19, who came to America as refugees in 2002. Tamerlan was arrested on charges of domestic violence in 2009. The Obama administration could have deported him after the arrest.[973] Why wasn't he deported then? Two years later, Tamerlan was interrogated by the FBI, at the request of the Russian government, regarding possible extremist ties.[974] A week after the bombings, sources found the Russian government warned the FBI "multiple times" about Tamerlan's radicalism, but the agency was "more concerned with al-Qaeda and other Middle Eastern terrorist groups" and overlooked the threat of Chechen terrorists.[975] Obama was eager to spy on Americans, as we've already discussed, yet Tamerlan, with his history of violence and extremism, was *not* under surveillance by the federal government. Why not?

Also, the day after the bombing, we found out the budget for domestic bomb prevention had been cut to $11 million by the Obama administration, down from $20 million during the Bush administration. Obama argued that a mere 2 percent reduction in government spending due to the sequestration that followed the 2011 debt ceiling negotiation would devastate the economy and public safety, yet he slashed funds for bomb prevention.

Obama was complacent about the threat of Islamist terrorism here in the United States, in part because he held a worldview that cast them in the role of victims. Obama steadfastly refused to link terrorism and Islamic extremism. On the evening of April 19, 2013, after Dzhokhar Tsarnaev was caught, Obama devoted nearly 20 percent of his televised statement to lecturing Americans on the dangers of Islamophobia and the need to avoid jumping to conclusions about the Tsarnaev brothers' motivation.[976] We knew Tamerlan had shared radical Islamic videos online in support of killing enemies of Islam, but Obama was blinded by an ideological filter that infested the administration's national security strategy.[977]

168. MISSING THE OPPORTUNITY TO DESTROY AL-QAEDA

The May 2011 death of Osama bin Laden was a great moment in the War on Terror, but it was also the biggest missed opportunity. Had Barack Obama been less interested in patting himself on the back and taking credit for bin Laden's death and more interested in defeating al-Qaeda, we could have crippled al-Qaeda and changed the course of history for the better.

In addition to bin Laden's body, the Marines found papers, hard drives, and thumb drives containing a treasure trove of intelligence in his lair. Bestselling author and award-winning investigative journalist Richard Miniter said the potential to wipe out al-Qaeda was lost because

"Obama ran to the cameras and raced to tell the world that bin Laden was dead." The data collected included "the whereabouts of al-Qaeda's senior commanders, the secret sources of funds, its hideouts, its sleeper cells, its pending plots."[978] Had Obama waited a few weeks for U.S. intelligence agencies to translate and analyze the captured documents, they had actionable intelligence good enough that "nearly every al-Qaeda leader could have been killed or captured."[979]

It gets worse. Not only did Obama miss the opportunity to wipe out al-Qaeda, but he deliberately misled America about al-Qaeda's supposed demise in order to get reelected. According to five senior U.S. intelligence officials, "the documents (captured from bin Laden) sat largely untouched for months—perhaps as long as a year."[980] At that point, the 2012 presidential election was six months away, and Obama's list of accomplishments numbered one item—this one. As he toured the country repeating the claim that al-Qaeda was on its heels, nothing could have been further from the truth and the captured documents proved that. Al-Qaeda, the documents showed, was alive and well and growing. To keep Americans in the dark about this before the election, the Obama administration limited the Defense Intelligence Agency's access to the documents "and instructed DIA officials to stop producing analyses based on them."[981]

The sad irony is, had Obama been less willing to fabricate a campaign talking point and less eager to claim credit for bin Laden's death, by the 2012 elections, al-Qaeda might well have been dead and gone. Instead, the narcissist in chief torpedoed his only foreign policy achievement of note, and al-Qaeda, free to expand and grow, overwhelmed Libya and perpetrated the Benghazi massacre that nearly sunk Obama's chances for reelection.

169. TERRORIST ATTACKS ON U.S. SOIL (AND OBAMA'S DENIALISM)

At least six terrorist attacks on U.S. soil were successful on Obama's watch: the Fort Hood shootings on November 5, 2009; the bombing of the Social Security building in Casa Grande, Arizona, on November 30, 2012; the Boston Marathon bombing on April 15, 2013; the July 16, 2015, Chattanooga, TN, attack; the shootings in San Bernardino, CA, in December 2015; and the June 12, 2016, mass shooting in Orlando, FL. There've been other potentially terror-related incidents, more limited in scope, including a pair of brutal murders of police officers in New York City, a beheading in Oklahoma City, the shooting that took place outside of Pamela Gellar's irreverent "Draw Mohammed" art contest in Garland, TX, and a drive-by shooting at a military base in Little Rock, AR. But even if you want to limit the count to the first six, that's a lot of bloodshed in the name of the prophet right here at home, and these are the attacks that succeeded. There were at least two others that could have been just as devastating and failed only because the perpetrators weren't competent in their execution of well-laid plans.

A plot by al-Qaeda leaders in Yemen to blow up a plane over Detroit on Christmas Day in 2009 was carried out by Abdul Farouk Umar Abdulmutallab, who had explosives sewn into his underwear. The attempt was nearly successful, but Abdulmutallab failed to detonate the explosives properly. He was subdued by passengers and arrested upon landing. This was a gross failure of the system. Abdulmutallab was on a U.S. terror watch-list, and his own father recognized his son's radicalism and informed the U.S. Embassy in Nigeria that his son was a potential threat to the United States.[982]

Less than six months later, there was another close call with an attempted car bombing in Times Square. On May 10, 2010, two street vendors noticed smoke coming from a parked car in Times Square. The car bomb had ignited but failed to explode. The bomb squad disarmed the device, and no one was hurt or killed. Faisal Shahzad, who had been trained at a Pakistani terror training camp, was arrested two days later. The Pakistani Taliban financed and orchestrated the plot.[983]

The Washington Times reported in May 2010 that Shahzad "was on the Department of Homeland Security's Traveler Enforcement Compliance System list in 2008. The Obama administration *removed* him from that list. The National Joint Terrorism Task Force also investigated Shahzad until the Obama administration waved it off the case." Had Shahzad been a more competent terrorist, the Obama administration would have had to answer a lot of question about their actions.

Adding insult to injury, while all of this bloodshed occurred, Obama steadfastly refused to acknowledge the source of the violence. In the run-up to his reelection effort in 2012, Obama couldn't risk the political ramifications of having successful terrorist attacks in the U.S. on his watch, and so the Fort Hood and Social Security incidents (which occurred during his first term) were *not* classified as terrorism, despite all the evidence that these were, in fact, acts of terror.

Nidal Malik Hasan, the U.S. Army major who shot and killed thirteen people and wounded many others, was in contact with Anwar al-Awlaki, a radical American-born imam under investigation by U.S. intelligence agencies for years. In December 2011, Obama's Department of Defense classified the shooting as "workplace violence."[984] Even Obama would not describe the shooting as terrorism.[985]

Abdullalltif Ali Aldosary, the Iraqi refugee who created a homemade explosive and bombed a Social Security building, was denied U.S. citizenship for "terror-related activity." Aldosary planned the bombing in advance and researched terrorist bombs. Documents on how to build bombs were hidden behind a picture in his home, and he tried to obtain information on how to create RDX, a powerful military high-yield explosive used in many terrorist plots.[986] Despite all this, Aldosary was not charged with terrorism. Instead he was charged with "maliciously damaging federal property by means of explosives" and with illegal possession of a firearm[987]

After the election, and despite no serious risk to Obama or his party, Obama still refused to refer to the term "radical Islamic terrorism" or "Jihadist" and insisted on calling the San Bernardino and Orlando attacks bouts of gun violence, as though they were common crime to be dealt with by our justice system and not acts of war. If the government didn't recognize a terror attack as a terror attack, then Obama could keep his legacy free of terror attacks. But calling it "workplace violence" or "damaging federal property" fools *no one.*

170. WHITEWASHING ISLAMIC TERRORISM

While Obama's refusal to link blatant acts of terrorism with radical Islam is well documented, and, honestly, quite disturbing, his Orwellian attempts to censor references to Islamic terrorism had far worse implications. On March 31, 2016, President Obama and French President Hollande gave joint remarks to the press on terrorism. Video of the remarks were posted on the White House website, then briefly removed, then reposted. The reposted video edited out portions of Hollande's remarks where he referred to "Islamist terrorism."[989] Obama's policy of not referring to Islamic terrorism now included altering audio and video to remove references to Islamic terrorism.

But perhaps the worst example came in the wake of the Orlando mass shooting. The public was already aware through earlier media reporting of eyewitness accounts that the gunman had pledged allegiance to Allah and ISIS, but that didn't stop the Obama administration from trying to frame the incident as a bigoted act of gun violence rather than an act of Islamic terror. Their denialism eventually turned into full-fledged revisionism. A week after the shooting, the FBI released edited transcripts of the 911 calls made by gunman Omar Mateen, omitting all references to Islam and ISIS. The FBI and Justice Department released the full transcripts later the same afternoon after serious backlash.[990] Despite the fact Mateen's motives were crystal clear, the day after the full transcripts were released, Attorney General Loretta Lynch declared that Mateen's motives may never be known.[991]

Obama's attempts to keep such information from the public only made us less safe. With terror attacks on U.S. soil a new reality on Obama's watch, he should have been more concerned with protecting us than with protecting radical Islamists and his own reputation.

171. INTELLIGENCE FAILURES IN THE SAN BERNARDINO AND ORLANDO MASS SHOOTINGS

As mentioned, two bloody mass shootings rocked the nation in the final year of Obama's presidency. One was in San Bernardino, CA, involving Syed Rizwan Farook and Tashfeen Malik, a married couple who'd been radicalized in Afghanistan and took their jihad to a Christmas party with their colleagues.[992] The other was a lone gunman who held an Orlando gay nightclub hostage and slaughtered fifty young men and women, then called police to declare his allegiance to ISIS.[993] We do not blame Barack Obama for these incidents—even a well-oiled intelligence machine is going to miss a plot every now and then. Instead we intend to highlight massive failures of the intelligence apparatus and demonstrate the connection of those failures to the

Obama administration's politically correct policy toward radical Islam.

Following the San Bernardino attack, during which fourteen people were killed and twenty-two were injured, as Barack Obama took to the airwaves in a rare televised address from the Oval Office to denounce the "gun violence" and insist that conservatives get behind "common sense gun reforms," real questions about the effectiveness of our domestic terrorism prevention apparatus began to surface. In the wake of the chaos, we found out Malik had been granted a green card despite the fact that her public writings and social media presence, while in Afghanistan, revealed a strong radical streak.[994] On top of that, neighbors observed a host of deeply troubling behavior from the young couple—massive shipments of supplies to their garage, strangers coming and going at odd hours, and the like—and chose not to report it to police for fear of being branded racists for engaging in "profiling."[995] Following up on any leads they might have gained from Farook's cellphone became impossible when agents investigating the attack blundered into locking the phone with no way to recover it.[996]

Then, in the summer of 2016, following the grisly murder of fifty innocent people in Orlando, FL, the jihadi attacker's history came to light and cast further doubts on the seriousness of Obama's security policy. The man responsible, Omar Mateen, had twice before been on the FBI's radar as a possible terrorist threat, and no action was taken. They even interviewed him three times in 2013 and 2014 due to his contacts with suspected terrorists.[997]

In fact, the FBI dropped their investigation of Mateen after concluding that concerns over his terroristic threats were the result of the anti-Muslim bigotry by his coworkers.[998]

But Mateen left plenty of clues about his radical leanings and mental instability in his final years, including harassing his colleagues, spewing racist and sexist slurs at work, being arrested for beating his ex-wife, and leaving an extensive social media trail between him and jihadis. It's also worth noting that Mateen's father was, at the time of the shooting, running for the presidency—of Afghanistan—as a pro-Taliban figure with years of social media propagandizing for the Taliban behind him. But the real kicker is that Mateen was a member of a radical mosque in Orlando that some in the intelligence community wanted to investigate for its radical preaching and ties to terrorist affiliates. But Obama senior officials ignored the threat posed by this mosque.

172. INCREASE IN ELECTRONIC GOVERNMENT SPYING

Obama, like many Democrats, was a loud and vocal opponent of the Bush administration's efforts to intercept communications between persons inside the United States and suspected terrorists overseas. He described it as a sinister attempt to eavesdrop on American citizens at random and a gross violation of civil liberties. Alas, once Obama became president, he sang a different tune.

In 2010, *The New York Times* reported the Obama administration wanted to make it easier for the government to monitor domestic internet communications.[999] According to the American Civil Liberties Union (ACLU), there has been a 64 percent growth in electronic spying by the United States government since Obama took office in 2009.[1000] In September 2012 in federal court, the Obama administration argued in that the public has no "reasonable expectation of privacy" regarding their cellphone location data and that the government can obtain these records without a warrant.[1001]

Further blemishing Obama's record on civil liberties, his administration green-lighted a giant government database of information on millions of citizens, even ones not suspected of terrorism or any crime at all. *The Wall Street Journal* first reported on this in December 2012:

> *Top U.S. intelligence officials gathered in the White House Situation Room in March to debate a controversial proposal. Counterterrorism officials wanted to create a government dragnet, sweeping up millions of records about U.S. citizens—even people suspected of no crime.*
>
> *Not everyone was on board. "This is a sea change in the way that the government interacts with the general public," Mary Ellen Callahan, chief privacy officer of the Department of Homeland Security, argued in the meeting, according to people familiar with the discussions.*
>
> *A week later, the attorney general signed the changes into effect.*[1002]

Why did Obama want to make it easier to read your email or listen to your phone calls? For someone who once taught constitutional law, he showed little concern for the Fourth Amendment. And yet, he still couldn't catch the terrorists before they killed Americans.

173. THE NSA/PRISM SCANDAL

As a U.S. Senator, Barack Obama was a critic of domestic surveillance and worked to pass legislation that would have seriously reigned in the power of the government to collect data on the American people without a specific reason.[1003] His position on domestic surveillance did not change during his first campaign for president—he vowed to fight such things as a renewal of the Foreign Intelligence Surveillance Act (FISA).[1004] But, once Obama reached the White House, his position "evolved." Under President Obama, Bush-era programs to intercept intelligence about foreign enemies of the United States "evolved" into a massive data collection free-for-all that scooped up masses of information from just about everybody—without cause or a warrant.

In April 2013, a top-secret FISA court order was made forcing Verizon to provide the National Security Agency (NSA) information on all calls on its systems. Not just calls between the United States and other countries, but domestic calls as well. The details of the secret order were leaked by former NSA contractor Edward Snowden and revealed by *The Guardian* in June 2013—a month after the IRS scandal broke.[1005] Sources familiar with the NSA's operations told *The Wall Street Journal* that other telecom companies and internet service providers were also covered by the program.[1006]

The surveillance program, called PRISM, was created in 2007, but experienced "exponential growth" under Obama, according to *The Washington Post*. This expansion changed surveillance practices "away from individual suspicion in favor of systematic, mass collection techniques."[1007] Under the expanded PRISM program, the NSA and FBI were "tapping directly into the central servers" of Microsoft, Yahoo, Google, Facebook, PalTalk, AOL, Skype, YouTube, and Apple, "extracting audio and video chats, photographs, emails, documents, and connection logs that enable analysts to track foreign targets."[1008]

Even *The New York Times* editorial board couldn't hold back criticism of Obama. "Essentially, the administration is saying that without any individual suspicion of wrongdoing, the government is allowed to know whom Americans are calling every time they make a phone call, for how long they talk and from where."[1009]

The Obama administration defended the expanded program as a crucial tool in the fight against terrorism, though they could not cite a single instance where an imminent terrorist attack was prevented because of it. A federal court ruled in May 2015 that the bulk collection of Americans' phone records was indeed a violation of the Constitution.[1010]

As Obama went from being a critic of domestic surveillance to becoming the embodiment of Big Brother, our country ceased to look like the America envisioned by the Founding Fathers and became much more like China or Soviet Russia.

174. THE BENGHAZI ATTACK AND COVER-UP

There is much we don't know about what happened on September 11, 2012, when the American consulate in Benghazi, Libya, was attacked, along with the U.S. Embassy in Cairo, Egypt. We know that in Benghazi four Americans were killed, including U.S. Ambassador to Libya, Christopher Stevens. And we know that the circumstances behind the run-up to the attack, the lack of support the consulate received before and during the attack, and the government response in the aftermath thereafter stink to high heaven. Here is what we learned after years of investigation and debate:

- *The attack was clearly carried out by terrorists linked to al-Qaeda, and this fact was known in the administration within hours of the attack.*[1011]
- *The murdered ambassador in Benghazi had called repeatedly for additional security for our diplomatic posts in Benghazi.*[1012]
- *Former Defense Secretary Leon Panetta testified that he personally informed Obama that the consulate was under attack and that they didn't speak again for another six hours, contradicting previous claims by Obama that he was fully engaged with the response.*[1013]
- *Obama's former Secretary of State, Hillary Clinton, testified that she never read the cables from Libya insisting upon the need for greater security.*[1014]
- *Survivors of the attack remain under federal gag order, preventing them from discussing or testifying about what happened.*[1015]

- *A Senate Intelligence Committee report found that the State Department was negligent in failing to increase security, despite deteriorating safety conditions in the area.*[1016]
- *A House Armed Services Committee report also faulted the White House for not providing adequate security and for ignoring or failing to comprehend "the dramatically deteriorating security situation in Libya and the growing threat to U.S. interests in the region." The Defense Department knew that it was terrorist attack "nearly from the outset."*[1017]
- *The claim that an obscure, anti-Islamic video was the cause of a spontaneous demonstration that got out of hand was an outright lie, but the Obama administration used the video connection as a talking point anyway.*[1018] *This was proven in April 2014, when a declassified email revealed by Judicial Watch showed that the White House played a central role in falsely blaming the video in order to protect Obama. Charles Krauthammer called the email "a classic cover-up of a cover-up" and a "serious offense."*[1019]
- *Emails between Hillary Clinton and her daughter, Chelsea, also surfaced wherein Hillary told Chelsea there was a terrorist attack in progress.*[1020]
- *State Department documents, released in June 2015, also confirmed that the White House was immediately involved in crafting the "blame the video" strategy.*[1021]

The attack occurred two months before the presidential election, and it is quite clear that the White House cared more about getting Obama reelected than about the four Americans who died because of the Obama administration's incompetence. Protecting Obama trumped everything, especially the truth. The Obama administration was willing to deliberately deceive the entire country rather than risk political fallout. What happened in Benghazi was preventable, and the cover-up that followed was positively Nixonian.

175. FAILURES OF INACTION

In addition to his failures in places like Iraq and Afghanistan detailed elsewhere in this book, Obama's intellectual blind spots in the Middle East and the surrounding countries took a significant toll on the entire region. The Middle East is difficult for any president, but the setbacks resulting from Obama's policies were particularly severe.

In June 2009, millions of Iranians took peacefully to the streets in the "Green Revolution," demanding democracy. Obama made no effort to back the Iranian people—claiming he didn't want to meddle in Iranian affairs—and ignored Iranian freedom fighters' request for aid.[1022] The Iranian government slaughtered those moderates and freedom fighters in the streets, crushing any hope America had of procuring an ally in the region and feeding into Islamic propaganda claiming that the U.S. is no friend to freedom, only intervening when they have something to gain.

While Obama didn't want to help the Iranians free themselves of a dictatorship, Obama was perfectly content to push former Egyptian President Hosni Mubarak, an ally of the United States, to step down in 2011 during the Arab Spring uprisings, thus ushering in a terrorist, Muslim Brotherhood government. Obama then helped the Muslim Brotherhood government by waiving human rights requirements, thus allowing for continued military aid to Egypt, despite horrific human rights violations. One could argue that, with or without American intervention, Mubarak's days were numbered, but the real failure here was one of inaction. When the Muslim Brotherhood government was at risk of being ousted by popular revolt backed by Egypt's military, Obama first backed the Brotherhood, threatening to cut military aid in response to the uprising.[1023] Then, as chaos and violence erupted in the country, Obama chose to step back and wash his hands of it, declaring, "America cannot determine the future of Egypt."[1024] The people of Egypt and their military joined hands to rid their home of the cancerous Muslim Brotherhood, with no help or encouragement from President Obama. Obama's incoherent strategy in Egypt diminished America's standing and influence in the country, leaving the moderates now in control of the nation to wonder whether it's in their best interests to ally with the U.S. or whether they should join with Saudi Arabia instead.

As previously noted, Obama's inaction in Syria, following Assad's use of sarin gas on rebels in 2013, led to the formation of an alliance between Iran and Assad, while simultaneously convincing many rebels to join with ISIS as their only viable ally against Assad, playing into the local belief that the U.S. is not a reliable ally. Leon Panetta, who had previously served as Obama's CIA Director and Secretary of Defense, said Obama damaged the credibility of the United States by drawing a red line then failing to follow through.[1025] According to Panetta, Obama's failures in Syria and his early withdrawal from Iraq, against the advice of his cabinet, led to the rise of ISIS in both countries.[1026] In Afghanistan, Obama's 2010 troop surge failed to stop the Taliban's momentum there, as he wasn't committed to an aggressive military posture.[1027]

Obama's counterterrorism strategy in Yemen also collapsed with the fall of the U.S.-backed Yemeni government in January 2015. Months earlier, Obama dubbed the strategy a successful model for fighting the Islamic State in Iraq and Syria.[1028] Those who triumphed in Yemen were Iranian-backed Islamists. In fact, the alliance was so threatening to Yemen's neighbors that Saudi Arabia launched a military campaign to roll back the Iranian-backed forces. Likewise, as the sectarian violence in Lebanon worsened in 2014 and 2015,[1029] spurred on by ISIS fighters in the region, Obama took no action, resulting in the collapse of security in Beirut—one of the most economically crucial cities in the Middle East.[1030]

All these failures in the region added up. James Jeffrey, Obama's former U.S. Ambassador to Iraq, said, in March 2015, that the Middle East destabilized faster under Obama than at any point in recent history. "The situation has gotten worse, and the recipes that we have tried to use to stem the violence and to stem the destabilization, the basic challenge to the nation states in the region, by one or another Islamic religious movement, be it the Iranians, be it ISIS and al-Qaeda, have not been successful, and now we're at a crisis point."[1031] Robert Gates, who served as Obama's first Secretary of Defense, said in an interview in May 2015 that he didn't think the Obama administration had any Middle East strategy. "We're basically sort of playing this day to day."[1032]

176. THE ISIS INTELLIGENCE SCANDAL

As a U.S. Senator, Barack Obama joined the chorus of liberal politicians claiming that George W. Bush manipulated intelligence about Iraq in order to justify going to war in 2002. As president, he found himself embroiled in an intelligence scandal of his own.

In the summer of 2015, the press reported the Pentagon inspector general was investigating claims that high-ranking military officials were manipulating intelligence assessments of the war against ISIS.[1033] According to a report by *The Daily Beast*, more than fifty CENTCOM intelligence analysts formally complained their intelligence reports regarding ISIS were being "inappropriately altered by senior officials." According to the analysts, the administration manipulated intelligence reports to portray ISIS as weaker than it really was, so that the intelligence mirrored "the administration's public line that the U.S. is winning the battle both against ISIS and al Nusra, al-Qaeda's branch in Syria."[1034]

Barack Obama's intelligence chief, James Clapper, was directly implicated in the scandal for having had "frequent and unusual contact" with the military intelligence officer responsible for editing the reports, Army

Major General Steven Grove. Clapper—who in 2013 gave false testimony to the Senate about the scope of domestic surveillance—was speaking daily with Grove, telling him the administration's perception on the outlook of the war and questioning CENTCOM's assessments. All of this raises questions about how much Obama knew about the manipulation of intelligence.[1035]

Obama, true to form, claimed he was unaware of the details of the investigation. During a press conference, Obama claimed, "What I do know is my expectation, which is the highest fidelity to facts, data—the truth." But according to retired Lt. Gen. Michael Flynn, Obama's former top military intelligence official, "Where intelligence starts and stops is at the White House. The president sets the priorities and he's the number one customer."[1036] Flynn also told CNN, in 2011 and 2012, Obama ignored intelligence reports warning about the rise of ISIS because they did not fit the narrative of his reelection campaign.[1037]

While pre-war intelligence about Iraq may have been incorrect, there is actual evidence that intelligence about ISIS was deliberately doctored to benefit Obama's reelection campaign. While this may have prevented Obama from answering for the destabilization of the Middle East before he was reelected, there's no telling what damage was done because of it. It is one thing for a politician to spin a situation to obtain maximum political advantage or damage control, but to put the lives of the men and women of our armed forces at risk in order to support a political narrative is nothing short of criminal.

177. BOKO HARAM

Ranked by the Global Terrorism Index as one of the world's most deadly terrorist forces,[1038] Boko Haram in Nigeria rocketed to international attention with the kidnapping of hundreds of schoolgirls in April 2014.[1039] It swiftly became known that Boko Haram either sold the girls into slavery or forced them to marry Boko Haram fighters. The people of the world were justly outraged by this, but Boko Haram wasn't new to the scene.

While the origins of the group go back to the early 2000s, it wasn't until 2009 that Boko Haram was able to start cutting a bloody swath through Nigerian society, which is divided about equally between Muslim and Christian citizens. Between 2009 to 2014, Boko Haram murdered thousands of people in scores of terrorist attacks, with the targets predominantly Christian churches during services. For years, lawmakers, U.S. officials, and outside groups called on the Obama administration to label Boko Haram as a terrorist organization,[1040] but no action was taken until after the school kidnapping.[1041]

Why did the Obama administration ignore Boko Haram and refuse to allocate any resources to its defeat? There were some in Nigeria who accused Obama and his senior adviser David Axelrod of conspiring to harm the Nigerian economy and hand the northern part of the country to Boko Haram in the hopes of ousting sitting Nigerian President Jonathan, whose challenger was backed by AKPD, a Nigerian consulting group funded by Axelrod.[1042] This theory is speculative and more than a little far-fetched, but the bloody mayhem enabled by Obama's inaction against Boko Haram is as clear as day.

After ignoring the problem for years and only taking notice when the situation escalated enough to potentially embarrass him, Obama made vigorous statements about how the United States would react forcefully against Boko Haram.[1043] The only action that followed was First Lady Michelle Obama tweeting a photo of herself holding up a sign with "#BringBackOurGirls" printed on it in May 2014. In fact, Boko Haram's murders increased by 300 percent from 2014 to 2015, despite Michelle Obama's tweet.[1044] Indeed, experts believed Boko Haram benefited significantly from the State Department's inaction.[1045]

A bloody price was paid by Obama's blasé response to Boko Haram. Boko Haram's death toll is now in the thousands, and the organization is claiming enormous influence over Africa's most prosperous nation. Whether or not he had personal reasons to ignore this group, there is no justification for failing to act, refusing to provide arms and intelligence at the request of the Nigerian government, and sealing the fates of thousands of Christians.

178. OBAMA'S NUCLEAR DEAL WITH IRAN

Over a period from 2013 to 2015, Obama engaged in a series of negotiations with Iran—the world's leading sponsor of terrorism—to, theoretically, prevent Iran from developing nuclear weapons. That is, until Obama started negotiating; then it became something else entirely.

It began in 2013 when Iran promised to start, over a period of months, to slow down nuclear weapons development in return for the immediate easing of economic sanctions crippling the country.[1046] But the terms of the deal allowed for Iran's nuclear infrastructure to remain intact. This first step agreement merely gave the mullahs of Iran short-term cover and economic relief, and the world was no more secure.

Maybe Obama didn't realize this, but the Iranian government did. Despite the deal, they declared their intention to continue their nuclear program.[1047] Iranian Foreign Minister Mohammad Javad Zarif claimed that the Obama administration publicly mischaracterized the terms of the deal, telling CNN, "We did not agree to dismantle anything."[1048] Iranian president Hassan Rouhani said of the deal that "world powers surrendered to Iranian nation's [sic] will."[1049]

Congress was justifiably skeptical of Iran, and bipartisan sanctions legislation progressed from committee. This prompted Obama to declare during his 2014 State of the Union address that he would veto any bill passed by Congress that levied sanctions on Iran.[1050] Yet the worst was still to come.

The capstone of Obama's pro-Iranian foreign policy came on July 14, 2015, with a nuclear deal between Iran and six world powers. In return for an unenforceable agreement to curtail their nuclear program, Iran got a bonanza of benefits at the expense of the safety and security of the United States and its allies in the Middle East. The deal lifted economic sanctions against Iran, freeing $150 billion in fresh capital. Even Obama's Ambassador to the U.N., Susan Rice, and Secretary of State, John Kerry, agreed the loot could fuel military and terrorist activities.[1051]

What happened? How did such a rotten deal come to be? Former Secretary of State Henry Kissinger said what began as a multilateral negotiation to prevent Iran from developing nuclear weapons became "an essentially bilateral negotiation over the scope of that capability."[1052] And the resulting deal had America's allies in the Middle East—including Israel, Saudi Arabia, and Egypt—afraid that Obama abandoned them in favor of a mutual enemy.[1053]

Obama's claim that the deal made America safer couldn't be further from the truth. He was so desperate to achieve a deal, any deal, with Iran, that he reportedly gave in to 80 percent of Iran's demands.[1054] The deal does not prevent Iran from obtaining a nuclear weapon and leaves their enrichment infrastructure intact. The deal also allows Iran to block inspections of nuclear sites and allows Russia and China to supply Iran with weapons.[1055] Oh, and Iran, by secret side-deal with the U.N., was allowed to self-inspect some of its most sensitive facilities. Some of those same facilities are currently being expanded by the Iranian government. What could possibly go wrong?

There was absolutely no reason to trust Iran...or the Obama administration, for that matter. They were fully aware that Iran was no more than three months away from producing enough enriched fissile material to make a nuclear weapon but kept that information secret, claiming publicly that Iran was more than a year away from being able to make a nuclear bomb.[1056]

And then there is the question of the legitimacy of the deal. The Constitution is quite clear about international treaties. According to Article II, Section 2, Clause 2, the president "shall have power, by and with the advice and consent of the Senate, to make treaties, provided two-thirds of the Senators present concur..." But Obama knew he wasn't going to get the Senate to approve the treaty and claimed that he didn't need Senate approval, then kept Congress in the dark about various aspects of the deal.[1057]

Even though he didn't bother with Senate approval, he still needed people to think that the deal was in America's best interest, so he turned to his foreign policy guru, Ben Rhodes, a failed novelist with zero foreign policy experience. Rhodes was tasked with convincing Obama's media allies that the deal was good[1058] and created a media echo-chamber where the mainstream press mindlessly repeated Rhodes' false talking points until they became "conventional wisdom." Rhodes spun a fabulous story that Iran was run by "moderates" whom the United States could trust and only hate-filled, war-mongering Republicans could have a problem with the deal.

To the surprise of none by Obama's sycophants, Iran didn't play ball. When Secretary of State Kerry was asked what might constitute a violation of the deal, he admitted that Iran could purchase conventional weapons, violating a U.N. embargo, without violating the nuclear deal—a loophole Iran immediately took advantage of. And when Iran's spiritual leaders held rallies where the Iranian people celebrated the deal with chants of "death to America!" Obama, for reasons that simply cannot be explained, downplayed it.[1059] By 2017, Iran got sick of pretending to care about the deal and blamed the United States for its collapse.

To sum up this sad story, Obama cut a nuclear deal with Iran that did nothing at all to deter their nuclear program, wrote them an enormous check to be used however they saw fit, gave them military aid from some of our most dangerous rivals in the region, and allowed them to dictate terms to the international community. For whatever reason, Obama was desperate to make this deal happen. What we knew then was bad enough...but more would come to light even after Obama left office.

THE FINAL MONTHS

THE FOLLOWING CHAPTERS PICK UP where the first edition of this book (published in July 2016) left off.

To complete our original work, we not only updated and reorganized the information in the previous chapters, but we've compiled new information that we've divided into two chapters. Here we cover the final months of Obama's presidency, including his last-minute power grabs and his attempts to undermine then-President Elect Trump. In the next chapter, we'll discuss the horrify, frustrating, and downright rage-inducing things we've learned since Obama left office.

The last seven months of Obama's tenure were among his most scandalous and frustrating. As the political left grew increasingly concerned about their electoral prospects, Obama and his acolytes got nastier. Far from giving us any reason to think better of him, the outgoing president dug in his heels and insisted on proving only that we underestimated his treachery and the damage he could cause when he set his mind to a goal.

Then Americans rejected Obama's heir-apparent and chose provocateur Donald Trump in an election that defied every poll-based electoral projection and analysis. Reactions by liberals in the wake of Trump's election ranged from absurd, to comical, to outright pathetic. While we can laugh at the meltdowns of liberal pundits on election night, or the pained cries of Hillary voters when Trump took the oath of office, some of the reactions from inside the Obama White House were...incredibly troubling. With so many predicting Hillary's inevitable victory, the election of Trump—a man intent on obliterating Obama from political relevance—put Obama's entire legacy in jeopardy.

With no electoral consequences to consider, and a successor who promised to undo his legacy, Obama went mad with unchecked power. The Obama administration, in his final weeks in office, rushed to fill "nearly 200 jobs announced after the election and scheduled to stop taking applicants before President-elect Donald Trump's inauguration." These were influential positions that would put Obama-approved people in positions where they could influence policy.[1060] In addition to stacking the federal government with as many of his own people as possible, Obama made several eleventh-hour policy changes and handed down dozens of costly new regulations by executive order.[1061] Of course, with a Republican Congress, Obama's final attempts to entrench his legacy were effectively written in pencil, not a pen, leaving them for his successor to either leave in place or overturn.

179. THE WAR ON COPS

Obama was never a friend to law enforcement, as he proved early in his presidency with his "beer summit" misadventure. But in the final months of his presidency, he openly embraced the core deceptions and social marxism of the Black Lives Matter movement. He moved from merely expressing solidarity with African-Americans' concerns over racism among the police to joining the chorus of radical activists in condemning the men in blue at every opportunity, even citing bogus or misleading statistics to bolster claims of racial bias.[1062]

William Johnson, the executive director of the National Association of Police Organizations, accused Obama of waging a war on cops after the shooting ambush of a squadron of police officers at a Dallas, Texas, protest in July 2016 that resulted in five murdered officers and nine others wounded. "I think [the Obama administration's] continued appeasements at the federal level with the Department of Justice, their appeasement of violent criminals, their refusal to condemn movements like Black Lives Matter, actively calling for the death of police officers, that type of thing, all the while blaming police for the problems in this country has led directly to the climate that has made Dallas possible." Johnson added, "It's a war on cops, and the Obama administration is the Neville Chamberlain of this war."[1063]

Statistics seem to support Johnson's claim. Ambush killings of police officers skyrocketed on Obama's watch, despite Obama's claims to the contrary. According to Justice Department statistics, ambushes of police climbed 25 percent between 2008 to 2013 over the previous ten-year period.[1064] And it only got worse from there. In 2016, Obama's last year in office, the number of police shot and killed in the line of duty increased an alarming 56 percent over the previous year. About a third of those fatally shot were victims of ambush attacks.[1065]

As the president of the United States, Obama used his position as the country's top executive and moral leader to tarnish the reputation of law enforcement as a racist institution. Rather than reserve judgment until all the facts were known or express confidence that any legitimate incidents of racial bias by law enforcement were exceptions to the rule, Obama helped promote the narrative that our system of justice is racist and used that bogus narrative to justify his record number of pardons and commutations of prison sentences.[1066]

180. THE WORST RECORD WITH CONGRESS

When President George W. Bush lost control of Congress after the 2006 midterms, and the new Democrat majority became hostile toward his agenda, despite having a Congress that was ideologically opposed to him, President Bush still managed to get congressional approval for his "surge" of military force in Iraq. Even before then, President Bush proved himself adept at working with Congress to get what he considered important work done with bipartisan support, including his tax cuts. It takes great patience to work together with a divided Congress, especially when the opposition party is in control. Where other presidents managed some success, Obama so thoroughly alienated Republicans that any major bipartisan reform was dead on arrival.

According to analysis from *The Washington Times*, "President Obama oversaw the deepest legislative malaise in modern political history." By their count, Obama only signed 1,227 bills into law—which is fewer than one-term presidents Carter and George H.W. Bush. "Digging deeper into the numbers, Congress spent less time in session, handled fewer business [sic] on the chamber floors and generally sputtered for much of Mr. Obama's tenure, according to *The Times*' index."[1067]

While some—including Obama—might blame Congress, Obama was unable to bring both sides together to achieve compromise; he didn't know the meaning of the word. According to Andrew Busch, a presidential scholar at Claremont McKenna College in California, the blame belongs to Obama. "The president was never good at reaching across the aisle. So when the composition of Congress changed relative to what it was in his first two years, he wasn't able to accommodate that very well," he explained. "He never accustomed himself to operating in a system where he was not the sole player."[1068]

As we noted earlier, Obama famously declared, in 2014, that he didn't need Congress to enact his agenda, insisting, "I've got a pen and I've got a phone."[1069] His agenda always trumped the constitutional process for achieving his goals. He would not negotiate or make any concessions. A president who governs like a dictator will not get far with the governing body he usurps.

181. THE IRAN RANSOM SCANDAL

On January 16, 2016, the Iranian government released five American hostages as one of the final actions necessary to completely enact the nuclear disarmament deal agreed to the previous summer.[1070] Although Americans were thankful to see their people return, they later learned that this "concession" came at a high price. In early August, the story broke that the Obama administration had arranged the transport of $400 million in cash by air to the government of Iran under the cover of darkness on the same day those hostages came home.

Barack Obama claimed that the money was actually just the first installment of a $1.7 billion dollar settlement deal critical to completing his pact with Iran to curb their nuclear weapons ambitions.[1071] Although Obama initially claimed the two events were unrelated, *The Wall Street Journal* later obtained info from U.S. intelligence officials briefed on the cash payment confirming that the cash was not delivered until the hostages were "wheels up" and on the way home and that both sides of the exchange were tightly scripted and undeniably linked.[1072]

As to whether a policy of paying ransom for hostages was good for the country, at least three additional hostages were seized by Iran after the terms of the exchange were met.[1073] In fact, according to a Department of Defense official who spoke anonymously with Fox News, incidents involving Iran threatening or taunting U.S. Navy personnel went up 50 percent in 2016 over the prior year.[1074] This was no surprise to astute observers of foreign policy. For decades, the United States has maintained a strict rule: we do not negotiate with abductors and we do not pay ransom. It only encourages bad actors around the world to capture more of our citizens, hoping for a ransom in return. This is all the more true for nations whose spiritual leaders incite chants of "death to America" during Friday afternoon prayers.

To add insult to injury, on September 9, 2016, *The Washington Free Beacon* reported that, throughout the negotiations over the nuclear deal, Iran was receiving $700 million dollar cash payments every month, totaling at least $11.6 billion in cash. They also received shipments of gold and precious metals, which may have increased the value of the payments, previously frozen by tough international sanctions, to as much as $33.6 billion.[1075] All of this gravy flowing freely from the U.S. to Iran, and we still needed to pay a ransom for the return of our own people? Obama's generosity truly is second to none—at least towards the world's number one sponsor of terrorism.

182. THE PART-TIME ECONOMY

The decline in labor force participation under Obama often drove the falling unemployment rate—and the unemployment rate is what usually makes headlines. And while there was (eventually) modest job growth under Obama, the quality of those new jobs was poor. For all of Obama's rhetoric about all the jobs he created, he never mentioned that they were largely part-time jobs.

And the bleeding of full-time jobs wasn't confined to the recession. In April 2012, approximately 812,000 full-time jobs were lost—the largest drop since March 2009—while part-time jobs increased by 508,000 in the same month.[1076] In May 2016, involuntary part-time employment sharply increased by 468,000.[1077] One contributing factor, of course, was Obamacare. The employer mandate incentivized the hiring of part-time workers over full-time. According to a Goldman Sachs economist, it was, at the very least, a modest contributing factor.[1078]

Alan Krueger, a former top White House economist under Obama, conceded that 94 percent of new jobs created under Obama were part-time jobs. "Workers seeking full-time, steady work have lost."[1079] This explains why wage growth was nonexistent under Obama despite the apparent recovery in the jobs market.[1080] By December 2016, there were 6.4 million part-time workers who would prefer to have full-time work but found no such jobs.[1081] The number of people holding multiple jobs also hit the highest number this century.[1082]

183. UNILATERALLY SIGNING THE PARIS CLIMATE CHANGE TREATY

As we've previously established, Obama was never one to let constitutional concerns thwart his agenda. With everyone predicting a landslide victory for Hillary, he assumed his legacy would never be undone, and he proceeded accordingly. His crowning achievement for his environmental policy was the Paris Climate Treaty...which was so flawed there was no chance of it passing the U.S. Senate, not that Obama cared.

Obama's top climate negotiator, Todd Stern, cooked up the idea that the Paris Treaty was nothing new—and not even a treaty, but an "agreement"—and brazenly declared that they could write the deal as a mere addendum to United Nations Framework Convention on Climate Change (UNFCCC), which was ratified by the Senate and signed by President Bill Clinton in 1993. Stern figured Obama wouldn't have to submit the new agreement to the Senate.[1083] And, in fact, the language of the treaty was carefully crafted to help Obama *pretend* he could bypass the Constitutional requirement of a two-thirds vote by the Senate in favor of ratification, much as he did when he ignored the rules governing recess appointments by declaring the Senate in recess when they were not.

But, according to expert Steven Groves, "The Senate gave its consent to ratification of the UNFCCC based on the executive branch's explicit promise that any future protocol 'containing targets and timetables' would be submitted to the Senate." Groves continued:

> *The 1992 agreement struck between the Democrat-controlled Senate and the Republican President made no exception for "non-binding" targets and timetables. Rather, the Senate relied on the good faith of future presidential Administrations to adhere to the "shared understanding" that future agreements "containing targets and timetables" be submitted to the Senate for advice and consent.*[1084]

In spite of the clear language of the agreement, Obama unilaterally approved the Paris Climate Treaty on September 3, 2016. After seven and a half years in office, Obama had lost none of his conviction that he was the glorious agent of fundamental transformation: his signing statement proclaimed, "Someday we may see this as the moment that we finally decided to save our planet."[1085]

Obama's audacity didn't end there. After the election of Donald Trump—who promised to tear up the Paris agreement—Obama warned him not to withdraw from the agreement, scolding, "The tradition has been you carry [international agreements] forward across the administrations."[1086] This would be true had the Senate approved the deal, but without their approval, Trump considered the treaty nonbinding and withdrew.

184. MEDAL OF FREEDOM ABUSE

The final entries in this chapter will cover Obama's actions in the aftermath of the surprise election of Donald Trump. A lame duck president on the verge of relinquishing his power to a new president determined to undo his legacy, Obama wasn't about to wind down upon his return to the private sector. There were still things left undone to help secure his legacy and reward his allies. With no electoral consequences to consider, he clearly felt a sense of liberation to abuse his power.

We'll start by marveling at his largesse. Obama set many records during his presidency, most of them manifestly unflattering. One seemingly innocuous example, however, is the record for the most Presidential Medals of Freedom of any other president.[1087] Upon further inspection, even this record is not irreproachable.

The Presidential Medal of Freedom is the nation's highest civilian award. Established by President John F. Kennedy in 1963, the award recognizes, at the president's discretion, "any person who has made an especially meritorious contribution to (1) the security or national interests of the United States, or (2) world peace, or (3) cultural or other significant public or private endeavors."[1088] Such a high honor ought to be reserved for people who have met those requirements. But such high standards didn't always apply. In 2009, Obama posthumously awarded the Presidential Medal of Freedom to Harvey Milk, an early gay rights activist who seduced underage boys and held radical views on other political issues most Americans would find abhorrent. "Harvey Milk's voice will forever echo in the hearts of all those who carry forward his timeless message,"[1089] Obama said. That message took the form of the *Communist Internacional*.

But his final Medal of Freedom Award giveaway was his *coup de grâce,* awarding the most medals ever in a single ceremony to a slate of celebrities that, as *The Washington Times* described it, was "a collection of entertainers, athletes and celebrities famous mostly for being famous, no doubt deserving of honor in their fields, but out of place in a ceremony to recognize devotion and excellence as envisioned for the nation's highest civilian award."[1090]

Many people were left scratching their heads as they scanned the massive list of mediocre recipients—most were about as deserving of their awards as Obama was when he received his Nobel Peace Prize. But the answer becomes much clearer when you discover that many of the people Obama decided were worthy of the highest civilian award donated big money to Obama and the Democratic Party. Ellen DeGeneres, Robert De Niro, Tom Hanks, and Robert Redford all received awards, as did singer-songwriter Bruce Springsteen, former basketball players Kareem Abdul-Jabbar and Michael Jordan, and Bill and Melinda Gates. All of them have donated big money or held fundraising galas for Obama or the Democratic National Committee. Architect Frank Gehry, who donated more than a quarter of a million dollars to Democrats over twenty years, including $80,000 to the Obama Victory Fund in 2012, was another recipient.[1091]

Lorne Michaels, creator and producer of *Saturday Night Live*, also received an award. Anyone who has seen *SNL* in recent years would agree that Michaels doesn't deserve any awards, let alone the nation's highest civilian award. But apart from being a frequent Obama donor, Michaels' influential show found it nearly impossible to satirize Obama and other Democrats while pulling no punches for their Republican rivals—in fact, they openly mourned Hillary's defeat with a haunting rendition of Leonard Cohen's "Hallelujah" performed by Kate McKinnon, the show's frequent Hillary Clinton stand-in. There are more examples, but you get the idea.

While Obama's policy decisions and unconstitutional acts are the more serious grievances compiled in this book, cheapening the Presidential Medal of Freedom as an honor that can be given to a known sexual predator or that can be bought with donations and celebrity status is pretty low too.

185. FEDERAL LAND GRABS

The designation of national monuments should not be controversial. Yet Obama made it so by creating more national monuments than any other president, increasing the amount of land and water now under strict federal control by over 550 million acres.[1092] Most of the controversial designations came during his final weeks in office, raising concerns he was abusing the Antiquities Act in order to impose extreme environmental restrictions on public land. Two examples of this abuse were the Bears Ears Monument in Utah and the Gold Butte Monument in Nevada. Together these designations put over a million acres under strict federal control despite opposition from local Navajo tribal members.[1093]

> *The Antiquities Act has been repeatedly abused beyond its intent, says economist Nicholas Loris.*
>
> *The tradition of presidents designating national monuments began in 1906 when President Theodore Roosevelt signed the Antiquities Act.*
>
> *That law was intended to prevent the looting of archaeological and Native American structures and objects, and it gave the federal government an expeditious path to do so.*
>
> *Unsurprisingly, its use has evolved into a federal power tool for making land grabs that cater to special interests, rather than welcoming input from local affected parties, such as the outdoor tourist industry, Native American tribes, or simply the people living in the community.*
>
> *[...]*

> *Contrary to the media spin, the issue at hand is not about environmental stewardship, but taking decisions away from states, private citizens, and local interests.*[1094]

In April 2017, President Trump ordered reviews of twenty-seven national monuments, arguing that his predecessors overstepped their authority under the Antiquities Act by designating monuments that weren't, as the law dictates, "confined to the smallest area compatible with proper care and management of the objects to be protected."[1095] In December 2017, Trump reduced the size of the Bears Ears monument from 1.35 million acres to 201,876 acres.[1096]

186. SURGE IN REFUGEES DESPITE SECURITY RISKS

The refugee crisis affecting Europe should have been a red flag for anyone advocating the increase of refugees from terror-sponsoring countries and other terrorist hotbeds in the Middle East. Germany, for example, has admitted thousands of "refugees" from Syria thanks to Angela Merkel's "open door" refugee policy, and violent crime in the country has skyrocketed, with the number "of suspected crimes by refugees, asylum-seekers and illegal immigrants" increasing an incredible 52.7 percent in 2016.[1097]

This is hardly something we should desire to replicate in the United States, and while there are certainly legitimately oppressed refugees in need of sanctuary, there are clearly violent, criminal elements taking advantage of "open door" policies and poor screening processes to gain entry into European countries and even the United States. In September 2016, State Department spokesman John Kirby admitted that ISIS terrorists were trying to integrate themselves into refugee populations overseas to enter the United States: "I wouldn't debate the fact that there's the potential for ISIS terrorists to try to insert themselves, and we see that in some of the refugee camps in Jordan and in Turkey, where they try to insert themselves into the population."[1098] Rather than put the safety of Americans citizens first by reducing the number of refugees from countries until a proper vetting procedure could be implemented, Obama doubled down, announcing plans to *increase* the number of refugees allowed into the United States by 30 percent.[1099] After Trump was elected, Obama sped up the "refugee" resettlement process to ensure as many so-called refugees could be welcomed into the United States before Trump took office.[1100] He cared nothing for the risk of letting in an unknown number of ISIS terrorists and didn't mind letting his successor deal with the consequences.

187. OUTLAWING STATES FROM CUTTING FUNDS TO PLANNED PARENTHOOD

Abortion is a sacred cow for the political left, and any attempts to restrict it are met with outrage and allegations of a so-called war on reproductive rights or the blanket accusation of sexism. Once the liberal mantra was that abortion should be safe, legal, and *rare*. Now, they consider anything less than completely unrestricted and taxpayer-funded abortion on demand to be a violation of civil rights.

With his departure from the White House imminent, Obama gave the abortion lobby one final gift, issuing a federal regulation prohibiting state agencies from denying funds to organizations that provide abortion services[1101] following various state-led efforts to deny funding specifically to Planned Parenthood. If abortion is a sort of sacrament on the left, Planned Parenthood is the left's holy temple. As transparent as this foolish kowtowing to the abortion lobby was, unilateral executive actions are only as permanent as the next president wants them to be, and the regulation was reversed by Donald Trump in April 2017.[1102]

188. RECORD MIDNIGHT REGULATIONS

As we noted earlier in this book, Obama loved regulations. After the 2016 election went for Trump, Obama, sensing it would be a long time before Democrats would have another chance to strangle the American people any further, knew he had to get in as many new rules as he could before leaving office—such last-minute executive actions are commonly called "midnight regulations," and Obama took these to a whole new level.

In fact, he issued 145 separate regulations that cost over $100 million during his lame duck period—the most of any president in a generation, according to a study by the American Action Forum. The cost of these regulations came to $21 billion and would require more than twenty-one million hours of paperwork annually, according to AAF director of regulatory policy Sam Batkins.[1103]

Obama's constitutionally questionable govern-by-executive-pen approach will take years to unravel, but the Trump administration is doing its level best. The new president withdrew twenty-four of Obama's economically significant regulations in his first week in office and delayed the publication of $181 billion Obama-era regulations, including all of his remaining "midnight" regulations.[1104]

189. ELECTION POWER GRAB

In the aftermath of Donald Trump's election, liberals were looking for any excuse to explain how they lost to such a polarizing figure. Liberals have a Seinfeldian "Excuse Rolodex" to give both preemptive and postmortem excuses for losing elections: voter suppression, Fox News, talk radio, and racism are all quite common excuses. After Trump won, they added sexism, the Electoral College, James Comey, and, of course, Russia, to the list. After a few days, they focused their energy on the last one in particular.

The Obama administration took accusations of Russian hacking of the Democratic National Committee and colluding with the Trump campaign as an excuse to attempt a major federal takeover of our elections—completely disregarding Article 1, Section 4, Clause 1 of the Constitution, which states, "the times, places and manner of holding elections" shall be determined by the states. With only two weeks before Trump's inauguration, Obama's Homeland Security Secretary Jeh Johnson used a report on the alleged Russian hacking of the DNC to designate state and local voting systems "pieces of critical infrastructure" that put them under the jurisdiction and control of the Department of Homeland Security.[1105] Your polling place was now owned by Uncle Sam.

Legal experts said the move would set a dangerous precedent. "The Department of Homeland Security does not have the legal authority to interfere with states' election systems without their permission," said John Yoo, law professor at UC Berkeley School of Law. "While the federal government has the general power to protect the nation's cyber infrastructure, it cannot intrude into areas of state sovereignty without clear constitutional mandate."[1106]

"There is no federal power to control or secure elections. Each state administers its own elections, restricted only by constitutional protections for voting rights," agreed Illya Shapiro of the CATO Institute. He added, "It may make sense for states to request federal support here, but it would set a dangerous precedent for a federal agency to unilaterally take over state electoral processes." Hans von Spakovsky, a senior legal fellow at The Heritage Foundation, agreed. "It is unnecessary and uncalled for and potentially unconstitutional since the federal government doesn't have the authority to administer elections, only to set the time, place, and manner of congressional elections."[1107] Georgia Secretary of State Brian Kemp accused Jeh Johnson of using security "as an excuse to subvert the Constitution and establish the basis for federal encroachment into election systems."[1108]

In light of the hack that exposed the personal data of millions of current and former federal employees held by the Office of Personnel Management, it's quite clear that the federal government is no more capable of protecting voting systems than state and local governments. Officials from both parties opposed the power grab. According to John Fund, coauthor of *Who's Counting: How Fraudsters and Bureaucrats Put Your Vote at Risk*, there's good reason. They know "a decentralized U.S. election system makes large-scale hacking almost impossible." In a telephone conference with state officials, Jeh Johnson conceded there was "no credible threat of a successful cyberattack on the voting and ballot-counting process."[1109]

190. HAMPERING THE TRUMP TRANSITION

At a campaign rally in October 2016, Hillary Clinton, responding to Donald Trump's suggestion that he would need to know the circumstances of the election outcome to know whether he would accept the results without challenge, said the "peaceful transition of power is one of the things that sets us apart. It's how we hold our country together no matter who is in charge."[1110] President Obama, the day after the election, even promised a smooth transition to the Trump administration.[1111] On the same day, House Minority Leader Nancy Pelosi (D-CA) also said that a peaceful transition of power is a "cornerstone of our democracy."[1112] So everyone is on the same page publicly: ensuring the smooth transition of power from one administration to another as American as apple pie. But, as in so many other statements about the normal, American way of doing things we now have to add: "until Obama became President."

For Barack Obama, much more was at stake in the 2016 election than keeping the White House under Democratic Party control. Donald Trump campaigned aggressively against key elements of Obama's agenda, so Obama's entire legacy was on the line. He made no attempt to deny it. Electing Donald Trump "would be an insult to my legacy," he said less than two months before Election Day while speaking at the Congressional Black Caucus gala, urging them to get out and vote for Hillary.[1113]

Obama benefited from a smooth transition from an outgoing administration that he constantly attacked during the long and bitter presidential campaign that preceded it; he had nothing but positive things to say about the process. "Throughout the current transition, President Bush and his Administration have extended the hand of cooperation, and provided invaluable assistance to my team as we prepare to hit the ground running on January 20th," Obama said. "Transitions remind us that what we hold in common as Americans far outweighs our political differences."[1114] Yet cooperation and assistance for the incoming Trump administration gave way to the same partisan, divisive behavior that stained his entire presidency.

» Obama asserted that had he been able to run in 2016, he would have beaten Trump.
» In an interview with *Rolling Stone*, he blamed "Fox News in every bar and restaurant in big chunks of the country" for Trump's victory.[1115]

- » White House spokesman Josh Earnest spent four consecutive days during the transition attacking Trump and accusing Russia of trying to help Trump win the election.[1116]
- » Obama didn't just blame Russia for interfering with and influencing the election, but sanctioned Russia for doing so—despite lack of conclusive evidence—expelling thirty-five Russian diplomats in retaliation, in a thinly veiled attempt to delegitimize Trump's election.[1117]
- » Michelle Obama claimed that the election of Trump meant we "lost hope."
- » Rather than hold back criticism of his successor, as past presidents have typically done, Obama said he would speak out against President Trump if he felt it necessary.[1118]
- » Obama met with Congressional Democrats to discuss how to save Obamacare and thwart Trump's agenda.[1119]
- » He converted political appointees into permanent, civil service employees, in order to complicate the transition and hamper Trump's ability to have his own people guiding administration policy.[1120]
- » Obama began raising money to "help Democrats fight back" and "stand up to Trump and the GOP" after leaving office.[1121]

» He took several unilateral actions that, according to *The Hill*, "appear designed to box in President-elect Donald Trump." Incoming White House press secretary Sean Spicer told conservative radio host Hugh Hewitt, "Both the regulatory stuff, the executive orders that are on the way out...that [is] something that I believe, you know, makes it a little bit tougher in terms of the transition on the policy side."[1122]

Trump accused Obama of sacking the transition, tweeting, "Doing my best to disregard the many inflammatory President O statements and roadblocks. Thought it was going to be a smooth transition - NOT!"[1123]

We teach our children that cooperation is an important part of effective government and, even if you don't agree with a newly elected official, you need to give them a chance to succeed. Sadly, even after eight years in the Oval Office, Obama couldn't find it in his heart to be presidential and ensure a smooth transition. Former Speaker of the House Newt Gingrich compared President Obama's actions to a petulant god in a Wagnerian opera.[1124] Rather than making the transition smooth in the interests of the American people, President Obama was determined to cause as much trouble as he could for the new president. He and other Democratic Party leaders even crafted a strategy of blanket opposition and gave it a catchy hashtag name: #Resist. Obama ended his presidency exactly as he started it: he divided Americans into warring factions and made our lives worse.

191. THE FINAL INSULT TO ISRAEL

We discussed Obama's disdain for the Jewish state earlier, so it comes as no shock that he took another jab at them before leaving office. It has been long-standing U.S. policy that the fate of the West Bank, Gaza, and the eastern part of Jerusalem is to be decided by negotiations between the Israelis and the Palestinians. Obama undermined this with his call for a return to the 1967 borders, but what he did via the U.N. is far worse. On December 23, 2016, the United States, at Obama's direction, abstained from a Security Council resolution stating that *all* territory taken by Israel in 1967 is occupied territory and that Israel must not build any settlements on such land.[1125] With the U.S. abstention, the resolution passed through the U.N. Security Council, thus making it official United Nations policy.

Obama's U.N. ambassador, Samantha Powers, tried to claim the administration was merely continuing U.S. policy against increased settlements, but all one has to do is realize that the resolution makes the Wailing Wall *and the Jewish Quarter of Jerusalem* "occupied territory" to understand the absurd scope of this UN resolution. The Jewish Quarter was ethnically cleansed of its Jews in the aftermath of the 1948 Arab-Israeli War, and Jews were only permitted back into that part of Jerusalem when Israel reclaimed the territory in 1967.[1126] How can the Jews of Israel be the illegal occupiers of the *Jewish* Quarter of Jerusalem?

Within days, we learned Obama's intention all along was to abstain and allow the resolution to pass; he directed that the United States abstain from the vote.[1127] In fact, the Israeli government was certain that the Obama administration "helped craft and promote the resolution" condemning Israel.[1128] They were right. Both Secretary of State John Kerry and Vice President Joe Biden had a hand in pushing approval of the resolution.[1129] The resolution was Obama's *coup de grâce* for Israel, removing all doubt that Obama was an enemy to Israel.

192. CONTROVERSIAL ACTS OF CLEMENCY

Most modern presidents issued pardons some Americans disliked. George H. W. Bush pardoned key figures in the Reagan-era Iran-Contra Scandal, Bill Clinton pardoned Marc Rich on his last day in office, and George W. Bush commuted the sentence of I. Lewis "Scooter" Libby. All of those pardons faced opposition and criticism. But Obama didn't pardon a handful of people for political reasons; his actions were much less constrained. On his last day in office, he issued 330 commutations, setting the record for the largest number of commutations in a single day and bringing his total number of commutations to 1,385, which the White House lauded as "the most grants of commutation issued by any President in this nation's history." Obama also granted sixty-four pardons, bringing his final tally to 212 pardons.[1130] The White House was proud of this "accomplishment," as seen in White House counsel Neil Eggleston's statement:

> *While the mercy the President has shown his 1,597 clemency recipients is remarkable, we must remember that clemency is an extraordinary remedy, granted*

> *only after the President has concluded that a particular individual has demonstrated a readiness to make use of his or her second chance. Only Congress can achieve the broader reforms needed to ensure over the long run that our criminal justice system operates more fairly and effectively in the service of public safety.*[1131]

Many of Obama's pardons and commutations went to felons who had committed violent crimes and/or individuals who wound up back in prison. But we'll focus on two of his worst eleventh-hour commutations—FALN terrorist Oscar Lopez-Rivera and former Army Private Chelsea (Bradley) Manning.

Lopez-Rivera is a decorated Vietnam veteran who became radicalized after the war. He became a community organizer and eventually a recruiter, instructor, and bomb-maker for the terrorist Armed Forces of National Liberation (FALN)—a Stalinist organization dedicated to separating Puerto Rico from the United States and installing a Communist dictatorship on the island. Over a period of nine years in the 1970s and 1980s, FALN carried out 120 attacks, resulting in the deaths of five people.[1132] Lopez-Rivera was sentenced to serve fifty-five years for a variety of crimes and terrorist acts connected to FALN.[1133] He expressed no remorse for his actions or the deaths caused by them.[1134] Naturally, his radical views and causes made him a hero to some on the political left.[1135]

And then there's Private Manning, an intelligence analyst for the Army who leaked thousands of secret military documents to WikiLeaks in 2010 and was consequently arrested, tried, convicted, and sentenced to thirty-five years in prison.[1136] Obama's commutation of his sentence was unusual—his administration targeted leakers more than any other. Perhaps it has something to do with the fact that, after his sentencing, Manning announced he was transgender[1137] and sought taxpayer-funded "gender reassignment" surgery,[1138] making him a darling of the LGBT rights movement and a leftist icon.

The editors at *National Review* explained why this commutation was a horrible injustice:

> *He downloaded, copied, and passed along to WikiLeaks several hundred thousand files that comprehensively detailed American military and diplomatic activities in Iraq, Afghanistan, and beyond.*
>
> *These files not only disclosed the identities of individuals working with Americans and spotlighted vital and sensitive classified diplomatic efforts, they provided a comprehensive overview of American military operations in both Iraq and Afghanistan—including detailed descriptions of American tactics and strategies, right down to descriptions of the vehicles used in various missions, the purpose of the missions, and the targets of operations. In other words, to borrow a football analogy, it was like handing the opposition your playbook—except with lives on the line.*
>
> *During Manning's trial, prosecutors introduced evidence that al-Qaeda was not only gleeful about the*

> *leak (one of its spokesmen said, "By the grace of God, the enemy's interests are today spread all over the place"), Osama bin Laden himself "asked for and received" the "Afghanistan battlefield reports that WikiLeaks published."*[1139]

We don't doubt some of Obama's commutations and pardons went to people who deserved a second chance but commuting the sentence of an unrepentant terrorist and an American traitor raises serious doubts about his character and motivations. Did he really believe they were all worthy of a second chance or was he just out to please his core constituency? Regardless, Obama showed his utter contempt for the United States and the rule of law.

193. ELEVENTH-HOUR EXPANSION OF THE SURVEILLANCE STATE

We've previously covered several of Obama's Orwellian abuses of power during his eight years as president. Before he left office, he made things much worse for American civil liberties by dramatically expanding the surveillance state. It doesn't matter who you are or what party you belong to; this should concern you. About a week before leaving office, Obama issued Executive Order 12333, which *The New York Times* explained, "expanded the power of the National Security Agency to share globally intercepted personal communications with the government's 16 other intelligence agencies before applying privacy protections."[1140]

> *The new rules significantly relax longstanding limits on what the N.S.A. may do with the information gathered by its most powerful surveillance operations, which are largely unregulated by American wiretapping laws. These include collecting satellite transmissions, phone calls and emails that cross network switches abroad, and messages between people abroad that cross domestic network switches.*
>
> *The change means that far more officials will be searching through raw data. Essentially, the government is reducing the risk that the N.S.A. will fail to recognize that a piece of information would be valuable to another agency, but increasing the risk that officials will see private information about innocent people.*[1141]

The new rules under Obama's executive order mean that "if analysts stumble across evidence that an American has committed any crime, they will send it to the Justice Department."[1142] Surveillance reform expert Kate Tummarello called it "a huge and troubling shift in the way those intelligence agencies receive information collected by the NSA."[1143] She explained, "Domestic agencies like the FBI are subject to more privacy protections, including warrant requirements. Previously, the NSA shared data with these agencies only after it had screened the data, filtering out unnecessary personal information, including about innocent people whose communications were swept up the NSA's massive surveillance operations."[1144] Obama must've thought *1984* was an instruction manual rather than a warning.

POST-PRESIDENCY REVELATIONS

AS WE PREPARED THIS UPDATED edition, we faced a dilemma. When should we publish? Ordinarily, after a president leaves office, we'll only hear a trickle of new details about his administration—certainly nothing incredibly outrageous or scandalous. That's why we have a free press: to hold our leaders accountable while they're in office. But with Obama, the media completely failed to do that while he was still in power. Now, a veritable flood of toxic new details is pouring out, revealing just how many layers of corruption Obama hid behind his hope and change facade.

If you thought Obama's presidency was a cesspool of incompetence and scandal before, you might want to hold your nose, because you're dealing with an entire sewer. New odious slime is bubbling up every day. No matter when we stop adding to this book, more will have surfaced by the time you read it, but we had to draw the line somewhere. Roughly a year after the end of the worst presidency in American history, let's take stock of just how bad it really was.

194. LOSING OTTO WARMBIER TO KIM JUNG-UN

In January 2016, twenty-two-year-old college student Otto Warmbier was arrested in North Korea while traveling with a tour group. North Korean thugs alleged Warmbier stole a propaganda poster, a serious crime in the country. He was sentenced to fifteen years of hard labor. He would not be freed until June 2017; by the time he arrived in the U.S., he'd been comatose for many months. He died six days later, having never regained consciousness. American doctors were unable to determine the cause of his neurological injuries, but U.S. officials believe the North Korean government was directly responsible for his death.[1145]

Days after his death, President Trump criticized Barack Obama for not doing enough to bring Warmbier back home. "It should never, ever be allowed to happen. And frankly, if he were brought home sooner, I think the results would have been a lot different," Trump told reporters.[1146]

Trump had plenty of reasons to be critical. Upon Otto's belated return to the United States, his father, Fred Warmbier, criticized how the Obama administration handled Otto's imprisonment. In March 2016, Obama's press secretary Josh Earnest was asked how the administration was going to respond to Otto's imprisonment, and he said, "We strongly urge the North Korean government to pardon him and grant him special amnesty and immediate release."[1147] The empty words of the Obama administration carried little weight with the North Korean regime, and as they failed to secure Otto's release, they told the Warmbier family to stay silent and maintain a low profile so as to not upset the North Koreans.

According to Fred Warmbier, "When Otto was first taken, we were advised by the [Obama] administration to take a low profile while they worked to obtain his release.

We did so without result."[1148] Warmbier visited Washington, D.C., several times to meet with lawmakers but he was never given the opportunity to have a face-to-face meeting with President Obama about his son's imprisonment.[1149] Seeing that maintaining a low profile wasn't producing any results, the Warmbiers finally went public, and after spending seventeen months in captivity, Otto came home with the help of the new Trump administration.

Fred Warmbier praised the Trump administration's more effective efforts in bringing Otto back. When asked about whether he thought the Obama administration could have done more for his son, Warmbier said, "I think the results speak for themselves."[1150] He added, "We received a very nice phone call from President Trump, who told us that Secretary of State Tillerson worked hard to help bring Otto home. We are extremely grateful for their efforts and concern."[1151] The Trump administration succeeded where the Obama administration failed, but it was too late for Otto. Obama was so concerned about upsetting North Korea that his administration failed Otto Warmbier, and a young life was needlessly lost. This was not the first time Obama's fear of offense emboldened an enemy of the United States, nor even the only time his cowardice got Americans killed.

195. IRS TARGETING OF PRO-ISRAEL GROUPS

We covered the IRS's documented illegal targeting of conservative groups earlier in this book, but, on February 1, 2018, we learned that Obama's IRS had other groups in its crosshairs as well. It turns out that favoring Israel was a good way to find your group trapped in limbo. Consistent with Obama's antagonistic policy toward Israel, also covered earlier in this book, the IRS falsely considered Israel a state linked to terrorism—to deny pro-Israel groups tax-exempt status.

The pro-Israeli nonprofit organization Z Street published a full rundown of their IRS nightmare in *The Wall Street Journal*.[1152] According to founder Lori Lowenthal Marcus, the group began in 2009 with a mission of educating the U.S. about Israel's efforts to defend itself from foreign aggression. The group applied for 501(c)(3) tax exempt status and, like dozens of conservative groups applying at that time, they got the runaround. When they contacted the IRS to inquire as to their status, they were informed that Z Street was being scrutinized due to Israel's supposed links to terrorism. Z Street then sued the IRS for violating their constitutional rights and, in response, the tax juggernaut claimed that it had corrected the "error" but because the application was now the subject of ongoing litigation, it was frozen until the matter was settled.

That settlement didn't come for more than seven long years. In February 2018, the IRS and Z Street settled the case, with Z Street collecting damages and the IRS finally approving their application for tax-exempt status.[1153] It wasn't until Z Street publicized their ordeal that the IRS issued a hollow apology.[1154]

But don't imagine that this was an isolated incident. In fact, Z Street's lawsuit produced evidence exposing years of efforts by Obama administration officials to weaponize the IRS against pro-Israel groups. Marcus explained:

> *Within weeks of President Obama's inauguration, IRS and State Department officials began considering whether they could deny or revoke tax-exempt status for organizations that provided material support to Jews living across the Green Line—the nonborder that delineates pre-1967 Israel from the territories Israel acquired in the Six Day War. The theory was that a Jewish presence in those areas is inconsistent with U.S. policy. The IRS drew up lists of such organizations based on information from anti-Israel websites such as Electronic Intifada and MondoWeiss.*
>
> *[...]*
>
> *While no formal policy was released barring U.S. tax-exempt entities from supporting Jewish activity over the Green Line, Obama IRS officials tried three times between 2009 and 2012 to create such a policy, and IRS employees made sure the effort wasn't documented. One emailed her supervisor saying that she would answer his questions about IRS policy relating to Israeli settlements only orally. "Not doing email on this," she explained.*[1155]

Just like the targeting of conservative groups, the IRS tried to cover up their anti-Israel bias.

Z Street was just one unlucky victim of an Obama-era policy of discriminating against pro-Israeli groups, and the rationale given was that those groups didn't advocate ideas consistent with official government policy regarding

Israel's acquisition of territories in the Six-Day War. In short, disagree with Obama, and you don't get the same rights as everyone else. It's stunning that his administration felt comfortable enough in their illegal scheming to leave this sort of evidence behind. Given what we know about Obama, perhaps we shouldn't be surprised.

196. IRAN NUCLEAR DEAL FALLOUT

We've already demonstrated what sorts of ethically questionable choices Barack Obama made in his pursuit of a nuclear disarmament deal with Iran, from bankrolling the world's number one sponsor of terrorism to trading money for hostages to turning a blind eye to acts of war against the U.S. Navy. But in the last days of 2017, we learned just how far Obama was willing to go to kowtow to Iran. In a blockbuster report, *Politico* investigative journalist Josh Meyer revealed the Obama administration shielded Hezbollah-linked criminal gangs from prosecution and covered up a billion-dollar international money laundering operation.[1156] Why? Because Obama had to protect Iran's allies to make sure that nothing stood in the way of his precious nuclear deal, and his counterterrorism expert, John Brennan, had convinced him that Hezbollah—a terrorist group—could be mainstreamed and its "moderate" voices built up.

In 2008, the Drug Enforcement Administration opened an investigation that was dubbed Project Cassandra after evidence mounted suggesting that Hezbollah had morphed from a paramilitary force to an international crime syndicate. The objective was to round up drug-runners and other bad actors linked to Hezbollah. By 2011, in fact, the task force managed to link one of the largest drug rings under the microscope to Hezbollah by way of a massive money laundering conspiracy valued at nearly half a billion dollars. But the Obama administration didn't act. In fact, they kept throwing up roadblocks to hinder its progress. These stall tactics ranged from the Department of Justice refusing to file criminal charges against key operatives to the State Department denying requests for assistance in luring prime suspects to countries where they might be arrested and interrogated.[1157] As a result, the years-long investigation didn't achieve its objectives, and hundreds of known members of a vast international drug trafficking ring linked to a terrorist organization with global reach remain free.

Thanks to the *Politico* report, in January 2018, Attorney General Jeff Sessions launched a new investigation into Hezbollah-backed drug-trafficking and money-laundering schemes.[1158] We can hope that this new effort will bring a just end to the entire sordid affair, but the new task force is starting from scratch. It took Project Cassandra years to uncover Hezbollah's worldwide network, only to have the Iran-appeasing Obama administration squander their efforts and allow tons of cocaine to enter the United States.

197. OBAMA THE SPY

The more we learn about Obama, the clearer it is that the Constitution was written to protect us from people like him. The Founding Fathers may not have predicted Obama's election 220 years before it happened, but they understood, even then, that the people needed to be protected from an all-powerful government with the resources to violate our civil rights. In May 2017, we found out that the National Security Agency had been conducting illegal searches on Americans for years, was rebuked by the Foreign Intelligence Surveillance Court (FISC), and covered it up until just before the 2016 election.

According to a classified report examined by *Circa*, "More than 5 percent, or one out of every 20 searches seeking upstream Internet data on Americans inside the NSA's so-called Section 702 database violated the safeguards Obama and his intelligence chiefs vowed to follow in 2011." In fact, *Circa* reported there was "a three-fold increase in NSA data searches about Americans and a rise in the unmasking of U.S. person's identities in intelligence reports after Obama loosened the privacy rules in 2011." Obama's National Security Adviser Susan Rice and other Obama officials argued their actions were legal and that safeguards were preventing abuses, but according to the FISC, and NSA Inspector General, that simply wasn't the case—and so they tried to cover it up as long as they could before the 2016 election.[1159]

These violations are, according to the American Civil Liberties Union, some of the most serious Fourth Amendment abuses ever documented.[1160] And they happened on Barack Obama's watch—Obama, the former "constitutional law professor" who claimed to "respect the Constitution."

198. PROTECTING HILLARY FROM JUSTICE

Did the Obama administration protect Hillary from being held accountable in order to protect Obama's heir apparent? All the evidence points in that direction. Before the 2016 election, *The Washington Times* revealed that the Obama administration "rejected requests from three FBI field offices that wanted to open public corruption cases involving the Clinton Foundation and Democratic presidential nominee Hillary Clinton."[1161] In the wake of the dubious exoneration of Hillary Clinton's mishandling of classified information with her private, unsecured email server, this raises serious questions about bias in the Justice Department.

Obama protected Hillary for a long time. In March 2016, Obama's State Department announced they would put off completing their review of classified information on Clinton's secret email server until after the election in November.[1162] A month later, the State Department admitted that a key Benghazi email of Hillary's had been withheld from watchdog group Judicial Watch since 2014. Had the disclosure of the email not been delayed, it would have exposed Hillary's private server before Hillary had thousands of her emails deleted.[1163]

In the summer of 2016—in the middle of the presidential campaign—as the lengthy FBI investigation neared its conclusion, Attorney General Loretta Lynch met former President Bill Clinton on the tarmac of Sky Harbor International Airport in Phoenix in an allegedly chance meeting.[1164] On July 1, 2016, Attorney General Lynch announced that she would accept whatever recommendation the FBI made on the matter.[1165] On July 5, FBI director James Comey publicly exonerated Clinton of any wrongdoing, after describing, at length, actions that would have likely had anyone else facing criminal charges of mishandling classified information.

Many suspected something was amiss. But it wasn't until after Obama left office that we learned just how far the Obama administration went to protect Hillary before the election. In October 2017, damning evidence that the entire investigation was a sham came to light when we learned that Comey's exoneration of Hillary was drafted *before* Hillary and other key witnesses were even interviewed by the FBI.[1166] Peter Strzok, the lead investigator on the case, softened the language of Comey's exoneration statement, changing the description of Clinton's actions from "grossly negligent" (a term that had legal implications) to "extremely careless." Strzok was also responsible for officially opening the investigation of Russian meddling into the 2016 election.[1167] According to text messages revealed in 2018, Strzok, a rabidly anti-Trump Clinton supporter, described the Russian collusion investigation as "an insurance policy" just in case Trump won.[1168]

And then there's the Uranium One deal, tainted by donations to the Clinton Foundation and an administration cover-up of illicit dealings before the Obama administration signed off. In order to protect Hillary, not to mention covering for the entire administration, officials placed an FBI informant under a gag order to prevent him from testifying about alleged bribery and racketeering prior to the approval of the Uranium One deal. According to the informant's lawyer, "He can tell what all the Russians were talking about during the time that all these bribery payments were made." In response, Obama's Justice Department threatened the informant with prosecution if he attempted to testify about what he knew.[1169]

Who was in charge of the FBI when this went down? None other than Robert Mueller—yup, the same Robert Mueller who, at the time of this writing, is still "investigating" allegations of collusion between the Trump campaign and Russia in 2016. Mueller's connection to the Uranium One bribery cover-up raised alarms for many who believe that it compromises his ability to investigate Hillary's opponent in the 2016 election.[1170]

Make no mistake, in protecting Hillary, Obama was also protecting the entire administration. Hillary would guarantee Obama's legacy would be preserved. Donald Trump ran on promises to undo Obama's legacy and see that justice would be done regarding Obama-era corruption. The fact that so much has been exposed since Obama left office tells us Hillary's defeat has given us the best chance to see justice served.

199. URANIUM ONE

We alluded to the infamous Russian business deal above, but let's take a closer look. The Uranium One deal, which saw 20 percent of the United States' uranium supply sold to Russia, actually dates to 2010 when the Obama administration foolishly and inexplicably approved the deal (despite national security concerns and Republican opposition). But revelations about the deal since Obama left office have shed new light on the controversial deal, prompting new investigations in what has become a full-blown scandal.

Questions over the connection between the Uranium One deal and large donations to the Clinton Foundation have been asked since well before the 2016 election, but in October 2017, media sources showed even before the deal was approved, the FBI had learned that "Russian nuclear industry officials were engaged in bribery, kickbacks, extortion and money laundering designed to grow Vladimir Putin's atomic energy business inside the United States." The Obama administration covered this up by not bringing charges and prolonging the investigation—keeping it hidden from both the American people and Congress.[1171] Congress and the Justice Department under Donald Trump have since begun new investigations.[1172] The investigation has already led to one indictment in January 2018. Judicial Watch president Tom Fitton believes more scrutiny is warranted. "There's tens of millions of dollars that were laundered by Russians into the Clinton operation that needs to be thoroughly investigated in order for the American people to rest assured that our uranium industry hasn't been compromised."[1173]

But perhaps the biggest bombshell came with the testimony of FBI informant Douglas Campbell in February 2018. Campbell was under a gag order and threatened by the Obama administration, as we previously mentioned, but the Trump administration released him from that order and cleared him to speak to Congress. Campbell testified Russian actors routed millions of dollars to the United States to benefit the Clinton Global Initiative while then-Secretary of State Hillary Clinton was driving a "reset" in America's relations with Russia. The Obama administration, Campbell explained in his written statement, was making decisions benefiting Russia's nuclear industry as Russia was attempting to monopolize the global uranium market and achieve a geopolitical advantage over the United States. Russian nuclear officials monitored by the FBI were recorded boasting about "how weak the U.S. government was in giving away uranium business and were confident that Russia would secure the strategic advantage it was seeking in the U.S. uranium market." Campbell also testified he had provided the FBI evidence of illegal activities months before the Obama administration unanimously approved the Uranium One deal. Despite attempts by Democrats to attack Campbell's credibility, the FBI rewarded him for his undercover work in 2016—which Obama knew, Campbell claimed. "My FBI handlers praised my work. They told me on various occasions that details from the undercover probe had been briefed directly to FBI top officials. On two occasions, my handlers were particularly excited, claiming that my undercover work had been briefed to President Obama as part of his daily presidential briefing," he testified. The decision to approve the Uranium One deal frustrated Campbell. "I expressed these concerns repeatedly to my FBI handlers. The response I got was that politics was somehow involved."[1174]

With Obama, politics always seems to be involved.

200. TRUMP SURVEILLANCE AND FISA-GATE SCANDALS

In March 2017, President Donald Trump declared on Twitter that he was informed Trump Tower was wiretapped during the 2016 presidential campaign—calling out Barack Obama by name. Democrats and the media alike laughed it off as a delusional conspiracy theory. *How dare he accuse Barack Obama of such a crime!* The left-wing fact-checking site *Politifact* was quick to declare the claim false.[1175] But it would eventually become clear that Trump's campaign had indeed been targeted for surveillance by the Obama administration. The more we learned as time passed, the worse it looked.

Let's step back a bit first to the presidential campaign. Donald Trump's victory took everyone by surprise, and Hillary Clinton loyalists struggled to explain what happened. Hillary Clinton couldn't have lost legitimately! Within days of the election, Democrats across the political-media complex began assembling a narrative: Donald Trump must have colluded with the Russians to undermine Hillary Clinton and steal the election.

Ten days before Trump's inauguration, *Buzzfeed* published what is now known as the Steele Dossier—written by former British spy Christopher Steele—which supposedly documented collusion between the Russian government and the Trump campaign.[1176] Experts in Russian intelligence operations from both the U.S. and Russia registered doubts over the accuracy of the dossier, which was rife with unsubstantiated and salacious allegations and claims that were easily debunked. For example,

Steele claimed Trump family attorney Michael Cohen had frequented Prague and held meetings there at specific times. Cohen not only denied ever having been to Prague, but there was no evidence he had ever been there.[1177] The next day, reports proved the Obama Justice Department had indeed sought a FISA request to monitor the Trump campaign in June 2016—a request that was originally denied.[1178] The FISA court is not known to reject many requests, having turned down eleven out of more than 33,900 requests as of 2013.[1179] A second, revised request was approved by the court in October 2016.[1180]

A year later, we learned that the Steele Dossier had been funded by the Democratic National Committee and the Hillary Clinton campaign as opposition research against Trump.[1181] Following this revelation, several Democrats who had been touting the dossier as ironclad proof of collusion began backpedaling and downplaying its significance—even Fusion GPS, which hired Steele, began to distance themselves from it.[1182] In January 2018, we learned, when Christopher Steele gave the FBI his files on Trump in October 2016, he also delivered a second memo, this one authored by Clinton operative Cody Shearer. The Shearer memo is, as of this writing, still being "assessed" by the FBI.[1183] Longtime politicos may remember Cody Shearer as the man responsible for starting the false and utterly laughable rumor that former Vice President Dan Quayle had purchased cocaine to bolster Bill Clinton's chances in the 1992 election.

Given the political motivations behind the creation of the dossier, one might ask how the FBI determined it was reliable enough to use as a major piece of evidence against Trump. FBI operative Bruce Ohr, whose wife was on the payroll for Fusion GPS, was in close contact with Steele and others responsible for creating the dossier in the months leading up to its release. In fact, Ohr leaked bits of the tall tale to the mainstream press prior to the release of the fraudulent report, and the FBI then used those media reports to "corroborate" it.

Meanwhile, two key members of the team investigating Trump, Peter Strzok and Lisa Page, traded anti-Trump text messages throughout the summer and fall of 2016, all while conducting an illicit affair at the office. Some of those messages suggested the investigation was an "insurance policy" in case he won the election.[1184] Another message infamously suggested that they wanted to form a "secret society" to battle Trump, though we suspect that comment was meant in jest. The texts betrayed an undeniably politicized culture in the FBI.

Page also sent a text message to Strzok informing him that Obama "wants to know everything we're doing." Original reports suggested she was referring to the Hillary private email server investigation—Director Comey would reopen the case roughly a month later. Later, some sources claimed she meant the investigation of Russian meddling in the 2016 election. Judicial Watch president Tom Fitton argued neither option looked good. "Either way you see President Obama being intensely involved in wanting to know everything about either the Clinton email investigation or Russia investigation. Pick your poison, in terms of presidential involvement in the sensitive criminal investigations." He added that President Trump "...is being criminally investigated about his communication with the FBI director about a criminal investigation. Why isn't [sic] there similar inquiries into what President Obama was doing?"[1185]

And then there was former Deputy Director of the FBI, Andrew McCabe. Ari Fleischer thinks McCabe tolerated no criticism of former FBI Director Jim Comey; he learned this in person when he was turned away from a counterterrorism training seminar at which he was to be the keynote speaker following mildly critical remarks about Comey's decision to leak FBI memos to *The New York Times.*[1186] And, in December 2017, McCabe testified that the Steele Dossier was the exclusive piece of evidence used in their FISA warrant request, and the request made no mention of its politically motivated history. He also said the bureau would not have sought a FISA warrant against Carter Page without the dossier. That month, he admitted the agency had yet to verify any of the accusations of bribery or collusion in the dossier. McCabe resigned from the FBI when this information appeared in a memo crafted by House Intelligence Committee chairman Devin Nunes.[1187]

The Nunes memo contained a number of other bombshells that cast doubt on the integrity of the FBI and exposed just how politicized the Department of Justice and the FBI became under Barack Obama. For example, the bureau's star witness, Christopher Steele, was dismissed as a reliable source just nine days after the FISC granted a warrant to surveil Carter Page. Steele bragged to *Mother Jones* about his association with the FBI in direct violation of FBI policy regarding material witnesses. Such grandstanding makes it hard to take him at his word, yet, in three subsequent filings for extensions on the Page warrant, the FBI neglected to inform the court about Steele's new status.

The Nunes memo was attacked relentlessly by Democrats. They tried everything from suggesting its release would cause a constitutional crisis to claiming, once it was released, that there wasn't much substance to it, or even questioning its accuracy. But the Nunes memo was further substantiated by an eight-page brief from Republican Senators Chuck Grassley, chairman of the Senate Judiciary Committee, and Lindsey Graham, chairman of the Judiciary Committee's subcommittee on crime and terrorism. This document, dubbed the Grassley/Graham memo, was attached to a letter to Deputy Attorney General Rod Rosenstein and FBI Director Chris Wray and recommended that Christopher Steele be indicted for lying to the FBI. The Grassley/Graham memo verified that the Steele dossier "formed a significant portion of the FBI's warrant application," that the FISA application "relied more heavily on Steele's credibility than on any independent verification or corroboration for his claims." It also revealed that Clinton associates were sources used to concoct Steele's anti-Trump dossier—some speculating that one source was Hillary Clinton confident Sidney Blumenthal. According to the memo, "[i]t is troubling enough that the Clinton Campaign funded Mr. Steele's work, but that these Clinton associates were contemporaneously feeding Mr. Steele allegations raises additional concerns about his credibility."[1188]

Just before Valentine's Day 2018, we got another hint at the depth of this deception when we learned of a previously undisclosed secret meeting on January 5, 2017, between FBI Director James Comey, Vice President Biden, National Security Advisor Susan Rice, Deputy Attorney General Sally Yates, and President Obama. We only know about because Rice sent herself a bizarre and unsettling email on Inauguration Day 2017 uncovered during the Senate investigation into Obama-era bias by the FBI and DOJ. Comey never mentioned this meeting when asked about conversations with the White House on the Trump probe under oath. But Rice's email described how Obama asked Comey "to inform him if anything changes in the next few weeks that should affect how we share classified information with the incoming team." According to Rice's email, "Comey said he would."[1189] What exactly did the Obama administration want to hide from the incoming Trump administration? Andrew McCarthy at National Review believes it was about classified information regarding the Obama administration's Trump-Russia investigation.

> *The dilemma was that the Obama administration had placed "the incoming team"—in particular, President-elect Trump—under investigation. Remember, Obama's law-enforcement agencies believed the Steele dossier. No, the FBI had not been able to corroborate it; but, as former FBI director Comey told Congress, the bureau deemed its author, Christopher Steele, to be a reliable source. Steele, moreover, had collaborated*

> *on the project with Nellie Ohr, the wife of Bruce Ohr, Yates's top aide at the Justice Department. Even if the Justice Department and the FBI could not prove Steele's allegations, at least not yet, they still believed that Trump was compromised and that the Russians could be blackmailing him. If they had not believed those allegations were credible, they would not have put them in a warrant application to the FISA Court.*
>
> *So we arrive at the knotty question for Obama political and law-enforcement officials: How do we "engage with the incoming team" of Trump officials while also determining that "we cannot share information fully as it relates to Russia"? How do we assure that an investigation of Trump can continue when Trump is about to take over the government?*[1190]

When you string together this entire filthy web of deceit, obfuscation, and political opportunism, the shape it takes is startling. The FBI used a piece of opposition research with highly questionable origins as its primary evidence in an investigation of Donald Trump and to justify spying on his campaign. Donald Trump wasn't just a presidential candidate, but the opponent of Obama's heir apparent, Hillary Clinton—Obama's only hope in ensuring that his legacy would remain intact after he left office. This effort to use federal power, in what can only be described as an attempt to overrule the will of the American electorate and eventually undermine his future presidency is outrageous. This is the same organization that cleared

Hillary Clinton of wrongdoing in the private email server investigation months before even interviewing her. It has never been clearer that justice was entirely absent under Barack Obama. Former Secret Service agent Dan Bongino called it the "most consequential political scandal in the history of the United States."[1191] Joe DiGenova, former U.S. Attorney for the District of Columbia, called the scandal "the largest law enforcement scandal in history" because, he explained, "the activities of McCabe and others and Bruce Ohr and others were designed to subvert the Constitution and a national election, the most serious offense under our Constitution."[1192] Victor Davis Hanson called it "a more worrisome scandal than either Watergate or Iran-Contra," in part because the media is now "defending such actions, not uncovering them."[1193]

CONCLUSION

HOW WILL THE HISTORIANS OF the future assess the presidency of Barack Obama? He would like to be remembered as the president who saved America from another Great Depression, the president who ushered in a new era of government transparency and accountability, the president who cut taxes for the middle class and lowered the cost of healthcare while providing coverage for all Americans. He'll want history to remember him for making America safer from the threat of terrorism, all while improving the nation's standing in the world. He'll expect the shortcomings of his presidency to be blamed on his predecessor, his own unblemished presidency a success beyond all debate.

It would be a great legacy, if any of it were true.

As patriotic Americans, we felt it was our duty to document the truth about Obama's presidency so that his legacy is defined by the facts, not by his false narrative.

We saw an economy hobble along thanks to a failed stimulus, new taxes, and regulations. We saw more people leave the workforce during the so-called "recovery" than the recession that preceded it. We saw more people live in poverty and put on welfare, disability, and food stamps. We saw a signature healthcare policy that exploded the cost of care for the average American, crippled the nation's network of hospitals and clinics, and buried doctors alive in paperwork. Obama broke the engine of economic growth, and Americans got poorer and less able to build wealth. Are these the results of successful economic policy?

Obama was also a spectacular failure abroad. Obama raved about the death of Al-Qaeda during his 2012 reelection campaign while enabling its ascent to new heights. His misguided policies directly caused the rise of ISIS and the destabilization of the Middle East. He abandoned Israel and sided with Iran and terrorist groups like Hezbollah and Hamas. He empowered Russian expansion, ignored socialist advances in the Americas, and bowed to the United Nations even as they denigrated America and revealed a deep and disturbing lack of morality. He offended and alienated our allies, kowtowed to our enemies, and Americans felt less safe after eight years of Obama than they did after 9/11.

Obama's lust for executive power came at a huge price. He treated our inalienable human rights as privileges to be granted by the state and the Constitution like a loose set of guidelines rather than the law of the land. When Obama realized his agenda wouldn't make it through Congress, he imposed it via executive fiat. If he didn't like a law, he simply wouldn't enforce it. His administration weaponized the IRS, Department of Justice, and FBI against Obama's political enemies. Obama sought the power to indefinitely detain American citizens and build a government spying program unbound by any oversight. Gross abuses of power threatened our freedom of speech, religion, the press, and other civil liberties we hold dear.

The "great uniter" was, instead, a brutally divisive president who relied on racial and class-based rhetoric to justify most of his actions. He never missed an opportunity to scold conservatives and everyday Americans. As a result, by the time Obama left office, we were more divided than at any time since the Civil War, and Americans lost pride in our heritage and history, believing our best times were behind us and our problems were the "new normal."

The worst thing about Obama's time in office was he was never personally held accountable for his policy failings or corruption. The Democratic Party suffered the loss of over a thousand elected offices in state and federal government and countless more in local government—the most in American history to be lost from the party of the sitting president. But Obama remained personally popular. Even now, Obama is still canonized by his supporters in the media, academia, and Hollywood, who will stop at nothing to maintain the illusion that Obama was not just a good and successful president, but one of the best, if not *the* best. We can't let that happen.

As we survey the disaster of Obama's presidency, it is vitally important that the next generation—who will have to pay for the mistake of electing Obama *twice*—fully understands his record and shows better judgment in the voting booth, placing a higher value on America's deeper principles and on a coherent sense of reason and purpose going forward. America can rise again—we can once again be the beacon of economic and personal freedom for the world, the shining city on a hill, if we reject the regressive, failed ideas still promulgated by the left. We just need to remind ourselves: we've seen this before.

ENDNOTES

1. Nolan D. McCaskill, "Obama: I'm not responsible for Trump," *Politico*, 11/15/2016; (https://www.politico.com/story/2016/11/obama-trump-not-my-fault-231411)
2. "Democrats lost over 1,000 seats under Obama," Fox News, 12/27/2016; (http://www.foxnews.com/politics/2016/12/27/democrats-lost-over-1000-seats-under-obama.html)
3. P.J. Gladnick, "60 Minutes Broadcast Edits Out Laughable Obama Claim as 4th Best President", *Newsbusters*, 12/16/2011; (http://newsbusters.org/blogs/pj-gladnick/2011/12/16/60-minutes-broadcast-edits-out-laughable-obama-claim-4th-greatest-presi)
4. Michael D. Shear and Gardiner Harris, "With High-Profile Help, Obama Plots Life After Presidency", *New York Times*, 8/16/2015; (http://www.nytimes.com/2015/08/17/us/politics/with-high-profile-help-obama-plots-life-after-presidency.html)
5. Huma Khan, "What Does One Get a Queen?" *ABC News*, 04/01/2009, (http://abcnews.go.com/blogs/politics/2009/04/what-does-one-g/)
6. Toby Harnden, "Barack Obama's gift for the Queen: an iPod, your Majesty," *The Telegraph*, 04/01/2009, (http://blogs.telegraph.co.uk/news/tobyharnden/9355453/Barack_Obamas_gift_for_the_Queen_an_iPod_your_Majesty/)
7. Emily Yoffe, "Today We Are Gathered ... To Hear More About Me," *Slate*, 12/21/2012, (http://www.slate.com/articles/news_and_politics/politics/2012/12/barack_obama_s_eulogy_to_daniel_inouye_told_us_more_about_the_president.html)
8. Mike Flynn, "To Honor Neil Armstrong, Obama Posts Photo of Himself," *Breitbart*, 8/26/2012 (http://www.breitbart.com/Big-Government/2012/08/26/to-honor-neil-armstrong-obama-posts-a-picture-of-himself)
9. "President Obama Honors Rosa Parks Anniversary With Picture of...Himself," *Fox News*, 12/02/2012, (http://nation.foxnews.com/obama/2012/12/02/president-obama-honors-rosa-parks-anniversary-picture-himself)

10. The White House (WhiteHouse) "President Obama on President Kennedy and the American spirit —> http://go.wh.gov/j4dUY6 #JFK, pic.twitter.com/1irDH153L1" 22 November 2013 11:34 a.m. Tweet
11. The White House (WhiteHouse) "Rest in peace, Nelson Mandela. pic.twitter.com/4qlqsXLp6e" 5 December 2013 3:07 p.m. Tweet
12. William Bigelow, "Obama Honors Pearl Harbor Dead with Picture of Himself" *Breitbart*, 12/8/2013 (http://www.breitbart.com/Big-Government/2013/12/07/Obama-Inserts-Picture-of-Himself-to-Honor-Pearl-Harbor-Dead)
13. Seth Mandel, "Obama Drops His Name Into the Other Presidential Biographies," *Commentary*, 05/15/2012, (http://www.commentarymagazine.com/2012/05/15/obama-drops-his-name-into-presidential-biographies/)
14. Ian Schwartz, "Obama Criticizes Sending Children to Private Schools: 'Contributes To Less Opportunity For All Our Kids'," *Real Clear Politics*, 5/13/2015; (https://www.realclearpolitics.com/video/2015/05/13/obama_criticizes_children_attending_private_schools_contributes_to_less_opportunity_for_all_our_kids.html)
15. Steven Mufson and Greg Jaffe, "Under fire for inaction, Obama orders flags lowered for Chattanooga victims," *The Washington Post*, 7/21/2015; (https://www.washingtonpost.com/politics/obama-orders-flags-to-half-staff-for-victims-of-chattanooga-rampage/2015/07/21/aac952a6-2fdb-11e5-8353-1215475949f4_story.html)
16. Peggy Noonan, "A New Kind of 'Credibility' Gap" *The Wall Street Journal*, 9/2/2013 (http://online.wsj.com/news/articles/SB10001424127887323808204579085560400501346)
17. Kate Hicks, "Awkward: Obama Blames Bush for Economy While Standing Next to Him," *Townhall*, 05/31/2012, (http://townhall.com/tipsheet/katehicks/2012/05/31/awkward_obama_blames_bush_for_economy_while_standing_next_to_him)
18. Matthew Mosk and Brian Ross. "Solyndra Hearing: Blame It On Bush, Say Obama Officials" ABC News. 12/26/2012. (http://abcnews.go.com/Blotter/solyndra-blame-bush-obama-officials/story?id=14513389#.UNsIa2_AcsI)

19. Mary Bruce, "Obama Blames GOP for Inability to Pass Immigration Reform," ABC News, 09/20/2012, (http://abcnews.go.com/blogs/politics/2012/09/obama-blames-gop-for-inability-to-pass-immigration-reform/)
20. Darlene Superville, "Obama Appeals for an End to Partisan Politics – With a Jab at GOP," Associated Press, 10/30/2010, (http://www.msnbc.msn.com/id/39922794/ns/politics-decision_2010/t/obama-appeals-end-partisan-politics-jab-gop/)
21. Fred Hiatt, "Next Time, Obama May go Over Congress' Head," *The Washington Post*, 09/04/2012, (http://www.washingtonpost.com/blogs/post-partisan/post/next-time-obama-may-go-over-congresss-head/2012/09/04/9073eb30-f6ba-11e1-8398-0327ab83ab91_blog.html)
22. Ibid.
23. Ewen MacAskill, "Barack Obama Accused of Giving Partisan Inauguration Speech," *The Guardian*, 01/22/2013, (http://www.guardian.co.uk/world/2013/jan/22/obama-inauguration-speech-republican-compromise)
24. Liz Goodwin, "Conservatives React to Obama Inaugural Speech," *Yahoo News*, 01/22/2013, (http://news.yahoo.com/blogs/ticket/conservatives-react-obama-inaugural-speech-161537952--election.html)
25. Sarah Tanksalvala, "Obama's Inaugural Address Quotes Constitution While Misrepresenting Opposition," *Examiner*, 01/23/2013, (http://www.examiner.com/article/obama-s-inaugural-address-quotes-constitution-while-misrepresenting-opposition)
26. Yuval Levin, "Obama's Second Inaugural," *National Review*, 01/22/2013, (http://www.nationalreview.com/corner/338366/obama-s-second-inaugural-yuval-levin)
27. Ron Fournier, "Post-Partisan No More: Who Is the New Obama?" *National Journal*, 1/22/2013, (http://www.nationaljournal.com/politics/post-partisan-no-more-who-is-the-new-obama-20130122)
28. David Ignatius, "A flat, partisan and pedestrian speech," *The Washington Post*, 1/21/2013, (http://www.washingtonpost.com/blogs/post-partisan/wp/2013/01/21/obama-inaugurala-flat-partisan-and-pedestrian-speech/)
29. Ibid.

30. CQ Transcripts, "Sens. Obama and Biden Deliver Remarks in Springfield, IL," *The Washington Post*, 08/23/2008, (http://www.washingtonpost.com/wp-dyn/content/article/2008/08/28/AR2008082803216.html)
31. "Bring Democrats and Republicans Together to Pass an Agenda," *Tampa Bay Time Politifact*, 08/31/2012, (http://www.politifact.com/truth-o-meter/promises/obameter/promise/522/bring-democrats-and-republicans-together-pass-agen/)
32. Gallup Daily: Obama Job Approval, (http://www.gallup.com/poll/113980/Gallup-Daily-Obama-Job-Approval.aspx)
33. Jeffry M. Jones, "Obama Job Approval Ratings Most Politically Polarized by Far," Gallup, 1/25/2017; (http://news.gallup.com/poll/203006/obama-job-approval-ratings-politically-polarized-far.aspx)
34. Byron York, "In defeat, Obama tells GOP: My mandate is bigger than yours," *The Washington Examiner*, 11/6/14; (http://www.washingtonexaminer.com/in-defeat-obama-tells-gop-my-mandate-is-bigger-than-yours/article/2555866)
35. Walter Hickey, "Obama Really Wishes He Never Gave This Speech About the Debt Ceiling," *Business Insider*, 01/14/2013 (http://www.businessinsider.com/obama-voted-against-debt-ceiling-increase-2006-2013-1)
36. Talman Bradley, "Obama White House Discloses Two More Lobbyist Waivers Granted," ABC News, 03/10/2009, (http://abcnews.go.com/blogs/politics/2009/03/obama-white-hou/)
37. "Support Human Mission to Moon by 2020," *Politifact*, 02/15/2010, (http://www.politifact.com/truth-o-meter/promises/obameter/promise/339/support-human-mission-to-moon-by-2020/)
38. "Reduce earmarks to 1994 levels," *Politifact*, 2/19/2010, (http://www.politifact.com/truth-o-meter/promises/obameter/promise/431/reduce-earmarks-to-1994-levels/)
39. "No Proposal to End Taxes for Seniors Making Less Than $50,000," *Politifact*, 04/15/2009, (http://www.politifact.com/truth-o-meter/promises/obameter/promise/24/end-income-tax-for-seniors-making-less-than/)

40. Josh Gerstein, "President Obama Hails Return to PAYGO," *Politico*, 02/13/2010, (http://www.politico.com/news/stories/0210/32921.html)
41. Mary Bruce, "Obama Argues Rising Gas Costs are Not His Fault," ABC News, 02/25/2012, (http://abcnews.go.com/blogs/politics/2012/02/obama-argues-rising-gas-costs-are-not-his-fault/)
42. "Obama Unveils Plan to Wean Americans Off Foreign Oil," *Montreal Gazette*, 8/5/2008, (http://www.canada.com/story.html?id=9ffe2146-39a6-4aa2-bd31-5c868b744214)
43. "Pipeline Politics: Misguided Obama Blocks Keystone Pipeline," *Chicago Tribune*, 01/19/2012, (http://www.chicagotribune.com/news/opinion/editorials/ct-edit-pipeline-20120119,0,3017097.story)
44. Greg McDonald, "Flashback: Obama Argued Against Mandate in 2008," *Newsmax*, 03/29/2012, (http://www.newsmax.com/Newsfront/Obamacare-Clinton-mandate-court/2012/03/29/id/434199)
45. Todd Beamon, "Rules Issued for Obamacare's Individual Mandate," *Newsmax*, 01/30/2013, (http://www.newsmax.com/Newsfront/individual-manage-regulations-issued/2013/01/30/id/488132)
46. Elizabeth White, "Obama Says Gitmo Facility Should Close," *The Washington Post*, 6/24/2007, (http://www.washingtonpost.com/wp-dyn/content/article/2007/06/24/AR2007062401046_pf.html)
47. Michael McAuliff, "Indefinite Detention Ban Stayed by Appeals Judge in NDAA Case," *Huffington Post*, 09/18/2012, (http://www.huffingtonpost.com/2012/09/18/indefinite-detention-ban-_n_1893652.html)
48. Jenny Percival, "Barack Obama compares oil spill to 9/11," *The Guardian*, 6/14/2010, (http://www.guardian.co.uk/environment/2010/jun/14/barack-obama-oil-spill-911)
49. Joe Newby, "Tucson event more political rally than memorial service," *Examiner*, 1/13/2011, (http://www.examiner.com/article/tucson-event-more-political-rally-than-memorial-service)
50. Jim Hoft, "Gross. Barack Obama Uses Sandy Hook Massacre to Push Tax Hikes (Video)," *Gateway Pundit*, 12/19/2012, (http://www.thegatewaypundit.com/2012/12/

gross-barack-obama-uses-sandy-hook-massacre-to-push-tax-hikes-video/)

51. Perry Chiaramonte, "Forgotten by FEMA: Staten Island's Sandy victims vent over lack of aid," Fox News, 11/8/2012, (http://www.foxnews.com/us/2012/11/08/volunteers-step-in-for-fema-in-storm-ravaged-nyc-borough)
52. Kate Zernike, "Gasoline Runs Short, Adding Woes to Storm Recovery", *The New York Times*, 11/1/2012; (http://www.nytimes.com/2012/11/02/nyregion/gasoline-shortages-disrupting-recovery-from-hurricane.html)
53. Lisa L Colangelo, "Exclusive: City Controller Scott Stringer Launching Audit of Build it Back Hurricane Sandy Home Re-Building Program", *New York Daily News*, 4/17/2014; (http://www.nydailynews.com/new-york/exclusive-city-audit-build-back-article-1.1759058)
54. Billy Hallowell, "Hurricane Sandy Victim Who Hugged Obama in Viral Photo Claims He Broke Aid Promise, Sent Her 'Disturbing' Form Letter," *The Blaze*, 1/4/2013 (http://www.theblaze.com/stories/2013/01/04/hurricane-sandy-victim-in-viral-photo-claims-obama-broke-aid-promise-sent-her-disturbing-form-letter-response/)
55. Keith Koffler, "Election Over, Obama Returns to Golf," *White House Dossier*, 11/10/2012, (http://www.whitehousedossier.com/2012/11/10/election-obama-returns-golf/)
56. Roger Runningen and Margaret Talev, "Obama Promising Millions in Aid for California's Drought," *Bloomberg*, 2/14/2014 (http://www.bloomberg.com/news/2014-02-14/obama-promising-millions-in-aid-for-california-s-drought.html)
57. Pete Kasperowitz, "House passes California drought bill to override Obama on environment," *The Hill*, 2/5/2014 (http://thehill.com/blogs/floor-action/votes/197585-house-picks-people-over-fish-with-california-drought-bill)
58. Central Valley Project. (n.d.). In Wikipedia. Retrieved March 30, 2014, from http://en.wikipedia.org/wiki/Central_Valley_Project
59. Pete Kasperowitz, "House passes California drought bill to override Obama on environment," *The Hill*, 2/5/2014 (http://thehill.com/blogs/floor-action/

votes/197585-house-picks-people-over-fish-with-california-drought-bill)

60. Bobby Jindal. *Leadership and Crisis.* Washington D.C.: Regnery Pub, 2010. Print.
61. Karl Rove, "Yes, the Gulf Spill is Obama's Katrina," *The Wall Street Journal*, 5/27/2010, (http://online.wsj.com/article/SB10001424052748704717004575268752362770856.html)
62. John M. Broder, "Report Slams Administration for Underestimating Gulf Spill," *The New York Times,* 10/6/2010, (http://www.nytimes.com/2010/10/07/science/earth/07spill.html)
63. "Editorial: Obama's race-baiting," *Washington Times*, 5/3/2010; (http://www.washingtontimes.com/news/2010/may/3/obamas-race-baiting/)
64. "Interview with President Obama," *The New York Times*, 7/27/2013; (http://www.nytimes.com/2013/07/28/us/politics/interview-with-president-obama.html)
65. David Remnick, "Going The Distance: On and Off The Road with Barack Obama," *The New Yorker*, 1/27/2014; (http://www.newyorker.com/reporting/2014/01/27/140127fa_fact_remnick)
66. Neil Munro, "Hope and Change: Obama Uses Racial Politics to Justify Marijuana Legalization," *The Daily Caller*, 1/20/2014; (http://dailycaller.com/2014/01/20/hope-and-change-obama-uses-racial-politics-to-justify-marijuana-legalization/)
67. "Obama: Police who arrested professor 'acted stupidly'," *CNN*, 7/23/2009, (http://www.cnn.com/2009/US/07/22/harvard.gates.interview/)
68. Stephanie Condon, "Obama: 'If I Had a Son, He'd Look Like Trayvon'," CBS News, 03/23/2012, (http://www.cbsnews.com/8301-503544_162-57403200-503544/obama-if-i-had-a-son-hed-look-like-trayvon/)
69. Susan Jones, "Sebelius: Obamacare Opponents Are Like Those Who Opposed Civil Rights," CNS News, 7/17/2013; (http://cnsnews.com/news/article/sebelius-obamacare-opponents-are-those-who-opposed-civil-rights)
70. Tiffany Madison, "MADISON: Holder's Department of Justice is racist, lawless," *The*

Washington Times, 8/20/2013; (http://communities.washingtontimes.com/neighborhood/citizen-warrior/2013/aug/20/madison-holders-department-justice-racist-lawless/)

71. Don Lee, "Obama calls for persistence in confronting 'deeply rooted' racism," *Los Angeles Times*, 12/7/2014;, (http://www.latimes.com/nation/la-na-obama-race-police-bet-interview-20141207-story.html)
72. "Advisory: NPR News Interview With President Obama," NPR, 12/27/2014; (http://www.npr.org/about-npr/372903748/advisory-npr-news-interview)
73. Brian MacQuarrie, "Racial Divide Expected to Persist in U.S.," *The Boston Globe*, 11/20/2012, (http://www.bostonglobe.com/news/nation/2012/11/20/despite-obama-presidency-racial-divide-expected-persist-united-states/ONPO9LRIasUfGrLYWM3m7H/story.html)
74. Julie Bykowicz, "Most Americans See Race Relations Worsening Since Obama's Election," *Bloomberg*, 12/7/2014; (http://www.bloomberg.com/politics/articles/2014-12-07/bloomberg-politics-poll-finds-most-americans-see-race-relations-worsening-since-obamas-election/)
75. Jim Norman, "U.S. Worries About Race Relations Reach a New High," Gallup, 4/11/2016; (http://www.gallup.com/poll/190574/worries-race-relations-reach-new-high.aspx)
76. The White House, The Press Office. (2013) Executive Order -- White House Initiative on Educational Excellence for African Americans. Retrieved from http://www.whitehouse.gov/the-press-office/2012/07/26/executive-order-white-house-initiative-educational-excellence-african-am
77. Neil Munro, "Obama backs race-based school discipline policies," *The Daily Caller*, 7/27/2012, (http://dailycaller.com/2012/07/27/obama-backs-race-based-school-discipline-policies/)
78. Michael Meyers, "Obama's Executive Order Puts Blacks In the Corner At the U.S. Department of Education," *The Huffington Post*, August 7, 2012, (http://www.huffingtonpost.com/michael-meyers/obamas-hbcu-executive-order_b_1726291.html)
79. Jessica Vaughn, "ICE Document Details 36,000 Criminal Alien Releases in 2013," Center for

Immigration Studies, May 12, 2014 (http://www.cis.org/ICE-Document-Details-36000-Criminal-Aliens-Release-in-2013)

80. Stephen Dinan, "Feds released hundreds of immigrant murderers, drunk drivers, sex-crimes convicts," *The Washington Times*, 5/12/20142 (http://www.washingtontimes.com/news/2014/may/12/feds-released-hundreds-immigrant-murderers-drunken/?page=2)
81. Jessica Vaughn, "ICE Document Details 36,000 Criminal Alien Releases in 2013," Center for Immigration Studies, May 12, 2014 (http://www.cis.org/ICE-Document-Details-36000-Criminal-Aliens-Release-in-2013)
82. Tony Lee, "Obama: Amnesty Bill That Rewards Illegals Means 'Everyone Play The Same Rules'," *Breitbart*, 3/26/2014 (http://www.breitbart.com/Big-Government/2014/03/26/Obama-Amnesty-Bill-that-Rewards-Illegals-Means-Everyone-Plays-By-the-Same-Rules)
83. Charles C. Johnson and Ryan Girdusky, "As college student, Eric Holder participated in 'armed' takeover of former Columbia University ROTC office," *The Daily Caller*, 9/30/2012 (http://dailycaller.com/2012/09/30/as-college-sophomore-eric-holder-participated-in-armed-takeover-of-former-columbia-university-rotc-office/)
84. Patrick Howley, "Al Sharpton Talking to White House About New Attorney General Pick", *The Daily Caller*, 9/25/2014; (http://dailycaller.com/2014/09/25/al-sharpton-talking-to-the-white-house-about-new-attorney-general-pick/)
85. Patrick Howley, "Obama Attorney General Pick: Voter ID Laws Are About Taking Back What Dr. King Won', *The Daily Caller*, 11/9/2014; (http://dailycaller.com/2014/11/09/obama-attorney-general-pick-voter-id-laws-are-about-taking-back-what-dr-king-won/)
86. Judson Phillips, "Loretta Lynch and the GOP surrender caucus", *Washington Times*, 1/30/2015; (http://www.washingtontimes.com/news/2015/jan/30/judson-phillips-loretta-lynch-and-gop-surrender-ca/?page=all)
87. Matthew Boyle, "Loretta Lynch: Illegal Aliens Have Right to Work As Much As American Citizens", *Breitbart*, 1/28/2015; (http://www.

breitbart.com/big-government/2015/01/28/loretta-lynch-illegal-aliens-have-right-to-work-as-much-as-american-citizens/)

88. Ginger Gibson, "Attorney General Nominee Omitted HSBC Interview From Senate Questionnaire", *International Business Times*, 1/27/2015; (http://www.ibtimes.com/attorney-general-nominee-loretta-lynch-omitted-hsbc-interview-senate-questionnaire-1796924)
89. Dana Bash and Emily Sherman, "Sotomayor 'Wise Latina' Quote Used on Multiple Occasions," *CNN Politics*, 06/05/2009, (http://politicalticker.blogs.cnn.com/2009/06/05/sotomayor-wise-latina-quote-used-on-multiple-occasions/)
90. Ed Whelan, "Former Puerto Rican Nationalist Nominated to North American Supreme Court," *National Review Online – Bench Memos,* (http://www.nationalreview.com/bench-memos/49993/former-puerto-rican-nationalist-nominated-north-american-supreme-court/ed-whelan)
91. Ed Morrissey, "New DHS Folly: the Domestic Extremism Lexicon." *Hot Air,* 05/01/2009, (http://hotair.com/archives/2009/05/01/new-dhs-folly-the-domestic-extremism-lexicon/)
92. Ben Conery, "Kagan Kicked out Campus Recruiters at First Chance," *The Washington Times,* 05/12/2010, (http://www.washingtontimes.com/news/2010/may/12/kagan-kicked-out-campus-recruiters-at-first-chance)
93. John Byrne, "Kagan Helped Shield Saudis from 9/11 Lawsuits," *Raw Story*, 05/11/2010, (http://www.rawstory.com/rs/2010/05/11/kagan-helped-shield-saudis-911-lawsuits/)
94. Guatham Nagesh, "U.S. Plans to Give Up Oversight of Web Domain Manager," *The Wall Street Journa*l, 3/14/2014 (http://online.wsj.com/news/articles/SB10001424052702303546204579439653103639452)
95. L. Gordon Crovitz, "America's Internet Surrender," *The Wall Street Journal*, 3/18/2014 (http://online.wsj.com/news/articles/SB10001424052702303563304579447362610955656)
96. Ibid.
97. bid.

98. "FCC Official Warns Obama-backed Net Neutrality Plan Would Bring 'Immediate' Internet Tax", Fox News, 11/17/2014; (http://www.foxnews.com/politics/2014/11/17/fcc-official-warns-obama-backed-net-neutrality-plan-will-bring-backdoor-tax-on/)
99. Phil Kerpen, "Obama's Taxing Plan to Regulate the Internet," *CNSNews*, 11/13/2014; (http://cnsnews.com/commentary/phil-kerpen/obama-s-taxing-plan-regulate-internet)
100. Michael Mandel, "Obama's Plan to Regulate the Internet Would Do More Harm Than Good", *The Washington Post*, 11/14/2014; (http://www.washingtonpost.com/opinions/obamas-internet-rules-would-do-more-harm-than-good/2014/11/14/64a795d0-6b82-11e4-a31c-77759fc1eacc_story.html)
101. Brendan Sasso, "Republican FCC Commissioner: Public Is Being Misled About Net-Neutrality Plan", *National Journal*, 2/10/2015; (http://www.nationaljournal.com/tech/republican-fcc-commissioner-public-is-being-misled-about-net-neutrality-plan-20150210)
102. "61% Oppose Federal Regulation of the Internet" *Rasmussen Reports*, 11/13/2014; (http://www.rasmussenreports.com/public_content/lifestyle/general_lifestyle/november_2014/61_oppose_federal_regulation_of_the_internet)
103. Alina Selyukh and Roberta Rampton, "Exclusive: White House says net neutrality legislation not needed," Reuters, 1/15/2015; (http://www.reuters.com/article/2015/01/15/us-usa-internet-neutrality-exclusive-idUSKBN0KO2JO20150115)
104. Brian Hughes, "Net neutrality approved," *The Washington Examiner*, 2/26/2015; (http://www.washingtonexaminer.com/net-neutrality-approved/article/2560759)
105. Matthew Vadum, "National Endowment for the Arts is Trying to Create a Cult of Obama," *The American Spectator*, 09/01/2009, (http://spectator.org/blog/2009/09/01/national-endowment-for-the-art)
106. Ibid
107. Ben Shapiro, "At Least 6 Federal Laws and Regulations Violated by the NEA Conference Call," *Breitbart*, 09/22/2009, (http://www.breitbart.com/Big-Hollywood/2009/09/22/At-Least-6-Federal-Laws-and-Regulations-Violated-By-the-NEA-Conference-Call)

108. Motoko Rich " 'No Child' Law Whittled Down by White House," *The New York Times*, 07/06/2012, (http://www.nytimes.com/2012/07/06/education/no-child-left-behind-whittled-down-under-obama.html)
109. Lindsey Burke, Brittany Corona, Jennifer A. Marshall, Rachel Sheffield and Sandra Stotsky "Common Core National Standards and Tests: Empty Promises and Increased Federal Overreach Into Education," *The Heritage Foundation*, 10/7/2013 (http://www.heritage.org/research/reports/2013/10/common-core-national-standards-and-tests-empty-promises-and-increased-federal-overreach-into-education)
110. Brittany Corona, "No Child Left Behind Waivers: Tethers to the Feds," *The Heritage Foundation*, 10/6/2013 (http://www.heritage.org/research/reports/2010/01/a-smarter-path-to-a-race-to-the-top-in-education-reform)
111. Blaine Greteman, "Federal Bureaucrats Declare 'Hunger Games' More Complex Than 'The Grapes of Wrath' ", *The New Republic*, 10/29/2013; http://www.newrepublic.com/article/115393/common-core-standards-make-mockery-novels-complexity
112. Fr. John Zuhlsdorf, "Obama Math: 'Common Core' Curriculum to Infect Catholic Schools?", *Fr Z's Blog*, 8/19/2013; http://wdtprs.com/blog/2013/08/obamamath-common-core-curriculum-to-infect-catholic-schools/
113. Al Baker, "Common Core Curriculum Now Has Critics on the Left," *The New York Times*, 2/16/2014 (http://www.nytimes.com/2014/02/17/nyregion/new-york-early-champion-of-common-core-standards-joins-critics.html?hp&_r=3)
114. "Tuition Costs of Colleges and Universities," National Center for Education Statistics, accessed 12/08/2012
115. Mary Beth Marklein, "College Costs Going Up At Slower Rate," *USA Today*, 10/24/12, (http://www.usatoday.com/story/news/nation/2012/10/23/college-tuition-costs/1643921/)
116. Kathleen Kingsbury, "College Costs Stall As Borrowing Falls, Study Says," Reuters, 10/24/12, (http://www.reuters.com/article/2012/10/24/us-education-college-costs-idUSBRE89N06R20121024)

117. Jordan Weissmann, "53% of Recent College Grads Are Jobless or Underemployed—How?", *The Atlantic*, 4/23/2012; (http://www.theatlantic.com/business/archive/2012/04/53-of-recent-college-grads-are-jobless-or-underemployed-how/256237/)
118. Lynn Adler, "U.S. 2009 Foreclosures Shatter Record Despite Aid," Reuters, 01/14/2010, (http://www.reuters.com/article/2010/01/14/us-usa-housing-foreclosures-idUSTRE60D0LZ20100114)
119. "1.8 Million U.S. Properties With Foreclosure Filings in 2012," *RealtyTrac*, 01/14/2013
120. "2012 Foreclosure Activity Up in 57 Percent of Metro Areas...," *RealtyTrac*, 01/28/2013
121. Les Christie, "Foreclosures Hit 6 Year Low in 2013," CNN Money, 1/16/2014; http://money.cnn.com/2014/01/16/real_estate/foreclosure-crisis/
122. Brena Swanson, "Realty Trac: Monthly Foreclosure Filings Reverse Course, Rise 8%", *Housing Wire*, 2/13/2014; http://www.housingwire.com/articles/28952-realtytrac-foreclosure-filings-reverse-course-rise-8
123. Binyamin Appelbaum, "Cautious Moves on Foreclosures Haunting Obama," *The New York Times*, 08/19/2012, (http://www.nytimes.com/2012/08/20/business/economy/slow-response-to-housing-crisis-now-weighs-on-obama.html)
124. Chris Isidore, "Home Prices Rebound," CNN Money, 9/25/2012 (http://money.cnn.com/2012/09/25/real_estate/home-prices/index.html)
125. Edward J. Pinto, "The Next Housing Bailout? Big Trouble Brewing at the FHA," *The Atlantic*, 11/16/2012, (http://www.theatlantic.com/business/archive/2012/11/the-next-housing-bailout-big-trouble-brewing-at-the-fha/265359/)
126. Margaret Chadbourn, "U.S. Federal Housing Administration to tap $1.7 bln in taxpayer fund," Reuters, 9/27/2013 (http://www.reuters.com/article/2013/09/27/usa-housing-bailout-idUSW1N0G702P20130927)
127. Abby Ohlheiser, "Activists release a fourth undercover video as the battle over Planned Parenthood intensifies," *The Washington Post*, 7/30/2015; (https://www.washingtonpost.com/news/acts-of-faith/wp/2015/07/30/activists-release-a-fourth-undercover-video-as-the-battle-over-planned-parenthood-intensifies/)

128. Lena H. Sun, "Obama officials warn states about cutting Medicaid funds to Planned Parenthood," *The Washington Post*, 4/19/2016; (https://www.washingtonpost.com/news/post-nation/wp/2016/04/19/obama-officials-warn-states-about-cutting-medicaid-funds-to-planned-parenthood/)
129. Steven Ertelt, "Obama Punishes Kansas for De-Funding Planned Parenthood by Cutting Its Title X Funding," LifeNews, 8/26/2015; (http://www.lifenews.com/2015/08/26/obama-punishes-kansas-for-de-funding-planned-parenthood-by-cutting-its-medicaid-funding/)
130. Julian Pecquet, "Health Plans Ordered to Cover Birth Control Without Co-Pays," *The Hill*, 01/20/2012, (http://thehill.com/blogs/healthwatch/health-reform-implementation/205413-obama-administration-orders-health-plans-to-cover-birth-control-without-co-pays)
131. "HHS Mandate Information Central," The Becket Fund, (http://www.becketfund.org/hhsinformationcentral/)
132. "Attorney: Hobby Lobby to Defy Morning-After Pill Insurance Requirement While Lawsuit is Pending," Associated Press, 12/27/2012, (http://www.newser.com/article/da3ee7s01/attorney-hobby-lobby-to-defy-morning-after-pill-insurance-requirement-while-lawsuits-pending.html)
133. Andre Tartar, "David Axelrod Talks with John Heilmann: A Constitutional Amendment to Overturn Citizens United?," *New York Magazine*, 06/12/2012, (http://nymag.com/daily/intel/2012/06/david-axelrod-on-how-to-overturn-citizens-united.html)
134. "U.S. Supreme Court: Citizens United v Federal Election Commission"; 12/21/2010, PDF Document retrieved from http://www.supremecourt.gov/opinions/09pdf/08-205.pdf
135. Eugene Volokh, "The 'People's Rights Amendment' and the Media," *The Volokh Conspiracy*, 4/26/2012, (http://www.volokh.com/2012/04/26/the-peoples-rights-amendment-and-the-media/)
136. "JW Obtains Records Detailing Obama administration's Warrantless Collection of Citizens' Personal Financial Data," *Judicial Watch*, 6/27/2013 (http://www.judicialwatch.org/press-room/press-releases/

jw-obtains-records-detailing-obama-administrations-warrantless-collection-of-citizens-personal-financial-data/)
137. Richard Pollock, "CFPB's data-mining on consumer credit cards challenged in heated House hearing," *The Washington Examiner*, 9/13/2013 (http://washingtonexaminer.com/cfpbs-data-mining-on-consumer-credit-cards-challenged-in-heated-house-hearing/article/2535726)
138. Richard Pollock, "Federal Consumer Bureau Data-Mining Hundreds of Millions of Consumer Credit Card Accounts, Mortgages," *The Washington Examiner*, 1/28/2014, (http://washingtonexaminer.com/federal-consumer-bureau-data-mining-hundreds-of-millions-of-consumer-credit-card-accounts-mortgages/article/2543039)
139. US Energy Information Administration, http://www.eia.gov/coal/ accessed 12/08/2012
140. Steve Mufson, "The Last Minute Obama-McCain Coal Debate," *The Washington Post*, 11/3/2008, (http://newsweek.washingtonpost.com/postglobal/energywire/2008/11/the_last_minute_obama-mccain_c.html)
141. Michael Bastasch, "Report: More Than 200 Coal-Fired Generators Slated for Shutdown," *The Daily Caller*, 09/21/2012 (http://dailycaller.com/2012/09/21/report-more-than-200-coal-fired-generators-slated-for-shutdown/)
142. "Obama Administration Imposes Five-Year Drilling Ban on Majority of Offshore Areas," House Natural Resources Committee, Press Release, 11/08/2011 (http://naturalresources.house.gov/news/documentsingle.aspx?DocumentID=267985)
143. Wendy Koch, "Obama bans offshore oil drilling in Atlantic waters," *USA Today*, 12/2/2010, (http://usatoday30.usatoday.com/news/washington/environment/2010-12-02-oildrill02_ST_N.htm)
144. Julie Seymour, "Pump Prices Running Out of Gas - Fall Below $3 for First Time in More than Three and a Half Years", CNS News, 11/1/2014, (http://cnsnews.com/mrctv-blog/julia-seymour/pump-prices-running-out-gas-fall-below-3-first-time-more-three-and-half)

145. "Obama threatens to wield veto pen to counter GOP-led Congress" Fox News, 12/29/2014; (http://www.foxnews.com/politics/2014/12/29/obama-threatens-to-wield-veto-pen-to-counter-gop-led-congress/)
146. Juliet Eilperin and Katie Zezima, "Obama vetoes Keystone XL bill," *The Washington Post*, 2/24/2015; (http://www.washingtonpost.com/news/post-politics/wp/2015/02/24/keystone-xl-bill-a-k-a-veto-bait-heads-to-presidents-desk/)
147. JulietEilperinandStevenMufson,"StateDepartmentreleasesKeystone XL final environmental impact statement," *The Washington Post*, 1/31/2014; (https://www.washingtonpost.com/business/economy/state-to-release-keystones-final-environmental-impact-statement-friday/2014/01/31/3a9bb25c-8a83-11e3-a5bd-844629433ba3_story.html)
148. Kelly David Burke, "Obama administration cuts back oil shale development", Fox News, 6/22/2013; (http://www.foxnews.com/politics/2013/06/22/obama-administration-cuts-back-oil-shale-development/)
149. Mike Brownfield, "EPA Blocks Oil Drilling in Alaska," *Daily Signal*, 4/25/2011; (http://dailysignal.com/2011/04/25/epa-blocks-oil-drilling-in-alaska/)
150. "Oil and Gas Production on Federal Lands Still a Disappointment," Institute for Energy Research, 4/24/2014 (http://instituteforenergyresearch.org/analysis/oil-and-gas-production-on-federal-lands-still-a-disappointment/)
151. Darrell Issa, "Obama's Bad Policy, Harmful Regulations Add to Gas Prices," *US News and World Report*, 05/27/2011, (http://www.usnews.com/opinion/articles/2011/05/27/obamas-bad-policy-harmful-regulations-add-to-gas-prices)
152. "Obama and Reid's Energy Tax Puts Ideology Above Economics," Pete Sepp, *US News and World Report*, 03/07/2012, (http://www.usnews.com/opinion/blogs/on-energy/2012/03/07/obama-and-reids-energy-tax-puts-ideology-above-economics)
153. "American economy stronger than Obama incompetence," *The Washington Times*; 1/1/2015; (http://www.washingtontimes.com/news/2015/jan/1/editorial-american-economy-stronger-than-obama-inc/)

154. "Barack Obama's Acceptance Speech," *The New York Times*, 8/28/2008; (http://www.nytimes.com/2008/08/28/us/politics/28text-obama.html)
155. Jerome Hudson, "22 Times Obama Admin Declare Climate Change a Greater Threat Than Terrorism," *Breitbart*, 11/14/2015; (http://www.breitbart.com/big-government/2015/11/14/22-times-obama-admin-declared-climate-change-greater-threat-terrorism/)
156. Melanie Hunter, "Obama Links Islamic Terrorism to Climate Change", CNS News, 5/20/2015; (http://cnsnews.com/news/article/melanie-hunter/obama-links-islamic-terrorism-climate-change)
157. Stephen Dinan, "Obama clean energy loans leave taxpayers in $2.2 billion hole," *The Washington Times*, 4/27/2015; (http://www.washingtontimes.com/news/2015/apr/27/obama-backed-green-energy-failures-leave-taxpayers/)
158. Rowan Scarborough; "Pentagon orders commanders to prioritize climate change in all military actions," *The Washington Times*, 2/7/2016; (http://www.washingtontimes.com/news/2016/feb/7/pentagon-orders-commanders-to-prioritize-climate-c/)
159. Andrew Follett, "Obama's NASA Budget Is All About Global Warming, Not Space," *The Daily Caller*, 2/10/2016; (http://dailycaller.com/2016/02/10/obamas-nasa-budget-is-all-about-global-warming-not-space/)
160. Marita Noon, "Killing Coal: The Obama Administration's Intentional Assault on an Industry," *Breitbart*, 1/19/2016; (http://www.breitbart.com/big-government/2016/01/19/killing-coal-the-obama-administrations-intentional-assault-on-an-industry/)
161. Hans von Spokovsky, "Attorney General Lynch Looks Into Prosecuting 'Climate Change Deniers,' " *The Daily Signal*, 3/10/2016; (http://dailysignal.com/2016/03/10/attorney-general-lynch-looking-into-prosecuting-climate-change-deniers/)
162. Rowan Scarborough; "Pentagon wrestles with bogus climate warnings as funds shifted to green agenda," *The Washington Times*, 6/1/2014; (http://www.washingtontimes.com/news/2014/jun/1/pentagon-wrestles-with-false-climate-predictions-a/)

163. Keith Johnson, "How Carbon Dioxide Became a 'Pollutant,' " *The Wall Street Journal*, 4/18/2009; (http://www.wsj.com/articles/SB124001537515830975)
164. Nicholas Loris, "EPA Formally Declares CO2 a Dangerous Pollutant," *The Daily Signal*, 12/7/2009; (http://dailysignal.com/2009/12/07/epa-formally-declares-co2-a-dangerous-pollutant/)
165. Evan Lehmann, "Senate Abandons Climate Effort, Dealing Blow to President," *The New York Times*, 7/23/2010; (http://www.nytimes.com/cwire/2010/07/23/23climatewire-senate-abandons-climate-effort-dealing-blow-88864.html)
166. Keith Goldberg, "High Court Stay Could Spell Doom For EPA's Clean Power Plan," *Law360*, 2/16/2016; (http://www.law360.com/articles/757509/high-court-stay-could-spell-doom-for-epa-s-clean-power-plan)
167. Jim DeMint, "How Obama will celebrate 'Earth Day,' " *The Washington Times* 4/21/2016; (http://www.washingtontimes.com/news/2016/apr/21/jim-demint-obama-bypasses-senate-approval-of-paris/)
168. Sen James Lankford, "Obama Raided $500M for Zika to Finance UN's Green Climate Fund," *The Daily Signal*, 5/23/2016; (http://dailysignal.com/2016/05/23/obama-raided-500m-for-zika-to-finance-uns-green-climate-fund)
169. Frank Newport, "Americans Downbeat on State of U.S., Prospects for Future," Gallup, 1/21/2013, (http://www.gallup.com/poll/160046/americans-downbeat-state-prospects-future.aspx)
170. Ibid.
171. Ibid.
172. "Direction of our Country," *RealClearPolitics*, Accessed 1/30/2018 (https://realclearpolitics.com/epolls/other/direction_of_country-902.html).
173. The White House, The Press Office. Memorandum For The Heads of Executive Departments and Agencies. Retrieved from http://www.whitehouse.gov/the-press-office/freedom-information-act
174. The White House, The Press Office (2009). Executive Order 13489 -- Presidential Records. Retrieved from http://www.whitehouse.gov/the_press_office/ExecutiveOrderPresidentialRecords

175. Jim Snyder & Danielle Ivory, "Obama Cabinet Flunks Disclosure Test With 19 in 20 Ignoring Law," *Bloomberg*, 9/27/2012 (http://www.bloomberg.com/news/2012-09-28/obama-cabinet-flunks-disclosure-test-with-19-in-20-ignoring-law.html)
176. Tom Schoenberg, "Obama Visitor Logs Must be Made Public, Lawyer Tells Court," *Bloomberg*, 09/18/2012, (http://www.bloomberg.com/news/2012-09-18/obama-visitor-logs-must-be-public-lawyer-tells-court.html)
177. Hadas Gold, "Media protest White House photo ban," *Politico*, 11/21/13; (http://www.politico.com/blogs/media/2013/11/whca-protests-white-house-photo-ban-178077.html)
178. "'We did not know': 9 times the Obama administration was blindsided", Fox News, 6/19/2014; (http://www.foxnews.com/politics/2014/06/20/obama-administration-caught-by-surprise/)
179. "Obama says he learned of Clinton using private email through news reports", Fox News, 3/8/2015; (http://www.foxnews.com/politics/2015/03/08/obama-says-learned-clinton-private-emails-news-reports/)
180. Edward-Isaac Dovere, "White House alerted to potential Clinton email problem in August," *Politico*, 3/6/15; (http://www.politico.com/story/2015/03/hillary-clinton-emails-delays-115824.html)
181. Pablo Martinez Monsivais, "Blindsided by Arab Spring, US sees changes in Mideast influence," NBC News, 12/12/2011; (http://worldnews.nbcnews.com/_news/2011/12/12/9381833-blindsided-by-arab-spring-us-sees-changes-in-mideast-influence)
182. Joshua Berlinger, "BLINDSIDED: Obama's Asia Team Reportedly Partying When North Korea Launched Rocket," *Business Insider*, 12/14/2012; (http://www.businessinsider.com/report-obamas-asia-team-was-partying-when-north-korea-launched-its-rocket-2012-12)
183. " 'We did not know': 9 times the Obama administration was blindsided," Fox News, 6/19/2014; (http://www.foxnews.com/politics/2014/06/20/obama-administration-caught-by-surprise/)
184. "Official: U.S. intelligence surprised by collapse of Yemen government," CBS News, 2/13/2015; (http://www.cbsnews.com/news/obama-administration-surprised-by-collapse-of-yemen-government/)

185. Zachary A. Goldfarb, "Male-female pay gap remains entrenched at White House," *The Washington Post*, 7/1/2014; (http://www.washingtonpost.com/politics/male-female-pay-gap-remains-entrenched-at-white-house/2014/07/01/dbc6c088-0155-11e4-8fd0-3a663dfa68ac_story.html)
186. Ibid.
187. "Michelle Obama's August 2010 Vacation in Spain...," *Judicial Watch*, 04/26/2012, (http://www.judicialwatch.org/press-room/press-releases/michelle-obamas-august-2010-vacation-in-spain-cost-american-taxpayers-467585-according-to-records-obtained-by-judicial-watch/)
188. Paul Bedard, "Michelle Obama's Africa Trip Cost More Than $424,142," *US News and World Report*, 10/04/2011, (http://www.usnews.com/news/blogs/washington-whispers/2011/10/04/michelle-obamas-africa-vacation-cost-more-than-432142)
189. Malia Zimmerman, "Residents Alerted to Obamas' Hawaiian Holiday Plans," *Hawaii Reporter*, 11/27/2012, (http://www.hawaiireporter.com/residents-alerted-to-obamas-hawaiian-holiday-plans/123)
190. Keith Koffler, "Obama Returns to Hawaii at an Added Cost of Over $3 Million," *White House Dossier*, 01/02/2013;, (http://www.whitehousedossier.com/2013/01/02/obama-returns-hawaii-added-cost-3-million/)
191. Tony Lee, "Media Ignores Lavish Obama Vacations, Slammed Bush for Mountain Biking," *Breitbart*, 3/26/2013; (http://www.breitbart.com/big-journalism/2013/03/26/obamas-vacation-more-lavishly-than-bushes/)
192. "Documents Obtained by Judicial Watch Reveal Obama 2013 Vacations, Leno Show Appearance, Cost Taxpayers $7,396,531 for Flight Expenses," *Judicial Watch*, 2/27/2014 (http://www.judicialwatch.org/press-room/press-releases/2013-vacations-cost-taxpayers/)
193. Greg Campbell, "Obamas to Take Third Vacation in Three Months," *TPNN*, 2/16/2015; (http://www.tpnn.com/2015/02/16/obamas-to-take-third-vacation-in-three-months/)
194. Morgan Chalfant, "Obama Books $12M Martha's Vineyard Mansion for Penultimate Presidential Vacation," *The Washington*

Free Beacon, 7/7/2015: (http://freebeacon.com/politics/obama-books-12m-marthas-vineyard-mansion-for-penultimate-presidential-summer-vacation/)

195. "Judicial Watch: Obama Travel Cost Now $105,662,975.27," Judicial Watch, 9/14/2017 (http://www.judicialwatch.org/press-room/press-releases/2013-vacations-cost-taxpayers/)
196. (n.d.). Retrieved from http://en.wikipedia.org/wiki/Staycation
197. Hugo Gye and Louise Boyle, "Obama Fund-Raises $4.5 Million from Celebs in Just 8 Hours in NY," *Daily Mail Online*, 06/14/2012, (http://www.dailymail.co.uk/news/article-2159554/Barack-Obama-New-York-President-jets-evening-star-studded-fundraisers.html)
198. Toby Harnden, "Is the Taxpayer Funding Obama's Reelection Campaign?," *Daily Mail Online*, 04/26/2012, (http://www.dailymail.co.uk/news/article-2135763/This-does-pass-straight-face-test-Obama-accused-wasting-taxpayers-money-fund-raising-events-election.html)
199. Brett LoGiurato, "Republicans Have Filed A Formal Complaint Into Obama's 'Misuse Of Taxpayer Dollars,' " *Business Insider*, 4/25/2012, (http://www.businessinsider.com/rnc-complaint-on-obama-travel-2012-4)
200. Jeffrey Klein, "Obama Leaves Cities on Hook for Expensive Fundraiser Security Costs," *Examiner*, 08/22/2012, (http://www.examiner.com/article/obama-leaves-cities-on-hook-for-expensive-fundraiser-security-costs)
201. Elizabeth Dinan, "Obama refuses to pay Portsmouth $30K for campaign visit costs," *Seacost Online*, 12/20/2012, (http://www.seacoastonline.com/articles/20121220-NEWS-212200416)
202. "City Demands Obama Team Pay Police Tab," *The Wall Street Journal*, 8/2/2012, (http://online.wsj.com/article/SB10000872396390443545504577563152319884314.htm)
203. Dave Levinthal, "Obama's 2012 campaign is watching you," *Politico*, 3/16/2012, (http://www.politico.com/news/stories/0312/74095.html)
204. Ethan Roeder, "I Am Not Big Brother," *The New York Times*, 12/5/2012, (http://www.nytimes.com/2012/12/06/opinion/i-am-not-big-brother.html)

205. Ed Lasky, "Big Brother Obama is Watching," *American Thinker*, 03/17/2012, (http://www.americanthinker.com/blog/2012/03/big_brother_obama_is_watching.html)
206. Reid J. Epstein, "Division over platform at DNC," *Politico*, 9/5/2012, (http://www.politico.com/news/stories/0912/80801.html)
207. Awr Hawkins, "Obama Admin Gave Classified Info to Bin Laden Filmmakers," *Breitbart*, 11/15/2012, (http://www.breitbart.com/Big-Peace/2012/11/15/Obama-Admin-Discussed-Classifed-Information-With-Osama-bin-Laden-Filmmakers)
208. "Obama's Speech on Economic Policy," *The New York Times*, 10/13/2008; (http://www.nytimes.com/2008/10/13/us/politics/13obama-text.html?pagewanted=print&_r=0)
209. Glenn Greenwald, "The Real Story Of How 'Untouchable' Wall Street Execs Avoided Prosecution," *Business Insider*, 1/23/2013; (http://www.businessinsider.com/why-wall-street-execs-werent-prosecuted-2013-1)
210. "News Conference by the President" The White House, 10/6/2011; (http://www.whitehouse.gov/the-press-office/2011/10/06/news-conference-president)
211. Glenn Greenwald, "The Real Story Of How 'Untouchable' Wall Street Execs Avoided Prosecution," *Business Insider*, 1/23/2013; (http://www.businessinsider.com/why-wall-street-execs-werent-prosecuted-2013-1)
212. Paul H. Kupiec, "Dodd-Frank doesn't end 'too big to fail,' " *The Hill*, 7/3/2014; (http://thehill.com/opinion/op-ed/213871-dodd-frank-doesnt-end-too-big-to-fail)
213. Matthew Boyle, "Report: Cronyism, Political Donations Likely Behind Obama, Holder Failure to Charge any Bankers After 2008 Financial Meltdown," *The Daily Caller*, 08/07/2012, (http://dailycaller.com/2012/08/07/report-cronyism-political-donations-likely-behind-obama-holder-failure-to-charge-any-bankers-after-2008-financial-meltdown)
214. Ibid
215. "Justice Inaction: The Department of Justice's Unprecedented Failure to Prosecute Big Finance," Government Accountability Institute, 08/2012; Retrieved at http://g-a-i.org/wp-content/uploads/2012/08/DOJ-Report-8-61.pdf

216. The White House, Office of the Press Secretary. (2012). Remarks by the President in State of the Union Address [Press release]. Retrieved from http://www.whitehouse.gov/the-press-office/2012/01/24/remarks-president-state-union-address
217. Daniel Greenfield, "Obama Donors Got $21,000 in Government Money for Every $1 They Gave," *Frontpage Magazine*, 11/25/2012, (http://frontpagemag.com/2012/dgreenfield/obama-donors-got-21000-in-government-money-for-every-1-they-gave/)
218. Ronnie Green and Matthew Mosk, "Green Bundler With the Golden Touch," The Center for Public Integrity, 03/30/2011, (http://www.publicintegrity.org/2011/03/30/3845/green-bundler-golden-touch/)
219. Devin Dwyer, "Watchdogs Question Obama Donor Influence in 'Fiscal Cliff' Meetings," ABC News, 11/28/2012, (http://abcnews.go.com/blogs/politics/2012/11/watchdogs-question-donor-influence-in-obama-fiscal-cliff-meetings/)
220. Dave Levinthal, "Obama Inauguration Sponsors Spent Millions Influencing Government," Center for Public Integrity, *TruthOut*, 01/21/2013, (http://truth-out.org/news/item/14037-obama-inauguration-sponsors-spent-millions-influencing-government)
221. Ashley Portero, "Obama's Organizing for Action Could Lead to Government Corruption, Watchdogs Fear," *International Business Times*, 02/20/2013; http://www.ibtimes.com/obamas-organizing-action-could-lead-government-corruption-watchdogs-fear-1095592)
222. T.W. Farnam, "The Influence Industry: Obama gives administration jobs to some big fundraisers," *The Washington Post*, 3/7/2012, (http://articles.washingtonpost.com/2012-03-07/politics/35447935_1_bundlers-obama-administration-steve-spinner)
223. Lachlan Markar, "Report: 80% of DOE Green Energy Loans Went to Obama Backers," *The Foundry*, 11/14/2011, (http://blog.heritage.org/2011/11/14/report-80-of-doe-green-energy-loans-went-to-obama-backers/)
224. Mike McIntire and Michael Luo, "White House Opens Door to Big Donors, and Lobbyists Slip In," *The New York Times*, 04/14/2012,

(http://www.nytimes.com/2012/04/15/us/politics/white-house-doors-open-for-big-donors.html)
225. Ibid.
226. Matthew Boyle, "LightSquared CEO Made Curious Max Donation to DNC While Seeking White House Audience," *The Daily Caller*, 02/24/2012, (http://dailycaller.com/2012/02/24/lightsquared-ceo-made-curious-max-donation-to-dnc-while-seeking-white-house-audience/)
227. Matthew Boyle, "LightSquared CEO Resigns Amid Revelations of Company's Proximity to Obama White House," *The Daily Caller*, 02/28/2012, (http://dailycaller.com/2012/02/28/lightsquared-ceo-resigns-amid-revelations-of-companys-proximity-to-obama-white-house/)
228. Matthew Boyle, "Documents: LightSquared Shaping up as FCC's Solyndra," *The Daily Caller*, 02/21/2012, (http://dailycaller.com/2012/02/21/documents-lightsquared-shaping-up-as-the-fccs-solyndra/)
229. David Willman, "Cost, Need Questioned in $433 Million Smallpox Drug Deal," *Los Angeles Times*; 11/13/2011, (http://articles.latimes.com/2011/nov/13/nation/la-na-smallpox-20111113)
230. Chuck Neubauer, "Obama Donors Got Deal; Depositors Get 'Stiffed Again'," *The Washington Times*, 06/10/2012, (http://www.washingtontimes.com/news/2012/jun/10/obama-donors-get-deal-depositors-get-stiffed-again/)
231. Wynton Hall, "Democrats Blast Obama's Bundler-Turned-Treasury Nominee," *Breitbart*, 12/28/2014; (http://www.breitbart.com/big-government/2014/12/28/democrats-blast-obamas-bundler-turned-treasury-nominee/)
232. Vince Coglianese, "White House Won't Deny $500,000 Purchases Access to President Obama," *The Daily Caller*, 02/25/2013, (http://dailycaller.com/2013/02/25/white-house-wont-deny-500000-purchases-access-to-president-obama-video/)
233. Nicholas Confessore, "Obama's Backers Seek Big Donors to Press Agenda," *The New York Times*, 02/22/2013, (http://www.nytimes.com/2013/02/23/us/politics/obamas-backers-seek-deep-pockets-to-press-agenda.html?_r=3&)

234. Nicholas Confessore and Sheryl Gay Stolberg, "Well-Trod Path: Political Donor to Ambassador," *The New York Times*, 01/18/2013, (http://www.nytimes.com/2013/01/19/us/politics/well-trod-path-political-donor-to-ambassador.html)
235. "List of Ambassadorial Appointments," American Foreign Service Association, Accessed 6/2/2016; (http://www.afsa.org/ambassadorlist.aspx)
236. Fred Lucas, "23: That's How Many Obama Bundlers Have Been Nominated for Ambassadorships — And Now a Democrat Is Speaking Out," *The Blaze*, 2/7/2014 (http://www.theblaze.com/stories/2014/02/07/23-thats-how-many-obama-bundlers-have-been-nominated-for-ambassadorships-and-now-a-democrat-is-speaking-out/)
237. Tim Cavanaugh, "Konnichi-Whaa? Experts debate Caroline Kennedy's Japan cred," *The Daily Caller*, 4/3/2013 (http://dailycaller.com/2013/04/03/konnichi-whaa-experts-debate-caroline-kennedys-japan-cred/)
238. "Obama's ambassador pick for Norway bobbles Senate history test, but still likely to nab job," Fox News, 1/23/2014 (http://www.foxnews.com/politics/2014/01/23/obama-ambassador-pick-for-norway-fails-senate-history-test-but-still-likely-to/)
239. Eyder Peralta, "Ambassador To Argentina Nominee Has Never Been To the Country," *The Two-Way*, 2/7/2014 (http://www.npr.org/blogs/thetwo-way/2014/02/07/273106029/ambassador-to-argentina-nominee-has-never-been-to-the-country)
240. Al Kamen, "Obama ambassador nominees — Baucus, Bell and Tsunis — hit bumps in hearings," *The Washington Post*, 1/30/2014 (http://www.washingtonpost.com/politics/obama-ambassador-nominees--baucus-bell-and-tsunis--hit-bumps-in-hearings/2014/01/30/824d6b40-89e8-11e3-a5bd-844629433ba3_story.html)
241. Ibid.
242. "Obama far outpaces predecessors in appointing donors to foreign posts," Fox News, 2/10/2014 (http://www.foxnews.com/politics/2014/02/10/obama-far-outpaces-predecessors-in-appointing-donors-to-foreign-posts/)

243. Henri J. Barkey, "Obama's ambassador nominees are a disservice to diplomacy," *The Washington Post*, 7/6/2014 (http://www.washingtonpost.com/opinions/obamas-ambassador-nominees-are-a-disservice-to-diplomacy/2014/02/06/2273ef9e-8e86-11e3-b227-12a45d109e03_story.html)
244. Michael Isikoff, "Facing Opposition, Obama Intel Pick Pulls Out," *Newsweek*, 3/9/09 (http://www.newsweek.com/facing-opposition-obama-intel-pick-pulls-out-76211)
245. "Intelligence Failures," *National Review*, 3/4/2009 (http://www.nationalreview.com/articles/227003/intelligence-failure/editors)
246. Chris Jacobs, "Donald Berwick's Rationed Transparency", *The Heritage Foundation*, 6/27/2013 (http://www.heritage.org/research/commentary/2013/6/donald-berwicks-rationed-transparency)
247. Paul Mirengoff, "Boring From Within", *Powerline*, 3/29/2010 (http://www.powerlineblog.com/archives/2010/03/025876.php)
248. Mario Trujlio, "Obama nomination of Mumia Abu Jamal lawyer stirs controversy," *The Hill*, 1/9/2014 (http://thehill.com/blogs/blog-briefing-room/news/194950-obama-nomination-of-mumia-abu-jamal-lawyer-stirs-controversy)
249. Burgess Everett, "Democrats help block Obama's DOJ pick," *Politico*, 3/5/2014 (http://www.politico.com/story/2014/03/senate-blocks-debo-adegbile-justice-department-104297.html)
250. "Obama's DHS pick a major Democratic donor, senators question credentials," Fox News, 10/18/2013 (http://www.foxnews.com/politics/2013/10/18/obamas-dhs-pick-major-democratic-donor-senator-questions-credentials/)
251. Stephen Dinan, "DHS nominee Jeh Johnson lacks immigration experience," *The Washington Times*, 10/18/2013 (http://www.washingtontimes.com/news/2013/oct/18/dhs-jeh-johnson-nominee-lacks-immigration-experien/)
252. Jess Bravin and Jared A. Favole, "Surprised Pick for Homeland Security," *The Wall Street Journal*, 10/17/2013 (http://online.wsj.com/news/articles/SB20001424052702303680404579141881388674454)
253. Jordan Schachtel, "Official Who Claimed al Qaeda 'On The Run' Obama's Pick to Head DHS," *Breitbart*, 10/24/2013

(http://www.breitbart.com/Big-Peace/2013/10/24/President-Obama-s-Left-Hand-Man-Appointed-to-Lead-DHS)

254. Tom Gardner, "Illegal immigrants have 'earned the right to be U.S. citizens', says Homeland Security Secretary," *Daily Mail*, 1/27/2014
255. Andrew Malcolm, "Obama's green jobs czar Van Jones quits under fire," *Los Angeles Times*, 9/6/2009 (http://latimesblogs.latimes.com/washington/2009/09/obama-adviser-van-jones.html)
256. Chip Johnson, "Timing Of Protest Is Suspect / Mumia supporters disrupt youth event," *San Francisco Gate*, 10/9/1999 (http://www.sfgate.com/bayarea/johnson/article/Timing-Of-Protest-Is-Suspect-Mumia-supporters-2903851.php)
257. Tony Lee, "Radical Obama Regulatory Chief Cass Sunstein Resigns," *Breitbart*, 8/5/2012 (http://www.breitbart.com/Big-Government/2012/08/05/Radical-Obama-Regulatory-Chief-Cass-Sunstein-Resigns)
258. Adam Brickley, "Obama Appoints Pro-Gay Activist Who Promotes Pro-Gay Clubs in Public Schools to be 'Safe Schools' Czar," CNSNews, 6/17/2009 (http://www.cnsnews.com/news/article/obama-appoints-pro-gay-activist-who-promotes-pro-gay-clubs-public-schools-be-safe)
259. Kerry Picket, "Kevin Jennings's longtime foe, 'Mass Resistance'," *The Washington Times*, 12/8/2009 (http://www.washingtontimes.com/weblogs/watercooler/2009/dec/08/kevin-jennings-longtime-foe-time-mass-resistance/)
260. Kathy Shaidle, " 'Science Czar' John P. Holdren's disturbing beliefs about America, capitalism and humanity" *Examiner*, 7/16/2009 (http://www.examiner.com/article/science-czar-john-p-holdren-s-disturbing-beliefs-about-america-capitalism-and-humanity)
261. Benjamin Lesser and Greg B. Smith, "Buildings sprang up as donations rained down on Bronx Borough President Adolfo Carrion," *New York Daily News*, 3/1/2009 (http://www.nydailynews.com/new-york/bronx/buildings-sprang-donations-rained-bronx-borough-president-adolfo-carrion-article-1.367969)

262. Michelle Malkin, "Czar Wars: The Phantom Menaces," *New York Post*, 7/26/2009 (http://nypost.com/2009/07/26/czar-wars-the-phantom-menaces/)
263. Michelle Malkin, "The Trouble with Obama's Energy Czar," *Human Events*, 12/12/2008 (http://www.humanevents.com/2008/12/12/the-trouble-with-obamas-energy-czar/)
264. "Browner is an environmental radical - and a socialist (seriously)," *The Washington Examiner*, 1/7/2009 (http://washingtonexaminer.com/browner-is-an-environmental-radical-and-a-socialist-seriously/article/25170)
265. Seton Motley, "New FCC 'Chief Diversity Officer' Co-Wrote Liberal Group's 'Structural Imbalance of Political Talk Radio'," *Newbusters*, 8/6/2009 (http://newsbusters.org/blogs/seton-motley/2009/08/06/new-fcc-chief-diversity-officer-co-wrote-liberal-groups-structural-imb)
266. Seton Motley, "Audio: FCC's Diversity Czar: 'White People' Need to be Forced to 'Step Down' 'So Someone Else Can Have Power'," *Newbusters*, 8/6/2009 (http://newsbusters.org/blogs/seton-motley/2009/09/23/fccs-diversity-czar-white-people-need-be-forced-step-down-so-someone-0)
267. Jesse Byrnes, "McCain: Ebola czar does not 'fit the bill' " *The Hill*, 10/17/2014; (http://thehill.com/policy/healthcare/221157-mccain-ebola-czar-does-not-fit-the-bill)
268. "ISIS Czar a Terrorist Sympathizer Once Fired by Obama for Hamas Ties," *Judicial Watch*, 12/2/2015 (http://www.judicialwatch.org/blog/2015/12/isis-czar-a-terrorist-sympathizer-once-fired-by-obama-for-hamas-ties/)
269. Eric Owens, "Supremes Smack Down Obama Administration 9-0 For 13th TIME SINCE 2012," *The Daily Caller*, 6/27/2014 (http://dailycaller.com/2014/06/27/supremes-smack-down-obama-administration-9-0-for-13th-time-since-2012/)
270. Ilya Shapiro, "Obama's Abysmal Record Before the Supreme Court," CATO Institute, 2/11/2016 (http://www.cato.org/blog/obamas-abysmal-record-supreme-court)
271. Jonathan Weisman, "Appointments Challenge Senate Role, Experts Say," *The New York Times*, 01/07/2012 (http:// www.

nytimes.com/2012/01/08/us/politics/experts-say-obamas-recess-appointments-could-signify-end-to-a-senate-role.html)

272. Stephen Dinan, "Obama Recess Appointments Unconstitutional," *The Washington Times*, 1/25/2013 (http://www.washingtontimes.com/news/2013/jan/25/federal-court-obama-broke-law-recess-appointments/)
273. Julian Hattern, "Obama dealt second court defeat over NLRB recess appointments," *The Hill*, 5/16/2013 (http://thehill.com/blogs/regwatch/labor/300273-court-rules-against-nlrb-recess-appointment)
274. Larry O'Dell. "NLRB Recess Appointments Ruled Unconstitutional By Virginia Appeals Court," Associated Press, 7/17/2013 (http://www.huffingtonpost.com/2013/07/17/nlrb-appointments-unconstitutional_n_3613034.html)
275. Robert Barnes, "Supreme Court questions Obama's recess appointment power," *The Washington Post*, 1/13/2014 (http://www.washingtonpost.com/politics/2014/01/13/15869f86-7c87-11e3-9556-4a4bf7bcbd84_story.html)
276. Marc Ambinder, "Obama Won't go to Court Over Defense of Marriage Act," *National Journal*, 02/24/2011, (http://www.nationaljournal.com/obama-won-t-go-to-court-over-defense-of-marriage-act-20110223)
277. Robert Pear, "Fewer Youths to Be Deported in New Policy," *The New York Times*, 08/18/2011, (http://www.nytimes.com/2011/08/19/us/19immig.html)
278. Ibid.
279. Donna St. George and Brady Dennis, "Growing Share of Hispanic Voters Helped Push Obama to Victory," *The Washington Post*, 11/07/2012, (http://www.washingtonpost.com/politics/decision2012/growing-share-of-hispanic-voters-helped-push-obama-to-victory/2012/11/07/b4087d0a-28ff-11e2-b4e0-346287b7e56c_story.html)
280. Julia Preston, "In Big Shift, Latino Vote Was Heavily for Obama," *The New York Times*, 11/06/2008, (http://www.nytimes.com/2008/11/07/us/politics/07latino.html)
281. Dr. Milton R. Wolf, "ObamaCare Waiver Corruption Must Stop," *The Washington Times*, 05/20/2011, (http://

www.washingtontimes.com/news/2011/may/20/obamacare-waiver-corruption-must-stop/)

282. Jeffrey H. Anderson, "Obama Continues to Violate His Own 'Stimulus' Law by Not Releasing Quarterly Reports", *The Weekly Standard*, 1/26/2013. (http://www.weeklystandard.com/article/obama-continues-violate-his-own-stimulus-law-not-releasing-quarterly-reports/697896)
283. Grace-Marie Turner, "70 Changes to ObamaCare... -So Far", Galen Institute, 1/28/2016; (http://galen.org/newsletters/changes-to-obamacare-so-far/)
284. Josh Rogin, "Exclusive: Obama Declines to Add Names to Russian Sanction List," *The Daily Beast*, 12/19/2013, (http://www.thedailybeast.com/articles/2013/12/19/exclusive-obama-declines-to-add-names-to-russian-sanction-list.html)
285. "Obama's Magnitsky Walkback", *The Wall Street Journal*, 1/5/2014, (http://online.wsj.com/news/articles/SB10001424052702304591604579290880748745144)
286. Joe Cunningham, "Obama's Iran Deal Violates A Law Obama Signed In 2012," *RedState*, 10/8/2015; (http://www.redstate.com/joesquire/2015/10/08/obamas-iran-deal-violates-law-obama-signed-2012/)
287. James Rosen, "EXCLUSIVE: U.S. officials conclude Iran deal violates federal law," Fox News, 10/9/2015; (http://www.foxnews.com/politics/2015/10/08/exclusive-us-officials-conclude-iran-deal-violates-federal-law.html)
288. John Nolte, "Obama Pivots to Economy for 21st Time," *Breitbart*, 11/8/2013 (http://www.breitbart.com/Big-Government/2013/11/08/obama-pivots-to-economy-for-20th-time)
289. Foon Rhee, "Obama vows line-by-line budget review," Political Intelligence, 11/25/2008 (http://www.boston.com/news/politics/politicalintelligence/2008/11/obama_vows_line.html)
290. Chris Jacobs, "The Final Obama Budget: Better Never Than Late?" *Conservative Review*, 2/9/2016; (https://www.conservativereview.com/commentary/2016/02/the-final-obama-budget-better-never-than-late)

291. Jeff Cox, "Average College Debt Rose to $24,000 in 2009," *The New York Times*, 10/21/2010; (http://www.nytimes.com/2010/10/22/education/22debt.html)
292. Jeff Cox, "Student debt load growing, so are delinquencies," CNBC, 3/8/2016; (http://www.cnbc.com/2016/03/08/student-debt-load-growing-so-are-delinquencies.html)
293. Kim Parker, "The Boomerang Generation," Pew Research Center, 3/15/2012; (http://www.pewsocialtrends.org/2012/03/15/the-boomerang-generation/)
294. Alan M. Collinge, "President Obama's horrible, terrible legacy on student loans," *The Hill*, 5/13/2016; (http://thehill.com/blogs/congress-blog/education/279512-president-obamas-horrible-terrible-legacy-on-student-loans)
295. Ibid.
296. Julie Pace, "Obama to propose tax hikes for the wealthy, free community college," *The Christian Science Monitor*, 1/18/2015; (http://www.csmonitor.com/USA/Latest-News-Wires/2015/0118/Obama-to-propose-tax-hikes-for-the-wealthy-free-community-college-video)
297. "Breakthrough White Paper: Four Year Colleges vs. Community Colleges," Breakthrough Collaborative, (https://www.breakthroughcollaborative.org/sites/default/files/BTResearch-4yr_vs_2yr_colleges.pdf)
298. David Eldrige, "Report Flunks Obama's 'Free' Community College Plan," *Inside Sources*, 1/7/2016; (http://www.insidesources.com/report-flunks-obamas-free-community-college-plan/)
299. "Car Allowance Rebate System", Wikipedia, accessed 12/18/2012; http://en.wikipedia.org/wiki/Car_Allowance_Rebate_System
300. Edmunds, (2015). "Cash for Clunkers Results Finally In: Taxpayers Paid $24,000 per Vehicle Sold, Reports Edmunds.com. (http://www.edmunds.com/about/press/cash-for-clunkers-results-finally-in-taxpayers-paid-24000-per-vehicle-sold-reports-edmundscom.html)
301. Jennifer Santis, "The Cash for Clunkers Conundrum," *EMagazine*, 1/2/2013; (http://www.emagazine.com/blog/the-cash-for-clunkers-conundrum)

302. Nick Bunkley, "Government Will End Clunker Program Early," *The New York Times*, 8/20/2009; (http://www.nytimes.com/2009/08/21/business/21clunkers.html)
303. Peter Ferrara, "President Obama: The Biggest Government Spender In World History," *Forbes*, 6/14/2012; (http://www.forbes.com/sites/peterferrara/2012/06/14/president-obama-the-biggest-government-spender-in-world-history/)
304. "Examiner Editorial: Big-spending Obama frames himself as scrooge," *The Washington Examiner*, 5/24/2012; (http://www.washingtonexaminer.com/examiner-editorial-big-spending-obama-frames-himself-as-scrooge/article/650536)
305. Government data from http://www.usgovernmentspending.com/spending_chart_1929_2017USk_11s1li011mcn_G0f_Deficits_In_Inflation-adjusted_Dollars
306. Ibid.
307. "The Debt to the Penny and Who Holds It," Treasury Direct, Accessed 1/23/2016 (http://www.treasurydirect.gov/NP/debt/current)
308. "U.S. Debt Reaches 100 Percent of Country's GDP," Fox News, 8/4/2011 (http://www.foxnews.com/politics/2011/08/04/us-debt-reaches-100-percent-countrys-gdp/)
309. "United States Gross Federal Debt to GDP" Trading Economics, Accessed 1/30/2018 (https://tradingeconomics.com/united-states/government-debt-to-gdp)
310. Zachary Goldfarb, "S&P downgrades U.S. credit rating for first time," *The Washington Post*, 8/6/2011; (http://www.washingtonpost.com/business/economy/sandp-considering-first-downgrade-of-us-credit-rating/2011/08/05/gIQAqKeIxI_story.html)
311. Office of Speaker John Boehner, (Press Release) 12/03/2012. House GOP Leaders Make New Offer to Avert Fiscal Cliff. Retrieved from, http://www.speaker.gov/press-release/house-gop-leaders-make-new-offer-avert-fiscal-cliff
312. Kathleen Hennessy, "Obama Rejects GOP 'Fiscal Cliff' Offer, Says Tax Rates Must Rise," *Los Angeles Times*, 12/04/2012, (http://

www.latimes.com/news/politics/la-pn-obama-rejects-fiscal-cliff-offer-20121204,0,3064040.story)

313. Richard Sisk, "Hagel Says Cuts to Pay and Benefits are Needed," *Military.com News*, 11/5/2013 (http://www.military.com/daily-news/2013/11/05/hagel-says-cuts-to-pay-and-benefits-are-needed.html?comp=7000024213943&rank=1)
314. "Number of Military Families on Food Stamps Has Nearly Doubled Since Obama Took Office," Fox News *Insider*, 2/18/2014 (http://foxnewsinsider.com/2014/02/18/number-military-families-food-stamps-has-nearly-doubled-obama-took-office)
315. Chris Edwards, "Overpaid Federal Workers," *Downsizing The Federal Government*, 8/2013 (http://www.downsizinggovernment.org/overpaid-federal-workers)
316. Elizabeth Harrington, "Food Stamp Rolls in America Now Surpass the Population of Spain," CNS News, February 13, 2013, (http://cnsnews.com/news/article/food-stamp-rolls-america-now-surpass-population-spain)
317. Alan Bjerga, "Food-Stamp Usage Climbs to Record, Reviving Campaign Issue," *Bloomberg*, 9/4/2012, (http://www.bloomberg.com/news/2012-09-04/food-stamp-use-climbed-to-record-46-7-million-in-june-u-s-says.html)
318. Brittany Stepniak, "Food Stamp Growth: 75X Greater Than Job Growth," *Wealth Wire*, 11/2/2012, (http://www.wealthwire.com/news/economy/4098)
319. https://www.fns.usda.gov/pd/supplemental-nutrition-assistance-program-snap Accessed 2/9/2016
320. Caroline May, "Exclusive: Robert Rector Details 370 Percent Increase of Able-Bodied Adults Without Dependents on Food Stamps," *Breitbart*, 1/14/2016, (http://www.breitbart.com/big-government/2016/01/14/exclusive-robert-rector-details-370-increase-of-able-bodied-adults-without-dependents-on-food-stamps/)
321. Joe Schoffstall, "Cost of Food Stamp Fraud More Than Doubles In Three Years," CNS News, 4/1/2013, (http://cnsnews.com/blog/joe-schoffstall/cost-food-stamp-fraud-more-doubles-three-years)
322. Ed O'Keefe, "Obama administration targeting food stamp fraud as program reaches record highs," *The Washington Post*,

12/06/2011, (http://www.washingtonpost.com/blogs/federal-eye/post/obama-administration-targeting-food-stamp-fraud-as-program-reaches-record-highs/2011/12/05/gIQAfdM3XO_blog.html)
323. Walter Hamilton, "Disability Claims Rise Even As Work Injuries Decline," *Los Angeles Times*, 8/22/2012) (http://articles.latimes.com/2012/aug/22/business/la-fi-mo-disability-claims-20120822)
324. Source: Social Security Administration extracted on: February 9, 2018
325. Stephen Olmacher, "Social Security Awarding Disability Benefits Without Adequately Reviewing Applications: Report," *The Huffington Post*, 9/13/2012 (http://www.huffingtonpost.com/2012/09/13/social-security-disability-benefits_n_1879791.html)
326. David Jackson, "Obama: Income inequality threatens American Dream," *USA Today*, 12/4/2013 (http://www.usatoday.com/story/news/politics/2013/12/04/obama-income-inequality-speech-center-for-american-progress/3867747/)
327. David Jackson, "Obama: More work remains in 'war on poverty'," *USA Today*, 1/8/2014 (http://www.usatoday.com/story/theoval/2014/01/08/obama-statement-war-on-poverty-lyndon-johnson/4370259/)
328. Christopher Ingraham, "Child Poverty in the U.S. is Among the Worst in the Developed World," *The Washington Post*, 10/29/2014 (http://www.washingtonpost.com/blogs/wonkblog/wp/2014/10/29/child-poverty-in-the-u-s-is-among-the-worst-in-the-developed-world/)
329. Tanzina Vega, "2 out of 5 Black Children are Living in Poverty," CNN Money, 7/14/2015; (http://money.cnn.com/2015/07/14/news/economy/black-children-poverty/)
330. Terrence P. Jeffrey, "65 Percent of Children Live in Households on Federal Aid Programs," CNS News, 12/10/2014; (http://cnsnews.com/commentary/terence-p-jeffrey/65-percent-children-live-households-federal-aid-programs)
331. David Boyer, "That's rich: Poverty level under Obama breaks 50-year record," *The Washington Times*, 1/7/2014

(http://www.washingtontimes.com/news/2014/jan/7/obamas-rhetoric-on-fighting-poverty-doesnt-match-h/)

332. Peter Ferrara, "Obama's Rising Inequality," *The American Spectator*, 5/8/2013; http://spectator.org/articles/55646/obamas-rising-inequality

333. "Income Inequality Grew Faster Under Obama, According to One Measure," *The Huffington Post*, 9/1/2013; http://www.huffingtonpost.com/2013/09/01/income-inequality-obama_n_3853183.html

334. Bret Baier, "As Obama Hammers 'Income Inequality,' Gap Grows Under His Presidency," Fox News, 1/21/2014; http://www.foxnews.com/politics/2014/01/21/as-obama-hammers-income-inequality-gap-grows-under-his-presidency/

335. Nick, Timiraos, "U.S. Incomes End 6-Year Decline, Just Barely," *The Wall Street Journal*, 9/16/2014; (http://www.wsj.com/articles/u-s-incomes-edge-higher-as-sluggish-recovery-persists-1410878730)

336. Angelo Young, "Despite Falling US Unemployment, Numbers Of Long-Term Unemployed And Those Who've Given Up On Work Remain High," *International Business Times*, 1/9/2015, (http://www.ibtimes.com/despite-falling-us-unemployment-numbers-long-term-unemployed-those-whove-given-work-1778990)

337. "Average (Mean) Duration of Unemployment," Federal Reserve Bank of St. Louis, Accessed 1/23/2015, (http://research.stlouisfed.org/fred2/series/UEMPMEAN/)

338. Brad Plumer, "7 reasons why Congress's failure to extend unemployment insurance matters," *Wonkblog*, 1/14/2014, (http://www.washingtonpost.com/blogs/wonkblog/wp/2014/01/14/an-extension-of-unemployment-insurance-just-failed-in-the-senate/)

339. Labor Force Statistics from the Current Population Survey," Bureau of Labor Statistics, Accessed 2/9/2018; (https://data.bls.gov/timeseries/LNS13008636)

340. "Labor Force Statistics from the Current Population Survey," Bureau of Labor Statistics, Accessed 6/09/2015; (http://data.bls.gov/timeseries/LNS11300000)

341. James Sherk, "Not Looking for Work: Why Labor Force Participation Has Fallen During the Recovery," *The Heritage Foundation*, 9/4/2014; (http://www.heritage.org/research/reports/2014/09/

not-looking-for-work-why-labor-force-participation-has-fallen-during-the-recovery)

342. "Alternative Measures of Labor Underutilization," Bureau of Labor Statistics, accessed 6/09/2015; (http://www.bls.gov/news.release/empsit.t15.htm)
343. "Labor Force Statistics from the Current Population Survey," Bureau of Labor Statistics, accessed 1/31/2018; (http://data.bls.gov/timeseries/LNS11300000)
344. Terence P. Jeffrey, "It's Official: Federal Debt Tops $16 Trillion," CNS News, 9/4/2012, (http://cnsnews.com/news/article/its-official-federal-debt-tops-16-trillion)
345. Asche Schow, "President Obama's Taxpayer-Backed Green Energy Failures," The Heritage Foundation, 10/18/2012, (http://blog.heritage.org/2012/10/18/president-obamas-taxpayer-backed-green-energy-failures/)
346. Dave Boyer, "That's rich: Poverty level under Obama breaks 50-year record," *The Washington Times*, 1/7/2014; (http://www.washingtontimes.com/news/2014/jan/7/obamas-rhetoric-on-fighting-poverty-doesnt-match-h/)
347. David Rosen, "Looking Beyond Hurricane Sandy," *Counterpunch*, 11/15/2012, (http://www.counterpunch.org/2012/11/15/looking-beyond-hurricane-sandy/)
348. Stephanie Condon, "Obama: 'No Such Thing as Shovel-Ready Projects,' " CBS News, 10/13/2010; (http://www.cbsnews.com/news/obama-no-such-thing-as-shovel-ready-projects/)
349. James Pethokoukis, "Well, I Think We Have a Final Verdict on the Obama Stimulus," *AEI Ideas*, 12/18/2012, (http://www.aei-ideas.org/2012/11/well-i-think-we-have-a-final-verdict-on-the-obama-stimulus/)
350. James Sherk, "Not Looking for Work: Why Labor Force Participation Has Fallen During the Recovery", The Heritage Foundation, 9/4/2014; (http://www.heritage.org/research/reports/2014/09/not-looking-for-work-why-labor-force-participation-has-fallen-during-the-recovery)
351. Ibid.
352. Wynton Hall, "Richer Democratic States with Lower Unemployment Got Bulk of Obama Stimulus," *Breitbart*, 4/20/2012;

(http://www.breitbart.com/big-government/2012/04/20/richer-democratic-states-with-lower-unemployment-got-bulk-of-obama-stimulus/)

353. "Startup America," The White House, 1/31/2011; (http://www.whitehouse.gov/economy/business/startup-america)
354. Jim Clifton, "American Entrepreneurship: Dead or Alive?," Gallup, 1/13/2015; (http://www.gallup.com/businessjournal/180431/american-entrepreneurship-dead-alive.aspx)
355. Ibid.
356. "Liberal Study Finds Entrepreneurs Dying Under Obama," *Investors Business Daily*, 5/7/2014; (http://news.investors.com/ibd-editorials/050714-700002-liberal-study-finds-obamanomics-killed-the-american-entrepreneur.htm)
357. Max Velthoven, John Kartch, and Ryan Ellis, "Obama has Proposed 442 Tax Hikes Since Taking Office," Americans for Tax Reform, 4/14/2014; (http://www.atr.org/obama-has-proposed-442-tax-hikes-taking-office)
358. Angie Drobnic Holan, "No family making less than $250,000 will see any form of tax increase.'," *The Obamater*, 4/8/2010 (http://www.politifact.com/truth-o-meter/promises/obameter/promise/515/no-family-making-less-250000-will-see-any-form-tax/)
359. Robert Stacy McCain, "Obama Cut Your Taxes, and Other Lies Frank Rich Wants You to Believe In," *The Other McCain*, 10/24/2010; (http://theothermccain.com/2010/10/24/obama-cut-your-taxes-and-other-lies-frank-rich-wants-you-to-believe-in/)
360. Glenn Kessler, "Obama's whopper of a claim on tax cuts," *The Washington Post*, 9/7/2011; (http://www.washingtonpost.com/blogs/fact-checker/post/obamas-whopper-of-a-claim-on-tax-cuts/2011/09/06/gIQAmL2h7J_blog.html)
361. Jason, Russell, "All seven of Obama's budgets have proposed tax hikes," *The Washington Examiner*, 2/1/2015; (http://www.washingtonexaminer.com/all-seven-of-obamas-budgets-have-proposed-tax-hikes/article/2559596)
362. Michelle Jamrisko, "U.S. Economy Expands to 0.5% Pace, Weakest in Two Years," *Bloomberg*, 4/28/2016; (http://www.

realclearmarkets.com/articles/2016/02/01/barack_obamas_sad_record_on_economic_growth_101987.html)

363. Lucinda Shen, "Donald Trump Says U.S. Never Hit 3% GDP Growth Under Obama — But It's Misleading," *Fortune*, 8/30/2017; (http://fortune.com/2017/08/30/donald-trump-springfield-mo-3-gdp/)
364. Louis Woodhill, "Barack Obama's Sad Record on Economic Growth," *Real Clear Markets*, 2/1/2016; (http://www.realclearmarkets.com/articles/2016/02/01/barack_obamas_sad_record_on_economic_growth_101987.html)
365. Ibid.
366. "Starving North Koreans Forced to Survive on Diet of Grass and Tree Bark," *Amnesty International*, 7/15/2010, (http://www.amnesty.org/en/news-and-updates/starving-north-koreans-forced-survive-diet-grass-and-tree-bark-2010-07-14)
367. Gerard Hunt, "From Bread Basket to Basket Case: Land Seizures from White Farmers Have Cost Zimbabwe 7 Billion Pounds," *The Daily Mail*, 08/03/2011, (http://www.dailymail.co.uk/news/article-2022014/Mugabes-land-seizures-white-farmers-cost-Zimbabwe-7bn.html)
368. Charlies Devereaux and Raymond Colitt, "Venezuelans Faring Better but Economy is Crumbling," *Bloomberg*, 03/08/2013, (http://www.dispatch.com/content/stories/national_world/2013/03/08/venezuelans-faring-better-but-economy-is-crumbling.html)
369. Terry Miller, "U.S. Economic Freedom Continues to Fade," *The Wall Street Journal*, 1/31/2016; (http://www.wsj.com/articles/u-s-economic-freedom-continues-to-fade-1454281752)
370. "Economic Freedom," The Fraser Institute, (https://www.fraserinstitute.org/economic-freedom/)
371. James Sherk, "Not Looking for Work: Why Labor Force Participation Has Fallen During the Recovery," The Heritage Foundation, 9/4/2014; (http://www.heritage.org/research/reports/2014/09/not-looking-for-work-why-labor-force-participation-has-fallen-during-the-recover
372. "Labor Force Statistics from the Current Population Survey: Civilian labor force participation rate," Bureau of Labor Statistics, Accessed 1/30/2018; (http://data.bls.gov/timeseries/LNS11300000)

373. "Labor Force Statistics from the Current Population Survey: Employment-population ratio," Bureau of Labor Statistics, Accessed 1/21/2015; (http://data.bls.gov/timeseries/LNS12300000)
374. Jim Hoft, "Gallup CEO: Number of Full-Time Jobs as Percent of Population Is Lowest It's Ever Been (Video)," *Gateway Pundit*, 2/5/2015; (http://www.thegatewaypundit.com/2015/02/gallup-ceo-number-of-full-time-jobs-as-percent-of-population-is-lowest-its-ever-been-video/)
375. Jason Lange, "Obama trumpets rising U.S. wages; data has a more somber tone," Reuters, 1/21/2015; (http://www.reuters.com/article/2015/01/21/us-usa-obama-economy-idUSKBN0KU0BC20150121)
376. "Annual growth of the Real Gross Domestic Product (GDP) of the United States from 1990 to 2014," *Statista*, Accessed 2/9/2015; (http://www.statista.com/statistics/188165/annual-gdp-growth-of-the-united-states-since-1990/)
377. P. J. Gladnick, "CNBC Hosts by Guest's Unwelcome Economic Forecast," *NewsBusters*, 2/11/2015; (http://linkis.com/newsbusters.org/blog/Z9WtE)
378. Howard Schneider, "Middle class decline looms over final years of Obama presidency," Reuters, 1/18/2015; (https://ca.news.yahoo.com/middle-class-decline-looms-over-final-years-obama-130212665--business.html)
379. Neil Irwin, "You Can't Feed a Family With G.D.P.," *The New York Times*, 9/16/2014; (http://www.nytimes.com/2014/09/17/upshot/you-cant-feed-a-family-with-gdp.html)
380. Annie Lowrey, "Recovery Has Created Far More Low-Wage Jobs Than Better-Paid Ones," *The New York Times*, 4/27/2014; (http://www.nytimes.com/2014/04/28/business/economy/recovery-has-created-far-more-low-wage-jobs-than-better-paid-ones.html)
381. Prashant Gopal, "U.S. home ownership percentage declines to 1995 level," *Columbus Dispatch*, 10/29/2014; (http://www.dispatch.com/content/stories/business/2014/10/29/ownership-percentage-declines-to-1995-level.html)
382. Michael Snyder, "On The Verge Of The Next Economic Crisis, 62 Percent Of Americans Are Living Paycheck To Paycheck," The Economic Collapse, 1/7/2015; (http://theeconomiccollapseblog.

com/archives/verge-next-economic-crisis-62-percent-americans-living-paycheck-paycheck)

383. Gayle Trotter, "How Women Have Suffered Under Obama's Policies," *The Hill*, 5/30/2014; (http://thehill.com/blogs/congress-blog/civil-rights/207468-how-women-have-suffered-under-obamas-policies
384. "Monthly Labor Review," *Bureau of Labor Statistics*, 4/2014; (http://www.bls.gov/opub/mlr/2014/article/the-rise-in-women-share-of-nonfarm-employment.htm)
385. Neil Shah, "U.S. Wealth Is Near a Record, Yet Racial Gap Has Widened Since Recession", *Real Time Economics*, 12/12/2014; (http://blogs.wsj.com/economics/2014/12/12/u-s-wealth-is-near-a-record-yet-racial-gap-has-widened-since-recession/)
386. Young America's Foundation. (2010). Youth Misery Index Grows More Than 50% Under Obama Administration [Press release]. Retrieved from http://www.yaf.org/YouthMiseryIndexGrowsMoreThan50PercentUnderObamaAdministration.aspx
387. Michael Novak, "Obama's Legend," *National Review*, 8/14/2012; (http://www.nationalreview.com/articles/313899/obama-s-legend-michael-novak)
388. "Ben Shapiro: Fracking Saved the Obama Economy," *Front Page Magazine*, 1/16/2015; (http://www.frontpagemag.com/2015/truthrevolt-org/ben-shapiro-fracking-saved-the-obama-economy/)
389. Mark J. Perry, "Texas, the 'great American job machine,' is solely responsible for the +1.2M net US job increase since 2007," American Enterprise Institute, 1/23/2015; (http://www.aei.org/publication/texas-great-american-job-machine-solely-responsible-1m-net-us-job-increase-since-2007/)
390. "Obama's Economic Growth Gap Now Tops $2 Trillion," *Investor's Business Daily*, 7/30/2015; (http://www.investors.com/tepid-gdp-growth-leaves-economy-even-further-behind-the-pace/)
391. Joel Gehrke, "Obama threatens vetoes of bills requiring him to follow the law," *The Washington Examiner*, 3/12/2014 (http://washingtonexaminer.com/obama-threatens-vetoes-of-bills-requiring-him-to-follow-the-law/article/2545545)

392. Sam Stein, "Top Obama Adviser Tackles 2014, 'The Wire,' Vetoes, Obamacare And Weed," *The Huffington Post*, 12/29/2014 (http://www.huffingtonpost.com/2014/12/29/drinking-and-talking-dan-pfeiffer-obama_n_6373596.html)
393. "Top Organization Contributors," *Open Secrets*, 3/25/2013; (https://www.opensecrets.org/orgs/list.php?cycle=2012)
394. James Sherk, "How Union Card Checks Block Workers' Free Choice," The Heritage Foundation, 2/21/2007; (https://www.heritage.org/jobs-and-labor/report/how-union-card-checks-block-workers-free-choice)
395. Stacy Swimp, "Did President Obama Malign Right to Work Laws?," *The Washington Times*, 5/2/2012, (http://communities.washingtontimes.com/neighborhood/frederick-douglass-model-ages/2012/may/2/did-president-obama-malign-right-work-laws/)
396. Mark J. Perry, "Since 2009, Right to Work States Created 4x as Many Jobs as Forced Union States...," American Enterprise Institute, 11/24/2012, (http://www.aei-ideas.org/2012/11/since-2009-right-to-work-states-have-created-4x-as-many-jobs-as-forced-union-states-and-may-have-help-obamas-re-election/)
397. Ibid.
398. Macon Phillips, "Facts Are Stubborn Things," The White House Blog, 8/4/2009, (http://www.whitehouse.gov/blog/Facts-Are-Stubborn-Things)
399. "Big Brother Obama is Watching," *The Washington Times*, 9/14/2011, (http://www.washingtontimes.com/news/2011/sep/14/big-brother-obama-is-watching/)
400. "Gov't Says Wood is Illegal if U.S. Workers Produce It," Gibson Guitar: Press release, 08/25/2011, (http://www.gibson.com/absolutenm/templates/FeatureTemplatePressRelease.aspx?articleid=1340&zoneid=6)
401. Ibid.
402. Victor Keith, "What Gibson Guitars Did with the Wood the Government Returned," *American Thinker*, 2/2/2014 (http://www.americanthinker.com/blog/2014/02/what_gibson_guitars_did_with_the_wood_the_government_returned.html)

403. Anthony Martin, "Federal Raid on Gibson Guitars – Retaliatory Harassment?," *Examiner*, 08/29/2011, (http://www.examiner.com/article/federal-raid-on-gibson-guitars-retaliatory-harassment)
404. Becket Adams, "Feds Drop Case After Gibson Guitar Agrees to Pay $300k Penalty," *The Blaze*, 08/06/2012, (http://www.theblaze.com/stories/2012/08/06/feds-drop-case-after-gibson-guitars-agrees-to-pay-300k-penalty/)
405. Victor Keith, "What Gibson Guitars Did with the Wood the Government Returned," *American Thinker*, 2/2/2014 (http://www.americanthinker.com/blog/2014/02/what_gibson_guitars_did_with_the_wood_the_government_returned.html)
406. Mark Steyn, "Re: If Only Mitt Would Stop Preventing Us From Doing Our Jobs Sequel," *National Review Online – The Corner*, (http://www.nationalreview.com/corner/321063/re-if-only-mitt-would-stop-preventing-us-doing-our-jobs-sequel-mark-steyn#)
407. Colleen Curry, "Lawyers Rally in Defense of Anti-Muslim Filmaker," ABC News, 10/05/2012, (http://abcnews.go.com/US/jailed-anti-muslim-filmmaker-support-free-speech-lawyers/story?id=17397897)
408. "California Man Behind anti-Muslim Video Sentenced to Prison," The Associated Press, 11/07/2012, (http://www.foxnews.com/entertainment/2012/11/07/california-man-behind-anti-muslim-film-sentenced-to-prison/)
409. John F. Kennedy, Address, "The President and the Press" Before the American Newspaper Publishers Association, New York City. 04/27/1961, *The American Presidency Project*, (http://www.presidency.ucsb.edu/ws/index.php?pid=8093)
410. The White House, Office of the Press Secretary (2012) Remarks by the President at the Associated Press Luncheon [Press release] Retrieved from http://www.whitehouse.gov/the-press-office/2012/04/03/remarks-president-associated-press-luncheon
411. Michael Calderone, "Obama Turns to Local Media to Promote Reelection Message," *The Huffington* Post, 08/05/2012, (http://www.huffingtonpost.com/2012/08/05/obama-local-media-reelection_n_1741983.html)

412. Keith Koffler, "White House Sets Ground Rules for Local Interviews," *White House Dossier*, 08/21/2012, (http://www.whitehousedossier.com/2012/08/21/white-house-sets-ground-rules-local-interviews/)
413. Greta Van Susteren, "OBAMA ADMINISTRATION has some EXPLAINING TO DO," *Gretawire*, 1/16/2014 (http://gretawire.foxnewsinsider.com/2014/01/16/obama-administration-and-new-york-times-have-some-explaining-to-do/?dtoc)
414. Ajit Pai, "The FCC Wades Into the Newsroom," *The Wall Street Journal*, 2/10/2014; http://online.wsj.com/news/articles/SB10001424052702304680904579366903828260732
415. Michael Hausam, "First Amendment Victory! FCC Pulls Plug on News Monitoring Program," *Independent Journal Review*, 2/21/2014, http://www.ijreview.com/2014/02/116865-breaking-fcc-pulls-proposed-monitoring-program/
416. "Transparency and Open Government," The White House, (http://www.whitehouse.gov/the_press_office/TransparencyandOpenGovernment)
417. Margaret Sullivan, "Leak Investigations Are an Assault on the Press, and on Democracy, Too," *The New York Times*, 5/14/2013 (http://publiceditor.blogs.nytimes.com/2013/05/14/leak-investigations-are-an-assault-on-the-press-and-on-democracy-too/)
418. Bob Woodward, "Obama's Sequester Deal-Changer," *The Washington Post*, 02/22/2013, (http://articles.washingtonpost.com/2013-02-22/opinions/37238840_1_jack-lew-treasury-secretary-rob-nabors)
419. Brett LoGiurato, "Bob Woodward: A 'Very Senior' White House Person Warned Me I'd 'Regret' What I'm Doing," *Business Insider*, 02/27/2013, (http://www.businessinsider.com/bob-woodward-obama-sequester-white-house-reporting-price-politics-2013-2)
420. Maureen Callahan, "Beat the Press," *New York Post*, 03/03/2013, (http://www.nypost.com/p/news/opinion/opedcolumnists/beat_the_press_96lFrUNync5zuBZTiZ6aUL)
421. Ron Fournier, "Why Bob Woodward's Fight With the White House Matters to You," *National Journal*, 02/28/2013, (http://www.nationaljournal.com/politics/

why-bob-woodward-s-fight-with-the-white-house-matters-to-you-20130228)
422. "WMAL Exclusive: Woodward's Not Alone – Fmr. Clinton Aide Davis Says He Received White House Threat," *WMAL AM 630*, 02/28/2013, (http://www.wmal.com/common/page.php?pt=WMAL+EXCLUSIVE%3A+Woodward%27s+Not+Alone+-+Fmr.+Clinton+Aide+Davis+-Says+He+Received+White+House+Threat&id=8924&is_corp=0)
423. Mark Sherman, "Gov't Obtains Wide AP Phone Records in Probe," Associated Press, 5/13/2013 (http://www.ap.org/Content/AP-In-The-News/2013/Govt-obtains-wide-AP-phone-records-in-probe)
424. Ibid.
425. Mackenzie Weinger, "AP boss: Sources won't talk anymore," *Politico*, 6/19/2013 (http://www.politico.com/story/2013/06/ap-sources-93054.html)
426. Ann E. Marimow, "A rare peek into a Justice Department leak probe," *The Washington Post*, 5/19/2013 (http://www.washingtonpost.com/local/a-rare-peek-into-a-justice-department-leak-probe/2013/05/19/0bc473de-be5e-11e2-97d4-a479289a31f9_story.html)
427. Michael Isikoff, "DOJ confirms Holder OK'd search warrant for Fox News reporter's emails," NBC News, 5/27/2013 (http://investigations.nbcnews.com/_news/2013/05/23/18451142-doj-confirms-holder-okd-search-warrant-for-fox-news-reporters-emails)
428. Michael Barone, "Michael Barone: More than all past presidents, Obama uses 1917 Espionage Act to go after reporters," *The Washington Examiner*, 5/22/2013 (http://washingtonexaminer.com/michael-barone-more-than-all-past-presidents-obama-uses-1917-espionage-act-to-go-after-reporters/article/2530340)
429. "The Obama administration and the Press," Committee to Protect Journalists, 10/10/2013, (http://cpj.org/reports/2013/10/obama-and-the-press-us-leaks-surveillance-post-911.php)
430. Ibid.
431. Joel Pollack, "Obama Now Scapegoating Jewish Donor Adelson," *Breitbart*, 08/08/2012, (http://

www.breitbart.com/Big-Government/2012/08/08/Obama-Now-Scapegoating-Jewish-Donor-Adelson)

432. Christopher Bedford, "Obama Steps Up Anti-Koch Campaign With Online Petition," *The Daily Caller*, 02/29/2012, (http://dailycaller.com/2012/02/29/obama-steps-up-anti-koch-campaign-with-online-petition/)
433. Doug Schoen, "The Obama Campaign's Nixonian 'White House Enemies List'," *Forbes*, 05/14/2012, (http://www.forbes.com/sites/dougschoen/2012/05/14/the-obama-white-house-enemies-list/)
434. Jeff Zeleny, "Opponents Call Obama Remarks 'Out of Touch', " *The New York Times*, 4/12/2008, http://www.nytimes.com/2008/04/12/us/politics/12campaign.html?_r=0
435. Lachlan Markay, "An Extreme Position on Extremism," *The Washington Free Beacon*, 4/5/2013; http://freebeacon.com/an-extreme-position-on-extremism/
436. "Equal Opportunity and Treatment Incidents," Judicial Watch, http://www.judicialwatch.org/wp-content/uploads/2013/08/2161-docs.pdf
437. Charles Rollet, "Defense Department guide calls Founding Fathers 'extremist'," *The Daily Caller*, 8/23/2013 (http://dailycaller.com/2013/08/23/defense-department-guide-calls-founding-fathers-extremist/)
438. "Gallup Sued by DOJ After Unfavorable Obama Polls, Employment Numbers," *Breitbart*, 09/06/2012, (http://www.breitbart.com/Big-Government/2012/09/06/gallup-doj-axelrod)
439. Aruna Viswanatha and Lauren Tara Lacapra, "U.S. government slams S&P with $5 billion fraud lawsuit," Reuters, 2/5/2013, (http://www.reuters.com/article/2013/02/05/us-mcgrawhill-sandp-civilcharges-idUSBRE9130U120130205)
440. "Treasury chief Geithner sought revenge on S&P: McGraw," *New York Post*, 1/21/2014 (http://nypost.com/2014/01/21/treasury-chief-geithner-sought-revenge-on-sp-mcgraw/)
441. Aruna Viswanatha and Lauren Tara Lacapra, "U.S. government slams S&P with $5 billion fraud lawsuit," Reuters, 2/5/2013, (http://www.reuters.com/article/2013/02/05/us-mcgrawhill-sandp-civilcharges-idUSBRE9130U120130205)

442. Financial Fraud Enforcement Task Force Executive Director, Michael J. Bresnickat the Exchequer Club of Washington, D.C., 3/20/2013; (https://www.justice.gov/opa/speech/financial-fraud-enforcement-task-force-executive-director-michael-j-bresnick-exchequer)
443. "The Department of Justice's 'Operation Choke Point': Illegally Choking Off Legitimate Businesses?", U.S. House of Representatives Committee on Government Oversight and Reform (PDF), 5/29/2014; (http://oversight.house.gov/wp-content/uploads/2014/05/Staff-Report-Operation-Choke-Point1.pdf)
444. Kelly Riddell, "'High risk' label from feds puts gun sellers in banks' crosshairs, hurts business," *The Washington Times*, 5/18/2014; (https://www.washingtontimes.com/news/2014/may/18/targeted-gun-sellers-say-high-risk-label-from-feds/)
445. Frank Miniter, "FDIC Admits to Strangling Legal Gun Stores Banking Relationships," *Forbes*, 1/30/2015; (http://www.forbes.com/sites/frankminiter/2015/01/30/fdic-admits-to-strangling-legal-gun-stores-banking-relationships/#1a819a6027fd)
446. Victoria Guida, "Justice Department to end Obama-era 'Operation Choke Point'," *Politico*, 8/17/2017; (https://www.politico.com/story/2017/08/17/trump-reverses-obama-operation-chokepoint-241767)
447. Josh Blackman, "President Obama and arguments about pending Supreme Court cases," *Constitution Daily*, 6/17/2015; (http://blog.constitutioncenter.org/2015/06/president-obama-and-arguments-about-pending-supreme-court-cases/)
448. Elizabeth Slattery, "Obama's Attempt to Influence Supreme Court on Obamacare Case Breaks Precedent," *The Daily Signal*, 6/19/2015; (http://dailysignal.com/2015/06/19/obamas-attempt-to-influence-supreme-court-on-obamacare-case-breaks-precedent/)
449. *Stephen Dinan, "Email Tells Feds to Make Squester as Painful as Promised," The Washington Times*, 03/05/2013, (http://www.washingtontimes.com/news/2013/mar/5/email-tells-feds-make-sequester-painful-promised/)
450. Judson Berger, "Park Ranger: Supervisors Pushed Sequester Cuts That Visitors Would See," Fox News, 03/09/2013, (http://www.foxnews.com/politics/2013/03/08/

park-ranger-claims-supervisors-pushed-sequester-cuts-that-visitors-would-notice/)

451. Kathleen Hennessey, "Detained immigrants released; officials cite sequester cuts," *Los Angeles Times*, 2/26/13, (http://articles.latimes.com/2013/feb/26/news/la-pn-detained-immigrants-sequester-20130226)
452. Dylan Matthews, "Here is every previous government shutdown, why they happened and how they ended," *The Washington Post*, 9/25/13, (http://www.washingtonpost.com/blogs/wonkblog/wp/2013/09/25/here-is-every-previous-government-shutdown-why-they-happened-and-how-they-ended/)
453. "Closure of War Memorials Continues to Cause Conflict," *4 NBC Washington*, 10/4/2013 (http://www.nbcwashington.com/news/local/Closure-of-War-Memorials-Continues-to-Cause-Conflict-226481851.html)
454. Jillian Kay Melchior, "Park Service Knew World War II Veterans Would be Locked Out," *National Review Online*, 3/10/2014 (http://www.nationalreview.com/article/373015/park-service-knew-world-war-ii-veterans-would-be-locked-out-jillian-kay-melchior)
455. Elizabeth Shield, "Armed Guards Kick Senior Citizens Out of Yellowstone Park," *Breitbart*, 10/8/2013, (http://www.breitbart.com/InstaBlog/2013/10/08/Senior-Citizens-Kicked-Out-Treated-Harshly-at-Yellowstone-Park)
456. Warner Todd Huston, "Obama Forcing Shut Down of Parks the Feds Don't Even Fund," *Breitbart*, 10/4/2013, (http://www.breitbart.com/Big-Government/2013/10/03/Obama-Forcing-Shut-Down-of-Parks-the-Feds-Don-t-Even-Fund)
457. Jacqui Heinrich, "Lake Mead Property Owners Forced Out Until Shutdown Ends," *13 Action News*, 10/4/2013, (http://ktnv.com/news/local/Lake-Mead-Property-Owners-Forced-Out-Until-Gov-Shutdown-Ends-226557661.htm)
458. Ed O'Keefe, "Eleanor Holmes Norton Confronts Obama on D.C. Budget Bill," *The Washington Post*, 10/9/13 (http://www.washingtonpost.com/blogs/post-politics/wp/2013/10/09/eleanor-holmes-norton-confronts-obama-on-d-c-budget-bill/)
459. The White House, Office of the Press Secretary. (2009). News Conference by President Obama [Press release].

Retrieved from http://www.whitehouse.gov/the-press-office/news-conference-president-obama-40209
460. Matt Cover, "Obama Unsure, But State Department Says Egypt Is an Ally," CNS News, 9/13/2012, (http://cnsnews.com/news/article/obama-unsure-state-department-says-egypt-ally)
461. Rowan Scarborough, "Bush Policies he Reviled are Crux of Obama's Arsenal," *The Washington Times*, 05/15/2012, (http://www.washingtontimes.com/news/2012/may/15/bush-policies-he-reviled-part-of-obamas-arsenal/)
462. "Administration Reportedly Works Against Resolution to Recognize Deaths," *Politifact*, 03/05/2010, (http://www.politifact.com/truth-o-meter/promises/obameter/promise/511/recognize-armenian-genocide/)
463. Nile Gardiner, "The U-Turn President: Barack Obama's Top Ten Flip Flops," *The Telegraph*, 04/11/2011, (http://blogs.telegraph.co.uk/news/nilegardiner/100083104/the-u-turn-president-barack-obama-top-ten-flip-flops/)
464. "Flashback: Obama Calls Mubarak's Egypt 'Stallwart ally,' 'Force for Good," *Breitbart*, 09/13/2012, (http://www.breitbart.com/Breitbart-TV/2012/09/13/Flashback-Obama-Calls-Mubaraks-Egypt-Stallwart-Ally-Force-For-Good)
465. CNN Wire Staff, "Obama Says Egypt's Transition 'Must Begin Now'," CNN, 02/02/2011, (http://www.cnn.com/2011/POLITICS/02/01/us.egypt.obama/index.html)
466. Stephen Brown, "Obama's Disappearance on Darfur," *Frontpage*, 08/03/2012, (http://frontpagemag.com/2012/stephenbrown/obama%E2%80%99s-disappearance-on-darfur/)
467. Jennifer Rubin, "Obama to Israel: Never Mind," *The Washington Post*, 03/06/2012, (http://www.washingtonpost.com/blogs/right-turn/post/obama-to-israel-never-mind/2012/03/06/gIQA1T3BvR_blog.html)
468. "Trump has a chance to correct Obama's mistake on Venezuela," *The Washington Post*, 3/17/2017; (https://www.washingtonpost.com/opinions/global-opinions/trumps-chance-to-correct-obamas-mistake-on-venezuela/2017/03/17/8389943a-09aa-11e7-b77c-0047d15a24e0_story.html)

469. Chris Matthews, "Panama Papers: Why Did Clinton and Obama Flip Flop on Trade with Panama?," *Fortune*, 4/8/2016; (http://fortune.com/2016/04/08/panama-papers-sanders-clinton/)
470. Nina Easton, "Obama: NAFTA Not So Bad After All," *Fortune*, 6/18/08; (http://archive.fortune.com/2008/06/18/magazines/fortune/easton_obama.fortune/index.htm)
471. David Martosko, "Video Belies Obama 'Apology Tour' Denial," *The Daily Caller*, 10/22/2012, (http://times247.com/articles/video-belies-obama-s-apology-tour-denial)
472. The White House, Office of the Press Secretary. (2009). Remarks by President Obama at Strasbourg Town Hall [Press release]. Retrieved from http://www.whitehouse.gov/the-press-office/remarks-president-obama-strasbourg-town-hall
473. The White House, Office of the Press Secretary. (2009). Remarks by President Obama to the Turkish Parliament [Press release]. Retrieved from http://www.whitehouse.gov/the_press_office/Remarks-By-President-Obama-To-The-Turkish-Parliament
474. The White House, Office of the Press Secretary. (2009). Remarks by The President at The Summit of The Americas [Press release]. Retrieved from http://www.whitehouse.gov/the_press_office/Remarks-by-the-President-at-the-Summit-of-the-Americas-Opening-Ceremony
475. "Text of President Obama's Speech in Hiroshima, Japan," *The New York Times*, 5/27/2016; (http://www.nytimes.com/2016/05/28/world/asia/text-of-president-obamas-speech-in-hiroshima-japan.html)
476. Christian Datoc, "Obama: 'Hopefully, We Can Learn From' Cuba About Improving Human Rights In America," *The Daily Caller*, 3/21/2016; (http://dailycaller.com/2016/03/21/obama-hopefully-we-can-learn-from-cuba-about-improving-human-rights-in-america-video/)
477. Eugene Robinson, "George W. Bush's greatest legacy," *The Washington Post*, July 26, 2012 (http://articles.washingtonpost.com/2012-07-26/opinions/35487798_1_african-countries-pepfar-antiretroviral-treatment)
478. Jennifer Loven, "Africa Crowds Greet Bush With Hugs, Chants of Thanks," *The Boston Globe*, 02/19/2008, (http://

www.boston.com/news/world/articles/2008/02/19/africa_crowds_greet_bush_with_hugs_chants_of_thanks/)

479. AIDS Healthcare Foundation. (2012). Obama Budget Decimates Global AIDS Funding [Press release]. http://www.aidshealth.org/archives/news/obama-budget-decimates-global-aids-funding
480. "South Africa: 1,000 Protest Obama AIDS Funding Cuts, Says AHF", Press Release via Reuters, 03/18/2013, (http://www.reuters.com/article/2013/03/18/ca-potus-aids-funding-idUSnBw7gB6XQa+116+BSW20130318)
481. AIDS Healthcare Foundation. (2012). Obama Budget Decimates Global AIDS Funding [Press release]. http://www.aidshealth.org/archives/news/obama-budget-decimates-global-aids-funding
482. Tim Shipman, "Barack Obama Sends Bust of Winston Churchill on its Way Back to Britain," *The Daily Telegraph*, 02/14/2009, (http://www.telegraph.co.uk/news/worldnews/barackobama/4623148/Barack-Obama-sends-bust-of-Winston-Churchill-on-its-way-back-to-Britain.html)
483. Ian Drury, "To my special friend Gordon, 25 DVDs: Obama gives Brown a set of classic movies. Let's hope he likes the Wizard of Oz," *Daily Mail*, 3/6/2009, (http://www.dailymail.co.uk/news/article-1159627/To-special-friend-Gordon-25-DVDs-Obama-gives-Brown-set-classic-movies-Lets-hope-likes-Wizard-Oz.html)
484. Andrew Porter, "Barack Obama rebuffs Gordon Brown as 'special relationship' sinks to new low," *The Daily Telegraph*, 9/23/2009, (http://www.telegraph.co.uk/news/politics/gordon-brown/6224813/Barack-Obama-rebuffs-Gordon-Brown-as-special-relationship-sinks-to-new-low.html)
485. Z. Byron Wolf, "Awkward Moment During Obama Toast to Queen," ABC News, 5/24/2011, (http://abcnews.go.com/blogs/politics/2011/05/awkward-moment-during-obama-toast-to-queen/)
486. Nile Gardiner, "Barack Obama calls France America's strongest ally. The president gives Britain the boot again," *The Daily Telegraph*, 1/10/2011, (http://blogs.telegraph.co.uk/news/nilegardiner/100071241/barack-obama-france-is-americas-strongest-ally-the-president-gives-britain-the-boot-again/)

487. "Is the U.S.-U.K. 'special relationship' over?" *The Week*, 3/3/2010, (http://theweek.com/article/index/201339/is-the-us-uk-special-relationship-over)
488. Toby Harnden, "What does the USA think of the 'special relationship'?" *The Daily Telegraph*, 3/29/2010, (http://www.telegraph.co.uk/news/worldnews/northamerica/usa/7533241/What-does-the-USA-think-of-the-special-relationship.html)
489. Tim Walker and Nigel Morris, "Barack Obama says David Cameron allowed Libya to become a 's*** show'," *The Independent*, 3/10/2016; (http://www.independent.co.uk/news/uk/politics/barack-obama-says-david-cameron-allowed-libya-to-become-a-s-show-a6923976.html)
490. Dan Stewart, "Why the U.S.-U.K. Relationship Is Less Special than Ever," *TIME*, 3/11/2016; (http://time.com/4256202/why-the-u-s-u-k-relationship-is-less-special-than-ever/)
491. Alison Little, "Obama's Amazing Threat to Britain: UK Would be at the 'Back of the Queue' After Brexit", *Sunday Express*, 4/23/16; (http://www.express.co.uk/news/politics/663665/Barack-Obama-Britain-back-queue-Brexit)
492. Alastair Jamieson and Jon Schuppe, "Obama Brushes Off London 'Brexit' Backlash With Golf, Shakespeare", *NBC News*, 4/23/2016; (http://www.nbcnews.com/news/world/obama-brushes-london-brexit-backlash-golf-shakespeare-n560966)
493. The White House, Office of the Press Secretary. (2009). Remarks by President Obama [Press release]. Retrieved from http://www.whitehouse.gov/the_press_office/Remarks-By-President-Barack-Obama-In-Prague-As-Delivered/
494. Paul Kengor, "Obama, the Russians, and Missile Defense: Historical Parallels," *Townhall*, 4/1/,2012, (http://townhall.com/columnists/paulkengor/2012/04/01/obama_the_russians_and_missile_defense_historical_parallels/page/full/)
495. Ibid.
496. Nile Gardiner, "Barack Obama has insulted 38 million Poles with his crass and ignorant 'Polish death camp' remark," *Telegraph*, 5/30/2012, (http://blogs.telegraph.co.uk/news/nilegardiner/100161347/

barack-obama-has-insulted-38-million-poles-with-his-crass-and-ignorant-polish-death-camp-remark/)

497. "Obama skips Polish funeral, heads to golf course" *The Washington Times*, 4/18/2010, (https://www.washingtontimes.com/news/2010/apr/18/obama-skips-polish-funeral-heads-to-golf-course/)
498. Scott Wilson, "Where Obama Failed on Forging Peace in the Middle East," *The Washington Post*, 07/14/2012; (http://www.washingtonpost.com/politics/obama-searches-for-middle-east-peace/2012/07/14/gJQAQQiKlW_story.html)
499. Tom Cohen, "Obama Calls for Israel's Return to Pre-1967 Borders," CNN, 05/19/2011, (http://articles.cnn.com/2011-05-19/politics/obama.israel.palestinians_1_israel-palestinian-conflict-borders-settlements)
500. Robert Tait, "US Condemns 'Provocative' Israel Settlement Building," *The Daily Telegraph*, 12/19/2012, (http://www.telegraph.co.uk/news/worldnews/middleeast/israel/9756199/US-condemns-provocative-Israel-settlement-building.html)
501. Anne Bayefsky, "U.S to Legitimize U.N. Human Rights Council for Three More Years," *National Review*, 11/12/2012; (http://www.nationalreview.com/corner/333240/us-legitimize-un-human-rights-council-three-more-years-anne-bayefsky)
502. Jason Howerton, "Day After DNC 'Jerusalem' Controversy, State Department Still Refuses to Name Israel's Capital," *The Blaze*, 09/06/2012, (http://www.theblaze.com/stories/2012/09/06/day-after-dnc-jerusalem-controversy-state-dept-still-refuses-to-name-israels-capital/)
503. Sharona Schwartz, "Paper Details Obama Admin's Alleged Secret Note Sent to Iran: If Israel Attacks, We Won't Get Involved," *The Blaze*, 09/03/2012, (http://www.theblaze.com/stories/2012/09/03/paper-details-obama-admins-alleged-secret-note-sent-to-iran-if-israel-attacks-we-wont-get-involved/)
504. Keith Koffler, "Obama Insults Netanyahu; Press Fails to Report," *White House Dossier*, 11/08/2011, (http://www.whitehousedossier.com/2011/11/08/reuters-confirms-obama-insults-netanyahu/)
505. Roee Nahmias, "Hamas Says Asked by US to Keep Silent on Talks," *Ynet News*, 06/25/2010, (http://www.ynetnews.com/Ext/

Comp/ArticleLayout/CdaArticlePrintPreview/1,2506,L-3910714,00.html)

506. Anne Bayefsky, "Obama's Real Record on Israel," Fox News, 10/23/2012; (http://www.foxnews.com/opinion/2012/10/23/obama-real-record-on-israel/)
507. "Israel on the Outs, Again," *New York Post*, 07/14/2012; (http://www.nypost.com/p/news/opinion/editorials/israel_on_the_outs_again_U3SLVPX0LjPG4V8ojjqnpN)
508. Jonathan S. Tobin, "Will Obama Blame Israel for Abbas' 'No'?," *Commentary*, 3/7/14 (http://www.commentarymagazine.com/2014/03/07/will-obama-blame-israel-for-abbas-no-peace-process-jewish-state/)
509. Michael R. Gordon, "Kerry Expresses Regret After Apartheid Remark," *The New York Times*, 4/28/2014 (http://www.nytimes.com/2014/04/29/world/middleeast/kerry-apologizes-for-remark-that-israel-risks-apartheid.html)
510. Patrick Goodenoiugh, "State Dept. Slams Netanyahu: 'Overstated', 'Oversimplification', 'Scary"; CNS News, 3/4/2015; (http://cnsnews.com/news/article/patrick-goodenough/state-dept-slams-netanyahu-overstated-oversimplification-scary)
511. Thomas Rose, "Obama Campaign Team Arrives in Israel to Defeat Netanyahu in March Elections," *Breitbart*, 1/26/2015; (http://www.breitbart.com/big-government/2015/01/26/obama-campaign-team-arrives-in-israel-to-defeat-netanyahu-in-march-elections/)
512. Stephen Dinan, "Obama admin. sent taxpayer money to campaign to oust Netanyahu," *The Washington Times*, 7/12/2016; (https://www.washingtontimes.com/news/2016/jul/12/obama-admin-sent-taxpayer-money-oust-netanyahu/)
513. Hana Levi Julian, "US Declassifies Report, Exposes Details on Israel's Nuclear Program," *The Jewish Press*, 3/25/2015; (http://www.jewishpress.com/news/breaking-news/us-declassifies-report-exposes-details-on-israels-nuclear-program/2015/03/25/)
514. J.E. Dyer, "Obama Let 40 Year Old Oil Supply Guarantee to Israel Expire in November 2014," *The Jewish Press*, 3/17/2015; (http://www.jewishpress.com/indepth/analysis/j-e-dyer/obama-let-40-year-old-oil-supply-guarantee-to-israel-expire-in-november-2014/2015/03/17/)

515. Jennifer Rubin, "Backlash blows away FAA's Israel flight ban," *The Washington Post*, 7/24/2014; (https://www.washingtonpost.com/blogs/right-turn/wp/2014/07/24/backlash-blows-away-faas-israel-flight-ban/)
516. Adam Entous and Danny Yadron, "U.S. Spy Net on Israel Snares Congress," *The Wall Street Journal*, 12/29/2015 (http://www.wsj.com/articles/u-s-spy-net-on-israel-snares-congress-1451425210)
517. David Efune, "Ed Koch on Chuck Hagel Nomination: Obama's Reneging on His Conveyed Support for Israel Has Come Earlier Than I Thought," *Algemeiner*, 01/07/2013, (http://www.algemeiner.com/2013/01/07/ed-koch-on-chuck-hagel-nomination-obamas-reneging-on-his-conveyed-support-for-israel-has-come-earlier-than-i-thought/)
518. Mike Flynn, "Hagel Limps into Pentagon," *Breitbart*, 02/26/2013, (http://www.breitbart.com/Big-Government/2013/02/26/Hagel-Limps-into-Pentagon#disqus_thread)
519. Jordan Michael Smith, "How Hagel Angered the GOP," *The National Interest*, 01/11/2013, (http://nationalinterest.org/commentary/how-hagel-angered-the-gop-7957)
520. John Cornyn, "White I Can't Support Hagel," CNN Opinion, 01/11/2013, (http://www.cnn.com/2013/01/10/opinion/cornyn-hagel)
521. Republican Jewish Coalition. (2012). RJC: Appointment of Hagel Would Be A "Slap in the Face" for Pro-Israel Americans [Press release]. Retrieved from http://www.rjchq.org/2012/12/rjc-appointment-of-hagel-would-be-a-slap-in-the-face-for-pro-israel-americans/)
522. Paul Mirengoff, "Report: Hagel Said State Department Controlled by Israel," *Powerline*, 02/14/2013, (http://www.powerlineblog.com/archives/2013/02/report-hagel-said-state-department-controlled-by-israel.php)
523. Jennifer Rubin, "Hagel: Israel Heading Towards 'Apartheid'," *The Washington Post*, 02/19/2013, (http://www.washingtonpost.com/blogs/right-turn/wp/2013/02/19/hagel-israel-heading-toward-apartheid/)
524. "Ash Carter to be Defense Secretary nominee: reports," *The Washington Times*, 12/2/2014; (http://

www.washingtontimes.com/news/2014/dec/2/ash-carter-be-defense-secretary-nominee-reports/)

525. Jeff Duntz, "Krauthammer: Hillary Achieved Nothing As Secretary of State," *Truth Revolt*, 2/18/2014 (http://www.truthrevolt.org/news/krauthammer-hillary-achieved-nothing-secretary-state)

526. Jennifer Rubin, "Obama team admits failure on Russian reset," *The Washington Post*, 2/4/2014; (http://www.washingtonpost.com/blogs/right-turn/wp/2013/02/04/obama-team-admits-failure-on-russian-reset/)

527. John Sexton, "Senate Report Faults State Department for Lack of Security in Benghazi," *Breitbart*, 1/15/2014 (http://www.breitbart.com/InstaBlog/2014/01/15/Senate-Report-Faults-State-Department-for-Lack-of-Security-in-Benghazi)

528. Joel E Pollak, "Top Ten Worst John Kerry Foreign Policy Mistakes," *Breitbart*, 12/30/2012; (http://www.breitbart.com/national-security/2012/12/30/top-ten-worst-john-kerry-foreign-policy-mistakes/)

529. Noah Rothman, "John Kerry Still The Only Secretary Of State In 20 Years To Fail At Ceasefire Efforts In Mideast," *Hot Air*, 7/25/2014; (http://hotair.com/archives/2014/07/25/john-kerry-still-the-only-secretary-of-state-in-20-years-to-fail-at-cease-fire-efforts-in-mideast/)

530. Jeremy Bender, "US is Now in an 'Awkward' Position over Syria and Iraq," *Business Insider*, 12/2/2014; (http://www.businessinsider.com/us-sharing-skies-with-syria-and-iran-2014-12)

531. Michael R Gordon and Steven Erlanger, "U.S. EFforts to Broker Russia-Ukraine Diplomacy Fails," *The New York Times*, 3/5/2014; (http://www.nytimes.com/2014/03/06/world/europe/ukraine.html?_r=0)

532. "Kerry Makes Climate Change a 'Top-Tier Diplomatic Priority", *Fox News*, 3/12/2014; (http://www.foxnews.com/politics/2014/03/12/kerry-makes-climate-change-his-first-policy-initiative-top-tier-diplomatic/)

533. Mark Murray, "ISIS Threat: Fear of Terror Attack Soars to 9/11 High, NBC News/WSJ Poll Finds," NBC News, 9/9/2014; (http://www.nbcnews.com/politics/first-read/isis-threat-fear-terror-attack-soars-9-11-high-nbc-n199496)

534. Rick Maze, "Obama Plan Calls for New Tricare Fee Hikes," *Army Times*, 09/19/2011, (http://www.armytimes.com/article/20110919/NEWS/109190318/Obama-plan-calls-new-Tricare-fee-hikes)
535. Bill Gertz, "Trashing Tricare," *Washington Free Beacon*, 02/27/2012, (http://freebeacon.com/trashing-tricare/)
536. Ibid
537. Louise Radnofsky, "Military Families Balk at Health Fee," *The Wall Street Journal*, 10/10/2012, (http://online.wsj.com/article/SB10000872396390443294904578046873641438216.html)
538. Michael Graham, "Michael Graham: Women poor fit for fight," *Boston Herald*, 1/24/2013 (http://bostonherald.com/print/news_opinion/opinion/op_ed/2013/01/michael_graham_women_poor_fit_fight)
539. "Marines delay female fitness plan after half fail pull-up test," Associated Press, 1/2/2014 (http://www.foxnews.com/politics/2014/01/02/marines-delay-female-fitness-plan-after-half-fail-pullup-test/)
540. "Retired Marine says proposed unisex uniform change is 'appalling'," Fox News, 10/25/2013 (http://www.foxnews.com/politics/2013/10/25/retired-marine-proposed-unisex-uniform-change-is-appalling/?intcmp=latestnews)
541. Ken Klukowski, "Pentagon Taps Anti-Christian Extremist For Religious for Religious Tolerance Policy," *Breitbart*, 4/28/2013; http://www.breitbart.com/Big-Peace/2013/04/28/Pentagon-Consults-Extremist-Who-Calls-Christians-Monsters-and-Enemies-of-the-Constitution-to-Develop-Religious-Tolerance-Policyh
542. Ken Klukowski, "Pentagon May Court Martial Soldiers who Share Christian Faith," *Breitbart*, 5/1/2013; http://www.breitbart.com/Big-Peace/2013/05/01/Breaking-Pentagon-Confirms-Will-Court-Martial-Soldiers-Who-Share-Christian-Faith
543. Andrew Tilghman, "Bible verse sends former Marine back to court," *Military Times*, 5/27/2015; (http://www.militarytimes.com/story/military/2015/05/27/marine-monifa-sterling-bible-verse-court-case/28010365/)
544. Jim Kouri, "U.S. military is No. 1 Islamic terrorism target," *Examiner*, 12/8/2011 (http://www.examiner.com/article/u-s-military-is-no-1-islamic-terrorism-target)

545. Greg Botelho and Joe Sterling, "FBI: Navy Yard shooter 'delusional,' said 'low frequency attacks' drove him to kill," CNN, (http://edition.cnn.com/2013/09/25/us/washington-navy-yard-investigation/)
546. "Fort Hood shooter snapped over denial of request for leave, Army confirms," Fox News, 4/7/2014 (http://www.foxnews.com/us/2014/04/07/fort-hood-shooter-snapped-over-denial-request-for-leave-army-confirms/)
547. J.D. Gordon, "GORDON: Purging America's military," *The Washington Times*, 11/12/2013 (http://www.washingtontimes.com/news/2013/nov/12/gordon-transforming-the-us-military/)
548. Sara Carter, "Blaze Sources: Obama Purging Military Commanders," *The Blaze*, 10/23/2013 (http://www.theblaze.com/stories/2013/10/23/military-sources-obama-administration-purging-commanders/)
549. Ibid.
550. Ibid.
551. Ellie Hall, "Obama Told Military Leaders: Accept Gays in Military or Step Down, Admiral Says," *Buzzfeed*, 3/31/2014 (http://www.buzzfeed.com/ellievhall/obama-told-military-leaders-accept-gays-in-military-or-step)
552. Kerry Eleveld, "Obama Talks All Things LGBT With The Advocate," *The Advocate*, 12/23/2008 (http://www.advocate.com/news/2008/12/23/obama-talks-all-things-lgbt-the%C2%A0advocate?page=0,1)
553. Jeff Zeleny, "No 'Yes' Men, Obama Says," *The Caucus*, 12/27/2007 (http://thecaucus.blogs.nytimes.com/2007/12/17/no-yes-men-obama-says/)
554. Marion Blakey, "Out of Balance: Obama Cut Weapons Too Much, Personnel Not Enough," *AOLDefense*, 03/14/2012, (http://defense.aol.com/2012/03/14/out-of-balance-obama-cut-weapons-too-much-personnel-not-enough/)
555. Adam Kredo, "Obama to kill Navy's Tomahawk, Hellfire missile programs in budget decimation," *The Washington Times*, 3/25/2014 (http://www.washingtontimes.com/news/2014/mar/25/obama-kill-navys-tomahawk-hellfire-missile-program)
556. Ibid.

557. Jeff Daniels, "Obama once looked to downsize Tomahawk missile system used in Syria strike," CNBC, 4/7/2017, (http://defense.aol.com/2012/03/14/out-of-balance-obama-cut-weapons-too-much-personnel-not-enough/)
558. James Rosen, "Proposed Defense Cuts Would Hit Some Bases, Spare Others", *The Washington Post*, 2/24/2014; http://www.mcclatchydc.com/2014/02/24/219237/proposed-defense-cuts-would-hit.html
559. Ben Shapiro, "Obama's Historic Defense Cuts Spell Disaster," *Breitbart*, 2/25/2014 (http://www.breitbart.com/Big-Government/2014/02/25/defense-budget-cuts-history)
560. Saagar Enjeti, "US Military 'In A Death Spiral' After Obama-Era Cuts," *The Daily Caller*, 10/11/2017 (http://dailycaller.com/2017/10/11/us-military-in-a-death-spiral-after-obama-era-cuts/)
561. Dakota L. Wood, "The Storm Gathers and America is Unready," *War on The Rock*, 10/11/2017 (https://warontherocks.com/2017/10/the-storm-gathers-and-america-is-unready/)
562. William Bigelow, "Administration Defends Obama Trips to Tyrannical Regimes," *Breitbart*, 11/16/2012, (http://www.breitbart.com/Big-Government/2012/11/15/Administration-Defends-Obama-Trips-To-Tyrannical-Regimes)
563. Brian Knowlton, "4 Nations With Child Soldiers Keep U.S. Aid," *The New York Times*, 10/28/2010, (http://www.nytimes.com/2010/10/29/world/africa/29soldiers.html)
564. David Axe, "Questions Abound as China Unveils Another Stealth Jet," *Wired*, 09/16/2012, (http://www.wired.com/dangerroom/2012/09/questions-abound-as-china-unveils-another-stealth-jet/)
565. Marc S. Reisch, "China Accused of Stealing DuPont Trade Secrets," *Chemical and Engineering News*, 02/09/2011, (http://cen.acs.org/articles/90/web/2012/02/China-Accused-Stealing-DuPont-Trade.html)
566. Jeffrey Mervis, "GAO Says White House Broke the Law by Holding Science Meetings With China," *Science*, 10/12/2011, (http://news.sciencemag.org/scienceinsider/2011/10/gao-says-white-house-broke-the-law.html)

567. Tony Lee, "Palin Mocked in 2008 for Warning Putin May Invade Ukraine if Obama Elected," *Breitbart*, 2/28/2014; http://www.breitbart.com/Big-Peace/2014/02/28/Flashback-Palin-Mocked-in-2008-for-Warning-Putin-May-Invade-Ukraine-if-Obama-Elected-President
568. Laura Smith-Spark, Diana Magnay and Ingrid Formanek, "Russian Upper House Approves Use of Military Force in Ukraine", CNN, 3/1/2014; http://www.cnn.com/2014/03/01/world/europe/ukraine-politics/
569. "Krauthammer on Ukraine: 'Everybody is shocked by the weakness of Obama's statement," Fox News, 2/28/2014 (http://www.foxnews.com/politics/2014/02/28/krauthammer-on-ukraine-everybody-is-shocked-by-weakness-obama-statement/)
570. Daniel Harper, "Obama Skips National Security Team Meeting on Russia, Ukraine," *The Weekly Standard*, 3/1/2014 (http://www.weeklystandard.com/blogs/obama-skips-national-security-team-meeting-russia-ukraine_783659.html)
571. Kirit Radia, "Russian Deputy PM Laughs at Obama's Sanctions," ABC News, 3/17/2014 (http://abcnews.go.com/blogs/headlines/2014/03/russian-deputy-pm-laughs-at-obamas-sanctions/)
572. Michael Hastings, "How Obama Decided to Intervene in Libya," *Rolling Stone*, 10/13/2011; (http://www.rollingstone.com/politics/news/inside-obamas-war-room-20111013)
573. http://www.theatlantic.com/international/archive/2016/04/obamas-worst-mistake-libya/478461/
574. Bill Gertz, "Islamic State Rises in Libya," *The Washington Free Beacon*, 3/20/2015; (http://freebeacon.com/national-security/islamic-state-rises-in-libya/)
575. Dominic Tierney, "The Legacy of Obama's 'Worst Mistake'," *The Atlantic*, 4/15/2016; (http://www.theatlantic.com/international/archive/2016/04/obamas-worst-mistake-libya/478461/)
576. Garikai Chengu, "Libya: From Africa's Wealthiest Democracy Under Gaddafi to Terrorist Haven After US Intervention," *Counterpunch*, 10/20/2015; (http://www.counterpunch.org/2015/10/20/libya-from-africas-wealthiest-democracy-under-gaddafi-to-terrorist-haven-after-us-intervention/)

577. "Obama Defends Military Mission in Libya, Says U.S. Acted to 'Prevent a Massacre'," Fox News, 3/28/2011; (http://www.foxnews.com/politics/2011/03/28/obama-delivers-address-nation-libya-intervention.html)
578. "Obama warns Syria not to cross 'red line'," CNN, 8/21/2012 (http://www.cnn.com/2012/08/20/world/meast/syria-unrest/)
579. Alistair Dawber, "John Kerry says Assad's Syria regime HAS used sarin chemical weapons against rebels - despite Barack Obama insisting that was a 'red line' for US," *The Independent*, 4/25/2013 (http://www.independent.co.uk/news/world/middle-east/john-kerry-says-assads-syria-regime-has-used-sarin-chemical-weapons-against-rebels--despite-barack-obama-insisting-that-was-a-red-line-for-us-8588774.html)
580. Dianne Feinstein. (2013). Feinstein statement on Syria. [press release] 4/25/2013 (http://www.feinstein.senate.gov/public/index.cfm/press-releases?ID=4423d4a4-a602-4e7d-823f-77aade545e91)
581. Joby Warrick, "More than 1,400 killed in Syrian chemical weapons attack, U.S. says," *The Washington Post*, 8/30/2013 (http://www.washingtonpost.com/world/national-security/nearly-1500-killed-in-syrian-chemical-weapons-attack-us-says/2013/08/30/b2864662-1196-11e3-85b6-d27422650fd5_story.html)
582. Molly Hunter and Shushannah Walshe, "Britain Won't Join in a Syrian Attack," ABC News, 8/29/2013 (http://abcnews.go.com/International/britain-join-syrian-attack/story?id=20104801)
583. Paul Singer, "Opposition to Syria Attack Emerges in Congress", *USA Today*, 9/2/2013 (http://www.usatoday.com/story/news/politics/2013/09/01/congress-syria-rand-paul-kerry/2752965/
584. Jonathan Karl, "Obama on Syria: 'My Credibility Is Not on the Line'," ABC News, 9/4/2013 (http://abcnews.go.com/blogs/politics/2013/09/obama-on-syria-my-credibility-is-not-on-the-line/)
585. Paul Steinhauser and John Helton, "CNN Poll: Public Against Syria Strike Resolution," CNN, 9/9/2013 (http://www.cnn.com/2013/09/09/politics/syria-poll-main)
586. Olivier Knox, "Kerry Vows 'Unbelievably Small' Strike on Syria", *Yahoo News*, 9/9/2013 (http://news.yahoo.

com/-kerry-vows-%E2%80%98unbelievably-small%E2%80%99-strike-on-syria--150302777.html)

587. Joel Gehrke, "Obama waives ban on arming terrorists to allow aid to Syrian opposition," *The Washington Examiner*, 9/17/2013 (http://washingtonexaminer.com/obama-waives-ban-on-arming-terrorists-to-allow-aid-to-syrian-opposition/article/2535885)
588. Julian Pecquet, "Obama Administration Reaches Syria Weapons Deal With Russia," *The Hill*, 9/26/2013 (http://thehill.com/blogs/global-affairs/un-treaties/324999-obama-administration-reaches-syria-deal-with-russia)
589. Joby Warrick, "Syria blamed for missed deadline on chemical arsenal," *The Washington Post*, 12/30/2013 (http://www.washingtonpost.com/world/national-security/syria-blamed-for-missed-deadline-on-chemical-arsenal/2013/12/30/8356c350-719d-11e3-8b3f-b1666705ca3b_story.html)
590. Josh Rogin, "Senators: Kerry Admits Obama's Syria Policy Is Failing," *The Daily Beast*, 2/4/2014 (http://www.thedailybeast.com/articles/2014/02/03/senators-kerry-admits-obama-s-syria-policy-is-failing.html)
591. Elise Jordan, "How Obama Lost Afghanistan," *The Daily Beast*, 4/5/2014; http://www.thedailybeast.com/articles/2014/04/05/how-obama-lost-afghanistan.html
592. James Warren, "President Obama Lost Faith in Afghanistan Mission, Can't Stand President Karzai: Gates' Memoir," *New York Daily News*, 1/7/2014; http://www.nydailynews.com/news/politics/president-obama-lost-faith-afghanistan-mission-article-1.1569274
593. Data from iCasualties.org
594. David Zucchino, "Opium cultivation soars in Afghanistan, U.N. reports," *Los Angeles Times*, 11/13/2013 (http://articles.latimes.com/2013/nov/13/world/la-fg-wn-opium-cultivation-soars-afghanistan-20131113)
595. Associated Press, "Obama threatens Karzai with full US withdrawal," *New York Post*, 2/26/2014 (http://nypost.com/2014/02/26/obama-threatens-karzai-with-full-us-withdrawal/)
596. Matthew Rosenberg and Michael D. Shear, "In Reversal, Obama Says U.S. Soldiers Will Stay in Afghanistan to 2017," *The New York*

Times, 10/15/2015; (http://www.nytimes.com/2015/10/16/world/asia/obama-troop-withdrawal-afghanistan.html)

597. Elise Jordan, "How Obama Lost Afghanistan," *The Daily Beast*, 4/5/2014; http://www.thedailybeast.com/articles/2014/04/05/how-obama-lost-afghanistan.html
598. James Gordon Meek, "Barack Obama Purges Web Site Critique of Surge in Iraq," *New York Daily News*, 7/14/2008 (http://www.nydailynews.com/news/politics/barack-obama-purges-web-site-critique-surge-iraq-article-1.349828)
599. Josh Rogin, "How the Obama Administration Bungled the Iraq Withdrawal Negotiations," *Foreign Policy*, 10/21/2011 (http://thecable.foreignpolicy.com/posts/2011/10/21/how_the_obama_administration_bungled_the_iraq_withdrawal_negotiations)
600. "Obama Announces Complete Withdrawal of U.S. Forces From Iraq by End of 2011," Fox News, 10/21/2011 (http://www.foxnews.com/politics/2011/10/21/obama-to-speak-about-iraq-troop-levels/)
601. "Violence in Iraq Increases Following US Withdrawal," *Catholic Online*, 3/11/2012 (http://catholic.org/international/international_story.php?id=45135)
602. Liz Sly, "Al-Qaeda-Linked Force Captures Fallujah Amid Rise in Violence in Iraq," *The Washington Post*, January 3, 2014; http://www.washingtonpost.com/world/al-qaeda-force-captures-fallujah-amid-rise-in-violence-in-iraq/2014/01/03/8abaeb2a-74aa-11e3-8def-a33011492df2_story.html
603. Francesca Chambers, "Revealed: How Obama SET FREE the merciless terrorist warlord now leading the ISIS horde blazing a trail of destruction through Iraq," *Daily Mail (UK)*, 6/13/2014 (http://www.dailymail.co.uk/news/article-2657231/Revealed-Obama-RELEASED-warlord-head-ISIS-extremist-army-five-years-ago.html)
604. Nick Hallett, "Dirty Bomb Fears After ISIS Seize Uranium," *Breitbart*, July 11, 2014 (http://www.breitbart.com/Breitbart-London/2014/07/11/Dirty-Bomb-Fears-after-ISIS-Seize-Uranium)
605. Nile Gardiner, "Barack Obama is proving an embarrassing amateur on the world stage compared to George W. Bush," *The*

Daily Telegraph, 8/30/2013 (http://blogs.telegraph.co.uk/news/nilegardiner/100233454/barack-obama-is-proving-an-embarrassing-amateur-on-the-world-stage-compared-to-george-w-bush/)

606. Shadee Ashtari, "Americans View U.S. Power, Respect Slipping On Global Stage, Poll Shows," *The Huffington Post*, 12/4/2013 (http://www.huffingtonpost.com/2013/12/04/us-power-global_n_4385160.html)

607. Nico Hines, "Senior UK Defense Advisor: Obama Is Clueless About 'What He Wants To Do In The World'," *The Daily Beast*, 1/14/2013, (http://www.thedailybeast.com/articles/2014/01/15/senior-uk-defense-advisor-obama-is-clueless-about-what-he-wants-to-do-in-the-world.html)

608. Maayana Miskin, "Report: Israel, Saudi Arabia Plan Iran Strike," *Arutz Sheva* 7, 11/17/2013, (http://www.israelnationalnews.com/News/News.aspx/174092#.UrNDJuInip0)

609. Barbara Starr, "U.S., Chinese warships come dangerously close," CNN, 12/13/2013 (http://www.cnn.com/2013/12/13/politics/us-china-confrontation/)

610. "Iran Sending Warships Close To US Borders," Associated Press, 2/8/2014 (http://abcnews.go.com/International/wireStory/iran-sending-warships-close-us-borders-22424767)

611. Oren Dorell, "Iranian warships heading to USA to show reach," *USA Today*, 2/11/2014 (http://www.usatoday.com/story/news/world/2014/02/10/iran-warships-threat-to-usa-coast/5365335/)

612. "North Korea's Shadowy Arms Trade," The Associated Press, July 17, 2013; http://www.theguardian.com/world/2013/jul/18/history-north-korea-arms-dealing

613. "Philippines Accuse China of Military Buildup at South China Sea," *Agence France-Presse*, June 30, 2013; http://www.ndtv.com/article/world/philippines-accuses-china-of-military-build-up-at-south-china-sea-386029

614. Fred Dews, "Lessons From World War I: is Today's China the German of 1914? Where is the Next Global Flashpoint?", Brookings Institute, November 13, 2013; http://www.brookings.edu/blogs/brookings-now/posts/2013/11/lessons-world-war-one-china-germany-global-flashpoint

615. "Obama: Bush not respecting Constitution," NBC News, 3/30/2007; (http://www.nbcnews.com/id/17876280/ns/politics-decision_08/t/obama-bush-not-respecting-constitution/)
616. "Obama On Executive Actions: 'I've Got A Pen And I've Got A Phone'," CBS DC, 1/14/2014; (http://washington.cbslocal.com/2014/01/14/obama-on-executive-actions-ive-got-a-pen-and-ive-got-a-phone/)
617. Josh Siegal,"What's Driving the Latest Surge of Illegal Immigration From Central America," *The Daily Signal*, 12/29/2015; (http://dailysignal.com/2015/12/29/whats-driving-the-latest-surge-of-illegal-immigration-from-central-america/)
618. Brandon Darby, "Leaked DHS Report Reveals Obama Admin Deception on Border Crisis," *Breitbart*, 7/7/2014; (http://www.breitbart.com/Breitbart-Texas/2014/07/07/Leaked-Internal-DHS-Report-Admits-Lack-of-Deportation-Significant-Factor-in-Border-Crisis)
619. "Child Border Surge Includes Mara Salvatrucha Gang Elements," *Investor's Business Daily*, Editorial, 7/9/2014; (http://news.investors.com/ibd-editorials/070914-708067-border-surge-includes-significant-criminal-element.htm)
620. Todd Starnes, "Immigration Crisis: Tuberculosis Spreading at Camps," Fox News, 7/7/2014; (http://www.foxnews.com/opinion/2014/07/07/immigration-crisis-tuberculosis-spreading-at-camps/)
621. "U.S. General: Border Security an "Existential" Threat to National Security," CBS DC, 7/7/2014; (http://washington.cbslocal.com/2014/07/07/us-general-border-security-an-existential-threat-to-national-security/)
622. Jessia Chasmer, "Amid border crisis, Obama to take 15-day vacation in Martha's Vineyard," *The Washington Times*, 7/10/2014 (http://www.washingtontimes.com/news/2014/jul/10/amid-border-crisis-obama-take-15-day-vacation-mart/)
623. Jessica Vaughan, "Don't Blame the Border Crisis on a 'Bush-era' Law," *National Review*, 7/10/2014 (http://www.nationalreview.com/article/382463/dont-blame-border-crisis-bush-era-law-jessica-vaughan)

624. Susan Crabtree, "White House stands by claim that border security is stronger than ever," *The Washington Examiner*, 7/11/2014 (http://washingtonexaminer.com/white-house-stands-by-claim-that-border-security-is-stronger-than-ever/article/2550730)
625. Brandon Darby, "Leaked DHS Report Reveals Obama Admin Deception on Border Crisis," *Breitbart*, 7/7/2014 (http://www.breitbart.com/Breitbart-Texas/2014/07/07/Leaked-Internal-DHS-Report-Admits-Lack-of-Deportation-Significant-Factor-in-Border-Crisis)
626. Sarah Carter, "Gov't Confirms Authenticity of Contract Request for 'Escort Services for Unaccompanied Alien Children' at the Border," *The Blaze*, 6/20/2014, (http://www.theblaze.com/stories/2014/06/20/govt-confirms-authenticity-of-contract-request-for-escort-services-for-unaccompanied-alien-children-at-the-border/)
627. "TRANSCRIPT: President Obama's Remarks at Univision Town Hall," Fox News, 9/20/2012; (http://insider.foxnews.com/2012/09/20/transcript-president-obamas-remarks-at-univision-town-hall)
628. Aaron Blake, "Obama: I 'probably' can't legalize immigrants myself," *The Washington Post*, 7/17/2013; (http://www.washingtonpost.com/blogs/post-politics/wp/2013/07/17/obama-i-probably-cant-legalize-immigrants-myself/)
629. "President Obama Vows To Act Alone, Use Executive Powers To Tackle Immigration Reform," Fox News Latino, 6/30/2014; (http://latino.foxnews.com/latino/politics/2014/06/30/same-song-same-verse-president-obama-threatens-to-act-alone-on-immigration/)
630. Dave Boyer, "Obama offers amnesty to 5 million illegal immigrants, defies GOP," *The Washington Times*, 11/20/2014; (http://www.washingtontimes.com/news/2014/nov/20/obama-offers-amnesty-to-millions-of-illegal-immigr/)
631. Jonathan Karl, "Obama's Long Lost Campaign Promise," ABC News, 2/17/2014; (http://abcnews.go.com/blogs/politics/2014/02/obamas-long-lost-campaign-promise/)
632. "Transcript of President Barack Obama with Univision," *Los Angeles Times*, 10/25/2010; (http://latimesblogs.latimes.com/

washington/2010/10/transcript-of-president-barack-obama-with-univision.html)

633. Mark Krikorian, "Obama's Unprecedented Amnesty," *National Review*, 11/18/2014; (http://www.nationalreview.com/article/392887/obamas-unprecedented-amnesty-mark-krikorian)
634. Brandon Darby, "Catch and Release 2.0 - Leaks Highlight Teardown of Immigration Enforcement," *Breitbart*, 1/11/2015; (http://www.breitbart.com/big-government/2015/01/11/exclusive-catch-and-release-2-0-leaks-highlight-teardown-of-immigration-enforcement/)
635. Stephen Dinan, "Obama's Amnesty to Impose Billions in Costs on States, Lawsuit Alleges," *The Washington Times*, 1/11/2015; (http://www.washingtontimes.com/news/2015/jan/11/obama-amnesty-for-illegal-immigrants-to-impose-bil/)
636. Stephen Dinan, "IRS to Pay Back-Refunds to Illegal Immigrants Who Didn't Pay Taxes," *The Washington Times*, 2/11/2015; (http://www.washingtontimes.com/news/2015/feb/11/irs-pay-back-refunds-illegal-immigrants-who-didnt-/?page=all)
637. Peter Kirsanow, "After Obama's Amnesty, Illegal Aliens Could Decide U.S. Elections," *National Review*, 2/16/2015; (http://www.nationalreview.com/corner/398677/after-obamas-amnesty-illegal-aliens-could-decide-us-elections-peter-kirsanow)
638. Ben Kamisar and Kyle Balluck, "Judge Blocks Obama Order on Immigration," *The Hill*, 2/17/2015; (http://thehill.com/blogs/blog-briefing-room/232918-judge-blocks-obama-order-on-immigration)
639. Daniel Halper, "Obama: 'Consequences' for ICE Officials Who Don't Follow Executive Amnesty," *The Weekly Standard*, 2/25/2015; (http://www.weeklystandard.com/blogs/obama-consequences-ice-officials-who-dont-follow-executive-amnesty_866479.html)
640. Stephen Dinan, "Judge Accuses Obama Lawyers of Misleading Him, Refuses to Restart Amnesty," *The Washington Times*, 4/7/2015; (http://www.washingtontimes.com/news/2015/apr/7/obama-motion-immediately-restart-amnesty-rejected-/)
641. Ariane de Vogue and Tal Kopan "Deadlocked Supreme Court deals big blow to Obama immigration plan," CNN, 6/23/2016;

(https://www.cnn.com/2016/06/23/politics/immigration-supreme-court/index.html)
642. Jessica Gavora, "How Title IX Became a Political Weapon," *The Wall Street Journal*, 6/7/2015; http://www.wsj.com/articles/how-title-ix-became-a-political-weapon-1433715320)
643. John Hinderaker, "The Obama Justice Department's Insane Attack on North Carolina," *Power Line*; 5/4/2016; (http://www.powerlineblog.com/archives/2016/05/the-obama-justice-departments-insane-attack-on-north-carolina.php)
644. Ryan T. Anderson, "Obama Unilaterally Rewrites Law, Imposes Transgender Policy on Nation's Schools," *The Daily Signal*, 5/13/2016; (http://dailysignal.com/2016/05/13/obama-unilaterally-rewrites-law-imposes-transgender-policy-on-nations-schools/)
645. Julie Hirschfeld Davis, "Obama Defends Transgender Directive for School Bathrooms," *The New York Times*, 5/16/2016; (http://www.nytimes.com/2016/05/17/us/politics/obama-defends-transgender-directive-for-school-bathrooms.html)
646. Julie Hirschfeld Davis and Matt Apuzzo, "U.S. Directs Public Schools to Allow Transgender Access to Restrooms," *The New York Times*, 5/12/2016; (http://www.nytimes.com/2016/05/13/us/politics/obama-administration-to-issue-decree-on-transgender-access-to-school-restrooms.html)
647. Caleb Howe, "These 12 States Are Fighting Back Against Obama's Leftist Bathroom Bullying," *Redstate*, 5/15/2016; (http://www.redstate.com/absentee/2016/05/14/12-states-fighting-back-obamas-leftist-bathroom-bullying/)
648. Mario Loyola, "Obama's Dictatorial Transgender Proclamation," *National Review*, 5/16/2016; (http://www.nationalreview.com/article/435413/bathroom-wars-obamas-proclamation-dictatorial-unconstitutional)
649. "Obama to Order Expansion of Overtime Pay for Millions of Workers," Fox News, 3/12/2014; (http://www.foxnews.com/politics/2014/03/12/obama-to-reportedly-order-expansion-overtime-pay-for-millions-workers/)
650. Benjamin Goad, "Biz Stunned by Obama Overtime Move," *The Hill*, 3/12/2014; (http://thehill.com/blogs/regwatch/business/200658-biz-stunned-as-obama-gives-millions-overtime)

651. Brakkton Booker, "Federal Judge Blocks Obama Administration's Overtime Pay Rule," NPR, 11/22/2016; (http://thehill.com/blogs/regwatch/business/200658-biz-stunned-as-obama-gives-millions-overtime)
652. Kate Scanlon, "Can Obama Raise Your Taxes Without Congressional Approval?," *The Daily Signal*, 3/3/2015; (http://dailysignal.com/2015/03/03/can-obama-raise-taxes-without-congressional-approval/?utm_source=facebook&utm_medium=social&utm_campaign=tds03042015RAISETAXES)
653. Amy Payne, "Obama Wants Power to Raise Debt Limit by Himself, Anytime," *The Foundry*, 12/05/2012, (http://blog.heritage.org/2012/12/05/morning-bell-obama-wants-power-to-raise-debt-limit-by-himself-anytime/)
654. Steve Holland and Mark Felsenthal, "Obama's opening 'fiscal cliff' bid seeks debt limit hike, stimulus," Reuters, 11/29/2012, (http://www.reuters.com/article/2012/11/30/us-usa-fiscal-offer-idUSBRE8AT02C20121130)
655. Robert Rector, "The Effects of Welfare Reform," Heritage Foundation, 03/15/2001, (http://www.heritage.org/research/testimony/the-effects-of-welfare-reform)
656. John Nolte, "Media Fact Checkers Shill for Obama's Gutting of Welfare Reform," *Breitbart*, 8/21/2012, (http://www.breitbart.com/Big-Journalism/2012/08/21/Fact-Checkers-Flak-For-Obamas-Gutting-of-welfare)
657. Eric Pianin, "Why Obama's Welfare Waivers Have Both Sides Seething," *Fiscal Times*, 08/10/2012, (http://www.thefiscaltimes.com/Articles/2012/08/10/Why-Obamas-Welfare-Waivers-Have-Both-Sides-Seething.aspx)
658. Rep. Dave Camp and Rep. John Kline, "Obama's illegal scheme to end welfare work requirements," *The Washington Times*, 9/19/2012, (http://www.washingtontimes.com/news/2012/sep/19/obamas-illegal-scheme-to-end-welfare-work-requirem/)
659. Andrew Refferty, "American Drone Deaths Highlight Controversy," NBC News, 03/05/2013; (usnews.nbcnews.com/_news/2013/02/05/16856963-american-drone-deaths-highlight-controversy)

660. Jon Swaine, "Barack Obama 'Has Authority to Use Drone Strikes to Kill Americans on US Soil'," *The Daily Telegraph*, 03/06/2013, (http://www.telegraph.co.uk/news/worldnews/barackobama/9913615/Barack-Obama-has-authority-to-use-drone-strikes-to-kill-Americans-on-US-soil.html)
661. "Brennan: Due Process Not Necessary to Kill Americans for Potential Future Actions," *Breitbart*, 02/07/2013, (http://www.breitbart.com/Breitbart-TV/2013/02/07/Brennan-Killing-Americans-Without-Due-Process-Not-Because-of-What-They-Did-But-What-They%20Might%20Do)
662. Jake Miller, "Paul's Filibuster Provokes Answer From Holder," CBS News, 03/07/2013, (http://www.cbsnews.com/8301-250_162-57573102/pauls-filibuster-provokes-answer-from-holder/)
663. Glenn Greenwald, "Chilling Legal Memo From Obama DoJ Justifies Assassination of US Citizens," *The Guardian*, 2/5/2013; http://www.theguardian.com/commentisfree/2013/feb/05/obama-kill-list-doj-memo
664. Pete Kasperowicz, " 'Everything is Confidential': Obama Stiffs Congress on Details of Cuban Spy Swap," *The Blaze*, 12/22/2014, (http://www.theblaze.com/stories/2014/12/22/everything-is-confidential-obama-stiffs-congress-on-details-of-cuban-spy-swap/)
665. United States Senate Committee on Foreign Relations. (2014). Chairman Menendez's Statement on the Release of Alan Gross [Press release]. Retrieved from http://www.foreign.senate.gov/press/chair/release/chairman-menendezs-statement-on-the-release-of-alan-gross
666. Rebecca Kaplan, "Congress deeply divided over Obama's Cuba deal," CBS News, 12/17/2014; (http://www.cbsnews.com/news/congress-deeply-divided-over-obamas-cuba-deal/)
667. Dave Boyer, "Obama to lift Cuba from list of terrorist sponsors," *The Washington Times*, 4/14/2015; (http://www.washingtontimes.com/news/2015/apr/14/obama-removes-cuba-state-sponsor-terror-list/)
668. David Steinberg, "Day After Obama Removes Cuba from Terror Sponsor List, Terror Group Sponsored by Cuba Kills

10," *PJ Media*, 4/15/2015; (http://pjmedia.com/tatler/2015/04/15/day-after-obama-removes-cuba-from-terror-sponsor-list-terror-group-sponsored-by-cuba-kills-10/)

669. Keith Johnson, "The link between Venezuela and Cuba," *Tico Times* 2/27/2014; (http://www.ticotimes.net/2014/02/27/the-link-between-venezuela-and-cuba)
670. Girish Gupta, "Venezuela's role in warming Cuba - US relations," *The Christian Science Monitor*, 12/17/2014; (http://www.csmonitor.com/World/Americas/Latin-America-Monitor/2014/1217/Venezuela-s-role-in-warming-Cuba-US-relations-video)
671. "Going hungry in Venezuela," *BBC*, 7/29/2016; (http://www.bbc.com/news/magazine-36913991)
672. Alberto de la Cruz, "Cuba and North Korea send Special Forces to Venezuela to prop up dictatorship," *Babalú Blog*, 5/21/2016; (http://babalublog.com/2016/05/21/cuba-and-north-korea-send-special-forces-to-venezuela-to-prop-up-dictatorship/)
673. Ana Quintana, "Congressional Oversight Needed as Obama Administration Moves to Remove Cuba From State Sponsors of Terrorism List," The Heritage Foundation, 1/29/2015; (http://www.heritage.org/research/reports/2015/01/congressional-oversight-needed-as-obama-administration-moves-to-remove-cuba-from-state-sponsors-of-terrorism-list)
674. Paul Bedard, "Obama legacy: Most red tape, regulations ever," *The Washington Examiner*, 10/16/2016; (http://www.washington-examiner.com/obama-legacy-most-red-tape-regulations-ever/article/2604333)
675. Paul Bedard, "Obama breaks the record on imposing regulations, $2,496 per person hit," *The Washington Examiner*, 10/7/2016; (http://www.washingtonexaminer.com/obama-breaks-the-record-on-imposing-regulations-2496-per-person-hit/article/2603884)
676. Ibid.
677. Ibid.
678. Lisa Desjardins, "The War Over Coal Is Personal," CNN, 7/17/12, (http://www.cnn.com/2012/07/17/us/embed-america-energy-war)
679. "Potential Impacts Of EPA Air, Coal Combustion Residuals, And Cooling Water Regulations," NERA Economic Consulting,

September 2011 (http://www.americaspower.org/sites/default/files/NERA_Four_Rule_Report_Sept_21.pdf)

680. The White House, Office of the Press Secretary. (2013). Remarks by the President in the State of the Union Address [Press release]. Retrieved from http://www.whitehouse.gov/the-press-office/2013/02/12/remarks-president-state-union-address
681. Amy Harder, "EPA Set to Unveil Climate Proposal," *The Wall Street Journal*, 5/26/2014 (http://online.wsj.com/news/articles/SB10001424052702304811904579585843675203708)
682. Michael Bastasch, "Obama Unilaterally Pushes Cap-And-Trade On Unwilling States," *The Daily Caller*, 6/2/2014, (http://dailycaller.com/2014/06/02/obama-unilaterally-pushes-cap-and-trade-on-unwilling-states//)
683. Justin Sykes, "Nearly 4,000 EPA Regulations Issued Under President Obama," Americans for Tax Reform, 7/6/ 2016 (https://www.atr.org/nearly-4000-epa-regulations-issued-under-president-obama)
684. "US DOT Proposes Broader Use of Even Data Recorders to Help Improve Vehicle Safety," NHTSA 46-10, 12/07/2012, (http://www.nhtsa.gov/About+NHTSA/Press+Releases/U.S.+DOT+Proposes+Broader+Use+of+Event+Data+Recorders+to+Help+Improve+-Vehicle+Safety)
685. Ibid.
686. The National Center for Public Policy Research, (2012). Obama Administration Rushes "Creepy Black Box" Mandate on All New Car Buyers [Press release]. Retrieved from http://www.nationalcenter.org/PR-Black_Boxes_Cars_121312.html
687. C. J. Ciaramella, "Justice Dept. Proposes Lying, Hiding Existence of Records Under New FOIA Rule," *The Daily Caller*, 10/24/2011, (http://dailycaller.com/2011/10/24/justice-dept-proposes-lying-hiding-existence-of-records-under-new-foia-rule)
688. Mark Tapscott, " 'Most transparent' White House ever rewrote the FOIA to suppress politically sensitive docs," *Washington Examiner*, 3/18/2014; (http://www.washingtonexaminer.com/most-transparent-white-house-

ever-rewrote-the-foia-to-suppress-politically-sensitive-docs/article/2545824)

689. Ted Bridis and Jack Gillum, "US Cites security more to censor, deny records," Associated Press, 4/17/2014; (http://news.yahoo.com/us-cites-security-more-censor-deny-records-180650460.html)
690. Megan R. Wilson, "White House formally exempts office from FOIA regs," *The Hill*, 3/16/2015; (http://thehill.com/homenews/administration/235900-white-house-exempts-office-from-foia-regs)
691. http://pjmedia.com/blog/bombshell-justice-department-only-selectively-complies-with-freedom-of-information-act-pjm-exclusive/
692. Rick Ungar, "Here Are The 23 Executive Orders On Gun Safety Signed Today By The President," *Forbes*, 1/16/2013; (http://www.forbes.com/sites/rickungar/2013/01/16/here-are-the-23-executive-orders-on-gun-safety-signed-today-by-the-president/)
693. Dean Chambers, "State leaders resist President Obama's new gun control regulations," *Examiner*, 01/17/2013 (http://www.examiner.com/article/state-leaders-resist-president-obama-s-new-gun-control-regulations)
694. AWR Hawkins, "Obama Uses Executive Actions To Bypass Congress on Gun Control Again," *Breitbart*, 8/29/2013; (http://www.breitbart.com/big-government/2013/08/29/obama-uses-executive-actions-to-bypass-congress-enact-more-gun-control/)
695. Fred Lucas, "Obama administration's Two Quiet New Executive Actions on Who Can Buy a Gun," *The Blaze*, 1/3/2014; (http://www.theblaze.com/stories/2014/01/03/obama-administrations-two-quiet-new-executive-actions-on-who-can-buy-a-gun/)
696. Paul Bedard, "Obama to Ban Bullets by Executive Action, Threatens Top-Selling AR-15 Rifle," *The Washington Examiner*, 2/27/2015, (http://www.washingtonexaminer.com/article/2560750)
697. Mary Katherine Ham, "ATF on Proposed AR15 Ammo Ban: Nevermind, for Now," *Hot Air*, 3/10/2015; (http://hotair.com/archives/2015/03/10/atf-on-proposed-ar15-ammo-ban-nevermind-for-now/)

698. "Obama Issues Executive Actions on Guns" NRA-ILA, 1/8/2016; (https://www.nraila.org/articles/20160108/obama-issues-executive-actions-on-guns)
699. Rep. Steve Stockman (StockmanSenate), "Remember, when Republicans suggested delaying ObamaCare because the site doesn't work Democrats called that 'terrorism' and shut down govt." 10/21/2013, 9:45 PM. Tweet.
700. Ian Schwartz, "Howard Dean: I Wonder If Obama Has "The Legal Authority" To Fix Obamacare," *RealClearPolitics*, 11/14/2013 (http://www.realclearpolitics.com/video/2013/11/14/howard_dean_i_wonder_if_obama_has_the_legal_authority_to_fix_obamacare.html)
701. Eugene Kontorovich, "The Obamacare 'Fix' Is Illegal," *Politico*, 11/23/2013 (http://www.politico.com/magazine/story/2013/11/the-obamacare-fix-is-illegal-100254.html)
702. John Yoo, "ObamaCare debacle much worse for constitution, presidency than Katrina was for Bush," Fox News, 11/21/2013 (http://www.foxnews.com/opinion/2013/11/21/obamacare-is-no-katrina-it-much-worse/)
703. John Hayward, "Obama threatens to veto the measure he just called for," *Breitbart*, 11/14/2013 (http://www.breitbart.com/InstaBlog/2013/11/14/Obama-threatens-to-veto-the-measure-he-just-called-for)
704. John Fund, "Who Says Obama Hasn't United the Country?," *The Corner*, 12/20/2013 (http://www.nationalreview.com/corner/366828/who-says-obama-hasnt-united-country-john-fund)
705. Juliet Eilperin and Amy Goldstein, "White House delays health insurance mandate for medium-sized employers until 2016," *The Washington Post*, 2/10/2014 (http://www.washingtonpost.com/national/health-science/white-house-delays-health-insurance-mandate-for-medium-sized-employers-until-2016/2014/02/10/ade6b344-9279-11e3-84e1-27626c5ef5fb_story.html)
706. Elise Viebeck, "New O-Care Delay to Help Midterm Dems," *The Hill*, 3/3/2014; http://thehill.com/blogs/healthwatch/health-reform-implementation/199784-new-obamacare-delay-to-help-midterm-dems

707. Ian Schwartz, "Turley: Obama's 'Become The Very Danger The Constitution Was Designed To Avoid'," *RealClearPolitics*, 12/4/2013 (http://www.realclearpolitics.com/video/2013/12/04/turley_obamas_become_the_very_danger_the_constitution_was_designed_to_avoid.html)
708. Ronn Torossian, "Millions Paid to Liberal Public Relations Firms," *Frontpage Magazine*, 10/30/2012, (http://frontpagemag.com/2012/ronn-torossian/millions-paid-to-liberal-public-relations-firms/)
709. Tyler Durden, "Foodstamps Surge by Most in One Year to New All Time High, in Delayed Release," *Zero Hedge*, 11/10/2012, (http://www.zerohedge.com/news/2012-11-10/foodstamps-surge-most-one-year-new-all-time-record-delayed-release)
710. Juliet Eilperin, "White House Delayed Enacting Rules Ahead of 2012 Election to Avoid Controversy," *The Washington Post*, 12/13/2013 (http://www.washingtonpost.com/politics/white-house-delayed-enacting-rules-ahead-of-2012-election-to-avoid-controversy/2013/12/14/7885a494-561a-11e3-ba82-16ed03681809_story.html)
711. Ibid.
712. Mary Bruce and Jake Tapper, "At White House Request, Lockheed Martin Drops Plan to Issue Layoff Notices," ABC News, 10/01/2012, (http://abcnews.go.com/blogs/politics/2012/10/at-white-house-request-lockheed-martin-drops-plan-to-issue-lay-off-notices/)
713. Mike Flynn, "Obama Urges Companies to Break Federal Law for His Reelection," *Breitbart*, 10/2/2012, (http://www.breitbart.com/big-government/2012/10/02/obama-urges-companies-to-break-federal-law-for-his-reelection/)
714. Bill Sammon, Shannon Beam and Fox News Staff, "GOP Sounds Alarm Over Obama Decision to Move Census to White House," Fox News, 02/09/2009, (http://www.foxnews.com/politics/2009/02/09/gop-sounds-alarm-obama-decision-census-white-house/)
715. David Crary, "Census Counts Gay Marriages Even in States That Don't Allow Them," *The Huffington Post*, 04/05/2010, (http://www.huffingtonpost.com/2010/04/05/census-counts-gay-marriag_n_526396.html)

716. Meredith Simons, "Census Launches Campaign to Hear More From Latinos," *Houston Chronicle*, 10/01/2009, (http://www.chron.com/news/nation-world/article/Census-launches-campaign-to-hear-more-from-Latinos-1732032.php)
717. Michelle Malkin, "Obama's Politicized, Profligate US Census," *Michelle Malkin*, 04/07/2009, (http://michellemalkin.com/2010/04/07/obamas-politicized-profligate-u-s-census/)
718. Kenneth R. Bazinet and Michasel McAuliff, "Bill Clinton Made Joe Sestak Job Offer on Behalf of Administration to Leave Race, White House Says," *New York Daily News*, 05/28/2010, (http://www.nydailynews.com/news/politics/bill-clinton-made-joe-sestak-job-offer-behalf-administration-leave-race-white-house-article-1.178586)
719. Hans von Spakovsky, "Sestak Job Offer Violated Federal Law?," *The Foundry*, 06/01/2010, (http://blog.heritage.org/2010/06/01/sestak-job-offer-violated-federal-law/)
720. 18 U.S.C. 211: U.S. Code – Section 211: Acceptance or Solicitation to Obtain Appointive Public Office, FindLaw, accessed at, http://codes.lp.findlaw.com/uscode/18/I/11/211
721. John Bresnahan and Jake Sherman, "DoJ Nixes Sestak Special Counsel," *Politico*, 05/24/2010, (http://www.politico.com/news/stories/0510/37713.html)
722. Frank Ahrens, "Treasury Pick Misfiled Using Off-the-Shelf Tax Software," *The Washington Post*, 01/22/2009, (http://www.washingtonpost.com/wp-dyn/content/article/2009/01/21/AR2009012103552.html)
723. Carrie Budoff Brown, "Sebelius Paid Over $7,000 in Back Taxes," *Politico*, 03/31/2009, (http://www.politico.com/news/stories/0309/20728.html)
724. Matt Kelley, "Tax Snafus Add up for Obama Team," *USA Today*, 02/05/2009, (http://usatoday30.usatoday.com/news/washington/2009-02-05-solis-husband-taxes_N.htm)
725. Huma Khan, "Another Tax Problem for Obama Nominee," ABC News, 02/03/2009, (http://abcnews.go.com/blogs/politics/2009/02/another-tax-pro/)
726. Andrew Malcolm, "36 Obama Aids Owe $833,000 in Back Taxes," *Investor's Business Daily*, 01/26/2012, (http://news.investors.com/

politics-andrew-malcolm/012612-599002-obama-white-house-staff-back-taxes.htm)

727. Stephen Dinan, "Tax Cheats got $1.4 Billion in Stimulus Loans," *The Washington Times*, 06/27/2012, (http://www.washingtontimes.com/news/2012/jun/27/gao-1-billion-in-tax-credits-went-to-cheats/)
728. John Fund, "Holder's Black Panther Stonewall," *The Wall Street Journal*, 8/20/2013 (http://online.wsj.com/news/articles/SB10001424052970203550604574361071968458430)
729. Jan Crawford, "New Black Panther Case Spurs Civil Rights Commission to Challenge DOJ," CBS News, 07/14/2010 (http://www.cbsnews.com/8301-504564_162-20010581-504564.html)
730. Josh Gerstein, "Eric Holder: Black Panther Case Focus Demeans 'My People'," *Politico*, 3/1/2011; (http://www.politico.com/blogs/under-the-radar/2011/03/eric-holder-black-panther-case-focus-demeans-my-people-033839)
731. John Solomon, "Exclusive: FBI Blocked in Corruption Probe Involving Senators Reid, Lee," *The Washington Times*, 3/13/2014 (http://www.washingtontimes.com/news/2014/mar/13/fbi-blocked-in-corruption-probe-involving-sens-rei/)
732. Huma Khan, "President Obama Fires Controversial Inspector General," ABC News, June 12, 2009, (http://abcnews.go.com/blogs/politics/2009/06/president-obama-fires-controversial-inspector-general/)
733. The Cajun Boy, "Will Obama's Firing of an Inspector General Evolve Into a Major Scandal?," *Gawker*, June 16, 2009, (http://gawker.com/5292275/will-obamas-firing-of-an-inspector-general-evolve-into-a-major-scandal)
734. Robert Stacy McCain, "IG-Gate: 'Hush Money' Charge in Sacramento Mayor's Sex Scandal Was Part of Probe," *American Spectator*, November, 23 2009, (http://spectator.org/blog/2009/11/23/ig-gate-hush-money-charge-in-s)
735. John Kinsellagh, "Obama fires Inspector General Gerald Walpin without cause," *Examiner*, 6/18/2009, (http://www.examiner.com/article/obama-fires-inspector-general-gerald-walpin-without-cause)

736. Pete Williams and Frank Thorp, "Obama invokes executive privilege over DOJ documents," NBC News, 6/20/2012; (http://firstread.nbcnews.com/_news/2012/06/20/12317893-obama-invokes-executive-privilege-over-doj-documents)
737. "AP Exclusive: US Ordered Delay in Intern's Arrest," Associated Press, 01/15/2013, (http://news.yahoo.com/ap-exclusive-us-ordered-delay-interns-arrest-172424335.html)
738. Sally Goldenberg, "Sanitation Department's Slow Cleanup Was a Budget Protest," *New York Post*, December 30, 2010; http://nypost.com/2010/12/30/sanitation-departments-slow-snow-cleanup-was-a-budget-protest/
739. Jennifer Gould Keil and Frank Rosario, "De Blasio 'getting back at us' by not plowing: UES residents," *New York Post*, 1/21/2014 (http://nypost.com/2014/01/21/upper-east-side-residents-feel-spurned-after-plow-delay/)
740. Matthew Boyle, "Sebelius Violated Hatch Act and May be Fired, Obama Administration Lawyers Find," *The Daily Caller*, 09/12/2012, (http://dailycaller.com/2012/09/12/sebelius-violated-hatch-act-and-may-be-fired-obama-administration-lawyers-find/)
741. The White House, Office of the Special Counsel. Information on Hatch Act. Accessed at http://www.osc.gov/haFederalPenalties.htm
742. Matthew Boyle, "Priebus: Menendez's Allegedly Criminal Link to Democratic Megadonor 'Stinks to High Heaven', " *Breitbart*, 3/9/2015; (http://www.breitbart.com/big-government/2015/03/09/priebus-menendezs-allegedly-criminal-link-to-democratic-megadonor-stinks-to-high-heaven/)
743. Keith Laning, "Report: US Attorney Investigating Christie Bridge Scandal," *The Hill*, 1/9/2014 (http://thehill.com/blogs/transportation-report/highways-bridges-and-roads/194931-new-jersey-us-attorney-investigating)
744. Paul Bond, "'2016: Obama's America' Filmmaker Indicted for Violating Campaign Finance Laws," *The Hollywood Reporter*, 1/23/2014 (http://www.hollywoodreporter.com/news/2016-obamas-america-filmmaker-indicted-673670)
745. Jennifer G. Hickey and John Gizzi, Dershowitz, "Law Enforcement Experts Slam D'Souza Targeting," *Newsmax*,

1/29/2014 (http://www.newsmax.com/Newsfront/DSouza-Dershowitz-targeting-selective/2014/01/29/id/549845)

746. Andrew C. McCarthy, "Amnesty, but Not for D'Souza," *National Review*, 2/1/2014 (http://www.nationalreview.com/article/370097/amnesty-not-dsouza-andrew-c-mccarthy/)
747. Lee Stranahan, "Pigford: NYT Pegs Obama for Vote-Buying Scheme," *Breitbart*, April 25, 2013; http://www.breitbart.com/Big-Government/2013/04/26/New-York-Times-Reveals-Obama-s-Maneuvers-And-Motives-On-Pigford
748. Lee Stranahan, "New Obama 'Pigford' Farmers Settlement Designed for Fraud," *Breitbart*, September 25, 2012; http://www.breitbart.com/Big-Government/2012/09/25/New-Obama-Farmers-Settlements-Designed-For-Fraud
749. Sharon LaFraniere, "U.S. Opens Spigot After Farmers Claim Discrimination," *The New York Times*, April 25, 2013; http://www.nytimes.com/2013/04/26/us/farm-loan-bias-claims-often-unsupported-cost-us-millions.html
750. Ibid.
751. Ibid.
752. Joel Gehrke, "Emails Show Obama Admin Used DOE Loan Money to Help Harry Reid's 2010 Campaign," *Washington Examiner*, 10/31/2012, (http://washingtonexaminer.com/emails-show-obama-admin-used-doe-loan-money-to-help-harry-reids-2010-campaign/article/2512249)
753. Tom Schoenberg, "Car Companies XP Vehicles, Limnia Sue U.S. Over Loans," *Bloomberg*, 01/10/2013, (http://www.bloomberg.com/news/2013-01-10/car-companies-xp-vehicles-limnia-sue-u-s-over-loans.html)
754. Ronnie Green, "Obama administration Agreed to Solyndra's Loan Days After Insiders Foresaw Firm's Failure," The Center for Public Integrity, 09/14/2011, (http://www.publicintegrity.org/2011/09/14/6465/obama-administration-agreed-solyndra-loan-days-after-insiders-foresaw-firms-failure)
755. Michael Beckel, "Before Collapse and Government Investigations, Solar Company Solyndra Was a Rising Star," *OpenSecrets*,

09/14/2011, (http://www.opensecrets.org/news/2011/09/solar-company-solyndra-rising-star.html)
756. Jonathan Karl, "Exclusive: Jobs 'Saved or Created' in Congressional Districts That Don't Exist," ABC News, 11/6/2009, (http://abcnews.go.com/Politics/jobs-saved-created-congressional-districts-exist/story?id=9097853)
757. Bill McMorris, "$6.4 Billion Stimulus Goes to Phantom Districts," *Watchdog.org*, 11/17/2009, (http://watchdog.org/1530/6-4-billion-stimulus-goes-to-phantom-districts/)
758. Conn Carroll, "Morning Bell: The Fake Jobs of Obama's Failed Stimulus," *The Foundry*, 11/17/2009, (http://blog.heritage.org/2009/11/17/morning-bell-the-fake-jobs-of-obamas-failed-stimulus/)
759. Sean Gallagher, "Encryption 'Would Not Have Helped' at OPM, says DHS Official," *arstechnica*, 6/16/2015; (http://arstechnica.com/security/2015/06/encryption-would-not-have-helped-at-opm-says-dhs-official/)
760. Devlin Barrett, Danny Yadron and Damian Paletta, "U.S. Suspects Hackers in China Breached About 4 Million People's Records, Officials Say," *The Wall Street Journal*, 6/5/2015; (http://www.wsj.com/articles/u-s-suspects-hackers-in-china-behind-government-data-breach-sources-say-1433451888)
761. Priya Anand, "OM Hack May Have Affected 32 Million Government Employees," *Market Watch*, 7/7/2015; (http://www.marketwatch.com/story/opm-hack-may-have-affected-32-million-government-employees-2015-07-08)
762. Sean Gallagher, "Hack of Government Employee Records Discovered by Product Demo," *arstechnica*, 6/11/2015; (http://arstechnica.com/security/2015/06/report-hack-of-government-employee-records-discovered-by-product-demo/)
763. Paul Conway, "How Obama's Poor Judgment Led to the Chinese Hack of OPM," *The Daily Signal*, 7/27/2015; (http://dailysignal.com/2015/07/27/how-obamas-poor-judgment-led-to-the-chinese-hack-of-opm/)
764. David Boyer, "Obama still backs OPM chief despite massive data breach," *The Washington Times*, 6/17/2015;

("http://www.washingtontimes.com/news/2015/jun/17/obama-still-backs-opm-chief-despite-data-breach/)

765. http://dailycaller.com/2012/11/12/epa-chiefs-secret-alias-email-account-revealed/
766. Stephen Dinan, "Newly Released Emails Show EPA Director's Extensive Use of Fictional Alter Ego," *The Washington Times*, 6/2/2013, (http://www.washingtontimes.com/news/2013/jun/2/newly-released-emails-show-epa-directors-extensive/)
767. Kevin Freking, "Lisa Jackson Resigns: EPA Administrator Stepping Down," *The Huffington Post*, 12/27/2013, (http://www.huffingtonpost.com/2012/12/27/lisa-jackson-resigns-epa-administrator_n_2370019.html)
768. http://pjmedia.com/blog/epa-accused-of-waiving-foia-fees-for-left-wing-groups-over-conservative-ones/
769. Michael Bastasch, "Vitter: EPA FOIA scandal 'no different than the IRS disaster'," *The Daily Caller*, 5/17/2013, (http://dailycaller.com/2013/05/17/vitter-epa-foia-scandal-no-different-than-the-irs-disaster/)
770. http://blog.ap.org/2014/09/19/8-ways-the-obama-administration-is-blocking-information/
771. C J Ciaramella, "Senators Question Leak of Private Farmer Info," *The Washington Free Beacon*, June 6, 2013; http://freebeacon.com/senators-question-epa-leak-of-private-farmer-info/
772. Rob Gordon, "Exposing the EPA's Gold King Mine Cover-Up," *The Daily Signal*, 6/14/2017, (http://dailysignal.com/2017/06/14/exposing-epas-gold-king-mine-cover/)
773. Michael Bastach, "Report: EPA Tested Deadly Pollutants on Humans to Push Obama Admin's Agenda," *The Daily Caller*, 4/2/2014 (http://dailycaller.com/2014/04/02/report-epa-tested-deadly-pollutants-on-humans-to-push-obama-admins-agenda/)
774. Kerry Picket, "This is How the EPA Finds People for Pollution Exposure Experiments," *Breitbart*, 4/3/2014 (http://www.breitbart.com/Big-Government/2014/04/03/This-Is-How-The-EPA-Finds-People-For-Pollution-Exposure-Experiments)
775. Michael Bastach, "Report: EPA Tested Deadly Pollutants on Humans to Push Obama Admin's Agenda," *The Daily Caller*, 4/2/2014 (http://dailycaller.com/2014/04/02/

report-epa-tested-deadly-pollutants-on-humans-to-push-obama-admins-agenda/)
776. Ibid.
777. "Press Release: Obama Campaign Announces National Veterans Advisory Committee; 11/12/2007," The American Presidency Project, accessed 5/19/2014; (http://www.presidency.ucsb.edu/ws/?pid=91891)
778. Bob Brewin, "VA Comes Under Fire as Claims Backlog Tops 900,000, Again," *NextGov*, 3/27/13 (http://www.nextgov.com/defense/2013/03/va-comes-under-fire-claims-backlog-tops-900000-again/62124/)
779. Jamie Reno, "Veterans Die Waiting For Benefits As VA Claims Backlog Builds," *The Daily Beast*, 2/9/2013 (http://www.thedailybeast.com/articles/2013/02/09/veterans-die-waiting-for-benefits-as-va-claims-backlog-builds.html)
780. Aaron Glantz, "Number of Veterans Who Die Waiting for Benefits Claims Skyrockets," *The Daily Beast*, 12/20/2012 (http://www.thedailybeast.com/articles/2012/12/20/number-of-veterans-who-die-waiting-for-benefits-claims-skyrockets.html)
781. "Senators Call for Probe into VA Hospital Deaths Allegedly Tied to Delayed Care," Fox News, 4/24/2014, (http://www.foxnews.com/politics/2014/04/24/senators-call-for-probe-into-va-hospital-deaths-allegedly-tied-to-delayed-care/)
782. Geoff Dyer, "Veterans scandal risks engulfing Obama," *Financial Times*, 5/16/2014 (http://www.ft.com/intl/cms/s/0/328546c0-dd10-11e3-8546-00144feabdc0.html)
783. Becket Adams, "Eric Holder: No Immediate Plans to Investigate VA Scandal," *The Blaze*, 5/14/2014 (http://www.theblaze.com/stories/2014/05/14/eric-holder-no-immediate-plans-to-investigate-va-scandal/)
784. "Whistleblovers describe VA culture of retaliation to lawmakers at hearing," Fox News, 7/9/2014 (http://www.foxnews.com/politics/2014/07/09/whistleblowers-tell-lawmakers-there-is-culture-retaliation-at-va/)
785. Guy Benson, "Surprise: WH Says Obama Found Out About VA Scandal On the News," *Townhall*, 5/19/2014, (http://townhall.com/tipsheet/guybenson/2014/05/19/

number-nine-albuquerque-va-hospital-accused-of-manipulating-wait-times-n1840291)

786. Jim McElhatton, "He Knew! Obama Told of Veterans Affairs Health Care Debacle as far Back as 2008", *The Washington Times*, 5/18/2014; (http://www.washingtontimes.com/news/2014/may/18/obama-warned-about-va-wait-time-problems-during-20/)
787. Martin Matishak, "Report: One-third of vets on pending medical care list already dead," *The Hill*, 7/13/2015; (http://thehill.com/policy/defense/247752-report-one-third-of-vets-waiting-medical-care-already-dead)
788. Richard A. Serrano, "Gun Store Owner Had Misgivings About ATF Sting," *Los Angeles Times*, 09/11/2011, (http://www.latimes.com/news/nationworld/nation/la-na-atf-guns-20110912,0,7686272,full.story)
789. Ken Ellingwood, Richard A. Serrano and Tracy Wilkinson, "Mexico Still Waiting for Answers on Faśt and Furious Gun Program," *Los Angeles Times*, 09/19/2011, (http://articles.latimes.com/2011/sep/19/world/la-fg-mexico-fast-furious-20110920)
790. David Keene, "Fast and Furious Cover-Up at Holder's Justice," *The Washington Times*, 07/06/2012, (http://www.washingtontimes.com/news/2012/jul/6/fast-and-furious-cover-up-at-holders-justice/)
791. Alan Silverleib, "House Holds Holder in Contempt," CNN, 06/29/2012, (http://www.cnn.com/2012/06/28/politics/holder-contempt/index.html)
792. "Victimizing the Borrowers: Predatory Lending's Role in the Subprime Mortgage Crisis," *Knowledge @ Wharton*, 2/20/2008; (http://knowledge.wharton.upenn.edu/article/victimizing-the-borrowers-predatory-lendings-role-in-the-sub-prime-mortgage-crisis/)
793. Sean Higgins, "Bank of America gets 2-for-1 deal in Justice Dept. settlement," *The Washington Examiner*, 6/1/2016; (http://www.washingtonexaminer.com/bank-of-america-gets-half-off-its-justice-dept.-settlement/article/2592705)

794. Byron York, "Justice Department Steers Money to Favored Groups," *The Washington Examiner*, 8/5/2010; (http://www.washingtonexaminer.com/justice-department-steers-money-to-favored-groups/article/11539)
795. Sean Higgins, "Bank of America gets 2-for-1 deal in Justice Dept. settlement," *The Washington Examiner*, 6/1/2016; (http://www.washingtonexaminer.com/bank-of-america-gets-half-off-its-justice-dept.-settlement/article/2592705)
796. Sean Higgins, "Bank of America gets 2-for-1 deal in Justice Dept. settlement," *The Washington Examiner*, 6/1/2016; (http://www.washingtonexaminer.com/bank-of-america-gets-half-off-its-justice-dept.-settlement/article/2592705)
797. "DOJ ends Holder-era 'slush fund' payouts to outside groups," Fox News, 6/7/2017; (http://www.foxnews.com/politics/2017/06/07/doj-ends-holder-era-slush-fund-payouts-to-outside-groups.html)
798. Caitlin Dickson, "IRS Scandal's Central Figure, Lois Lerner, Described as 'Apolitical'," *The Daily Beast*, 5/14/2013,(http://www.thedailybeast.com/articles/2013/05/14/irs-scandal-s-central-figure-lois-lerner-described-as-apolitical.html)
799. Patrick Howley, "Twelve different IRS units nationwide targeted conservatives," *The Daily Caller*, 6/25/2013, (http://dailycaller.com/2013/06/25/twelve-different-irs-units-nationwide-targeted-conservatives/)
800. "Judicial Watch: New Documents Show IRS HQ Control of Tea Party Targeting," Judicial Watch, 5/14/2014, (http://www.judicialwatch.org/press-room/press-releases/judicial-watch-new-documents-show-irs-hq-control-tea-party-targeting/)
801. Kerry Picket, "IRS Employee: D.C. Told Us to Target Tea Party," *Breitbart*, 6/2/2013 (http://www.breitbart.com/Big-Government/2013/06/02/IRS-Employee-Washington-D-C-Told-Us-To-Target-Tea-Party-Oragnizations)
802. Stephen Dinan, "IRS officials thought Obama wanted crackdown on tea party groups, worried about negative press," *The Washington Times*, 9/17/2013, (http://

www.washingtontimes.com/news/2013/sep/17/report-irs-staff-acutely-aware-tea-party-antipathy)

803. Vince Coglianese, "IRS's Shulman Had More Public White House Visits Than Any Cabinet Member," *The Daily Caller*, 5/29/2013, (http://dailycaller.com/2013/05/29/irss-shulman-had-more-public-white-house-visits-than-any-cabinet-member)
804. Patrick Howley, "White House, IRS exchanged confidential taxpayer info," *The Daily Caller*, 10/9/2013, (http://dailycaller.com/2013/10/09/white-house-irs-exchanged-confidential-taxpayer-info/)
805. Paul Bedard, "Treasury: IRS targeted 292 Tea Party groups, just 6 progressive groups," *Washington Examiner*, 6/27/2013, (http://washingtonexaminer.com/article/2532456)
806. Patrick Howley, "IRS Agents' Testimony: No Progressive Groups Were Targeted by IRS," *The Daily Caller*, 4/7/2014, (http://dailycaller.com/2014/04/07/committee-staff-report-no-progressive-groups-were-targeted-by-irs/)
807. Stephan Dinan, "House Republicans find 10% of tea party donors audited by IRS," *The Washington Times*, 5/7/2014 (http://www.washingtontimes.com/news/2014/may/7/house-republicans-find-10-of-tea-party-donors-audi/)
808. Joel Gehrke, "Report: IRS denied tax-exempt status to pro-lifers on behalf of Planned Parenthood," *Washington Examiner*, 5/16/2013, (http://washingtonexaminer.com/article/2529750)
809. John Nolte, "Report: IRS Covered Up Scandal Until After Election," *Breitbart*, 5/17/2013, (http://www.breitbart.com/Big-Journalism/2013/05/17/Report-Irs-Covered-up-Scandal-before-Election)
810. James Pethokoukis, "Did the IRS's Tea Party suppression get Obama reelected?," American Enterprise Institute, 6/20/2013, (http://www.aei-ideas.org/2013/06/the-asterisk-president-did-the-irss-tea-party-suppression-get-obama-reelected/)
811. Neil Munro, "Covert cronies? Obama's attorney general appoints Obama donor to investigate Obama's IRS," *The Daily Caller*, 1/8/2014, (http://dailycaller.com/2014/01/08/covert-cronies-obamas-attorney-general-appoints-obama-donor-to-investigate-obamas-irs/)

812. Lauren French, "Two Democrats Call for Ethics Probe into J. Russell George's Work as IRS Inspector General," *Politico*, 2/7/14, (http://www.politico.com/morningtax/0214/morningtax12951.html)
813. Devlin Barrett, "Criminal Charges Not Expected in IRS Probe," *The Wall Street Journal*, 1/13/14 (http://online.wsj.com/news/articles/SB10001424052702303819704579318983271821584)
814. Staff Report, "Lois Lerner's Involvement in the IRS Targeting of Tax-Exempt Organizations," Committee on Oversight and Government Reform, 3/11/14 (http://oversight.house.gov/wp-content/uploads/2014/03/Lerner-Report1.pdf)
815. Katie Pavlich, "BREAKING: New Emails Show Lois Lerner Was in Contact With DOJ About Prosecuting Tax Exempt Groups," *Townhall*, 4/16/2014 (http://townhall.com/tipsheet/katiepavlich/2014/04/16/breaking-new-emails-show-lois-lerner-contacted-doj-about-prosecuting-tax-exempt-groups-n1825292)
816. Gregory Korte, "House holds former IRS official Lerner in contempt," *USA Today*, 5/7/2014 (http://www.usatoday.com/story/news/politics/2014/05/07/lois-lerner-contempt-of-congress/8815051/)
817. "The IRS Loses Lerner's Emails", *The Wall Street Journal, Review and Outlook*, 6/13/2014; (http://online.wsj.com/articles/the-irs-loses-lerners-emails-1402700540)
818. Allahpundit, "IRS Regulations Require E-Mails That are 'Federal Records' to be Stored in Separate, Permanent System," *Hot Air*, 6/17/2014; (http://hotair.com/archives/2014/06/17/irs-regulations-require-e-mails-that-are-federal-records-to-be-stored-in-separate-permanent-system/)
819. Patric Howley, "IRS CANCELLED Contract with Email-Storage Firm Weeks After Lerner's Computer Crash," *Breitbart*, 6/22/2014 (http://dailycaller.com/2014/06/22/irs-cancelled-contract-with-email-storage-firm-weeks-after-lerners-computer-crash/)
820. Dave Boyer, "Obama's 'phony' scandals line draws GOP retort," *The Washington Times*, 7/25/2013 (http://www.washingtontimes.com/news/2013/jul/25/obamas-phony-scandals-line-draws-gop-retort/)

821. Charlotte Davis, "Reconciliation and Obamacare A 'Bad Mix,' " *The Foundry*, 2/8/2010, (http://dailysignal.com/2010/02/18/reconciliation-and-obamacare-a-"bad-mix")
822. Ray Locker, "Republican's Health Vote a 'Decision of Conscience'," *USA Today*, 11/09/2009, (http://usatoday30.usatoday.com/news/washington/2009-11-08-cao-votes-yes-for-health-bill_N.htm)
823. Chip Reid, "Obama Reneges on Health Care Transparency," CBS News, 01/07/2010, (http://www.cbsnews.com/8301-18563_162-6064298.html)
824. Patrick Howly, "Obamacare Architect: Lack of Transparency Was Key Because 'Stupidity Of The American Voter' Would Have Killed Obamacare," *The Daily Caller*, 11/9/2014; (http://dailycaller.com/2014/11/09/obamacare-architect-lack-of-transparency-was-key-because-stupidity-of-the-american-voter-would-have-killed-obamacare/)
825. Richard Pollack, "Groups led by inside trader, child abuser got Obamacare co-op loans," *The Washington Examiner*, 4/3/2013, (http://washingtonexaminer.com/groups-led-by-inside-trader-child-abuser-got-obamacare-co-op-loans/article/2526140)
826. Ibid.
827. Richard Pollack, "Failed Iowa entrepreneur awarded $112 million for Obamacare co-ops," *The Washington Examiner*, 3/26/2013, (http://washingtonexaminer.com/failed-iowa-entrepreneur-awarded-112-million-for-obamacare-co-ops/article/2525456)
828. Richard Pollack, "U.S. gave troubled Florida firm $129 million for new Ohio Obamacare health insurance cooperative," *The Washington Examiner*, 3/5/2013, (http://washingtonexaminer.com/u.s.-gave-troubled-florida-firm-129-million-for-new-ohio-obamacare-health-insurance-cooperative/article/2523337)
829. Richard Pollack, "Insurer with NY's 'worst' record of complaints gets $340M Obamacare loan," *Examiner*, 2/21/2013, (http://washingtonexaminer.com/obama-ally-got-340-million-to-set-up-health-care-co-ops/article/2522229)

830. Rep. Phil Roe, M.D., "CO-OP failures put spotlight on ACA's many shortcomings," *The Hill*,1/14/2016, (http://thehill.com/special-reports/healthcare-january-14-2016/265827-co-op-failures-put-spotlight-on-acas-many)
831. Ali Meyer"19th Obamacare Co-Op Folds, Leaving only Four Operating in 2018," Fox News, 6/28/2017; (http://www.foxnews.com/politics/2017/06/28/19th-obamacare-co-op-folds-leaving-only-4-operating-in-2018.html)
832. Dan Mangan, "President: 7.1 million enrolled in Obamacare," CNBC, 4/1/2014 (http://www.cnbc.com/id/101543801)
833. Guy Benson, "Confirmed: Many of Obamacare's 'Eight Million Enrollments' are Duplicates," *Townhall*, 5/7/2014 (http://townhall.com/tipsheet/guybenson/2014/05/07/confirmed-many-of-obamacares-8-million-enrollees-are-duplicates-n1834786)
834. Avik Roy, "RAND Comes Clean: Obamacare's Exchanges Enrolled Only 1.4 Million Previously Uninsured Individuals," *Forbes*, 4/9/2014 (http://www.forbes.com/sites/theapothecary/2014/04/09/rand-comes-clean-obamacares-exchanges-enrolled-only-1-4-million-previously-uninsured-individuals/)
835. Avik Roy, "New McKinsey Survey: 74% of Obamacare Sign-Ups Were Previously Insured," *Forbes*, 5/10/2014, (http://www.forbes.com/sites/theapothecary/2014/05/10/new-mckinsey-survey-74-of-obamacare-sign-ups-were-previously-insured/)
836. "Report: Obamacare contractors paid to do nothing," CBS News, 5/14/2014 (http://www.cbsnews.com/news/report-obamacare-contractors-paid-to-do-nothing/)
837. Sarah Hurtubise, "Yet Another Obamacare Contractor Office Paid to do Nothing," *The Daily Caller*, 5/20/2014 (http://dailycaller.com/2014/05/20/yet-another-obamacare-contractor-office-paid-to-do-nothing/)
838. Bill Allison, "Good enough for government work? The contractors building Obamacare," Sunlight Foundation, 10/9/2013 (http://sunlightfoundation.com/blog/2013/10/09/aca-contractors/)
839. Akash Chougule, "White House Hired Sham Foreign Company for Obamacare, Employees 'Do Nothing'," *The Blaze*, 5/22/2014, (http://www.theblaze.com/contributions/

white-house-hired-sham-foreign-company-for-obamacare-employees-do-nothing/)

840. David Morgan "U.S. administration defends Obamacare contractor after UK probe," Reuters, 7/16/2013 (http://www.reuters.com/article/2013/07/16/us-usa-healthcare-serco-idUSBRE96F18J20130716)
841. Brett Norman and David Nather, "Obamacare delay sparks new mandate fight," *Politico*, 2/10/2014 (http://www.politico.com/story/2014/02/obamacare-employer-mandate-delay-103338.html)
842. James Taranto, "OmertàCare," *The Wall Street Journal*, 2/12/2014 (http://online.wsj.com/news/articles/SB10001424052702304888404579378833508471324)
843. Chris Stirewalt, "Thought Police: Firms must swear ObamaCare not a factor in firings," Fox News, 2/11/2014 (http://www.foxnews.com/politics/2014/02/11/thought-police-firms-must-swear-obamacare-not-factor-in-firings/)
844. Sam Baker, "HHS finalizes over 1,200 waivers under health-care reform law," *The Hill*, 01/06/12, (http://thehill.com/blogs/healthwatch/health-reform-implementation/202791-hhs-finalizes-more-than-1200-healthcare-waivers)
845. Paul Conner, "Labor unions primary recipients of Obamacare waivers," *The Daily Caller*, 1/6/2012, (http://dailycaller.com/2012/01/06/labor-unions-primary-recipients-of-obamacare-waivers/)
846. Charlie Spierling, "Interior Secretary nominee Sally Jewell received Obamacare waiver for REI," *The Washington Examiner*, 2/7/2013, (http://washingtonexaminer.com/interior-secretary-nominee-sally-jewell-received-obamacare-waiver-for-rei/article/2520821)
847. Andrew Dugan, "Cost Still Delays Healthcare for About One in Three in U.S.," Gallup, 11/30/2015; (http://news.gallup.com/poll/187190/cost-delays-healthcare-one-three.aspx)
848. Ibid.
849. Rebecca Riffkin, "Cost Still a Barrier Between Americans and Medical Care," Gallup, 11/28/2014; (http://news.gallup.com/poll/179774/cost-barrier-americans-medical-care.aspx)

850. Andrew Dugan, "Cost of Healthcare Is Americans' Top Financial Concern," Gallup, 6/23/2017; (http://news.gallup.com/poll/212780/cost-healthcare-americans-top-financial-concern.aspx)
851. Lori Montgomery and Shailagh Murray, "In Deal With Stupak, White House Announces Executive Order on Abortion," *The Washington Post*, 3/21/10 (http://voices.washingtonpost.com/44/2010/03/white-house-announces-executiv.html)
852. Rep. Bart Stupak Announces His Retirement After Health Care Controversy, Fox News, 4/09/10 (http://www.foxnews.com/politics/2010/04/09/rep-bart-stupak-retire/)
853. Caroline May, "$1 abortion surcharge in Obamacare," *The Daily Caller*, 3/13/2012 (http://dailycaller.com/2012/03/13/1-abortion-premium-in-obamacare/)
854. Sean Higgins, "Bart Stupak: 'Perplexed and disappointed' that White House undid Obamacare abortion compromise," *The Washington Examiner*, 9/5/2012 (http://washingtonexaminer.com/bart-stupak-perplexed-and-disappointed-that-white-house-undid-obamacare-abortion-compromise/article/2507073)
855. Paige Winfield Cunningham, "Threats, Deals Got Drug Companies on Board With Obama," *The Washington Times*, 05/31/2012, (http://www.washingtontimes.com/news/2012/may/31/threats-deals-got-drug-companies-on-board-with-oba)
856. Kim Palmer, "Cleveland Clinic announces job cuts to prepare for Obamacare," Reuters, 9/18/2013 (http://www.reuters.com/article/2013/09/18/us-usa-health-clevelandclinic-idUSBRE98H14V20130918)
857. Paul Davidson and Barbara Hansen, "A job engine sputters as hospitals cut staff," *USA Today*, 10/13/2013 (http://www.usatoday.com/story/money/business/2013/10/13/hospital-job-cuts/2947929/)
858. Sarah Hurtubise, "Fourth Georgia hospital closes due to Obamacare payment cuts," *The Daily Caller*, 2/18/2014 (http://dailycaller.com/2014/02/18/fourth-georgia-hospital-closes-due-to-obamacare-payment-cuts/)
859. Cheryl K Chumley, "New York Doctors Flee ObamaCare: 'I Plan to Retire,' " *The Washington Times*, 10/29/2013;

http://www.washingtontimes.com/news/2013/oct/29/new-york-doctors-flee-obamacare-i-plan-retire/

860. David Carton, "Obamacare Is Killing Rural Hospitals and Their Patients,' " *The American Spectator*, 1/9/2017; (https://spectator.org/obamacare-is-killing-rural-hospitals-and-their-patients/)
861. Jeffrey Young, "Health Care Costs To Exceed A Record $20,000 Per Year For Families With Insurance, Study Says," *The Huffington Post*, 5/15/12, (http://www.huffingtonpost.com/2012/05/15/health-care-costs-record_n_1516380.html)
862. Jeffrey Young, "Health Care Costs To Exceed A Record $20,000 Per Year For Families With Insurance, Study Says," *The Huffington Post*, 5/15/12, (http://www.huffingtonpost.com/2012/05/15/health-care-costs-record_n_1516380.html)
863. Janean Chun, "John Metz, Denny's Franchisee And Hurricane Grill & Wings Owner, Imposes Surcharge For Obamacare," *The Huffington Post*, 11/14/2012, (http://www.huffingtonpost.com/2012/11/13/john-metz-hurricane-grill-wings-dennys_n_2122412.html)
864. 2012 Annual Report Of The Boards Of Trustees Of The Federal Hospital Insurance And Federal Supplementary Medical Insurance Trust Funds," Social Security & Medicare Trustees Report
865. Ricardo Alonso-Zaldivar, "Medicare Official Doubts Health Care Law Savings," Associated Press, 1/26/11, (http://www.nbcnews.com/id/41277495/ns/health-health_care/t/medicare-official-doubts-health-care-law-savings)
866. Jonathan Easley, "Obama backs down on cuts to Medicare," *The Hill*, 4/7/2014; (http://thehill.com/policy/healthcare/202897-obama-backs-down-on-cuts-to-medicare)
867. Ibid.
868. Kathryn Nix, "Obamacare and the Budget: Playing Games with Numbers," The Heritage Foundation, 2/21/2011; (https://www.heritage.org/health-care-reform/report/obamacare-and-the-budget-playing-games-numbers)
869. "The GOP's New York Spanking," *The Wall Street Journal*, 5/26/11, (http://online.wsj.com/article/SB10001424052702304520804576345442590223566.html)

870. Editorial, "Return Control To The Patient," *The Tampa Tribune*, 10/15/11, (http://www2.tbo.com/news/opinion/2011/oct/15/meopino1-return-control-to-the-patient-ar-272052/)
871. Julie Reiskin, "The wrong way to fix Medicare spending," *The Denver Post*, 5/5/2011, (http://www.denverpost.com/opinion/ci_17993137)
872. Steve Gelsi, "Boeing Cutting 30% of Executives at Defense Unit," *Marketwatch*, 11/2/2012; (http://www.marketwatch.com/story/boeing-cutting-30-of-executives-at-defense-unit-2012-11-07)
873. Kavita Kumar, "Energizer to Slash Workforce by 10 Percent, Close Three Factories," *St Louis Post-Dispatch*, 11/08/2012; (http://www.stltoday.com/business/local/energizer-to-slash-workforce-by-percent-close-three-factories/article_2a72c60e-29e8-5a71-94c9-2d4a3b34a0fe.html)
874. Steven Mufson, "After Obama Reelection, Murray Energy CEO Reads Prayer, Announces Layoffs," *The Washington Post*, November 9, 2012, (http://articles.washingtonpost.com/2012-11-09/business/35505834_1_coal-slurry-prayer-web-site)
875. Henry Blodget, "Exclusive: Layoffs at Groupon," *Business Insider*, 11/08/2012, (http://www.businessinsider.com/groupon-layoffs-2012-11)
876. Scott Sloan, "Stanford Brake to Layoff 75," *Lexington Herald-Leader*, 11/07/2012, (http://www.kentucky.com/2012/11/07/2398967/brake-company-in-stanford-laying.html)
877. Gregory J. Wilcox, "Updated: Rocketdyne Lays Off 100 – Mostly in San Fernando Valley," *LA Daily News*, 11/08/2012, (http://www.dailynews.com/business/ci_21952197/rocketdyne-lays-off-100-mostly-san-fernando-valley)
878. Paul Bedard, "Jobs shock: Mass layoffs at 3-year high," *The Washington Examiner*, 1/2/2013 (http://washingtonexaminer.com/jobs-shock-mass-layoffs-at-3-year-high/article/2517456#.UOY377njk44)
879. Neil Shirley, "Shirley: Medical Device Tax Will Impact Jobs and Costs," *Ventura County Star*, 10/27/2012, (http://www.vcstar.com/news/2012/oct/27/shirley-medical-device-tax-will-impact-jobs-and/)

880. Dan Mangan, "99% of Obamacare applications hit a wall," CNBC, 10/4/2013 (http://www.cnbc.com/id/101087965)
881. Devin Dwyer, "Memo Reveals Only 6 People Signed Up for Obamacare on First Day," ABC News, October 31, 2013, (http://abcnews.go.com/blogs/politics/2013/10/memo-reveals-only-6-people-signed-up-for-obamacare-on-first-day/)
882. "Less Than Half of One Percent of HealthCare.gov Visitors Complete Obamacare Enrollment," *Breitbart*, October 16, 2013, (http://www.breitbart.com/Big-Government/2013/10/16/one-half-one-percent-obamacare-enrollment)
883. Joe Johns and Z. Byron Wolf, "First on CNN: Obama administration warned about health care website," CNN, October 30, 2013 (http://www.cnn.com/2013/10/29/politics/obamacare-warning/)
884. Elizabeth Harrington, "Obama administration Knew of Healthcare.gov Security Risks Before Launch," *The Washington Free Beacon*, 12/19/2013 (http://freebeacon.com/obama-admin-knew-of-healthcare-gov-security-risks-before-launch/)
885. Staryl Attkisson, "High security risk found after HealthCare.gov launch," CBS News, 12/20/2013 (http://www.cbsnews.com/news/high-security-risks-found-after-healthcaregov-launch/)
886. Associated Press, "Obamacare site can't handle it when you have a baby," *New York Post*, 1/3/2014 (http://nypost.com/2014/01/03/adding-a-baby-to-obamacare-plan-not-easy/)
887. Patrick Howley, "Michelle Obama's Princeton classmate is executive at company that built Obamacare website," *The Daily Caller*, 10/25/2013 (http://dailycaller.com/2013/10/25/michelle-obamas-princeton-classmate-is-executive-at-company-that-built-obamacare-website/)
888. Avik Roy, "Obama Officials In 2010: 93 Million Americans Will Be Unable To Keep Their Health Plans Under Obamacare" *Forbes*, 10/31/2013 (http://www.forbes.com/sites/theapothecary/2013/10/31/obama-officials-in-2010-93-million-americans-will-be-unable-to-keep-their-health-plans-under-obamacare/)
889. "Reid hammered by GOP after claiming all ObamaCare 'horror stories' untrue," Fox News, 2/27/2014 (http://www.foxnews.com/politics/2014/02/27/

reid-hammered-by-gop-after-claiming-all-obamacare-horror-stories-untrue/)

890. Sarah Kliff, "If You Like Your Health Plan, You Might Lose It. Again," *Vox*, 4/24/2014; (http://www.vox.com/2014/4/24/5641356/if-you-like-your-health-plan-you-might-lose-it-again)
891. Alexis Levinson, "Poll: If voters had known they'd lose insurance, Romney would have won," *The Daily Caller*, 11/22/2013 (http://dailycaller.com/2013/11/22/poll-if-voters-had-known-theyd-lose-insurance-romney-would-have-won/)
892. Neil Munro, "Obama denies 'you can keep it' videotaped promises," *The Daily Caller*, 11/5/2013 (http://dailycaller.com/2013/11/05/obama-denies-you-can-keep-it-videotaped-promises/)
893. Noel Sheppard, "CNN: White House Pressuring Insurance Companies to Not Criticize ObamaCare," *Newsbusters*, 10/29/2013 (http://newsbusters.org/blogs/noel-sheppard/2013/10/30/cnn-white-house-pressuring-insurance-companies-not-criticize-obamacar)
894. Larry O'Connor, "White House Bullied Beckel For Backing Obamacare Delay," *Breitbart*, 10/24/2013 (http://www.breitbart.com/Big-Journalism/2013/10/24/White-House-Bullied-Beckel-For-Backing-Obamacare-Delay)
895. "Students suffer ObamaCare sticker shock as premiums soar, plans get cut," Fox News, 11/18/2013 (http://www.foxnews.com/politics/2013/11/18/students-suffer-sticker-shock-from-obamacare/)
896. Andrew Adams, "New health care law makes finding cancer coverage difficult, family says," *KSL.com*, 11/29/2013 (http://www.ksl.com/?sid=27834668)
897. Lucy McCalmont, "A health care 'success story' that isn't," *Politico*, 11/19/13 (http://www.politico.com/story/2013/11/jessica-sanford-obamacare-100046.html)
898. Angie Drobnic Holan, "Lie of the Year: If you like your health care plan you can keep it'," *Politifact*, 12/12/2013 (http://www.politifact.com/truth-o-meter/article/2013/dec/12/lie-year-if-you-like-your-health-care-plan-keep-it/)

899. "An Analysis of Health Insurance Premiums Under the Patient Protection and Affordable Care Act," Congressional Budget Office, 11/30/2009, (http://www.cbo.gov/publication/41792)
900. "Obama administration confirms double-digit premium hikes," *Los Angeles Times*, 10/24/2016, (http://www.latimes.com/business/la-fi-healthcare-premiums-20161024-snap-story.html)
901. Aimee Picchi, "For some, Obamacare deductibles deliver sticker shock," CBS News, 12/9/2013 (http://www.cbsnews.com/news/obamacare-deductibles-deliver-hefty-sticker-shock/)
902. Patrick Howly, "Obama Adviser Jonathan Gruber In 2009: Obamacare Will NOT Be Affordable," *The Daily Caller*, 12/30/2014; (http://dailycaller.com/2014/12/30/obama-adviser-jonathan-gruber-in-2009-obamacare-will-not-be-affordable/)
903. "Review and Outlook: Its Up to the Voters, Now," *The Wall Street Journal*, 07/02/2012, (http://online.wsj.com/article/SB10001424052702304782404577490842520348690.html)
904. Kate Pavlich, "Obama: I Have Not Raised Taxes," *Townhall*, 09/24/2012, (http://townhall.com/tipsheet/katiepavlich/2012/09/24/obama_i_have_not_raised_taxes)
905. Alyene Senger and John Fleming, "ObamaCare's 18 New Tax Hikes," Heritage Foundation, 08/20/2012, (http://blog.heritage.org/2012/08/20/obamacares-18-new-tax-hikes/)
906. Qassim Adbul-Zahra, "Al-Qaeda Making Comeback in Iraq, Officials Say," The Associated Press, 10/09/2012; (http://www.usatoday.com/story/news/world/2012/10/09/al-qaeda-iraq/1623297/)
907. Jill Dougherty, "European Official: Al-Qaeda Threat in Northern Africa 'Spreading,' " CNN, 10/03/2012; (http://security.blogs.cnn.com/2012/10/03/al-qaeda-threat-in-northern-africa-spreading/)
908. Bridget Johnson, "General Tells Senators al-Qaeda Has 'Grown Fourfold in Last Five Years'," *PJ Media*, 1/27/2015; (http://pjmedia.com/tatler/2015/01/27/general-tells-senators-al-qaeda-has-grown-fourfold-in-last-five-years/)
909. Bridget Johnson, "General Tells Senators al-Qaeda Has 'Grown Fourfold in Last Five Years,' " *PJ Media*, 1/27/2015; (http://pjmedia.com/tatler/2015/01/27/general-tells-senators-al-qaeda-has-grown-fourfold-in-last-five-years/)

910. Amy Davidson, "John Brennan's Kill List," *The New Yorker*, 01/07/2013, (http://www.newyorker.com/online/blogs/closeread/2013/01/john-brennans-kill-list.html)
911. "Brennan: Due Process Not Necessary to Kill Americans for Potential Future Actions," *Breitbart*, 02/07/2013, (http://www.breitbart.com/Breitbart-TV/2013/02/07/Brennan-Killing-Americans-Without-Due-Process-Not-Because-of-What-They-Did-But-What-They%20Might%20Do)
912. Steve Emerson, "John Brennan Wrong for CIA," *Newsmax*, 02/05/2013, (http://www.newsmax.com/Emerson/John-Brennan-Wrong-for-CIA/2013/02/05/id/489057)
913. Ibid.
914. "National Security Hawks Call for Brennan's Resignation," Fox News, 09/29/2010, (http://www.foxnews.com/politics/2010/09/29/national-security-hawks-brennans-resignation/)
915. Joel B. Pollak, "Brennan Breaks Record: Most 'No' Votes Ever for a CIA Director," *Breitbart*, 03/08/2013, (http://www.breitbart.com/Big-Peace/2013/03/08/Brennan-Breaks-Record-Most-No-Votes-Ever-for-CIA-Director)
916. Larry O'Conner, "Flashback: Obama Sent Three Representatives to Michael Brown Funeral," *Truth Revolt*, 1/12/2015; (http://www.truthrevolt.org/news/flashback-obama-sent-three-representatives-michael-brown-funeral)
917. Ashley Collman and David Martosko, "America Snubs Historic Paris Rally," *The Daily Mail*, 1/11/2015; (http://www.dailymail.co.uk/news/article-2905678/America-snubs-historic-Paris-rally-Holder-skipped-early-Kerry-India-Obama-Biden-just-stayed-home-leave-no-U-S-presence-anti-terror-march-joined-global-leaders.html)
918. Ibid.
919. Patrick Howley, "'A PETULANT CHILD': Former Secret Service Agent Blasts Obama For Blaming Service For Skipping Paris March," *The Daily Caller*, 1/13/2015; (http://dailycaller.com/2015/01/13/a-petulant-child-former-secret-service-agent-blasts-obama-for-blaming-service-for-skipping-paris-march/)

920. Neil Munro, "White House Slams French Cartoons, Amid Election-Time Threats From Islamists," *The Daily Caller*, 9/19/2012; (http://dailycaller.com/2012/09/19/white-house-slams-french-cartoon-amid-election-time-threats-from-islamists/)
921. Katrina Trinko, "Obama: 'The Future Must Not Belong To Those Who Slander the Prophet of Islam,' " *National Review*, 9/25/2015; (http://www.nationalreview.com/corner/328483/obama-future-must-not-belong-those-who-slander-prophet-islam-katrina-trinko)
922. Andrew McCarthy, "Why It's So Hard for Obama to Call Terrorism *Terrorism*," PJ Media, 1/7/2015; (http://pjmedia.com/andrewmccarthy/2015/01/07/why-its-so-hard-for-obama-to-call-terrorism-terrorism/
923. The White House, Office of the Press Secretary. (2010). Remarks by President Obama and Prime Minister Cameron of the United Kingdom in Joint Press Availability [Press release]. Retrieved from http://www.whitehouse.gov/the-press-office/remarks-president-obama-and-prime-minister-cameron-united-kingdom-joint-press-avail
924. Jason Allardyce and Tony Allen-Mills, "Revealed: Document exposes US double-talk on Lockerbie," *The Sunday Times*, 7/25/2010, (http://www.thesundaytimes.co.uk/sto/news/uk_news/National/article353568.ece)
925. Thom Shanker and Rick Gladstone, "Iran Fired on Military Drone in First Such Attack, U.S. Says," *The New York Times*, 11/08/2012, (http://www.nytimes.com/2012/11/09/world/middleeast/pentagon-says-iran-fired-at-surveillance-drone-last-week.html)
926. "Iran Fired on U.S Drone Before Vote," *The Wall Street Journal*, 11/09/2012, (http://online.wsj.com/article/SB10001424127887324398045781071914296622874.html)
927. "The Muslim Brotherhood," Jewish Virtual Library, accessed 12/30/2012, (http://www.jewishvirtuallibrary.org/jsource/Terrorism/muslimbrotherhood.html
928. "Muslim Brotherhood Envoys Met With White House Officials in DC," Fox News, 04/05/2012, (http://www.foxnews.com/politics/2012/04/05/muslim-brotherhood-envoys-met-with-white-house-officials-in-dc/)

929. Steve Emerson and John Rossomando, "A Red Carpet for Radicals at the White House," IPT News, 10/21/2012; (http://www.investigativeproject.org/3777/a-red-carpet-for-radicals-at-the-white-house)
930. Caroline May, "Obama Admin Unilaterally Changes Law to Immigrants with 'Limited' Terror Contacts into US," *The Daily Caller*, 2/5/14;
931. Patricia Zengerle, "U.S. Eases Rules to Admit More Syrian Refugees, After 31 Last Year," Reuters, 2/5/2014; http://www.reuters.com/article/2014/02/05/us-syria-crisis-usa-refugees-idUSBREA141ZQ20140205
932. Laura Koran, "Obama pledge to welcome 10,000 Syrian refugees far behind schedule," CNN, 4/1/2016; (http://www.cnn.com/2016/04/01/politics/obama-pledge-10000-syrian-refugees-falling-short/)
933. "Obama Administration Assures Governors Refugee Vetting Is Rigorous," CBS *New York*, 11/21/2015; (http://newyork.cbslocal.com/2015/11/21/united-states-syrian-refugee-vetting)
934. Daniel Greenfield, "1 In 4 Swedish Women will be Raped As Sexual Assaults Increase 500%," *Frontpage*, 1/29/2013; (http://www.frontpagemag.com/point/175434/1-4-swedish-women-will-be-raped-sexual-assaults-daniel-greenfield)
935. "Guide to nationalist parties challenging Europe," BBC, 5/23/2016; (http://www.bbc.com/news/world-europe-36130006)
936. Chuck Ross, "FBI Director Admits US Can't Vet All Syrian Refugees For Terror Ties," *The Daily Caller*, 10/21/2015; (http://dailycaller.com/2015/10/21/fbi-director-admits-us-cant-vet-all-syrian-refugees-for-terror-ties-video/)
937. Matt Vespa, "31 States: North Dakota Joins Majority Of Governors Refusing To Relocate Syrian Refugees, Cites Security Concerns," *Townhall*, 11/18/2015; (http://townhall.com/tipsheet/mattvespa/2015/11/18/31-states-north-dakota-joins-majority-of-governors-refusing-to-relocate-syrian-refugees-cites-security-concerns-n2082522)
938. Jess Bravin and Gary Fields, "Terror Trial Likely to Leave New York City," *The Wall Street Journal*, 01/30/2010, (http://online.wsj.com/article/SB10001424052748703389004575033000474040096.html)

939. Jason Ryan and Huma Khan, "In Reversal, Obama Orders Guantanamo Military Trial for 9/11 Mastermind Khalid Sheikh Mohammed,' " ABC, 04/04/2011, (http://abcnews.go.com/Politics/911-master-mind-khalid-sheikh-mohammed-military-commission/story?id=13291750)
940. William Bigelow, "Report Faules Obama for Ignoring Persecution of Christians," *Breitbart*, 5/7/2014; (http://www.breitbart.com/national-security/2014/05/07/report-faults-obama-administra-tion-for-ignoring-persecution-of-christians/)
941. Barbara Boland, "Pew Study: Christians are the World's Most Oppressed Religious Group," CNS News; 2/6/2014; (http://cnsnews.com/news/article/barbara-boland/pew-study-christians-are-world-s-most-oppressed-religious-group)
942. Jeremy Reynalds, "Sudan Bombings Kill More Nuba Christians Around Christmas," Assist News Service, 12/31/2012)(http://www.assistnews.net/STOS/2012/s12120143.htmRIE
943. Mark Salmon and Sean Duffy, "Religious Persecution in Pakistan," *National Review Online*, 6/17/14; (http://www.nationalreview.com/article/380554/religious-persecution-pakistan-matt-salmon-sean-duffy)
944. Daniel Greenfield, "Christian Refugee From Mosul Describes Being Forced Out by Muslim Neighbors," *FrontPage*, 8/12/2014; (http://www.frontpagemag.com/2014/dgreenfield/christian-refugee-from-mosul-describes-being-forced-out-by-mus-lim-neighbors-video/)
945. Perry Chiaramonte, "Series of attacks in Egypt targeting Coptic Christians forces churches to close," Fox News, 11/2/2017; (http://www.foxnews.com/world/2017/11/02/series-attacks-in-egypt-targeting-coptic-christians-forces-churches-to-close.html)
946. Todd Starnes, "Team Obama Wins Fight to Have Christian Home-School Family Deported," Fox News, 3/3/14; http://www.foxnews.com/opinion/2014/03/03/team-obama-wins-fight-to-have-chris-tian-home-school-family-deported/
947. "Obama's New Asylum Decree Favors Muslims Over Christians," *Investor's Business Daily*, 2/21/14; http://news.investors.

com/ibd-editorials/022114-690860-obama-immigration-reforms-seem-to-come-with-religious-test.htm
948. Ed Morrissey, "Friday night news dump: Obama bypasses Congress, funds Palestinian Authority," *Hot Air*, 04/28/2012 (http://hotair.com/archives/2012/04/28/friday-night-news-dump-obama-bypasses-congress-funds-palestinian-authority/)
949. Steven Lee Meyers, "U.S. Move to Give Egypt $450 Million in Aid Meets Resistance," *The New York Times*, 09/28/2012, (http://www.nytimes.com/2012/09/29/world/middleeast/white-house-move-to-give-egypt-450-million-in-aid-meets-resistance.html)
950. Erick Stackelbeck, "Muslim Brotherhood: A Global Terrorist Influence," CBN News, February 1, 2011, (http://www.cbn.com/cbnnews/world/2011/february/muslim-brotherhood-a-global-terrorist-influence/)
951. "A short course 14: The Muslim Brotherhood's Strategic Plan," Shariah: The Threat To America; (http://shariahthethreat.org/a-short-course-1-what-is-shariah/a-short-course-14-the-muslim-brotherhood%E2%80%99s-strategic-plan/)
952. Matthew Lee, "US Oks Egypt Aid Despite Congressional Concerns," *The Guardian*, 3/22/2012; http://www.theguardian.com/world/feedarticle/10158648
953. "Millions of Egyptians Demand Morsi's Downfall," *Al Monitor*, 6/30/2013; http://www.al-monitor.com/pulse/originals/2013/06/egyptians-demonstrate-in-large-numbers-against-morsi.html
954. Jim Sciutto and Elise Labott, "U.S. to Cut Some Military Aid to Egypt After Coup, Turmoil," CNN, 10/9/2013; http://www.cnn.com/2013/10/08/us/egypt-aid/
955. The White House, "Executive Order: Review and Disposition of Individual's Detained at the Guantanamo Bay Naval Base and Closure of Detention Facilities," 01/22/2009, (http://www.whitehouse.gov/the_press_office/ClosureOfGuantanamoDetentionFacilities)
956. Matt Sledge and Ryan J. Reilly, "NDAA Signed Into Law By Obama Despite Guantanamo Veto Threat, Indefinite Detention Provisions," *The Huffington Post*, 1/3/2013 (http://www.huffingtonpost.

com/2013/01/03/ndaa-obama-indefinite-detention_n_2402601.html)

957. Helene Cooper, "Obama Nears Goal for Guantánamo With Faster Pace of Releases," *The New York Times*, 1/5/2015; (http://www.nytimes.com/2015/01/06/us/obama-nears-goal-for-guantanamo-with-faster-pace-of-releases.html?_r=0)
958. "Former CIA Officer: Admin's Release of Gitmo Prisoners Is 'Insane,' " Fox News *Insider*, 1/17/2015; (http://insider.foxnews.com/2015/01/17/former-cia-officer-obama-administrations-release-guantanamo-bay-terror-prisoners-insane)
959. " 'Extraordinary Admission' by Chuck Hagel as He Exits: He Was Pressured by WH to Release Terrorists," *BizPac Review*, 1/31/2015; (http://www.bizpacreview.com/2015/01/31/extraordinary-admission-by-chuck-hagel-as-he-exits-he-was-pressured-by-wh-to-release-terrorists-176765)
960. "5 Yemeni Detainees Released from Guantanamo," *The Week*, 1/14/2015; (http://www.theweek.com/speedreads/533663/5-yemeni-detainees-released-from-guantanamo)
961. Ed Royce, "The Midnight Push to Empty Out Guantanamo," *The Wall Street Journal*, m/dd/yyy; (https://www.wsj.com/articles/the-midnight-push-to-empty-out-guantanamo-1482795549)
962. Rebecca Kheel, "US official: Gitmo transfers have resulted in American deaths," *The Hill*, 3/23/2016; (http://thehill.com/policy/defense/274083-pentagon-official-americans-killed-by-former-gitmo-detainees)
963. Alissa J. Rubin, "Former Taliban Officials Say U.S. Talks Started," *The New York Times*, 01/28/2012, (http://www.nytimes.com/2012/01/29/world/asia/taliban-have-begun-talks-with-us-former-taliban-aides-say.html)
964. Judicial Watch Blog, "Obama Negotiates With Taliban Over Gitmo Prisoners," Judicial Watch, 02/02/2012, (http://www.judicialwatch.org/blog/2012/02/obama-negotiates-with-taliban-over-gitmo-prisoners/)
965. Robert Tilford, "Clinton Evasive About Listing Taliban as Terrorist Organization," *Examiner*, 09/12/2012, (http://www.examiner.com/article/clinton-evasive-about-listing-taliban-as-terrorist-organization)

966. Jake Tapper, "Fellow Soldiers Call Bergdahl a Deserter, Not a Hero," CNN, 6/4/2014; (http://www.cnn.com/2014/06/01/us/bergdahl-deserter-or-hero/)
967. Charles Spiering, "Former Officer: Soldiers were 'Threatened' if they Question Bergdahl Story," *Breitbart*, 6/2/2014 (http://www.breitbart.com/Big-Government/2014/06/02/Former-Officer-Soldiers-Were-Threatened-if-They-Questioned-Bergdahl-Story)
968. James Rosen, "EXCLUSIVE: Bergdahl declared jihad in captivity, secret documents show," Fox News, 6/6/2014 (http://www.foxnews.com/politics/2014/06/06/exclusive-bergdahl-declared-jihad-secret-documents-show/)
969. Mark Thompson, "The 6 U.S. Soldiers Who Died Searching for Bowe Bergdahl," *TIME*, 6/2/2014; (http://time.com/2809352/bowe-bergdahl-deserter-army-taliban/)
970. Justin Sink, "Bergdahl blame shifting to Hagel?," *The Hill*, 6/10/2014 (http://thehill.com/blogs/blog-briefing-room/208803-obama-shifting-blame-for-bergdahl-trade-to-hagel)
971. Barbara Starr, "Officials: Detainee swapped for Bergdahl suspected of militant activities," CNN, 1/29/2015; (http://edition.cnn.com/2015/01/29/politics/bergdahl-swap-prisoner-militant-activity/index.html)
972. Alex Horton, "Bowe Bergdahl, the former hostage who pleaded guilty to desertion, avoids prison," *The Washington Post* 11/3/2017; (https://www.washingtonpost.com/world/national-security/bowe-bergdahl-the-former-hostage-who-pleaded-guilty-to-desertion-avoids-prison/2017/11/03/4bde4e56-b8e4-11e7-a908-a3470754bbb9_story.html)
973. "Boston Bomber Could Have Been Deported After 2009 Arrest," *Judicial Watch Blog*, 04/29/2013, (http://www.judicialwatch.org/blog/2013/04/boston-bomber-could-have-been-deported-after-2009-conviction/)
974. "FBI Interviewed Dead Boston Bombing Suspect Years Ago," CBS News, 04/19/2013, (http://www.cbsnews.com/8301-201_162-57580534/fbi-interviewed-dead-boston-bombing-suspect-years-ago/)
975. Hillary Chabot and David Wedge, "FBI's concern was Qaeda, not Chechens, says Sen." *Boston Herald*, 4/24/2013, (http://

bostonherald.com/news_opinion/local_coverage/2013/04/fbi_s_concern_was_qaeda_not_chechens_says_sen)

976. "Boston Marathon Bombings: Barack Obama Statement on Suspect's Capture," *The Daily Telegraph*, 04/20/2013, (http://www.telegraph.co.uk/news/worldnews/barackobama/10007338/Boston-Marathon-bombings-Barack-Obama-statement-on-suspects-capture.html)
977. Robert Spencer, "Boston Jihad Bombers YouTube Page Features Videos by Sheikh Feiz Mohammed," *Jihad Watch*, 4/19/2013, (http://www.jihadwatch.org/2013/04/boston-jihad-bombers-youtube-page-features-videos-by-sheikh-feiz-mohammed-who-called-on-muslims-to-k.html)
978. Richard Miniter, "President Obama's Greatest Foreign Policy Failure: Killing bin Laden," *Forbes*, 9/13/2012; (http://www.forbes.com/sites/richardminiter/2012/09/13/president-obamas-greatest-foreign-policy-failure-killing-bin-laden/)
979. Ibid.
980. Stephen F. Hayes and Thomas Joscelyn, "How America Was Misled on al Qaeda's Demise", *The Wall Street Journal*, 3/5/2015; (http://www.wsj.com/articles/stephen-hayes-and-tomas-joscelyn-how-america-was-misled-on-al-qaedas-demise-1425600796)
981. Ibid.
982. Richard Esposito and Brian Ross, "Investigators: Northwest Bomb Plot Planned by Al-Qaeda in Yemen," ABC, 12/26/2009, (http://abcnews.go.com/Blotter/al-qaeda-yemen-planned-northwest-flight-253-bomb-plot/story?id=9426085)
983. Charlie Savage, "Holder Backs a Miranda Limit for Terror Suspects," *The New York Times*, 05/09/2010, (http://www.nytimes.com/2010/05/10/us/politics/10holder.html)
984. Catherine Herridge and Fox News Staff, "Lawmakers Blast Administration for Calling Fort Hood Massacre 'Workplace Violence'," Fox News, 12/07/2011, (http://www.foxnews.com/politics/2011/12/06/military-growing-terrorist-target-lawmakers-warn/)
985. The White House, Office of the Press Secretary (2009). Remarks by the President at Memorial Service at Fort Hood [Press Release].

Retrieved from http://www.whitehouse.gov/the-press-office/remarks-president-memorial-service-fort-hood

986. "Authorities: Man Charged in Blast at Ariz. Social Security Office Researched Terrorist Bombs," The Associated Press, 12/03/2012, (http://www.foxnews.com/us/2012/12/03/authorities-man-charged-in-blast-at-ariz-social-security-office-researched/)
987. Dave Gibson, "No Terrorism Charges for Iraqi Man Accused of Arizona Bomb Attack," *Examiner*, 12/04/2012, (http://www.examiner.com/article/no-terrorism-charges-for-iraqi-man-accused-of-arizona-bomb-attack)
988. Sean Gorman, "Cruz is right: Obama doesn't link Islam to terrorism," *Politifact*, 11/30/2015; (http://www.politifact.com/virginia/statements/2015/nov/30/ted-cruz/cruz-right-obama-doesnt-link-islam-terrorismerrori/)
989. Craig Bannister, "VIDEO: WH Censors French President Saying 'ISLAMIST Terrorism,' " MRCTV, 4/1/2016; (http://www.mrctv.org/blog/video-wh-censors-reference-islamist-terrorism-french-president)
990. Kevin Johnson and Mary Bowerman, "FBI, DOJ issue new transcript of Orlando 911 call amid outrage," *USA Today*, 6/20/2016; (http://www.usatoday.com/story/news/nation-now/2016/06/20/many-outraged-reference-isil-omitted-orlando-911-transcript/86139678/)
991. Jim Treacher, "Loretta Lynch: We May Never Know Why That Islamic Terrorist Killed All Those People," *The Daily Caller*, 6/21/2016; (http://dailycaller.com/2016/06/21/loretta-lynch-we-may-never-know-why-that-islamic-terrorist-killed-all-those-people/)
992. Meghan Keneally, "San Bernardino Shooting Investigated as 'Act of Terrorism,' " ABC News, 12/4/2015; (http://abcnews.go.com/US/san-bernardino-shooting-investigated-act-terrorism/story?id=35573368)
993. Ralph Ellis, Ashley Fantz, Faith Karimi and Eliott C. McLaughlin, "Orlando shooting: 49 killed, shooter pledged ISIS allegiance," CNN, 6/12/2016; (http://www.cnn.com/2016/06/12/us/orlando-nightclub-shooting/)

994. John R. Schindler, "The Intelligence Lessons of San Bernardino," *Observer*, 12/14/15; (http://observer.com/2015/12/the-intelligence-lessons-of-san-bernardino/)
995. Katie Pavlich, "Neighbor Didn't Report Suspicious Activity of San Bernardino Killers For Fear of Being Called Racist," *Townhall*, 12/3/2015; (http://townhall.com/tipsheet/katiepavlich/2015/12/03/neighbor-didnt-report-suspicious-activity-of-san-bernardino-killers-for-fear-of-being-called-racist-n2088543)
996. Cecilia Kang and Eric Lichtblau, "F.B.I. Error Locked San Bernardino Attacker's iPhone," *The New York Times*, 3/2/2016; (http://www.nytimes.com/2016/03/02/technology/apple-and-fbi-face-off-before-house-judiciary-committee.html)
997. Michael Daly, "Omar Mateen, Terrorist Who Attacked Orlando Gay Club, Had Been Investigated by FBI," *The Daily Beast*, 6/12/2016; (http://www.thedailybeast.com/articles/2016/06/12/omar-mateen-id-d-as-orlando-killer.html)
998. Christian Datoc, "FBI Called Off Investigation Of Orlando Shooter Because They Thought His Coworkers Were Racist," *The Daily Caller* 6/13/2016; (http://dailycaller.com/2016/06/13/fbi-called-off-investigation-of-orlando-shooter-because-they-thought-his-coworkers-were-racist/)
999. Charlie Savage, "U.S. Tries to Make It Easier to Wiretap the Internet," *The New York Times*, 09/27/2012, (http://www.nytimes.com/2010/09/27/us/27wiretap.html)
1000. Peter Yost, "Federal Surveillance Rises Sharply Under Obama," Associated Press, 10/01/2012, (http://www.washingtonguardian.com/big-brother-listening)
1001. David Kravets, "Feds Say Mobile-Phone Location Data Not 'Constitutionally Protected'," *Wired*, 9/5/2012, (http://www.wired.com/threatlevel/2012/09/feds-say-mobile-phone-location-data-not-constitutionally-protected/)
1002. Julia Angwin, "U.S. Terrorism Agency to Tap a Vast Database of Citizens," *The Wall Street Journal*, 12/13/2012, (http://online.wsj.com/article/SB10001424127887324478304578171623040640006.html)
1003. Kara Brandeisky, "The Surveillance Reforms Obama Supported Before He Was President," *ProPublica*, August 7, 2013; http://www.

propublica.org/article/the-surveillance-reforms-obama-supported-before-he-was-president

1004. James Risen, "Obama's Wiretapping Stand Enrages Many Supporters," *The New York Times*, July 2, 2008, http://www.nytimes.com/2008/07/02/world/americas/02iht-obama.1.14161755.html?_r=0
1005. Glenn Greenwald, "NSA Collecting Phone Records of Millions of Verizon Customers Daily," *The Guardian*, June 5th, 2013; http://www.thedailybeast.com/articles/2013/06/07/nsa-surveillance-program-explained-here-s-why-we-re-freaking-out.html
1006. Siobhan Gorman, Evan Perez and Janet Hook, "U.S. Collects Vast Data Trove," *The Wall Street Journal*, June 7, 2013; http://online.wsj.com/news/articles/SB100014241278873242991045785291122 89298922
1007. Barton Gellman and Laura Poitras, "U.S., British Intelligence Mining Data from Nine U.S. Internet Companies in Broad Secret Program," *The Washington Post*, June 6th, 2013; http://www.washingtonpost.com/investigations/us-intelligence-mining-data-from-nine-us-internet-companies-in-broad-secret-program/2013/06/06/3a0c0da8-cebf-11e2-8845-d970ccb04497_story_2.html
1008. Ibid.
1009. The Editorial Board, "President Obama's Dragnet," *The New York Times*, 6/6/2013; (http://www.nytimes.com/2013/06/07/opinion/president-obamas-dragnet.html)
1010. Charlie Savage and Jonathan Weisman "N.S.A. Collection of Bulk Call Data Is Ruled Illegal," *The New York Times*, 5/7/2015; (https://www.nytimes.com/2015/05/08/us/nsa-phone-records-collection-ruled-illegal-by-appeals-court.html)
1011. "Ex-CIA Chief Petraeus Testifies Benghazi Attack was al Qaeda-linked Terrorism," CNN, 11/16/2012, (http://www.cnn.com/2012/11/16/politics/benghazi-hearings/index.html)
1012. Jake Tapper, "Documents Back up Claims of Requests Requests for Greater Security in Benghazi," ABC, 10/19/2012, (http://abcnews.go.com/blogs/politics/2012/10/documents-back-up-claims-of-requests-for-greater-security-in-benghazi/)

1013. Awr Hawkins, "Panetta's Testimony Calls Obama's Benghazi Explanations in to Question," *Breitbart*, 02/09/2013; (http://www.breitbart.com/Big-Peace/2013/02/08/Panetta-s-Testimony-Calls-Obama-s-Benghazi-Explanations-Into-Question)
1014. Arshad Mohammed and Tabassum Zakaria, "Clinton Forcefully Defends Handling of Benghazi Attack," Reuters, 01/23/2013, (http://www.reuters.com/article/2013/01/23/us-usa-libya-clinton-idUSBRE90M0SM20130123)
1015. Kerry Picket, "Benghazi Survivors Remain Gagged by Federal Law," *Breitbart*, 02/20/2013, (http://www.breitbart.com/Big-Peace/2013/02/20/Benghazi-Survivors-Remained-Gagged-By-Federal-Law)
1016. Marina Koren, "We Now Know Who's to Blame for Benghazi," *National Journal*, 1/15/2014 (http://www.nationaljournal.com/congress/we-now-know-who-s-to-blame-for-benghazi-20140115)
1017. John Parkinson, "White House Failed to Protect Benghazi Mission, House Report Concludes," ABC News, 2/11/2014 (http://abcnews.go.com/Politics/white-house-failed-protect-benghazi-mission-house-report/story?id=22460489)
1018. "Libyan President to NBC: Anti-Islam Film Had 'Nothing to do with' US Consulate Attack," NBC News, 09/26/2012, (http://worldnews.nbcnews.com/_news/2012/09/26/14105135-libyan-president-to-nbc-anti-islam-film-had-nothing-to-do-with-us-consulate-attack)
1019. Brendan Bordelon, "Krauthammer: New Benghazi Email A 'Classic Cover-Up Of A Cover-Up,' " *The Daily Caller*, 4/29/2014 (http://dailycaller.com/2014/04/29/krauthammer-new-benghazi-email-classic-cover-up-of-a-cover-up-and-that-is-a-serious-offense/)
1020. Eugene Kiely, "The Benghazi Timeline, Clinton Edition," *Source*, 6/30/2016; (https://www.factcheck.org/2016/06/the-benghazi-timeline-clinton-edition/)
1021. "Judicial Watch: Newly Released Documents Confirm White House Officials Set Hillary Clinton's Benghazi Response," *Judicial Watch*, 6/29/2015; (http://www.judicialwatch.org/press-room/press-releases/

judicial-watch-newly-released-documents-confirm-white-house-officials-set-hillary-clintons-benghazi-response/)
1022. Sara A Carter, "Secret Memo Suggests White House Ignored SOS from Iranian Opposition," *The Washington Examiner*, 2/27/2012; (http://www.washingtonexaminer.com/article/318891)
1023. David French, "The Utter Chaos of the 's Egypt Policy," *National Review*, 7/2/2013; (http://www.nationalreview.com/corner/352604/utter-chaos-obama-administrations-egypt-policy-david-french)
1024. Zeke J. Miller, "Obama Condemns Egyptian Violence, But Doesn't Halt Aid," *TIME*, 8/15/2013; (http://swampland.time.com/2013/08/15/obama-condemns-egyptian-violence-but-doesnt-halt-aid/)
1025. S.A. Miller, "The knives are out: Panetta eviscerates Obama's 'red line' blunder on Syria," *The Washington Times*, 10/7/2014; (http://www.washingtontimes.com/news/2014/oct/7/panetta-decries-obama-red-line-blunder-syria/)
1026. Noah Rothman, "Panetta: Obama's bad decisions on Syria and Iraq led to rise of ISIS," *Hot Air*, 9/22/2014; (http://hotair.com/archives/2014/09/22/obama-syria-iraq-panetta/)
1027. Spencer Ackerman, "What Surge? Afghanistan's Most Violent Places Stay Bad, Despite Extra Troops," *Wired*, 8/23/2012; (http://www.wired.com/2012/08/afghanistan-violence-helmand/)
1028. Julie Pace and Ken Dilanian, "US Counterterrorism Strategy in Yemen Collapses Amid Chaos," Associated Press, (http://www.military.com/daily-news/2015/03/24/us-counterterrorism-strategy-in-yemen-collapses-amid-chaos.html)
1029. Council on Foreign Relations, "Sectarian Conflict in Lebanon," Accessed 6/14/2016; (http://www.cfr.org/global/global-conflict-tracker/p32137#!/conflict/sectarian-conflict-in-lebanon)
1030. David Schenker, "Lebanon Unstable and Insecure," The Washington Institute, 6/12/2014; (http://www.washingtoninstitute.org/policy-analysis/view/lebanon-unstable-and-insecure)
1031. Ian Hanchett, "Fmr. Obama Ambassador: Middle East Destabilizing More Rapidly Than Under Bush," *Breitbart*, 3/28/2015; (http://www.breitbart.com/video/2015/03/28/fmr-obama-amb-middle-east-destabilizing-more-rapidly-than-under-bush/)

1032. Nick Gass, "Bob Gates: U.S. has no Middle East strategy 'at all'," *Politico*, 5/19/2015; (http://www.politico.com/story/2015/05/robert-gates-us-no-middle-east-strategy-118083.html)
1033. Mark Mazzetti and Matt Apuzzo, "Inquiry Weighs Whether ISIS Analysis Was Distorted," *The New York Times*, 8/25/2015; (http://www.nytimes.com/2015/08/26/world/middleeast/pentagon-investigates-allegations-of-skewed-intelligence-reports-on-isis.html)
1034. Shane Harris and Nancy A. Yousef, "Exclusive: 50 Spies Say ISIS Intelligence Was Cooked," *The Daily Beast*, 9/9/2015; (http://www.thedailybeast.com/articles/2015/09/09/exclusive-50-spies-say-isis-intelligence-was-cooked.html)
1035. Pamela Engel, "'Something's wrong': The ISIS intelligence scandal just hit Obama's inner circle," *Business Insider*, 9/11/2015; (http://www.businessinsider.com/obama-administration-and-isis-intelligence-2015-9)
1036. Stephen F. Hayes, "Obama's Intel Scandal," *The Weekly Standard*, 12/7/2015; (http://www.weeklystandard.com/obamas-intel-scandal/article/1070543)
1037. Tom LoBianco, "Former intel chief says WH worried over re-elect 'narrative,'" CNN, 12/2/2015; (http://www.cnn.com/2015/12/01/politics/michael-flynn-obama-isis/)
1038. Global Terrorism Index 2015; Institute for Economics and Peace (PDF); (http://economicsandpeace.org/wp-content/uploads/2015/11/Global-Terrorism-Index-2015.pdf)
1039. Aminu Abubakar, "As Many as 200 Girls Abducted by Boko Haram, Nigerian Officials Say," CNN, 4/16/2014; (http://www.cnn.com/2014/04/15/world/africa/nigeria-girls-abducted/)
1040. Morgan Lorraine Roach, "Boko Haram: Addressing the Threat Before it Strikes," *Heritage Foundation Issue Brief 3549*, 3/22/2012; (http://www.heritage.org/research/reports/2012/03/boko-haram-threat-of-the-nigerian-islamist-insurgency)
1041. Josh Rogin, "Hillary's State Department Refused to Brand Boko Haram as Terrorists," *The Daily Beast*, 5/7/2014; (http://www.thedailybeast.com/articles/2014/05/07/hillary-s-state-department-refused-to-brand-boko-haram-as-terrorists.html)

1042. James Simpson, "Obama Accused of Obstructing Battle against Boko Haram to Promote Axelrod's Nigerian Muslim Client," Accuracy in Media, 3/24/2015; (http://www.aim.org/aim-column/obama-accused-of-obstructing-battle-against-boko-haram-to-promote-axelrods-nigerian-muslim-client/)
1043. Robert Marquand, "Obama Singles Out Boko Haram and Nigeria Declares 'Total War' on Shadowy Group," *The Christian Science Monitor*, 5/29/2014; (http://www.csmonitor.com/World/Africa/2014/0529/Obama-singles-out-Boko-Haram-and-Nigeria-declares-total-war-on-shadowy-group-video)
1044. Global Terrorism Index 2015; Institute for Economics and Peace (PDF); (http://economicsandpeace.org/wp-content/uploads/2015/11/Global-Terrorism-Index-2015.pdf)
1045. Charlotte Florence, "Boko Haram Benefitted from State Department Inaction," *The Daily Signal*, 5/12/2014; (http://dailysignal.com/2014/05/12/boko-haram-benefitted-state-department-inaction/)
1046. "Statement By The President On First Step Agreement On Iran's Nuclear Program," The White House, 11/23/2013; (https://www.whitehouse.gov/the-press-office/2013/11/23/statement-president-first-step-agreement-irans-nuclear-program)
1047. "Iran Say to Continue Building at Arak Nuclear Site Despite Deal," Reuters, November 27, 2013; http://www.reuters.com/article/2013/11/27/us-iran-nuclear-arak-idUSBRE9AQ0U120131127
1048. Tom Cohen, "Iran on Nuke Deal: 'We Did Not Agree to Dismantle Anything,' " CNN, January 23, 2014; http://www.cnn.com/2014/01/22/politics/iran-us-nuclear/index.html
1049. Daniel Halper, "Iran's Rouhani: 'World Powers Surrendered to Iranian Nation's Will,' " *The Weekly Standard*, January 14, 2014; http://www.weeklystandard.com/blogs/irans-rouhani-world-powers-surrendered-iranian-nations-will_774616.html
1050. Julian Pecquot, "Obama: 'I will veto' new Iran sanctions," *The Hill*, 1/28/2014 (http://thehill.com/blogs/global-affairs/middle-east-north-africa/196750-obama-to-congress-i-will-veto-your-iran)
1051. Daniel Bassali, "Wolf Blitzer Makes a Fool Out of Susan Rice on Iran Funding of Terrorists," *The Washington Free Beacon*, 7/15/2015; (http://freebeacon.com/national-security/

wolf-blitzer-makes-a-fool-of-susan-rice-on-iran-funding-terrorists/)

1052. Henry A. Kissinger, "Speeches and Public Statements; Opening Statement by Dr. Henry A Kissinger Before the United States Senate Committee on Armed Services", 1/29/2015; (http://www.henryakissinger.com/speeches/012915.html)
1053. Yaroslav Trofimov, "Like Israel, U.S. Arab Allies Fear Obama's Iran Nuclear Deal," *The Wall Street Journal*, 3/4/2015; (http://www.wsj.com/articles/like-israel-u-s-arab-allies-fear-obamas-iran-nuclear-deal-1425504773)
1054. Jordan Schachtel, "Report: Obama has Agreed to 80 percent of Iran's Demands in Nuclear Talks," *Breitbart*, 1/30/2015; (http://www.breitbart.com/national-security/2015/01/30/report-obama-agrees-to-80-percent-of-irans-demands-in-nuke-talks/)
1055. Winston Hall, "7 Devestasting Facts about Obama's Iran Nuclear Deal," *Breitbart*, 7/17/2015; (http://www.breitbart.com/national-security/2015/07/17/7-devastating-facts-about-obamas-iran-nuclear-deal/)
1056. Eli Lake, "Obama Kept Iran's Short Breakout Time Secret," *Bloomberg View*, 4/21/2015; (http://www.bloombergview.com/articles/2015-04-21/obama-kept-iran-s-short-breakout-time-a-secret)
1057. Christian Datoc, "White House, Obama Blocked Congress From Reviewing Secret Aspects Of Iran Deal," *The Daily Caller*, 7/22/2015; (http://dailycaller.com/2015/07/22/white-house-obama-blocked-congress-from-reviewing-secret-aspects-of-iran-deal/)
1058. Lee Smith, "Obama's Foreign Policy Guru Boasts of How the Administration Lied to Sell the Iran Deal," *Weekly Standard*, 5/5/2016; (http://www.weeklystandard.com/article/2002252)
1059. Guy Taylor and Ben Wolfgang, "Obama downplays Iran 'death to America' remarks, toes hard line on Benjamin Netanyahu," *The Washington Times*, 3/23/2015; (http://www.washingtontimes.com/news/2015/mar/23/obama-downplays-iran-death-to-america-remarks-toes/)
1060. Ethan Barton, "Obama Administration Is SCRAMBLING To Fill 200 New Policy-Making Jobs," *The Daily Caller*, 1/17/2017; (http://

dailycaller.com/2017/01/17/obama-administration-is-scrambling-to-fill-200-new-policy-making-jobs/)
1061. Juliet Eilperin and Brady Dennis, "With days left in office, President Obama ushers in dozens of policies. But will they stay seated?," *The Washington Post*, 1/14/2017; (https://www.washingtonpost.com/national/health-science/with-days-left-in-office-obama-ushers-in-dozens-of-policies-but-will-they-stay-seated/2017/01/14/30f56b4a-d8f9-11e6-9a36-1d296534b31e_story.html)
1062. John R. Lott Jr., "Obama's false racism claims are putting cops' lives in danger," *New York Post*, 7/8/2016; (https://nypost.com/2016/07/08/obama-should-stop-smearing-cops-by-calling-them-racist/)
1063. Bianca Padro Ocasio, "Police group director: Obama caused a 'war on cops'," *Politico*, 7/8/2016; (https://www.politico.com/story/2016/07/obama-war-on-cops-police-advocacy-group-225291)
1064. Ben Shapiro, "Obama's DOJ Admits Ambushes on Cops Are Up. Cops Can Thank President Obama.," *The Daily Wire*, 10/27/2015; (https://www.dailywire.com/news/722/obamas-doj-admits-ambushes-cops-are-cops-can-thank-ben-shapiro)
1065. "2016 saw increase in number of police killed in line of duty," *Source*, 12/29/2016; (https://www.cbsnews.com/news/police-killed-line-of-duty-increase-2016/)
1066. Lumumba Akinwole-Bandele and Monifa Akinwole-Bandele, "Race still matters in presidential pardons," *The Hill*, 1/17/2017; (http://thehill.com/blogs/pundits-blog/civil-rights/314564-race-still-matters-in-presidential-pardons)
1067. Stephen Dinan, "Obama scores the worst legislative record in history," *The Washington Times*, 1/17/2017; (https://www.washingtontimes.com/news/2017/jan/17/president-obama-scores-poorly-working-congress-leg/)
1068. Ibid.
1069. "Obama On Executive Actions: 'I've Got A Pen And I've Got A Phone'," CBS *DC*, 1/14/2014; (http://washington.cbslocal.com/2014/01/14/obama-on-executive-actions-ive-got-a-pen-and-ive-got-a-phone/)
1070. Nahal Toosi, "Iran releases 5 detained Americans, including Washington Post reporter," *Politico*, 1/16/2016; (https://www.politico.com/story/2016/01/iran-prisoners-217875)

1071. Elise Labott, Nicole Gaouette and Kevin Liptak, "US sent plane with $400 million in cash to Iran," CNN, 8/3/2016; (http://www.cnn.com/2016/08/03/politics/us-sends-plane-iran-400-million-cash/)
1072. Jay Solomon and Carol E. Lee, "U.S. Held Cash Until Iran Freed Prisoners," *The Wall Street Journal*, 8/18/2016; (https://www.wsj.com/articles/u-s-held-cash-until-iran-freed-prisoners-1471469256)
1073. Elise Labott, Nicole Gaouette and Kevin Liptak, "US sent plane with $400 million in cash to Iran," CNN, 8/3/2016; (http://www.cnn.com/2016/08/03/politics/us-sends-plane-iran-400-million-cash/)
1074. Lucas Tomlinson, "Defense official: Iran confrontations with US Navy up 50 percent this year," Fox News, 8/26/2016; (http://www.foxnews.com/politics/2016/08/26/defense-official-iran-confrontations-with-us-navy-up-50-percent-this-year.html)
1075. Adam Kredo, "Iran May Have Received as Much as $33.6 Billion in Cash, Gold Payments From U.S.," *The Washington Free Beacon*, 9/8/2016; (http://freebeacon.com/national-security/iran-may-received-much-33-6-billion-cash-gold-payments-u-s/)
1076. Tyler Durden, "The Two Scariest Charts From Today's NFP Report, Or The Real "New Part-Time Normal"," *Zero Hedge*, 5/4/2012, (https://www.zerohedge.com/news/two-scariest-charts-todays-nfp-report-or-real-new-part-time-normal)
1077. Joseph Lawler, "Involuntary part-time employment soars in May," *Washington Examiner*, 6/3/2016, (http://www.washingtonexaminer.com/involuntary-part-time-employment-soars-in-may/article/2592914)
1078. Greg Robb, "Obamacare has led to rise in involuntary part-time employment, Goldman Sachs finds," *MarketWatch*, 6/8/2016, (ttps://www.marketwatch.com/story/obamacare-has-led-to-rise-in-involuntary-part-time-employment-goldman-sachs-finds-2016-06-08)
1079. "Is Part-Time and Temporary Employment the 'New Normal'?," *Talent Daily*, 12/9/2016, (https://www.cebglobal.com/talentdaily/part-time-temporary-employment-new-normal/)
1080. Tyler Durden, "Top Ex-White House Economist Admits 94% Of All New Jobs Under Obama Were Part-Time," *Zero Hedge*, 12/25/2016,

(https://www.zerohedge.com/news/2016-12-23/top-white-house-economist-admits-94-all-new-jobs-under-obama-were-part-time)

1081. Aimee Picchi, "A new post-recession normal: working part time, unwillingly," CBS News, 12/5/2016, (https://www.cbsnews.com/news/a-new-economy-post-recession-normal-working-part-time-unwillingly/)
1082. Tyler Durden, "Top Ex-White House Economist Admits 94% Of All New Jobs Under Obama Were Part-Time," *Zero Hedge*, 12/25/2016, (https://www.zerohedge.com/news/2016-12-23/top-white-house-economist-admits-94-all-new-jobs-under-obama-were-part-time)
1083. Ronald Bailey, "Obama's Possible Paris Climate Agreement End Run Around the Senate," *Reason*, 12/10/2014; (http://reason.com/archives/2014/12/10/obamas-possible-paris-climate-agreement)
1084. Steven Groves, "The Paris Agreement Is a Treaty and Should Be Submitted to the Senate," *Source*, 3/15/2016; (http://www.heritage.org/research/reports/2016/03/the-paris-agreement-is-a-treaty-and-should-be-submitted-to-the-senate)
1085. Tanya Somander, "President Obama: the United States Formally Enters the Paris Agreement," The White House, 9/3/2016; (https://www.whitehouse.gov/blog/2016/09/03/president-obama-united-states-formally-enters-paris-agreement)
1086. Devin Henry, "Obama: Trump Should not end Paris Climate Agreement," *The Hill*, 11/14/2016; (http://thehill.com/policy/energy-environment/305950-obama-trump-should-not-end-paris-climate-agreement)
1087. E. Fletcher McClellan, Kyle C. Kopko, Christopher J. Devine, Jillian E. Casey and Julia L. Ward, "Obama has set the record for the most Presidential Medals of Freedom," *The Washington Post*, 11/22/2016; (https://www.washingtonpost.com/news/monkey-cage/wp/2016/11/22/obama-has-set-the-record-for-the-most-presidential-medals-of-freedom/)
1088. Wikipedia Contributors, "Executive Order 11085," Wikipedia: The Free Encyclopedia, 11/5/2010; (https://en.wikisource.org/wiki/Executive_Order_11085)
1089. hPatrick Howley, "Why Doesn't Obama Condemn Boy Rapist Harvey Milk?," *The Daily Caller*,

7/15/2015; (http://dailycaller.com/2015/07/15/why-doesnt-obama-condemn-boy-rapist-harvey-milk/)

1090. "Medals at a discount," *The Washington Times*, 11/22/2016; (https://www.washingtontimes.com/news/2016/nov/22/medal-of-freedom-not-what-it-used-to-be/)

1091. Morgan Chalfant, "Obama Hands Out Medals of Freedom to Major Democratic Donors, Supporters," *The Washington Free Beacon*, 11/21/2016; (http://freebeacon.com/politics/obama-hands-medals-freedom-major-democratic-donors-supporters/)

1092. Michael Bastasch, "Obama Issues More Last-Minute National Monument Designations," *The Daily Caller*, 1/13/2017; (http://dailycaller.com/2017/01/13/obama-issues-more-last-minute-national-monument-designations/)

1093. Michael Bastasch, "Obama Puts 1.6 Million Acres Under Stricter Federal Control Despite Intense Local Opposition," *The Daily Caller*, 12/28/2016; (http://dailycaller.com/2016/12/28/obama-puts-1-6-million-acres-under-stricter-federal-control-despite-intense-local-opposition/)

1094. Nicholas Loris, "Federal Land Grabs Have Gotten Out of Control. Why Trump's Executive Order Is a Positive Sign," The Heritage Foundation, 4/26/2017; (https://www.heritage.org/environment/commentary/federal-land-grabs-have-gotten-out-control-why-trumps-executive-order)

1095. Nadja Popovich, "Bears Ears National Monument Is Shrinking. Here's What Is Being Cut," *The New York Times*, 12/8/2017; (https://www.nytimes.com/interactive/2017/12/08/climate/bears-ears-monument-trump.html)

1096. Ibid.

1097. Justin Huggler, "Migrant crime in Germany rises by 50 per cent, new figures show," The Telegraph, 4/25/2017; (http://www.telegraph.co.uk/news/2017/04/25/migrant-crime-germany-rises-50-per-cent-new-figures-show/)

1098. Pete Kasperowicz, "State admits: Islamic State terrorists trying to pose as refugees," Washington Examiner, 1/27/2018; (http://www.washingtonexaminer.com/

state-admits-islamic-state-terrorists-trying-to-pose-as-refugees/article/2602405)

1099. Miriam Jordan, "President Obama to Increase Refugees Admitted to U.S. by 30%," The Wall Street Journal, 9/14/2016; (https://www.wsj.com/articles/president-obama-to-increase-refugees-admitted-to-u-s-by-30-1473818352)
1100. Michael F. Haverluck, "Obama speeds up influx of 'refugees' before Trump," One News Now, 12/22/2016; (https://www.onenewsnow.com/national-security/2016/12/22/obama-speeds-up-influx-of-refugees-before-trump)
1101. Kimberly Leonard, "Obama Administration Moves to Protect Planned Parenthood Funding", US News & World Report, 12/14/2016; (https://www.usnews.com/news/articles/2016-12-14/obama-administration-blocks-states-from-defunding-planned-parenthood)
1102. Colleen Shalby, "Trump signs law that allows states to deny funding to Planned Parenthood," Los Angeles Times, 4/13/2017; (http://www.latimes.com/politics/washington/la-na-essential-washington-updates-trump-signs-law-that-allows-states-to-1492129331-htmlstory.html)
1103. Dave Boyer, "The 'most transparent' president in history issues record number of 'midnight' regulations," The Washington Times, 1/5/2017 (https://www.washingtontimes.com/news/2017/jan/5/obama-issuing-record-number-midnight-regulations/)
1104. Michael Batasch, "Trump Targets $181 Billion Worth Of Obama-Era Regulations, And That's Only The Beginning," The Daily Caller, 2/13/2017; (http://dailycaller.com/2017/02/13/trump-targets-181-billion-worth-of-obama-era-regulations-and-thats-only-the-beginning/)
1105. John Fund, "Obama Is Using the Russians as an Excuse to Expand Federal Power over Elections," National Review, 1/8/2017; (http://www.nationalreview.com/article/443659/obamas-russia-excuse-expanding-federal-power-over-elections)
1106. Barbara Hollingsworth, "Legal Experts: Allowing DHS to Secure Elections Would Set a Dangerous Precedent," CNS News, 8/31/2016; (https://www.

cnsnews.com/news/article/barbara-hollingsworth/legal-experts-allowing-dhs-secure-elections-would-set-dangerous)
1107. Ibid.
1108. John Fund, "Obama Is Using the Russians as an Excuse to Expand Federal Power over Elections," National Review, 1/8/2017; (http://www.nationalreview.com/article/443659/obamas-russia-excuse-expanding-federal-power-over-elections)
1109. Ibid.
1110. "Clinton Says Trump Transition Comments Threaten 'Our Democracy,' " Bloomberg Politics, 10/21/2016; (https://www.bloomberg.com/politics/trackers/2016-10-21/clinton-says-trump-transition-comments-threaten-our-democracy)
1111. Maya Kosoff, "Obama Promises 'Peaceful Transition of Power' to Donald Trump," Vanity Fair, 11/9/2016; (http://www.vanityfair.com/news/2016/11/obama-promises-peaceful-transition-of-power-to-donald-trump)
1112. Amy B. Wang, "Pelosi: 'Peaceful Transfer of Power is the Cornerstone of Our Democracy,' " The Washington Post, 11/9/2016; (https://www.washingtonpost.com/politics/2016/live-updates/general-election/real-time-updates-on-the-2016-election-voting-and-race-results/pelosi-peaceful-transfer-of-power-is-the-cornerstone-of-our-democracy/?utm_term=.b2a6148e74ac)
1113. M J Lee, Dan Merica and Jeff Zelany; "Obama: Would be 'Personal Insult' to Legacy if Black Voters Don't Back Clinton," CNN, 9/17/2016; (http://www.cnn.com/2016/09/17/politics/obama-black-congressional-caucus/)
1114. "The President-Elect's Radio Address," The American Presidency Project, 1/17/2009; (http://www.presidency.ucsb.edu/ws/index.php?pid=85456)
1115. Jann S. Wenner, "The Day After: Obama on His Legacy, Trump's Win and the Path Forward," Rolling Stone, 11/29/2016; (https://www.rollingstone.com/politics/features/obama-on-his-legacy-trumps-win-and-the-path-forward-w452527)
1116. Cameron Cawthorne, "Earnest Attacks Incoming President to Unprecedented Degree During

Transition Period," The Washington Free Beacon, 11/14/2016; (http://freebeacon.com/politics/earnest-attacks-trump-unprecedented-degree-transition-period/)

1117. Evan Perez and Daniella Diaz, "White House announces retaliation against Russia: Sanctions, ejecting diplomats," CNN, 1/2/2017; (http://www.cnn.com/2016/12/29/politics/russia-sanctions-announced-by-white-house/)
1118. "Obama says he'll speak out against Trump if he thinks US ideals are at risk," Fox News Politics, 11/21/2016; (http://www.foxnews.com/politics/2016/11/21/obama-says-hell-speak-out-against-trump-if-thinks-us-ideals-are-at-risk.htm.html)
1119. Seung Min Kim; "Obama to Huddle With Hill Democrats on Saving Obamacare," Politico, 12/30/2016; (http://www.politico.com/story/2016/12/obama-to-huddle-with-hill-democrats-on-saving-obamacare-233062)
1120. Fred Lucas, "Obama Political Appointees to Continue as Career Employees Under Trump," The Daily Signal, 12/8/2016; (http://dailysignal.com/2016/12/08/obama-political-employees-to-continue-as-career-employees-under-trump/)
1121. Paul Bedard, "Obama raising war chest to 'fight' Trump," Washington Examiner, 12/16/2016; (http://www.washingtonexaminer.com/obama-raising-war-chest-to-fight-trump/article/2609844)
1122. Jordan Fabian, "Nearing exit, Obama seeks to tie Trump's hands," The Hill, 12/30/2016; (http://thehill.com/homenews/administration/312162-nearing-exit-obama-seeks-to-tie-trumps-hands)
1123. Donald Trump. Twitter Post. 12/28/2016 6:07 AM; (https://twitter.com/realDonaldTrump/status/814110460761018368)
1124. Michael D. Shear; "Obama's Last Days: Aiding Trump Transition, but Erecting Policy Roadblocks," The New York Times; 12/31/2016; (http://www.nytimes.com/2016/12/31/us/politics/obama-last-days-trump-transition.html?_r=0)
1125. Doug Stanglin, "U.S. Abstains on U.N Vote Condemning Israeli Settlements," USA Today, 12/23/2016; (http://www.usatoday.com/story/news/2016/12/23/un-set-vote-israeli-settlement-despite-trump-intervention/95796716/)

1126. Yarden Frankel, "The Ethnic Cleansing of Jerusalem," The Times of Israel, 9/19/2016; (http://blogs.timesofisrael.com/the-ethnic-cleansing-of-jerusalem/)
1127. Michael A. Memoli, "Obama Personally Authorized U.S. Abstention from U.N. Vote on Israeli Settlements," Los Angeles Times, 12/23/2016; (http://www.latimes.com/nation/politics/trailguide/la-na-trailguide-updates-obama-authorized-u-s-abstention-on-1482528162-htmlstory.html)
1128. Jason Squitieri, "Israel Says There is 'Ironclad' Proof Obama Pushed UN Vote," CNN, 12/26/2016; (https://www.cnn.com/2016/12/26/world/israel-benjamin-netanyahu-iron-clad-intel-erin-burnett-cnntv/index.html)
1129. Adam Kredo, "White House on Defense After Being Exposed as Architect of Anti-Israel U.N. Action," The Washington Free Beacon, 12/29/2016; (http://freebeacon.com/national-security/white-house-defense-exposed-architect-anti-israel-u-n-action/)
1130. Neil Eggleston, "President Obama Has Now Granted More Commutations than Any President in this Nation's History," The White House of Barack Obama, 1/17/2017; (https://obamawhitehouse.archives.gov/blog/2017/01/17/president-obama-has-now-granted-more-commutations-any-president-nations-history)
1131. Ibid.
1132. Wikipedia Contributors, "Oscar López Rivera," Wikipedia: The Free Encyclopedia, 1/8/2018; https://en.wikipedia.org/wiki/Oscar_L%C3%B3pez_Rivera)
1133. "Sentence FALN Terrorist to 55 Years in Jail," UPI, 8/11/1981; (http://www.upi.com/Archives/1981/08/11/Sentence-FALN-terrorist-to-55-years-in-jail/3540366350400/)
1134. Ronald Kolb, "Oscar Lopez-Rivera Doesn't Deserve a Pardon," National Review, 1/17/2017; (http://www.nationalreview.com/article/443920/oscar-lopez-rivera-puerto-rican-terrorist-doesnt-deserve-pardon)
1135. Alexander Nazaryan, "Oscar López Rivera: Terrorist To Some, Hero To Others," Newsweek, 6/7/2017; (http://www.newsweek.com/oscar-lopez-rivera-terrorist-some-hero-others-621949)

1136. Julie Tate, "Bradley Manning Sentenced to 35 Years in Wikileaks Case," The Washington Post, 8/21/2013; (https://www.washingtonpost.com/world/national-security/judge-to-sentence-bradley-manning-today/2013/08/20/85bee184-09d0-11e3-b87c-476db8ac34cd_story.html?utm_term=.0b6cf10f78a6)
1137. Aaron Blake and Julie Tate, "Bradley Manning Comes Out as Transgender: 'I am Female,' " The Washington Post, 8/22/2013; (https://www.washingtonpost.com/world/national-security/bradley-manning-comes-out-as-transgendered-i-am-a-female/2013/08/22/0ae67750-0b25-11e3-8974-f97ab3b3c677_story.html?utm_term=.85f8678c222d)
1138. Sandhya Somashekhar, "Chelsea Manning, who gave trove of U.S. secrets to WikiLeaks, leaves prison," The Washington Post, 5/10/2017; (https://www.washingtonpost.com/national/chelsea-manning-who-gave-trove-of-us-secrets-to-wikileaks-to-leave-prison/2017/05/17/c988b6f8-399a-11e7-a058-ddbb23c75d82_story.html)
1139. The Editors, "The Injustice of Commuting Manning's Sentence," National Review, 1/18/2017; (http://www.nationalreview.com/article/443965/chelsea-mannings-sentence-commuted-unjust-decision-obama)
1140. Charlie Savage, "N.S.A. Gets More Latitude to Share Intercepted Communications," The New York Times, 1/12/2017; (https://www.nytimes.com/2017/01/12/us/politics/nsa-gets-more-latitude-to-share-intercepted-communications.html)
1141. Ibid.
1142. Ibid.
1143. Kate Tummarello, "Obama Expands Surveillance Powers on His Way Out," Electronic Frontier Foundation, 1/12/2017; (https://www.eff.org/deeplinks/2017/01/obama-expands-surveillance-powers-his-way-out)
1144. Ibid.
1145. Wikipedia Contributors, "Arrest and death of Otto Warmbier," Wikipedia, the Free Encyclopedia, 2/6/2018; (https://en.wikipedia.org/wiki/Arrest_and_death_of_Otto_Warmbier)
1146. Jeremy Berke, "Trump appears to blame Obama for not doing more to bring Otto Warmbier home sooner," Business Insider,

6/20/2017; (http://www.businessinsider.com/trump-blames-obama-for-not-bringing-otto-warmbier-home-sooner-2017-6)
1147. "Press Briefing by Press Secretary Josh Earnest," The American Presidency Project, 3/16/2016; (http://www.presidency.ucsb.edu/ws/index.php?pid=115053)
1148. Tim Hains, "Father Of Otto Warmbier: Obama Admin Told Us To Keep Quiet, Trump Admin Brought Him Home," RealClearPolitics, 6/15/2017; (https://www.realclearpolitics.com/video/2017/06/15/father_of_otto_warmbier_obama_admin_told_us_to_keep_quiet_trump_admin_brought_him_home.html)
1149. Rebecca Savransky, "Father criticizes Obama administration for handling of son's imprisonment in North Korea," The Hill, 6/15/2017; (http://thehill.com/homenews/news/337926-father-criticizes-obama-administration-for-handling-of-sons-imprisonment-in)
1150. Ibid.
1151. Alex Lockie, "'They've crossed a line with my son': Father of US student detained by North Korea speaks out," Business Insider, 6/15/2017; (http://www.businessinsider.com/fred-warmbier-otto-north-korea-crossed-a-line-2017-6)
1152. Lori Lowenthal Marcus, "The IRS Campaign Against Israel—and Us," The Wall Street Journal, 2/1/2018; (https://www.wsj.com/articles/the-irs-campaign-against-israeland-us-1517505496)
1153. Katie Pavlich, "DOJ Settles Lawsuit With Pro-Israel Group Obama's IRS Targeted," Townhall, 2/1/2018; (https://townhall.com/tipsheet/katiepavlich/2018/02/01/doj-settles-lawsuit-with-proisrael-group-obamas-irs-targeted-n2443079)
1154. Adam Kredo, "IRS Apologizes to Pro-Israel Group for Biased Treatment," The Washington Free Beacon, 2/1/2018; (http://freebeacon.com/issues/irs-apologizes-pro-israel-group-biased-treatment/)
1155. Lori Lowenthal Marcus, "The IRS Campaign Against Israel—and Us," The Wall Street Journal, 2/1/2018; (https://www.wsj.com/articles/the-irs-campaign-against-israeland-us-1517505496)
1156. Josh Meyer, "The secret backstory of how Obama let Hezbollah off the hook," Politico, 12/18/2017; (https://www.politico.com/interactives/2017/obama-hezbollah-drug-trafficking-investigation/)

1157. Ibid.
1158. Greg Price, "Sessions Investigating Obama-Linked Hezbollah Drug-Dealing, Money-Laundering Schemes And Probe," Newsweek, 1/11/2018; (http://www.newsweek.com/sessions-obama-hezbollah-drugs-778161)
1159. "Obama intel agency secretly conducted illegal searches on Americans for years," Circa, 5/23/2017; (https://www.circa.com/story/2017/05/23/politics/obama-intel-agency-secretly-conducted-illegal-searches-on-americans-for-years)
1160. Ibid.
1161. S.A. Miller, "Obama admin blocked FBI probe of Clinton Foundation corruption: Report," The Washington Times, 8/11/2016; (https://www.washingtontimes.com/news/2016/aug/11/obama-admin-blocked-fbi-probe-clinton-foundation/)
1162. Stephen Dinan, "State Dept: Review of Hillary Clinton's emails may wait until after election", The Washington Times, 3/1/2016; (http://www.washingtontimes.com/news/2016/mar/1/review-clinton-emails-may-come-after-election/)
1163. "State Department Hid Key Clinton Benghazi Email from Judicial Watch," Judicial Watch, 4/26/2016; (http://www.judicialwatch.org/press-room/press-releases/state-department-hid-key-clinton-benghazi-email-from-judicial-watch/)
1164. Eli Watkins, "Bill Clinton Meeting Causes Headaches for Hillary," CNN, 6/30/2016; (http://www.cnn.com/2016/06/29/politics/bill-clinton-loretta-lynch/)
1165. Mark Landler, Matt Apuzzo and Amy Chozik, "Loretta Lynch to Accept F.B.I. Recommendations in Clinton Email Inquiry," The New York Times, 7/1/2016; (https://www.nytimes.com/2016/07/02/us/politics/loretta-lynch-hillary-clinton-email-server.html)
1166. Max Kutner, "Comey Drafted Statement Ending Clinton Email Investigation Months Before Interviewing Her, FBI Confirms," Newsweek, 10/16/2017; (http://www.newsweek.com/james-comey-fbi-clinton-emails-drafted-statement-686140)
1167. Laura Jarrett and Evan Perez, "FBI agent dismissed from Mueller probe changed Comey's description of Clinton to 'extremely

careless'," CNN, 12/4/2017; (https://www.cnn.com/2017/12/04/politics/peter-strzok-james-comey/index.html)

1168. Michael Goodwin, "Evidence suggests a massive scandal is brewing at the FBI," New York Post, 1/23/2018; (https://nypost.com/2018/01/23/evidence-suggests-a-massive-scandal-is-brewing-at-the-fbi/)

1169. "Clinton Uranium One deal: FBI informant blocked by Obama-era AG can unlock key info, attorney says," FOXBusiness, 10/23/2017; (http://www.foxbusiness.com/politics/2017/10/23/clinton-uranium-one-deal-fbi-informant-blocked-by-obama-era-ag-can-unlock-key-info-attorney-says.html)

1170. Josh Delk, "Key conservative: Mueller in a 'precarious position' over Uranium One deal," The Hill, 11/9/2017; (http://thehill.com/blogs/blog-briefing-room/359732-key-conservative-mueller-in-a-precarious-position-over-uranium-one)

1171. John Solomon and Alison Spann, "FBI uncovered Russian bribery plot before Obama administration approved controversial nuclear deal with Moscow," The Hill, 10/17/2017; (http://thehill.com/policy/national-security/355749-fbi-uncovered-russian-bribery-plot-before-obama-administration)

1172. Christopher Brennan, "Jeff Sessions interviewing FBI over Uranium One probe: report," New York Daily News, 12/21/2017; (http://www.nydailynews.com/news/national/jeff-sessions-interviewing-fbi-uranium-probe-report-article-1.3713249)

1173. "Fitton on Uranium One Indictment: DOJ Must 'Aggressively' Investigate Clintons & Russia," Fox News, 1/15/2018; (http://insider.foxnews.com/2018/01/15/fitton-uranium-one-indictment-russian-money-laundering-must-be-thoroughly-investigated)

1174. John Solomon "Uranium One informant makes Clinton allegations to Congress," The Hill, 2/7/2018; (http://thehill.com/homenews/administration/372861-uranium-one-informant-makes-clinton-allegations-in-testimony)

1175. Jana Heigl, "A timeline of Donald Trump's false wiretapping charge," Politifact, 3/21/2017; (http://www.politifact.com/truth-o-meter/article/2017/mar/21/timeline-donald-trumps-false-wiretapping-charge/)

1176. Ken Bensinger, "These Reports Allege Trump Has Deep Ties To Russia," Buzzfeed, 1/20/2017; (https://www.buzzfeed.com/kenbensinger/these-reports-allege-trump-has-deep-ties-to-russia)
1177. Paul Roderick Gregory, "The Trump Dossier Is Fake -- And Here Are The Reasons Why," Forbes, 1/13/2017; (https://www.forbes.com/sites/paulroderickgregory/2017/01/13/the-trump-dossier-is-false-news-and-heres-why)
1178. Andrew C. McCarthy, "FISA and the Trump Team," National Review, 1/11/2018; (http://www.nationalreview.com/article/443768/obama-fisa-trump-wiretap-may-have-been-sought)
1179. "Famously agreeable FISA court reportedly turned down FBI request to monitor Trump officials," The Week, 1/11/2017; (http://theweek.com/speedreads/672504/famously-agreeable-fisa-court-reportedly-turned-down-fbi-request-monitor-trump-officials)
1180. George Neumayr, "How Investigating the Trump Campaign Backfired on Obama's Embeds," The American Spectator, 3/14/2017; (https://spectator.org/how-investigating-the-trump-campaign-backfired-on-obamas-embeds/)
1181. Adam Entous, Devlin Barrett and Rosalind S. Helderman, "Clinton campaign, DNC paid for research that led to Russia dossier," The Washington Post, 10/24/2017; (https://www.washingtonpost.com/world/national-security/clinton-campaign-dnc-paid-for-research-that-led-to-russia-dossier/2017/10/24/226fabf0-b8e4-11e7-a908-a3470754bbb9_story.html)
1182. Paul Sperry, "Democrats' dishonest scramble to disown the Trump 'dossier'," New York Post, 1/4/2018; (https://nypost.com/2018/01/04/democrats-dishonest-scramble-to-disown-the-trump-dossier/)
1183. Stephanie Kirchgaessner and Nick Hopkins, "Second Trump-Russia dossier being assessed by FBI," The Guardian, 1/30/2018; (https://www.theguardian.com/us-news/2018/jan/30/trump-russia-collusion-fbi-cody-shearer-memo)
1184. Adam Shaw, "FBI's Strzok and Page spoke of 'secret society' after Trump election, lawmakers say," Fox News, 1/23/2018; (http://www.foxnews.com/politics/2018/01/23/

fbis-strzok-and-page-spoke-secret-society-after-trump-election-lawmakers-say.html)

1185. "Former US attorney: FBI officials will likely face charges," Fox News, 2/7/2018; (http://www.foxnews.com/transcript/2018/02/07/former-us-attorney-fbi-officials-will-likely-face-charges.html)
1186. Ari Fleischer, "My experience with Andy McCabe: No criticizing James Comey allowed," The Hill, 2/2/2018; (http://thehill.com/opinion/judiciary/371902-my-call-with-andrew-mccabe-proves-he-should-have-left-the-fbi-long-ago)
1187. Alex Pappas, Catherine Herridge, Brooke Singman, "House memo states disputed dossier was key to FBI's FISA warrant to surveil members of Team Trump," Fox News, 2/2/2018; (http://www.foxnews.com/politics/2018/02/02/house-memo-states-disputed-dossier-was-key-to-fbi-s-fisa-warrant-to-surveil-members-team-trump.html)
1188. John Malcolm, "The Plot Thickens: Grassley-Graham Letter Sheds New Light on Steele Dossier, Nunes Memo," The Heritage Foundation, 2/8/2018; (https://www.heritage.org/crime-and-justice/commentary/the-plot-thickens-grassley-graham-letter-sheds-new-light-steele)
1189. Richard Pollack, "BOMBSHELL: Comey Held Secret Obama White House Meeting Before The Inauguration," The Daily Caller, 2/13/2018; (http://dailycaller.com/2018/02/13/comey-obama-secret-meeting/)
1190. Andrew C. McCarthy "What Did Comey Tell President Trump about the Steele Dossier?," National Review, 2/13/2018; (https://www.nationalreview.com/2018/02/susan-rice-email-president-obama-russia-investigation/)
1191. Jordan Schachtel, "Dan Bongino: Obamagate is the 'most consequential political scandal' in US history," Conservative Review, 2/1/2018; (https://www.conservativereview.com/articles/dan-bongino-obamagate-consequential-political-scandal-us-history
1192. "Former US attorney: FBI officials will likely face charges," Fox News, 2/7/2018; (http://www.foxnews.com/transcript/2018/02/07/former-us-attorney-fbi-officials-will-likely-face-charges.html)

1193. Victor Davis Hanson, "FISA-Gate Is Scarier Than Watergate," National Review, 2/8/2018; (http://www.nationalreview.com/article/456183/fisa-memo-scarier-watergate)

ABOUT THE AUTHORS

Matt Margolis is an author, graphic designer, former architect, and a consumer of books and coffee. He lives with his family on a vineyard near Buffalo, New York.

Mark Noonan is a long-time blogger and author who resides in Las Vegas, Nevada. A U.S. Navy veteran, Mark lives with his wife, a small dog, and an astonishingly large number of books. Mark is currently working on his first novel.